ON THE EDGE OF THE FUTURE

Religion in North America
Catherine L. Albanese and
Stephen J. Stein, editors

ON
THE
EDGE
OF
THE
FUTURE

Esalen *and the Evolution of American Culture*

Edited by Jeffrey J. Kripal and Glenn W. Shuck

INDIANA UNIVERSITY PRESS

BLOOMINGTON & INDIANAPOLIS

This book is a publication of

Indiana University Press
601 North Morton Street
Bloomington, IN 47404-3797 USA

http://iupress.indiana.edu

Telephone orders 800-842-6796
Fax orders 812-855-7931
Orders by e-mail iuporder@indiana.edu

© 2005 by Indiana University Press

I

The paper used in this publication meets the
minimum requirements of American National
Standard for Information Sciences—Permanence of
Paper for Printed Library Materials, ANSI Z39.48-
1984.

Manufactured in the United States of America

Library of Congress Cataloging-in-Publication Data

On the edge of the future : Esalen and the evolution of
American culture / edited by Jeffrey J. Kripal and Glenn
W. Shuck.
        p. cm.—(Religion in North America)
    Includes bibliographical references and index.
    ISBN 0–253–34556–1 (hardcover : alk. paper)—
ISBN 0–253–21759–8 (pbk.: alk. paper)
    1. United States—Religion—Congresses.
2. Religion and culture—United States—Congresses.
3. Esalen Institute—Congress.   I. Kripal, Jeffrey
John   II. Shuck, Glenn W.   III. Series.
    BL2525.O5 2005
        158'.9—dc22   2004027042

1 2 3 4 5 10 09 08 07 06 05

For John and Idonna Kripal, who wanted to visit
Esalen and did; and for Dorothy Ida Ulrich, who
wanted to visit Esalen and could not, but journeyed
there many times in her mind.

Now it is apparent that whereas hierarchical cultures tend to structure-out the vertical element against the unremitting deferral of apotheosis, democracies constantly seek to precipitate apotheosis in the here and now.

—William Everson, *Archetype West: The Pacific Coast as a Literary Region*

There is an orientalism in the most restless pioneer, and the farthest west is but the farthest east.

—Henry David Thoreau as quoted by Frederic Spiegelberg

CONTENTS

Acknowledgments

As with all book projects, this one is indebted to more individuals and institutions that can be properly named in so brief a genre as an acknowledgment page. Still, we must try. First and foremost, we must acknowledge the support of Michael Murphy, cofounder of Esalen; the Esalen Institute itself, which sponsored my initial conference idea, "On the Edge of the Future: Locating Esalen in the Histories of American Religion, Psychology, and Culture" (March 30 to April 5, 2003); and Frank Poletti, who handled all of the logistics of the conference and has since gracefully guided and supported my own research in too many contexts to count. Mike and I officially hosted the conference event, bringing together twenty Esalen leaders and historians of American religion in order to explore the many dimensions of Esalen's story and then attempt to contextualize them in the broader sweeps of American and European religious history. Although the final product that you now hold in your hands is quite different than the original conference proceedings (not all the papers are represented and new essays were commissioned for the volume), it nevertheless remains true that there would be no such book had there been no such conference.

A special debt of gratitude must also be extended to Daniel Bianchetta, whose photos of Esalen grace both the cover and frontispiece of this book. Daniel worked with both me and the press with what can only be called a supernatural patience and charm. His unique contributions to the present volume, I think, are stunningly obvious. I would also like to thank in this same context Sterling Doughty, who graciously offered us the use of his striking historical photo of Richard Price, which appears in Chapter 5.

We are extremely grateful to Robert Sloan, Senior Editor at Indiana University Press. Bob showed real interest in the project from the beginning, patiently put up with some initial contract complexities, and guided us through many an editorial labyrinth. I personally would also like to take this occasion to thank Glenn Shuck. Glenn was an advanced Ph.D. candidate at Rice University when I arrived here a little over two years ago. I was quite happy to abuse my privileges as one of his professors and put him to work doing all those scholarly chores (from formatting papers to helping me with the technicalities of digitally recording interviews) for which I neither had the time or the patience. His wacky sense of humor and uncanny knowledge of things religious and American taught me a great deal along the way. I'm honored now to have him as a colleague in the field. Other individuals at Rice University played important roles: Profs. Gale Stokes and Gary Wihl, former and present Deans of the Humanities, extended generous initial and summer research support to me over the last two years as I have worked on this Esalen project; Prof. William Parsons, former Chair of the Department of Religious Studies, incessantly lobbied for my interests and causes; Mr. Hae Young Seong, one of my talented graduate students, wrote the marvelous index to the present volume; and Ms. Sylvia Louie, Coordinator of the Department, pretty much did everything else, including initiating me into the mysteries of my present administrative duties. Our little universe here, I suspect, would collapse without this beneficent deity.

Finally, we would like to thank one individual who—to my great regret and because of no fault but my own hopelessly lapsed memory—played no direct part in either our conference proceedings or the production of this volume but whose person and work nevertheless stand behind almost everything that is attempted here. That person is Walter Truett Anderson, and that work is *The Upstart Spring*, the first and to this date only substantive historical treatment of Esalen. If any of us see farther than Walt did back in 1983—and that itself is debatable—it is not because we are somehow smarter or more farseeing; it is because we have the benefit of twenty more years of hindsight and are standing solidly on the broad shoulders of his generous book. So thank you, Walt, for beginning and then nurturing what we have attempted in our own small ways to develop, extend, and enrich in the following pages. We all stand in your debt.

Jeffrey J. Kripal
October 1, 2004
Rice University

ON THE EDGE OF THE FUTURE

INTRODUCING ESALEN

Jeffrey J. Kripal and Glenn W. Shuck

Esalen is on the edge. Located in Big Sur, California, just off Highway 1, Esalen is, geographically speaking, a literal cliff hanging rather precariously over the Pacific Ocean. The Esselen Indians used the hot mineral springs here as healing baths for centuries before the European settlers arrived. In the first half of the last century, banned author Henry Miller homesteaded property nearby, while the Big Sur Heavies, a loose collection of marijuana-smoking mountain men, took over the hills, and homosexual men from San Francisco and Los Angeles arrived to meet in the bathtubs that the property's legal owner, Dr. Henry Murphy, had shipped in with the hope of creating a European-style spa. Today the place is adorned with a host of lush organic gardens; mountain streams; a cliffside swimming pool; an occasional Buddha or garden goddess; the same hot springs now embedded in a striking multimillion-dollar stone, cement, and steel spa; and a small collection of meditation huts tucked away in the trees. These are grounds that both constitute the very edge of the American frontier and look due west to see the East, as whales play just off the coast and sea otters can be heard cracking their shells over their bellies in the kelp-congested tide: cultural symbolism and nature's rhythms interpenetrate mysteriously here.

Founded in 1962 by two Stanford graduates, Michael Murphy and Richard Price, this idyllic place with a hint of danger and a sulfuric smell of sensuality (the mineral hot baths gurgle constantly with 120-degree water laced with sulfur, lithium, and an assorted collection of respectful naked bodies) quickly became one of the country's most important centers of religious experimentation. Since then, a host of intellectual, artistic, scientific, and religious figures have graced Esalen with an astonishingly rich fund of anecdotes, legends, and provocative teachings. Humanist psychologist Abraham Maslow unwittingly stumbled upon the place one night looking for a motel, only to find a community of American visionaries who had been reading and debating his recently published *Toward a Psychology of Being*. Former Episcopalian priest, American Zen Buddhist, and inspiring muse of the Beat Generation Alan Watts; psychedelic visionary Timothy Leary, the self-proclaimed "High Priest" of the 60s; Stanislav Grof, the transpersonal psychologist of LSD and the cosmic mysticism of the birth trauma; and Terrence McKenna, futurologist and philosopher of the mushroom, all visited the place. For them as well as others such as British-born novelist Aldous Huxley and mythologist Joseph Campbell, who would later celebrate his birthdays here, Esalen has played a major role in translating any number of influential psychological, religious, and speculative insights into American culture. Invited and excited by the charismatic presences of Murphy and Price; theologians Paul Tillich and Harvey Cox; novelist and anthropologist-turned-shaman Carlos Casteñeda; futurist visionary and architect Buckminster "Bucky" Fuller; psychologists Rollo May, J. B. Rhine, Carl Rogers, and B. F. Skinner; the enigmatic Fritz Perls; anthropologist and philosopher Gregory Bateson; biologist Rupert Sheldrake; and California governor Jerry Brown, among many others, came here to speak, listen, learn, and share their intellectual (and sometimes physical) wares.

From the beginning, Esalen's was a deeply psychological culture, informed by the basic principle that religious experiences of all kinds were essentially psychological in nature and so could be approached as more or less unified expressions of a shared human psyche. The 60s saw an emphasis on Abraham Maslow's humanistic psychology, the Gestalt psychology of Fritz Perls, the Esalen encounter groups of Will Schutz, and the gradual appearance of what Maslow called in 1967 the emerging fourth force of American psychology. That school of psychological thinking (after psychoanalysis, behaviorism, and humanistic psychology) saw as its goal the speculative construction of the human mind that could incorporate seriously and nonreductively the transcendent "peak experiences" beyond the ego or conscious persons that constitute the history of religions. These transcendent moments appear today among secularized individuals as near-death experiences, out-of-body flights, paranormal phenomena, and so forth. In the 60s, 70s, and 80s, this fourth force developed quickly into what is now called transpersonal psychology, perhaps best known through the work of Ken Wilber but hinted at earlier in the works of William James (who used the word "transpersonal" as early as 1905) and C. G. Jung (who wrote of the *Überpersönlich*) and developed most significantly by Richard Sutich in the 60s and 70s.[1] Jung's thought in particular has always dwelled in the background of both Esalen and the transpersonal movement as a kind of defining spirit of the way religious practice and psychology should be done. Accordingly, mythology, dream, vision, archetypal language, and a generally nonreductive but still quite psychological approach to religious experience have all been central in the workshops, authors, and arts of Esalen (and the latter should never be underestimated).

Similarly, although this aspect of its history is not generally known in the medical community, Esalen played a major role in the development of alternative and complementary medical practices in America. Indeed, Esalen's Program in Humanistic Medicine, initiated in 1972 under the leadership of Stuart and Sukie Miller, has been called both "the prototype of integrative medicine today" and "a Mayo Clinic for the New Age." Among many other ventures, the Millers worked with Senator Jacob Javits to pass a new national public policy in 1976 (PL-94–484) to encourage "humanism in health care centers" and offered a weeklong workshop to the American Medical Student Association of AMSA. The list of teachers in this same lineage who have taught or actually lived at Esalen reads like a Who's Who of the contemporary alternative medicine scene: Drs. Dean Ornish, Andrew Weil, Rachael Remen, Kenneth Pelletier, and Wayne Jonas, the second director of the Office of Alternative Medicine at the National Institutes of Health, to name just a few.[2]

Alongside these psychological, philosophical, and medical dimensions runs another more social, unabashedly ethical or prophetic thread. Esalen, for example, has strong intellectual and institutional roots in both the civil rights movement of the 50s and 60s[3] and the environmental movements of the 70s, 80s, and 90s. It also played a major role in American-Soviet relations. Among other events, Esalen sponsored Boris Yeltsin's 1989 tour of the United States that resulted in the politician's conversion to democratic and economic reform in a Houston mega–grocery store (he had repeatedly been told that such things only existed as American propaganda ploys) and his subsequent resignation from the Party upon his return to Moscow (more on this below). Esalen, finally, is also an institution of art and music. Artists such as Joan Baez; Bob Dylan; Crosby, Stills, and Nash; Simon and Garfunkel; Ravi Shankar; George Harrison; and Ringo Starr have all come to perform their music and check out the legendary grounds. (George and Ringo arrived in a helicopter that landed on the front lawn.) Little wonder, then, that Abraham Maslow called Esalen "potentially the most important educational institution in the world"[4] and named it first in his list of enlightened educational experiments in the second edition of his *Toward a Psychology of Being*. Whether Esalen is the most important educational institution in the world is certainly open to debate. But its popularity and cultural significance, particularly in California, is beyond question. At present approximately 10,000 people visit Esalen or attend a workshop there every year, and this with a firm policy that does not allow casual visitors to enter the grounds.

Despite the cultural significance of the place and the central roles it has played in what is often called the New Age movement, remarkably little has been written about Esalen itself, despite its impressive archives of video, audio, textual, and photographic materials. To use a California metaphor, there is a gold mine just waiting to be struck, further enriched by a still very living oral tradition over which any respectable historian of American religion might drool.

THE RULES OF THE GAME

How, precisely, shall we mine this glowing vein of historical gold lurking just beneath the cultural surface? And how, once located and mined, are we to refine or make some sense of what we find? That is, how are we to interpret Esalen and its many histories, individuals, and cultural contexts?

It can be said without too much exaggeration that there are at least three modern intellectual events—revolutions, really—that render virtually every traditional religious worldview and attending symbolic system problematic within the context of American society. First, the political economy of democracy, with its attending values of human equality, intellectual and religious freedom, rugged individualism, and laissez-faire capitalism, calls into question the implicit monarchical or radically hierarchical arrangements of the world religions. Second, the discoveries of modern science and Western critical thought in general have rendered literal understandings of traditional cosmologies untenable. Third, the growing global awareness of religious and cultural pluralism calls into question the obvious normativity of any single system of thought, unless, of course, a tradition chooses to isolate itself at the risk of obsolescence. Democracy, science, and pluralism. It is significant that all three revolutions of modern thought have found a unique and special incarnation in American history, a history defined by democratic experiment, a scientific and technologically oriented society, and a stunning, even bewildering, display of religious pluralism. It is in this uniquely American context that Esalen can best be located and understood as a utopian experiment suspended between the revelations and promises of religious tradition and the democratic, scientific, and pluralist revolutions of modernity and now postmodernity.[5]

Michael Murphy and Richard Price founded Esalen in 1962 and subsequently formed the place in their own images in the 60s and 70s. Murphy had been converted to a global Hindu worldview by Frederic Spiegelberg, a professor of Indian religions and culture at Stanford, and a bit later by a pilgrimage to India, where he lived for a year and a half in Sri Aurobindo's ashram in Pondicherry, meditating for up to eight hours a day. Inspired by Aurobindo's vision of the descending Supermind, the evolution of Spirit through the body, and the future union of Eastern and Western culture, Murphy envisioned Esalen as a kind of intellectual ashram where Western and Eastern thinkers and practitioners could meet in order to fuse the best of both cultural visions and create a new way of being (or indeed becoming) human. Price, on the other hand, came to the vision after suffering grievously at the hands of the psychiatric profession to which he had been committed by his father after a psychotic episode. While serving in the air force and frequenting the San Francisco renaissance scene of the North Beach area, Price had experienced an illuminating and energetic ecstatic state that military psychologists diagnosed as a psychotic break. After months in a military hospital and much more time undergoing brutal insulin and shock treatments at the Institute of Living, Price was finally released on Thanksgiving Day of 1957. He met Murphy in San Francisco in 1960. The two young men possessed very similar social, economic, educational, and even athletic backgrounds, and they found themselves now in very similar existential places. And yet Price's vision for Esalen was somewhat different than Murphy's. Rather than an Aurobindoan marriage of East and West, Price saw Esalen as a place of healing, as a refuge from the cruelties of Western culture where people could come to recover, voice their own anti-establishment experiences and visions, and be part of a nurturing experimental community.

Early on, both men set the rules of the game, by which they sought to ensure (a) that no single individual, however charismatic, would be allowed to dominate the culture and (b) that religious dogma would be treated as metaphorical—that is, as essentially psychological in nature and never taken literally. They captured these basic game-rules in two Esalen aphorisms or mantras—"No one captures the flag" and "We hold our dogmas lightly." A third mantra often uttered at Esalen speaks directly to the naysayers and those who seek to cast cold water on the experimental nature of Esalen by pointing out the innumerable failed experiments of the past. This third mantra? "Fuck history." By means of such mantras, Esalen leaders rejected authoritarianism and pessimism of every kind in favor of a more-democratic, more-individualistic, and more-hopeful approach to the spiritual life. Through these political principles, they helped to open a social space relatively free of doctrinal strictures. They welcomed radical religious experimentation and a whole host of competing, but never quite conquering, charismatic figures who would come to Esalen over the next forty years to sell their spiritual wares, celebrate the depths and creativity of the self, and forge a set of new mystical visions. The place may look haphazard, even chaotic, and perhaps in some sense it truly is, but the chaos, like all chaos, has a pattern, a set of rules, and so manifests itself within a certain predictable randomness.

Very much related to this belief in democracy and a psychologized individualism as the best organizers of the spiritual life is one of the little-known stories of Esalen: the story of its American-Soviet Exchange Program. Murphy had long been interested in parapsychology. Initially drawn to Russia for the legends surrounding its parapsychological researches as advertised in Ostrander and Schroeder's 1970 best-selling *Psychic Discoveries behind the Iron Curtain* and deeply concerned by the potential catastrophes of the Cold War, an Esalen entourage traveled there at the nadir of American-Russian relations in 1980 and helped initiate the Esalen Institute Soviet-American Exchange Program that same year.[6] Among other successes, this venture was responsible for bringing Boris Yeltsin to America for the first time in 1989 within a strategy the media liked to call "hot-tub diplomacy" but which both Esalen and the government prefer to call "citizen diplomacy," or "track-two diplomacy." Essentially, this meant Russians and Americans getting together on the grounds of Esalen and sitting in the hot tubs in an attempt to bridge the distances and emphasize the human commonalities of the two cultures. The Cold War in the hot tub—it is an interesting set of images, even if Yeltsin himself never actually made it to Esalen or those baths. Moreover, even by official government standards, such lay diplomacy worked and played an important role in ending the Cold War and initiating political reform within the Soviet Union. Certainly such attempts among the sulfurous fumes of the hot tubs fit into a larger pattern of acute social consciousness at Esalen. As Michael Murphy put it at the time, "Americans think foreign relations is for experts, but I think we can do for U.S.-Soviet relations what we did for civil rights, the women's movement and ecology."[7] And so they did.

REFLECTING ON THE GAME: THE NEW FRONTIER

The present volume is a collection of essays, most of which were originally written for an invitational conference one of us (Jeffrey Kripal) directed at Esalen in the spring of 2003 with the support of Esalen's research arm, the Center for Theory and Research (CTR). Although it is perhaps not obvious, the conference was in fact quite traditional Esalen fare, as such academic events have been held on the grounds, usually in the Big House (the former Murphy family vacation home), for the last forty years. Although, as it turned out, this was the first such Esalen conference to address directly the history of the Institute itself, in gathering a group of interested intellectuals to discuss shared interests, we were nevertheless doing what thousands of scholars, writers, artists, and intellectuals had done before us in the Big House: talk, meet, eat, drink, and relax together in the hope that our shared chemistry would catalyze some new perspectives or ideas. We were certainly not disappointed, as we hope the present volume of essays demonstrates.

In one of those coincidental but meaningful historical synchronicities, just as Esalen was getting off the ground in the fall of 1962 and dreaming of new untapped "human potentialities" to locate, name, and develop, President Kennedy was articulating his vision of a "New Frontier" and encouraging Americans weary of the Cold War and the imminent threat of nuclear annihilation to look beyond their own immediate concerns upward and outward toward the stars. On September 12, 1962, President Kennedy told a crowd assembled at Rice University in Houston, Texas (a few yards from where we are preparing the present Introduction), that the United States needed to send a human to the moon and back safely within the decade—despite the fact that the American space program lacked both the funding and knowledge at that point in time to accomplish such an ambitious goal. What Kennedy called for was an exploration into "the final frontier," as the popular *Star Trek* series put it.

Certainly such language and visions did not go unnoticed at Esalen in the following years; indeed, as Barclay James Erickson points out below, *psychonaut* became part of the spiritual vocabulary of Esalen in the 60s, and the discovery of new inner frontiers was the order of the day. And indeed, this "new frontier" of the embodied, mystically gifted but still-evolving human being is an übertheme running through many of the essays that follow. Where, after all, to go once one has reached the farthest frontier of the continental United States, when one indeed lives on that edge and can hear the ocean below?

Our reflections begin with deep and important historical contextualization, with an ancient form of Gnosticism that historian Wouter Hanegraaff describes as idealist (in the philosophical sense), highly contemptuous of the human body and its capacities, available only to the initiated few, and socially disengaged in its orientations. From Hanegraaff's chapter onward, we see a steady evolution into what we now know as Esalen: a growth center that merges insights from Eastern religions with a quintessentially American suspicion of hierarchies and guru traditions and a deep appreciation for the human body as the privileged site of the sacred. We thus find a sort of inverted Gnosticism, one that "cares for the self," as Michel Foucault once deemed it, while also remaining socially relevant. At the same time, we discover the acceptance of intellectual and corporeal practices side by side, intertwined so as to discourage any facile attempt to divide the matters of the heart from the head, the material from the spiritual, the self from the social, or the present from the future.

Wouter Hanegraaff's chapter, "Human Potential Before Esalen: An Experiment in Anachronism," eloquently introduces and historically contextualizes many of these basic themes and historical patterns for us. Hanegraaff acknowledges that the notion of human potential is inextricably linked with the work of Esalen, but what do we mean by "human potential"? A historical analysis reveals the protean nature of the phrase. Esoteric traditions—those which posit higher, often "secret" forms of knowledge beyond that of the mundane senses—have understood the human potential in vastly different ways since antiquity. Ancient Christian and Jewish Gnostics, for example, argued that humans remained "asleep" so long as they lingered in the embodied world of materiality, ignorant of their true selves. Although subsequent esoteric traditions increasingly modified this basic Gnostic position (which itself manifested wide variations in this ancient literature), its basic suspicion of corporeality and materiality remained. Nineteenth-century developments, however, signaled the turn toward inner experience and the psychologization of occult phenomena that would become critical to twentieth-century understandings of the human potential. Still, this falls well short of Esalen's well-known celebration of corporeality and this-worldly concerns. Thus, although one finds affinities between previous understandings of the human potential and what emerged at Esalen, one must note the discontinuities that problematize the lineage between esoteric traditions and Esalen. To understand the esoteric roots of Esalen, in other words, historians must first question any easy assumptions of continuity and universality in modern concepts such as "human potential."

Catherine L. Albanese also introduces background information critical to the history of Esalen in "Sacred (and Secular) Self-Fashioning: Transformations in the American Experience of Yoga." According to Albanese, Americans moved from a thorough revulsion to yoga in the early and middle years of the nineteenth century toward a cautious acceptance (among liberal elites) of certain aspects of meditation yoga, although they continued to disdain hatha yoga. In the twentieth century, the theosophical legacy combined with certain aspects of New Thought and a growing interest in aspects of Tantra to create a new and quintessentially American yogic product. This American yoga came to value the physical as a route to the transcendent. It also began to pay attention to the all-but-overlooked language of the Self in earlier American understandings of the Atman-Brahman equation. Hence, by the early and middle twentieth century, American yoga gave fuller—though still limited—acknowledgment to the Self. With the emergence of Esalen and the human potential movement in the 1960s, many Americans embraced what Albanese calls the enlightened body-self. American yoga became a thorough celebration of the healthy body that was also sensual, sexual, and beautiful. It became a celebration of the Self to which Americans could return for sustenance, consciousness, and bliss in meditative moments.

Timothy Miller takes an interesting look at one of Esalen's immediate predecessors in his "Notes on the Prehistory of the Human Potential Movement: The Vedanta Society and Gerald Heard's Trabuco College." From its beginnings in 1962, the Esalen Institute has been known, among other things, as a meeting ground between East and West and as a center for the translation of Asian religions into an American context. Although sources for Esalen include the nascent human potential movement and the evolutionary philosophy of Sri Aurobindo, an impulse among individuals connected to the Vedanta Society to build monasteries and religious communities along the West Coast also played a vital role. The Vedanta Society established a number of monasteries and retreat centers in California, although Gerald Heard's Trabuco College experiment near Los Angeles proved most influential for Esalen. Heard, a British writer, philosopher, editor, and BBC science commentator, founded Trabuco College in 1942. The austere religious community worked under the assumption that humanity stood at a crossroads of imminent transformation or death. Humanity required spiritual leaders, and Heard hoped to foster them at his spiritual training center. Although Trabuco soon closed, it, along with Heard, provided direct inspiration to Esalen's founders, Michael Murphy and Richard Price, who would later incorporate what Heard had learned at Trabuco into their new experiment at Esalen.

Jeffrey J. Kripal picks up and expands upon a number of issues raised by Albanese in his contribution, "Reading Aurobindo from Stanford to Pondicherry: Michael Murphy and the Tantric Transmission (1950–1957)." Many religious themes underpin the history of Esalen, including the frequently overlooked significance of Tantric philosophies and practices. That the latter have been generally missed or overlooked is not surprising, given that the Tantric traditions of Hinduism and Buddhism are often viewed as heterodox or even heretical within their own cultures, particularly for their (in)famous penchant for erotic images, meanings, and ritual practices and their dramatic embrace of the phenomenal world and the body as privileged sites of mystical liberation (*mukti*) and physical pleasure (*bhukti*). One can trace Esalen's own specific Tantric emphases on embodiment and this-worldly concerns to cofounder Michael Murphy's encounter with the writings of the Indian philosopher and guru Sri Aurobindo. Murphy's reading of Aurobindo combined the world-affirming elements of Aurobindo's integral philosophy with a healthy American suspicion of the hierarchy and authority found in such guru traditions. In this way and others, a spiritual culture gradually emerged at Esalen that emphasized personal quests and transformed traditional elements of Asian contemplative traditions into new democratic forms that addressed the needs of a specifically American audience. Murphy's American appropriation of Aurobindo thus helped extend the appeal and influence of Tantric practices to a Western audience.

Barclay James Erickson complements Kripal's insights into the life and work of Michael Murphy with his chapter on Esalen cofounder Richard Price, easily the most-developed and -extensive published contribution on the life and work of Price to date. Drawing extensively upon interviews with Price, his family, and his closest colleagues, Erickson's biographical essay provides an overall context from which to understand Richard Price's contributions to the founding of the Esalen Institute and to contextualize the development of his unique form of Gestalt therapy called "Gestalt practice." Erickson identifies some of the important recurring patterns, themes, and leitmotifs in the subjective life history of Price that serve to connect the different parts of his personal world into an intelligible whole.

11

The chapter begins by describing Price's childhood and adolescent years in Chicago, discusses his early adult years in college and in the military, documents his seminal life crisis at the Institute of Living (a private psychiatric hospital in Connecticut), describes his struggle to build an authentic life of his own through the cofounding of Esalen Institute and the home he created for himself there, and ends in a moving depiction of Price's sudden untimely death in a hiking accident in 1985.

Gordon Wheeler discusses the blend of theory and practice so unique and integral to Esalen in "Spirit and Shadow: Esalen and the Gestalt Model." Wheeler argues that after a century of unprecedented global wars and the proliferation of various fascisms and authoritarian statisms, the world could benefit substantially from insights generated from both Esalen and Gestalt psychology. Deeply interrelated with the experiment of Esalen itself, Gestalt in the 60s and 70s moved between the poles set forth by its principle spokespersons, Fritz Perls and Paul Goodman. At Esalen, Perls attempted to free individuals from social conformity, while from Goodman's perspective, this was only the first step in the journey toward the creation of healthier relationships at both the individual and social levels. Wheeler suggests that the divide between Perls and Goodman is now in the process of being healed at Esalen, as practitioners are realizing that the self is not important in itself. Rather, the self and the whole of our human experience are products of relational patterns, relationships which begin with how we perceive the world. By modifying our perceptions, then, we can, on an evolutionary model, change the very constitution of our world. In the 90s, Esalen has made great strides toward overcoming the initial divisions among Gestalt practitioners as well as between Gestalt and the emerging individual and collective goals of Esalen itself.

In his "Esalen and the Cultural Boundaries of Metalanguage," Robert C. Fuller suggests that a culture's fundamental vision is most succinctly captured in its notions of causation. Beliefs concerning what constitutes a "real" cause go to the heart of a culture's normative vision. Whereas Aristotle, for example, describes a number of causal agents, modern science has focused almost exclusively on "efficient causation"; that is, those causes discernible through the five senses that directly effect a result or product. Esalen, by contrast, also admits the possibility of what one might call "ultimate" or "metaphysical" causes and energies that precede observable or efficient causes. Esalen's cultural vision, in other words, suggests that the universe may have a different constitution from that ordinarily depicted by the physical sciences. Such a vision of metacausality has in turn helped transform cultural malaise into spiritual exploration by providing a language that helps reintegrate psychological and biological insights from mainstream science with an emerging body of evidence that suggests that the universe conceived by traditional science may encompass only part of the picture.

Ann Taves directly addresses Murphy's contributions to psychical research in "Michael Murphy and the Natural History of Supernormal Human Attributes." Taves argues that scholars have paid some, albeit limited, attention to the Esalen Institute, but they have yet to evaluate the work of cofounder Michael Murphy and the place of his research agenda within the larger intellectual framework of Esalen's Center for Theory and Research. More specifically, Taves demonstrates how Murphy describes his work as a Jamesian empiricist pursuing "a natural history of supernormal human attributes" and positions himself in a lineage that includes Frederic W. H. Myers, William James, and Herbert Thurston. One could describe such figures, among other things, as researchers of paranormal phenomena who assumed such phenomena were extensions of ordinary human functioning rather than supernatural occurrences. The relationship between Murphy's natural history of the supernormal and more traditional natural histories within the biological sciences is, for Taves, primarily a metaphorical one. That is to say, Murphy's comparative use of religious phenomena extracted from the intimate contexts of field and text employs the language of science to explore the possibilities of extraordinary human functioning outside the bounds permitted by traditional science and, by so doing, changes the possible meanings of the specimens under study.

Don Hanlon Johnson's chapter, "From Sarx to Soma: Esalen's Role in Recovering the Body for Spiritual Development," explores the rich history and centrality of Esalen to the discipline of Somatics. Somatics, or "body work"—Esalen's famed massage techniques serving as one of the best-known examples—attempts to overcome the mind-body dualism inherent in Western thought by reintegrating the physical body as a well-spring of physical and psychological well-being. Esalen brought together a handful of disparate Somatic practitioners during the 1960s, many of whom were German exiles. Although figures such as Charlotte Selver, Carola Spread, Fritz Perls, Marion Rosen, and Ida Rolf often differed to the point of open hostility, Esalen fostered a dialogue between the practitioners who came to understand the similarities among their approaches. It also permitted a cooperation that led to a heightened awareness of Somatics along with appeals to state legislators to recognize the discipline. Esalen helped heal other divisions as well. The line between theory and practice, for example, became irreparably blurred. Theory, in keeping with the thought of American pragmatists such as William James, emerged from practice. Those steeped in existentialism found practitioners at Esalen who were doing existentialism in practice, not just in theory. In this way, Esalen brought together leading figures from a nascent field and helped them to craft their ideas into the discipline of Somatics.

Glenn W. Shuck moves the volume in an unexpected direction, probing the potential response of as many as 60 million American evangelicals to Esalen and its programs in "Satan's Hot Springs: Esalen in the Popular Evangelical Imagination." The Esalen Institute stands at the center of twentieth-century developments in transpersonal psychology, the New Age movement, and the recent expansion of alternative spiritualities. Esalen also promotes a vision of human potential and a new era of global peace and cooperation. All of this has not gone unnoticed among conservative evangelicals, who associate Esalen with all sorts of conspiracies, demons, and debauchery. More specifically, popular evangelical authors such as Frank Peretti have condemned Esalen as a hotbed of the New Age movement, paving the way for the antichrist's ascent. One can explain much of this antipathy by highlighting the dynamics of popular American religiosity since the 60s. Mainline churches have lost members, while conservative Protestant ones have grown rapidly. As historians and sociologists have noted, however, ill-defined legions of "spiritual seekers" have also expanded, attracted to the New Age. Esalen offers a competing vision that runs antithetical to almost everything conservative evangelicals support. This translates to a competition for seekers on one level but also represents an alternative vision for the future of American culture that differs markedly from that imagined by conservative evangelicals.

Finally, Marion Goldman explores Esalen from a sociological perspective in her chapter "Esalen Institute, Essence Faiths, and the Religious Marketplace." Goldman's chapter discusses Esalen's close connections to elite essence religions in the United States, which she defines as religions that believe in a divine spark of divinity residing in everyone that can be developed and transformed through the appropriate spiritual practices. Goldman, however, locates such essence religions mainly within the liberal wings of mainline churches. The Institute's first decade, for example, involved close connections with both West Coast liberal religious leaders and the National Council of Churches. Esalen fosters networks that include liberal clergy and disaffiliated or loosely tied members of mainstream religions, which increases the overall impact of essence religions in the United States and helps to recharge mainline denominations otherwise waning in spiritual dynamism. Most significant, Goldman completes the volume precisely where Hanegraaff ends, identifying a democratized, Esalen-style Gnosticism ideally suited to the legions of American spiritual seekers, whether they are formally affiliated with church groups or not.

BEGINNING THE JOURNEY

As we have already noted and will soon have opportunity to see again (and again) in these eleven essays, Esalen challenges dualities of all sorts and pays no heed to the historical failures of similar experiments. Esalen is indeed on the edge of the future in which, despite its formal leadership, no one person or group guides or "captures the flag." It is as if Esalen constitutes what complexity theorists call an emergent entity, moving forward with a sense of purpose, even if one cannot define the source and nature of its trajectory. It is thus something of a liminal institution, constantly facing the dangers posed by acts of nature, financial troubles, and even periodic concerns over a potential loss of vision. Yet, as philosopher Mark C. Taylor—himself once a participant at Esalen—puts it, entities such as Esalen thrive at the tipping point, at the moment of chaos straddling the line beyond destruction and new, unprecedented growth. And this is how it must be. As Taylor puts it, "The equilibrium of satisfaction is a symptom of death; the turbulence of dissatisfaction is the pulse of life."[8] So too, the following essays—all original reflections prepared especially for this volume—amply demonstrate that Esalen continues to strike out into a new frontier, one whose bounds are ill defined, chaotic, and fraught with existential uncertainty. This, anyway, is where our journey begins.

Notes

1. Eugene Taylor, *Shadow Culture: Psychology and Spirituality in America* (Washington, D.C.: Counterpoint, 1999), 274.

2. We are relying here on Bill Benda and Rondi Lightmark, "The Birth of a New Paradigm: Esalen's Pioneer Program in Humanistic Medicine," *Friends of Esalen Newsletter* 16, no. 2 (Summer 2004): 4–5.

3. Leonard tells this story in his *Walking on the Edge of the World: A Memoir of the Sixties and Beyond* (Boston: Houghton Mifflin, 1988).

4. Quoted in George Leonard, "Encounters at the Mind's Edge," *Esquire,* June 1985, 314.

5. "Postmodernity" or "postmodernism," whichever form one prefers (the usage does make a difference to specialists but need not detain us here), is a helpful term but one nevertheless laden with controversy. Often skeptics use the notion of postmodernity to parody or to draw a caricature of philosophical currents that allegedly deny the "truth" of the empirical Cartesian world. Like most caricatures, however, there is a kernel of fact in such a description. Postmodernity does indeed call into question the limited vistas open to a Cartesian worldview. It draws attention to the "constructedness" of the modern world and recognizes a multiplicity of possible worlds—a notion already implicit in the concept of modernity. Our usage of the term, then, recognizes Esalen's openness to a future laden with new "postmodern" possibilities.

6. This project later morphed into The Russian-American Center (TRAC), which operated out of its own office in San Francisco under the leadership of Dulce Murphy, still, however, with close connections to Esalen. Together, over the last twenty-four years, TRAC and Esalen have been involved in an array of cross-cultural educational and political events too numerous to list here. More recently (that is, in the winter of 2004), TRAC transformed itself again into Track Two: An Institute for Citizen Diplomacy, with Dulce Murphy as executive director. This quarter-century story, running parallel as it were with Esalen's history, deserves far more scholarly attention than we have been able to give it in the present volume.

7. Quoted in Leonard, "Encounters at the Mind's Edge," 314.

8. Mark C. Taylor, *The Moment of Complexity: Emerging Network Culture* (Chicago: University of Chicago Press, 2002), 198.

HUMAN POTENTIAL BEFORE ESALEN: AN EXPERIMENT IN ANACHRONISM

Wouter J. Hanegraaff

In this opening chapter, we will look at the relationship between the human potential movement and the history of Western esotericism. In modern academic research, the latter term has come to be used, since the 1960s and particularly since the 1990s, as a general umbrella concept covering a variety of related currents in Western culture that had suffered serious neglect by previous generations of historians.[1] While the term "esotericism" as such is often used to refer to traditions of secrecy (whether in Western or non-Western contexts), the currents referred to by the more specific term "*Western* esotericism" often have not been secret. Their origins can be traced to the syncretistic Hellenistic culture of late antiquity, which produced phenomena such as Gnosticism, hermetism, and Neoplatonist theurgy. Modern Western esotericism more specifically includes the revival of hermetism and the so-called occult philosophy in the early modern period as well as its later developments, alchemy, Paracelsianism and Rosicrucianism, Christian Kabbalah and its later developments, theosophical and illuminist currents, and various occultist and related developments during the nineteenth and twentieth century, including mesmerism and various neomesmerist developments, up to and including phenomena such as the New Age movement.[2] Since the human potential movement is generally considered to be either a predecessor or simply a part of the New Age, it can be seen as belonging to the history of Western esotericism. In a recent article about the subject, Olav Hammer writes that the eclectic mix of therapies that are seen as belonging to the human potential movement

> must be regarded as belonging to the history of gnosis and Western eso-tericism both for historical reasons and because of doctrinal similarities: historically, since by mediation of the mind cure or New Thought move-ments, the intellectual foundations of the HPM may be found in the psy-chologization of Mesmerism during the 19th century; doctrinally, since the religious aspects of the HPM to a considerable extent can be characterized as the search for an existential experience of the "real self" and its essential divinity—a search for what traditionally is known as "gnosis."[3]

It will be useful to take as our point of departure the two terms high-lighted by Hammer, "gnosis" and "mesmerism," for indeed, they stand respectively for what might be considered the most general characteristic of Western esotericism across the centuries, on the one hand, and for a more specific and historically determined shape this tradition has taken since the eighteenth century, on the other.

Accordingly, I intend to highlight some of the main stations of "hu-man potential" in the context of gnosis and Western esotericism since late antiquity and look in somewhat greater detail at one highly representative example in the context of German mesmerism, the case of Justinus Kerner and the so-called Seeress of Prevorst. The story could be continued from there, but since other contributions to this volume already go into nineteenth- and twentieth-century traditions prior to Esalen, my overview will end with Kerner. It must be emphasized that what follows is no more than a preliminary exploration: I will highlight what seem to me some of the more important aspects of human potential before Esalen, but my se-lected examples are evidently no more than the tip of an iceberg, and in order to do justice to the subject a book-length discussion would be re-quired. Perhaps such a detailed history of Western esotericism from the perspective of human potential will one day be written, but my main con-cern in this chapter is with a theoretical problem that cannot be avoided in any such study: Is it at all possible to assume the existence of any universal constants in supranormal experiences and abilities discussed through the ages, or are they to be seen as strictly culture-specific? This question is inseparable from the problem of anachronistic interpretations: trying to interpret history from the perspective of a modern concept such as human potential may be fruitful as a heuristic procedure, but it also carries the risk of historical distortion if we assume too easily that by doing so we are discovering a universal constant untouched by historical change.

GNOSIS: THE SEARCH FOR THE HIGHER SELF

The Greek word "gnosis," as widely used in the context of late antiquity, meant knowledge, but this knowledge was of a special kind. Not to be confused with the rational type of knowledge better referred to as "episteme," it meant to refer to a suprarational and experiential insight into the true nature of the Self. Necessarily, any appeal to "gnosis" in this sense must rest on the assumption that our normal everyday consciousness is somehow limited and falls short of unfolding its full potential. If an experience of gnosis gives us access to our "true" and "higher" Self, it follows that as long as we are cut off and alienated from it, we find ourselves imprisoned by a "false" or "lower" kind of consciousness. In this sense, the search for gnosis might legitimately (albeit anachronistically) be referred to as a search for regaining one's full human potential.

The normal everyday state of alienation or limited consciousness was frequently referred to as a state of "sleep," "drunkenness," or simply "ignorance." The Gnostic "Hymn of the Pearl" illustrates this in the form of a beautiful myth. A prince is sent from the "wealth and splendor" of his father's kingdom in order to find the "one Pearl" that is hidden in the land of Egypt; very clearly, this is a metaphor of the true self who has to leave his heavenly home and descend into the impure and dangerous realm of matter. Having arrived in Egypt, the prince gradually forgets his true identity because he adopts the social identity of the Egyptians. We read:

> I clothed myself in their garments, lest they suspect me as one coming from without. . . . But through some cause they marked that I was not their countryman, and they ingratiated themselves with me, and mixed me [drink] with their cunning, and gave me to taste of their meat; and I forgot that I was a king's son and served *their* king. I forgot the Pearl for which my parents had sent me. Through the heaviness of their nourishment I sank into deep slumber.[4]

The transcendent soul falls under the spell of this world: by eating the food and the drink of the Egyptians and putting on their clothing, the prince falls spiritually asleep and forgets his true self. Similar references to sleep and drunkenness are frequent in Gnostic literature. Particularly important, furthermore, is the reference to clothing: the garments of the Egyptians stand for the impure body or, rather, several bodies of increasing density. Eventually the prince is awakened from his slumber by a message from above, which stands for the saving experience of gnosis: he remembers his true identity, finds the Pearl, and returns to his home. In order to do so, he has to leave the impure body behind: "their filthy and impure garment I put off, and left it behind in their land."[5] Clearly, then, while the Gnostic could awaken to his true human potential while still alive in the body, in order to function in complete freedom, the higher self had to free itself from the body and ascend to a nonmaterial realm of spirit. The Gnostics mostly believed that the material world was a prison designed by a lower deity in order to keep the soul from finding its way back to its spiritual home.

It has rightly been noted that the hermetists of late antiquity—the name derives from their mythical founding father Hermes Trismegistus, the Hellenized form of the Egyptian god Thoth—were far more positive about the material cosmos as such. While the Gnostics saw the cosmos as entirely opposed to God, in the hermetic writings we find a panentheist perspective. The eleventh tractate of the *Corpus Hermeticum* contains a particularly impressive example: it describes what in contemporary language might be referred to as a transpersonal experience of unity with the cosmos and illustrates how the full unfolding of human potential implies a realization that the self is divine:

> You must think of God in this way, as having everything—the cosmos, himself, [the] universe—like thought within himself. Thus, unless you make yourself equal to God, you cannot understand God; like is understood by like. Make yourself grow to immeasurable immensity, outleap all body, outstrip all time, become eternity and you will understand God. Having conceived that nothing is impossible to you, consider yourself immortal and able to understand everything, all art, all learning, the temper of every living thing. Go higher than every height and lower than every depth. Collect in yourself all the sensations of what has been made, of fire and water, dry and

wet; be everywhere at once, on land, in the sea, in heaven; be not yet born, be in the womb, be young, old, dead, beyond death. And when you have understood all these at once—times, places, things, qualities, quantities—then you can understand God.

But if you shut your soul up in the body and abase it and say "I understand nothing, I can do nothing; I fear the sea, I cannot go up to heaven; I do not know what I was, I do not know what I will be," then what have you to do with God?[6]

The literature contains several descriptions of how hermetists actually reached the goal: in the thirteenth tractate of the *Corpus Hermeticum,* the initiated pupil exclaims "I am in heaven, in earth, in water, in air; I am in animals, in plants, in the womb, before the womb, after the womb, everywhere."[7] And in the *Discourse on the Eighth and the Ninth,* which contains a particularly interesting description of a hermetic initiation, the initiator exclaims:

I see! I see indescribable depths. How shall I tell you. . . . How shall I describe the universe? I [am Mind and] I see another Mind, the one that [moves] the soul! I see the one that moves me from pure forgetfulness. You give me power. I see myself! . . . I have found the beginning of the power that is above all powers, the one that has no beginning. I see a fountain bubbling with life. I have said, my son, that I am Mind. I have seen! Language is not able to reveal this.[8]

In spite of their more positive view of the material cosmos, the hermetists agreed with the Gnostics (as well as with most of their contemporaries, whether Platonists, Stoics, or Church Fathers) in seeing the body and the senses in a negative light.[9] In the seventh tractate of the *Corpus Hermeticum,* the body ("the tunic that you wear") is even described in extreme terms as "the garment of ignorance, the foundation of vice, the bonds of corruption, the dark cage, the living death, the sentient corpse, the portable tomb."[10] If we, then, describe the late-antique search for the true self as a search for attaining one's full human potential and even find descriptions of what we would call transpersonal experiences, it would be a grave mistake to push the comparison too far. In the sharpest possible contrast with the body-oriented perspective typical of Esalen, the body, the senses, and sexuality were the natural enemies of human potential for Gnostics and hermetists in late antiquity.

MAN THE GREAT MIRACLE

This did not change very much when the hermetic writings were rediscovered in the early Renaissance and became the foundation for the modern tradition of Western esotericism. The *Corpus Hermeticum* had been lost during the Middle Ages, but in 1471 the great Florentine Platonist Marsilio Ficino published his translation of its first fourteen tracts into Latin, and this translation became a kind of spiritual-philosophical bestseller during the sixteenth century.[11] The remaining tractates were translated in the early 1480s by a less-famous contemporary, Lodovico Lazzarelli, and became available in print in the early sixteenth century.[12] Lazzarelli has left us a fascinating Christian hermetic text, the *Crater Hermetis*, devoted to the question of how to attain true self-knowledge, and he follows the authentic hermetic writings in emphasizing the necessity of transcending the bodily passions. For example, he writes:

> The Apostle [Paul] exclaims and admonishes us: "If you live according to the flesh, you shall die: but if you mortify the deeds of the body by way of the spirit, you shall live." And Hermes tells us: "The love of the body is the cause of death." For he who clings to the body, with ill-directed love, will err in the dark, and harvests the evils of death.[13]

Although the ascetic tradition of rejecting the body remained strong, the Renaissance is also known, of course, as a period during which the pleasures of the senses came to be evaluated much more positively than before, as demonstrated most clearly by the flowering of music and the visual arts. For example, a cautiously more nuanced approach to the senses may be found already in Ficino himself, who thought of the bodily senses as the five lower stages in a sevenfold hierarchy: from lowest to highest, the order was touching, tasting, smelling, hearing, seeing, imagination, and reason. In one fascinating discussion, Ficino discussed the senses in the context of a juxtaposition of Venus and Mercurius, who are pictured as competing for the allegiance of human beings. Venus stands for the senses, Mercurius for reason, and during the course of a person's life the power of Mercurius should gradually gain dominance over the power of Venus. Ficino warns his younger readers against the temptations of the flesh: "Venus comes before your face as a friend, secretly as an enemy."[14] Venus seeks to seduce you by the pleasures of touching (that is to say, bodily pleasure, or sex), but beware: she is not really interested in you; she merely uses you as an instrument for procreation:

> Venus endowed you with only one pleasure, and that harmful, with which she harms you but profits those to come, little by little draining you as it were through a secret pipe, filling and procreating another thing with your fluid, and leaving you finally as if you were an old skin of a cicada drained upon the ground, while she looks after the fresh cicada.[15]

Barely better than sexual pleasure is the second sense, taste, which Ficino seems to associate mostly with gluttony. These two pleasures ("promised, rather than given" by Venus) are ultimately "lethal" (*letiferas*). Ficino, however, has an alternative:

> But I promise you with the kindness of a father and a brother five pleasures, and five I give, pure, perpetual, and wholesome, of which the lowest is smelling; the higher, in hearing; the more sublime, in seeing; the more eminent, in the imagination; the higher and more divine in the reason.[16]

Thus, the rejection of the two lowest senses is compensated for by the addition of two higher, suprasensual pleasures. Three of the bodily senses at least are seen positively, as steps on a ladder toward the divine; but nevertheless, they will finally be transcended when the divine state itself has been reached.

Ficino's contemporary Giovanni Pico della Mirandola has left us a famous oration on the dignity of man, which has often been seen as the programmatic statement par excellence of the new positive view of man and his unlimited potential. Pico begins by quoting the hermetic *Asclepius,* which calls man "a great miracle": alone of all created beings, man has potentially unlimited freedom to shape his own destiny. Thus Pico has God address Adam as follows:

> The nature of all other beings is limited and constrained within the bounds of laws prescribed by Us. Thou, constrained by no limits, in accordance with thine own free will, in whose hand We have placed thee, shalt ordain for thyself the limits of thy nature. We have set thee at the world's center that thou mayest from thence more easily observe whatever is in the world. We have made thee neither of heaven nor of earth, neither mortal nor immortal, so that with freedom of choice and with honor, as though the maker and molder of thyself, thou mayest fashion thyself in whatever shape thou shalt prefer. Thou shalt have the power to degenerate into the lowest forms of

life, which are brutish. Thou shalt have the power, out of thy soul's judgment, to be reborn into the higher forms, which are divine.[17]

This can be seen as another dimension of human potential. Man has the potential of developing into whatever direction he chooses: he can sink to the state of an animal and become subhuman, but he can also attain a superhuman divine status. Obviously, it is in the latter direction that his true destiny lies. The ideal of the divinization of man was potentially heretical, and to proclaim it could be dangerous, particularly in combination—as was often the case in the context of Renaissance hermeticism—with references to magic.

So far, I have focused on two aspects of the concept of human potential in Western esotericism. First, there is the idea that man's consciousness is limited by the senses and social conditioning but that he has the potential of attaining conscious knowledge of his true or higher Self, which is divine. The implication is that while the experience of gnosis provides certainty of spiritual salvation, it is still no more than a foretaste: the true state of salvation and perfect gnosis will be attained when the physical body and our current social environment are left behind after death. And second, there is the idea that even while still living in *this* world, man has the potential of becoming whatever he wants to be. This should not be confused with man's intellectual potential for unveiling the mysteries of the natural world by scientific inquiry: while the relevance of Renaissance hermeticism to the emergence of modern science has received much attention by scholars since the 1960s, it is marginal to our present concerns. My present subject is, more precisely, early modern ideas of—to use another anachronism—what a fully realized human being might be.

In Cornelius Agrippa's famous *Three Books of Occult Philosophy*—the fundamental *summa* of Renaissance magic—we find the following passage attached to a discussion of image magic:

But know this, that such images work nothing, unless they be vivified in such a way that either a natural, or celestial, or heroic, or animastical, or demonic, or angelic virtue is in them or adheres to them. But who will give a soul to an image and make a stone to live, or metal, or wood, or wax, and "raise out of stones Children unto Abraham." Certainly no insensitive sculptor will come into the possession of this *arcanum*, nor will he be able to give what he does not have: nobody has [such powers], but he who has gained control over the elements, has overcome nature, has transcended the heavens and the angels, and attains to the Archetype itself, as a cooperator of which he can indeed do anything.[18]

Here we have an image of the Renaissance magus who has perfect magical control over nature and can "do anything." Agrippa makes quite clear, however, that such a full realization of human potential is possible only for he whose mind has transcended the material world and has achieved unity with God. The passage in question is almost certainly inspired by Lazzarelli's *Crater Hermetis*, already mentioned above, which culminates in a spectacular doctrine of self-knowledge: the person who achieves true gnosis, according to Lazzarelli, participates in the very creative powers of God himself and is even able to create souls.[19] Likewise, Agrippa suggests that the powers of the true magus are based upon his transcendence of the bodily passions and achievement of perfect gnosis. Although compared with traditional hermetic concepts there is a new emphasis on the possibility of operating on the material world, it is quite clear that the true goal lies elsewhere. In fact, from the perspective of the fully realized magus, according to Agrippa, the possibility of actually practicing magic in this world has lost its attraction: he has found something higher in a reality that transcends the realm of material creation.[20]

Before leaving the period of the Renaissance, something needs to be said about another possible dimension of human potential: the doctrine that man is a microcosm modeled after the macrocosmos. This idea is implicit in several of the pre-Socratic philosophers and has been discussed explicitly since Philo of Alexandria in the first century.[21] The implication that by means of self-knowledge we reach knowledge of the macrocosmos has been attributed to Porphyry in the third century;[22] but actually it is already in Gnostic, Manichaean, and hermetic sources that—in slightly different formulations—we find the statement that "who knows himself, knows the All,"[23] and we have seen that the *Corpus Hermeticum* did contain descriptions of gnosis leading to experiences of unity with all parts of the cosmos. At first sight, one might therefore expect that if man is a microcosmos reflecting the macrocosmos in all respects and if by means of gnosis one may have perfect knowledge of one's true self and experience unity with the cosmos, gnosis might be seen as giving us access to an interior universe no less complex and splendid than the outer one. Actually, however, such concepts of an interior universe and personal experiences of one's own microcosmic being seem to have made their appearance only during later historical periods. The reason for this is actually not hard to find. Within the macrocosmos as imagined during the Renaissance, there still existed a very clear ontological hierarchy between the "lower" realms of elementary nature, the intermediate reality of the celestial spheres, and the supreme supercelestial and divine realities. Even if God's presence was seen as somehow pervading the created universe, this would still be seen on the analogy of the human soul animating the human body. While God and the soul are infinite and immortal, the universe and the human body are finite and mortal, and only an infinite and immortal reality can be the object of gnosis. Just as even the most perfect knowledge of the macrocosm is therefore not to be confused with knowledge of God, likewise even the most perfect knowledge of the human microcosm is something very different from knowledge of one's real self. The human potential to which gnosis might give access is not some kind of interior universe, for such a universe is and remains material. Rather, man's human potential beyond his empirical self still remains what it had been since antiquity: a divine spiritual reality distinct from the body and materiality.

ALCHEMY AND THE ADAMIZATION OF HUMANITY

But what about the possibility that material creation *itself,* including the embodied human being, falls short of its true potential but is capable of attaining a state of perfection? In alchemical traditions since antiquity, we find the idea that impure matter can be transmuted to a higher state, referred to as gold. The founding father Zosimos of Panopolis (third and fourth centuries) associated strictly material procedures of metallurgical transmutation with soteriological processes and presented them as rituals of death and rebirth. For example, Zosimos describes a vision of a sacrificial priest standing at a bowl-shaped altar who describes how he suffered "intolerable violence" when his body was cut into pieces, his bones were mixed with his flesh, and both were burned in the fire. In this manner his coarse body was transmuted to a higher state, and he became "spirit."[24] Very clearly this vision refers to the material processes of transmutation that take place within the bowl-shaped altar: the material form must be violently annihilated and reduced to primary matter in order to be reborn on a higher level by means of transmutation. Clearly, too, these material processes are presented as parallel to a process of spiritual transmutation.

Carl Gustav Jung has famously argued that the true nature of alchemy did not have to do with chemical experimentation as such but, rather, "with something resembling psychic processes expressed in pseudo-chemical language."[25] Alchemical texts, according to Jung, may superficially look like chemistry but are actually about psychic processes; alchemy is about the transformation of the alchemist's psyche, and hence the actual substances employed in alchemical processes were of no real importance to him.[26] This interpretation has come under heavy attack by historians of alchemy, who have demonstrated that even in the case of some of Jung's favorite examples of spiritual alchemy (such as Eirenaeus Philalethes and Basilius Valentinus), their writings can be decoded as describing straightforward chemical procedures, the effects of which can be reproduced in a modern laboratory.[27] The spiritual interpretation of alchemy that was made famous by Jung in fact reflects religious convictions typical of nineteenth-century occultism and is not supported by the antique and medieval alchemical sources.[28] This does not mean, however, that spiritual interpretations of alchemical procedures did not exist. It was quite natural to use alchemical terminology allegorically in order to describe the mysteries of faith, and conversely, alchemists often took recourse to Christian terminology about such things as death and resurrection, exaltation and sublimation in order to describe chemical processes. However, as pointed out by William Newman and Lawrence Principe, none of this is evidence "that alchemical practices were concerned primarily or essentially with the spiritual enlightenment or development of the practitioner."[29]

For this reason my focus here is not on Jungian ideas of individuation and self-development expressed by alchemy (which have, as a matter of historical fact, strongly emphasized the countercultural milieu of which Esalen is one manifestation) but on alchemical perspectives on the potential of matter—particularly the human body—for attaining perfection. From the perspective of the study of Western esotericism, it is particularly important here to look at a dominant strand of German *Naturphilosophie* that can be traced from Paracelsus in the sixteenth century to Jacob Böhme in the early seventeenth and from there through an entire tradition of Christian theosophers up to the early nineteenth century.[30] In Paracelsus's cosmology,[31] creation has its origin in an uncreated divine center referred to as "Mysterium Magnum (The Great Mystery)," from which emerges a first materialization referred to as "Yliaster." Yliaster is the primary, as-yet-undifferentiated "stuff" from which the universe will be made. By complex processes of separation, referred to in chemical terms as condensation or coagulation, three principal forces come into existence, referred to as Sulphur, Mercurius, and Salt. A further continuation of the same processes results in the emergence of the four classical elements—earth, fire, water, and air—from which a multitude of beings comes into existence. Paracelsus describes this entire "yliastric" world as eternal and perfect. He describes our own imperfect material world, in sharp contrast, as a "cagastric" or fallen, world, which has resulted from the Fall of Lucifer and his angels. The human body is likewise cagastric, having come forth from the cagastric person of Eve. Adam, in contrast, originally had an yliastric body described as an "extract" and "representation" of the universe. He had no need of material nourishment and accordingly had no intestines. He was immortal and androgynous, reproducing himself magically without need of sexual intercourse. As a result of the Fall, however, he was plunged into a world of coarse matter, lost his immortality, and was split into male and female.

Most of Paracelsus's ideas about Adam were taken up by Jacob Böhme, who integrated them within a complex theosophical vision of the birth of God from a primordial *Ungrund* into a body of light referred to as "Eternal Nature."[32] In Eternal Nature, God's wrath (associated with the Father) is eternally being redeemed by God's love (associated with the Son), the two together resulting in a perfect world of light and harmony. Our own world comes into existence as a result of the Fall of Lucifer, and Adam's task is to restore the harmony. However, Adam falls as well (by falling asleep: an image again of the loss of divine knowledge), and present-day humanity is the offspring of his sexual unity with Eve. Our task as Adam's offspring is to effect a spiritual rebirth and thus to contribute to the cosmic process of reintegration by means of which the Fall must be reversed and creation restored to its original state of perfection. A particularly interesting aspect of Böhme's thought is that not only must human beings find the way back to salvation, but Nature must do so as well. God's body, called "Eternal Nature," was disrupted by Lucifer's Fall, and as a result we now find ourselves in a world of *temporal* Nature, which sighs and suffers under the effects of the Fall and longs to return to the lost state of harmony. Man's spiritual task therefore involves much more than just saving his own soul. His task is to liberate Nature herself from her state of suffering and thus to restore God's own body to its original state of bliss.

Böhme's prelapsarian Adam is very clearly a picture of the fully realized human being as imagined from a Christian theosophical point of view:

> Adam was a man and also a woman, and yet he was neither; but [he was] a virgin, full of chastity, discipline and purity, as the image of God: he had both tinctures of fire and light in himself, in the conjunction of which stood his own love, as the virginal center, as the beautiful paradisical rose-garden of pleasure, in which he loved himself. Like we will be at the resurrection of the dead, as Christ says in Matthew 22:30: that we will neither marry, nor be given in marriage, but will be like God's angels.[33]

For Böhme, Adam was originally created as a perfect harmony of the internal and the external world. Not only was his body a microcosm modeled after the macrocosm (for this remains the case even with his fallen offspring), but his spirit also actively participated in the divine world. The stars, which rule all the rest of material creation, had no power over him. His body was not subject to heat or cold, sickness or death, pain or fear. It was not coarse and heavy but heavenly and transparent, consisting of a subtle matter "of heavenly water" like the body of the angels. He had no hard bones and teeth, no intestines: he nourished himself from spiritual food. He had no eyelids and eyelashes: because his consciousness and perception was divine, he could see into the heart of all things without needing sunlight, and he never slept. He knew the natural language of God and the angels. He had no sexual organs because he procreated spiritually, without bodily pain or harm. He was naked, because he needed no other clothing than "the clarity and the power of God." As an image of God and the quintessence of the four elements, he had unlimited powers (like Agrippa's magus): for example, he could generate himself into an angel (but also into a devil), he could walk right through trees and stones, and all creatures had to obey him.[34]

Böhme clearly implies that when the great process of reintegration is completed, man will once more return to the prelapsarian Adamic state. He will live once more in the paradisical state of the restored "Eternal Nature," God's own body of light. While sexuality will clearly be transcended, the body will *not* be left behind: rather, the coarse and heavy material body will have been transmuted to a higher, more subtle and perfect one. Böhme's positive view of the body and the senses leads him, for example, to state that while angels have subtle bodies, the devils do not: having no body is seen as a divine punishment.[35] And while Christians have traditionally said that God sees and hears everything, Böhme includes all the senses: God is "an all-powerful, all-wise, all-knowing, all-seeing, all-hearing, all-smelling, all-feeling, all-tasting God."[36] This positive view of the body and the senses would remain a constant in later Christian theosophical traditions, culminating in the radically anti-idealist and consistently incarnational theosophy of the eighteenth-century Lutheran theologian Friedrich Christoph Oetinger, whose most famous statement is that "Corporeality is the end [goal] of God's works" (*Leiblichkeit ist das Ende der Werke Gottes*).[37]

In the alchemically oriented theosophy of Paracelsus and Böhme and the traditions that built on their work, then, we find a vision of human potential based upon the ideal picture of the prelapsarian Adam. The fact that we so tragically fall short of this ideal is explained by a double Fall: the Fall of Lucifer and the Fall of Adam (which stand, respectively, for hubris and ignorance). And spiritual self-realization in a Christian theosophical context refers to a process of psychological and physical reintegration (described largely according to alchemical models but crucially dependent on divine grace), by means of which we will regain the superhuman status of our first forbear. This future state of full self-realization is imagined neither on this earth nor in a purely spiritual otherworldly reality but in a purified and perfected bodily world referred to as "Eternal Nature."

Woman Potential in German Romanticism

Paracelsian and Christian theosophical traditions have exerted a very strong influence on both the hermetic *Naturphilosophie* of German Romanticism and the philosophy of animal magnetism linked to the name of Franz Anton Mesmer.[38] One highly characteristic representative of this tradition was the German poet and physician Justinus Kerner. Kerner's case is all the more relevant to us because his famous book about "The Seeress of Prevorst" (published in 1829)[39] is known as a pioneering contribution to the empirical study of occult phenomena in the context of early German psychiatry and parapsychology, and it must be seen as an immediate predecessor of the psychologization of mesmerism Olav Hammer sees as basic to the emergence of the human potential movement.

Die Seherin von Prevorst describes in great detail the case of a female patient of Kerner, Friederike Hauffe (1801–1829). Following a childhood and adolescence that must have been deeply traumatic in several respects, and having been pressured by her family into an arranged marriage, she fell into a severe illness that would continue until her death. She suffered from severe cramps and sweats, combined with a so-called magnetic or mesmeric trance state (or rather, various gradations of such states) in which she displayed a spectacular range of supranormal abilities. First, she displayed an extreme sensitivity to the imponderable spirit (*Geist*) of various physical substances; second, she reported a rich variety of visionary experiences that included routine visions of the spirits of the deceased; third, she continuously gave prescriptions for her own healing based upon clairvoyant observations of her own interior states and for healing of other persons, whose symptoms she tended to "take over" herself; and finally, she developed a complex "inner language" combined with an "inner arithmetic" and a system of "inner circles," to which I will return. Friederike Hauffe's fame as a spectacular somnambulist who was believed to "be in daily contact with the higher world" spread all over Germany, and people flocked to her sickbed in Kerner's house in Weinsberg, hoping to witness miracles and receive signs of higher realities.

Although Kerner claims to restrict himself to an objective account of facts (*Thatsachen*), he actually presents Friederike's visions and abilities as empirical proof of his own Romantic-Naturphilosophical worldview, deeply rooted in hermetic and occult traditions linked to the Paracelsian and Christian theosophical current. We have seen how the concept of "Eternal Nature" emerged in this tradition as God's own body, and it is against this background that we must interpret Kerner's own ideas about nature, which he had derived in particular from Gotthilf Heinrich von Schubert's influential *Ansichten von der Nachtseite der Naturwissenschaft* (*Views from the Night-Side of Natural Science*; 1808). Heinrich Straumann has conveniently summarized this perspective:

> Nature, for [Kerner], is . . . not simply the whole world of sense experience but the Whole as such, including all spiritual being; or rather, it seems that, for him, Nature means precisely *not* the world of sense experience, but its hidden spiritual forces. For it is from an intimate commerce with "Nature" (i.e., the attempt to neutralize the Fall) that human beings gain these occult faculties which amount to power over these hidden forces, and death means the complete union with Nature.[40]

Much of German *Naturphilosophie* was predicated on a system of polarities according to which nature, as a lower reality associated with the "female," was put in opposition with the Spirit as a superior reality associated with the "male." In Kerner, however, we find an alternative system of polarities that opposes "Nature" as the superior reality with mere social "Reality" as the lower one while retaining the association of Nature with the female. The result looks as follows:

Nature	—	Reality
Female	—	Male
The Heart-system	—	The Brain-system
Spiritual	—	Materialist
Sleeping State	—	Waking state
(being truly awake, a state of trance)		(being spiritually asleep)
Illness	—	Health

What we have here is the basic framework of a Romantic ideology of *Todessehnsucht* (nostalgia for death) as an alternative to Enlightenment rationalism and materialism, the influence of which can be traced in many variations through the history of religion and the arts of the nineteenth and twentieth centuries but which is also highly relevant to contemporary ideas about the relation between spirituality and mainstream society. Kerner himself, in a letter to a friend, describes his perspective as follows:

> Death I call the profoundest union with the Spirit of Nature; illness is striving for that union. Death is the highest glorification attained by man

in this life. Magnetic sleep, epilepsy . . . , catalepsy, ecstasy, madness (Pythia on the tripod), feeling for metals (siderism), organic destruction in single parts of the body, old scars which predict changes in the atmosphere: all these are conditions through which man comes closer to, and on more friendly terms with, the Spirit of Nature, a universal life, the life of the spirits and the stars. . . . However, this union, this inner commerce with Nature, this withdrawal, can never occur as long as the body is a bastion which is dominant, is *healthy*. . . . It requires disintegration in order for the autonomous frozen mass of ice to flow toward the sea as [a] blue and soft flood from the mother's breast. . . . In the profoundest commerce with Nature, one may be brought to feel minerals and water in the depths, look into the future, see spirits etc.: in short, to gain knowledge of everything which is concealed from the spirit by the merely autonomous, hard, bounded bastion of the body (by health, the condition which is so fully fit and proper for earthly life).

Woman (to be woman is really illness [*Weib zu sein ist eigentlich Krankheit*]) is already in a closer union with Nature than man, is therefore susceptible to more illnesses. . . . Even while still in the bastion of the body, she is in closer union with the stars, with the moon, and has a stronger talent for premonition [*Ahnungsvermögen*] than man.[41]

Kerner continues by evoking the image of the caterpillar that floats up into space as a butterfly after falling ill, degenerating, and dying: "In the still incomplete pupa there actually lies merely a decayed, melted matter, the caterpillar, from which the spiritual sylph slowly molds itself."[42] The fundamental idea of material disintegration and death as a necessary condition for spiritual transformation, which we already found in alchemy, is used here to support a worldview according to which illness is a first step toward union with "eternal Nature." The trance states of a female patient such as Friederike Hauffe are actually symptoms of her "awakening" to a higher world.

Clearly, then, Kerner's picture of human potential might as well be called woman potential! Women such as Friederike Hauffe give us a glimpse of the vast untapped potentials of which we are capable if only we unite with the Spirit of Nature and free ourselves from the limited and mind-numbing perspective of the rationalist, who perceives nothing but the brute world of social reality because what Kerner calls his "glass skull" (*tabula vitrea*) keeps him isolated from intuitions of a higher world. In this context it is revealing to see Kerner's open frustration, revealed in a letter to a friend, about his duties as a physician (emphasis in the original):

I have to heal her body, I have to *lead her downward* to *normal humanity*. I have to do this, difficult though I find it. . . . My job is pathetic [*Mein Geschäft ist erbärmlich*]—but I must fulfill it. To make sure that she can soon devour a calf's leg and dip a liver sausage in her coffee [*dass sie bald einen Kalbsschlegel fressen und eine Leberwurst in den Kaffee tauchen kann*], I must gather the shit around her body so that she may return to the *life of our State*, darn her husband's socks and wipe her child's behind; *after death she can live with the spirits*.[43]

We should note that most of the oppositions we find in Kerner's worldview were also basic—mutatis mutandis—to the human potential movement and the New Age movement after World War II: what keeps us from realizing our full human potential is the "right-brained" (masculine) materialist rationalist perspective that dominates social reality. What we need to do is develop our "left-brained" (feminine) intuitive capacities that give us access to a higher spiritual reality. The main difference is that in the context of the human potential movement, bodily illness is a symptom of disharmony, whereas in Kerner's perspective, it is a symptom of spiritual transcendence. Implicit in Kerner's worldview is a still relatively negative view of the strictly material body—as opposed to a higher "subtle" body—as something that needs to be transcended because our full human potential will be realized only in another reality after death. Twentieth-century ideas of "perfect body/soul harmony"—the body being understood here in organic, that is to say, material terms (let alone a positive view of sexuality in that context)—remain alien to his Christian and Romantic perspective.

In another respect, however, Kerner's (or rather, Friederike's) perspective is yet one step closer on a scale that will culminate in the implicit this-worldliness of Esalen. Whereas Renaissance concepts of macrocosm/microcosm left no room, as we saw, for experiences of an interior universe, we do find such experiences in the German Romantic context. At a certain moment, Friederike Hauffe began to draw complex circular diagrams which she referred to as her "Solar circle" and her "Circle of Life." On one level, the Solar circles may be characterized as circular calendars on which Friederike noted the various events in her life which had a bearing on her physical, mental, and spiritual condition (see Figure 1.1). This was, however, only part of their meaning. First, Friederike saw them not just as symbolic representations but actually experienced them as physically present on her chest:

> I feel the time period from when I fell asleep [i.e., the beginning of her magnetic state] until I awoke, as well as the other periods, as a ring which emerges from my heart region [*Herzgrube*] and spreads over the breast and is as though fixed against its left side. This ring weighs on me quite heavily and gives me pain (it itches). . . . Under this ring I feel five more such rings, and above it another, empty one, but I will speak only of this sixth one. This ring has twelve parts, and in them I see the major imprints of that which happened to me in this period. It has exactly the size of the ring which I have drawn here, and just as many points and segments in its periphery.
>
> More inwardly in this ring lies another, smaller one which, however, has more main segments than the large one, i.e., 13³/₄, and out of this one my arithmetic went over into the large ring.[44]

This last reference is to the Circle of Life (see below). From Friederike's subsequent descriptions it becomes clear that the sixth Solar circle referred to the year in which she found herself at the time; the five circles "under" it referred to the five previous years, while the circle "above" it referred to the coming (and therefore still "empty") year. Together, they formed a cycle of seven years. While a detailed analysis of Friederike's sixth-year Solar circle would take too much room here, I will mention some aspects. The movement of the year is counterclockwise. The two waving lines just inside the periphery refer to Kerner and his wife, whom Friederike perceived as two blue flames. Kerner's wife stopped her magnetic treatment at a certain moment, which is indicated by her line moving out of the circle; later, when Friederike "awoke" out of her magnetic state, the rapport with Kerner stopped too, as indicated by the second line moving out of the circle. Everything outside the circle indicates the outside world; the small indentations refer to human beings whose presence somehow disturbed her. Friederike refers to the space between periphery and the twelve smaller circles inside as her "dream circle" [*Traumring*]. Here it becomes apparent that the Solar circle is not just a calendar; it represents the entirety of her inner world. The dream circle is described as an "in-between realm" (*Zwischenreich*), which is also the realm of animal souls; the space in this circle is described as clearer than our days but of another kind of clarity: without light or shadows.[45] While she was in her magnetic state, Friederike felt that she could move freely in all directions through this dream circle: this is how she was able to look into the past as well as the future. When she awoke, however, she had lost this freedom and now felt imprisoned in time: "I cannot go backward, and of forward I have only the anxious feeling of *one* point."[46] The twelve smaller circles, representing the months, were used mainly in connection with Friederike's "inner arithmetic."[47] Whenever she felt frightened by things happening in the outside world, she could fly through her dream circle toward the center. In the circle with seven stars—which mean actual stars![48]—she felt good, for the stars are the abode of the lower glorified spirits. While she was there, she would speak with Kerner, mistakenly believing that he was the only person who could hear her.[49] The next circle, that of the moon, was decidedly unpleasant: "In the second ring I felt cold and shivering; it must be a cold world. I never spoke there, I just swam over it, and a few times I looked down and into it. What I saw I no longer know; I am frightened when I think about it. It is terribly cold and bad there. This ring has the light of the moon."[50] Friederike believed that Hades—the abode of spirits who are as yet neither saved nor damned (a Protestant version of purgatory)—was located on or around the moon. Finally, at the very center of the circle Friederike locates what she calls the *Gnadensonne* (Sun of Grace):

> The third ring is bright as the sun, but its center is even brighter than the sun. In it I perceived an impenetrable profundity [*eine nicht zu durchschauende Tiefe*]—the profounder, the brighter—in which I myself never came but into which I was allowed to gaze only, and this I would like to call the *Gnadensonne*. It seemed to me, as if many more spirits gazed with me into this profundity, and as though all that lives and moves, exists as sparks from this profundity.[51]

The solar circles have puzzled several commentators because of their paradoxical character: they are felt physically on the chest and have a precise size; yet they also refer to Friederike's inner world; *in* this inner world she visits the *real* stars and moon; and together with many other spirits she contemplates the mystery of the central divinity. Kerner himself denied that Friederike might have been influenced, via him or otherwise, by Pythagorean or Platonic speculation and referred his readers to the historian of mysticism Joseph von Görres for a correct interpretation of the circles.[52]

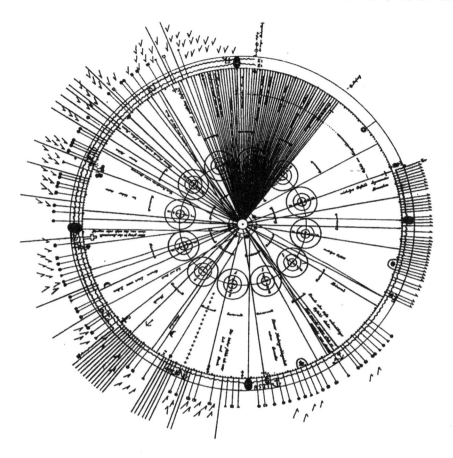

Fig 1.1. Friederike Hauffe's "Solar Circle." Created by Friederike
Hauffe. From *Die Seherin von Prevorst*, first edition 1829.

The Circle of Life (see Fig. 1.2) weighed less heavily on Friederike's
chest. While the Solar circle referred to life in this world, the Circle of
Life referred to another, higher world. The feelings and experiences which
Friederike noted in normal script on her Solar circle were written on this
Circle of Life in her "inner language."[53] Ultimately, all the signs on this
circle could be reduced to numbers, for "in the center of this circle sits
something which administers numbers and words, and that is the Spirit."[54]
Any movement from this spiritual center outward into the direction of

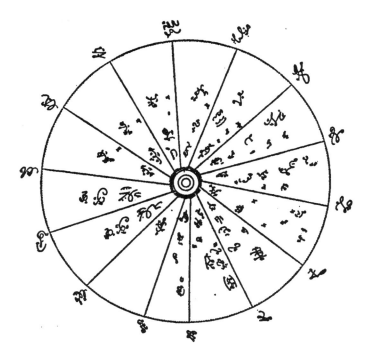

Fig 1.2. Friederike Hauffe's "Circle of Life." Created by Friederike Hauffe. From *Die Seherin von Prevorst,* first edition 1829.

physical existence—represented by the circle's periphery—implied a loss of purity.

INSTEAD OF A CONCLUSION

If a detailed history of Western esotericism from the perspective of human potential is ever written, it will likely illustrate how perceptions of the ideal human being have slowly moved on a scale from otherworldly to this-worldly.

• In ancient Gnosticism and hermetism, it was quite obvious that the body, the senses, and sexuality were alien to the higher Self and would have to be left behind: although a foretaste was possible in this life, one could only attain one's full human potential beyond the grave.

• In the Renaissance period we see a cautiously more positive view of the senses, but generally speaking the body and sexuality remain inimical to spiritual transformation. The Renaissance ideal of the magus does seem to imply a new concept of human potential as something that can be unfolded in this life, but the suprahuman powers of the magus are ultimately no more than a side effect of his having achieved spiritual union with the divine on a level that transcends this world.

• An important step toward a more concrete, sensual, and bodily oriented view of human transformation can be perceived in the alchemically inspired tradition of Paracelsianism and Christian Theosophy, which moves away from a purely idealistic view toward an incarnational perspective, culminating in Oetinger's motto *"Leiblichkeit ist das Ende der Werke Gottes."* Rather than being transcended altogether, the coarse body needs to be transmuted to a higher state: the full unfolding of human potential implies the development of a purified subtle body which will be an integral part of "Eternal Nature"—the Body of God.

• It is essentially on these foundations, then, that a German Romantic Naturphilosopher such as Kerner develops a worldview that sharply opposes a concept of "Eternal Nature" with the limited social reality of the rationalist and materialist. In Kerner's worldview there is no longer any room for the supernatural in the strict sense of the word (it is significant that he sharply rejects the interpretation of occult phenomena as miracles and insists that they are "nothing unusual, but something quite common, grounded in nature, thoroughly non-miraculous"[55]): the "higher world" has become a natural world, conceptualized as the "Nightside of Nature."[56] The divine no longer resides in an ontologically different world but has become a hidden (occult) dimension of one and the same world. Accordingly, it now becomes possible not only to "awaken" to the real nature of the macrocosm but also to envisage experiences of the microcosm, conceived of as an interior universe with the divine mystery at its very center.

In the early decades of the nineteenth century we stand on the threshold of a new chapter in the history of human potential, marked by two innovations that would eventually become basic to Esalen. First, it is well known that in the context of German Romanticism and mesmerism, the foundations were laid for the modern concept of the unconscious.[57] In many respects, the history of Western esotericism became entangled with the history of psychology in the nineteenth and twentieth centuries.[58] Second, the concept of a supernatural reality increasingly became alien and not understandable: even vocal opponents of materialism tend to naïvely describe "spiritual" realities in terms which in fact turn spirit into matter.[59] I would argue that both developments have eventually become basic to the understanding of human potential found in Esalen as well as in contemporary New Age spirituality. All of this means that a dramatic gulf yawns between how thinkers of late antiquity and the medieval and early modern periods understood "human potential" and how it has come to be understood since the early nineteenth century. Any attempt to write a history of human potential before Esalen will have to come to grips with this challenge to assumptions of continuity and universality.

NOTES

1. For an introduction to the field, see, for example, Wouter J. Hanegraaff, "Some Remarks on the Study of Western Esotericism," *Theosophical History* (March 1999): 223–232 [simultaneously in *Esoterica* 1, no. 1 (1999): 3–19, available on line at www.esoteric.msu.edu]; and Wouter J. Hanegraaff, "The Study of Western Esotericism: New Approaches to Christian and Secular Culture," in Peter Antes, Armin W. Geertz, and Randi Warne, eds., *New Approaches to the Study of Religion* vol. I (Berlin and New York: De Gruyter, 2004), 489–519. See also the academic periodical *Aries: Journal for the Study of Western Esotericism* (new series published by E. J. Brill since 2001).

2. For an overview and discussion of these currents, see Antoine Faivre, *Access to Western Esotericism* (Albany: State University of New York Press, 1994).

3. Olav Hammer, "Human Potential Movement," in Wouter J. Hanegraaff et al., eds., *Dictionary of Gnosis and Western Esotericism* (Leiden: Brill, 2005).

4. Translation in Hans Jonas, *The Gnostic Religion: The Message of the Alien God and the Beginnings of Christianity*, 2nd ed. (Boston: Beacon Press, 1958), 114.

5. Jonas, *The Gnostic Religion*, 115.

6. *Corpus Hermeticum* XI, 20–21. Translation in Brian P. Copenhaver, *Hermetica: The Greek Corpus Hermeticum and the Latin Asclepius in a New English Translation with Notes and Introduction* (Cambridge: Cambridge University Press, 1992), 41–42.

7. *Corpus Hermeticum* XIII, 11; in Copenhaver, ed., *Hermetica*, 51.

8. "The Discourse on the Eighth and the Ninth," NHC VI, in James M. Robinson, ed., *The Nag Hammadi Library in English*, 3rd rev. ed. (Leiden: Brill, 1988), 324–325.

9. On the differences and similarities between Gnosticism and Hermetism, see Roelof van den Broek, "Gnosticism and Hermetism in Antiquity: Two Roads to Salvation," in Roelof van den Broek and Wouter J. Hanegraaff, eds., *Gnosis and Hermeticism from Antiquity to Modern Times* (Albany: State University of New York Press, 1998), 1–20.

10. *Corpus Hermeticum* VII, 2; in Copenhaver, ed., *Hermetica*, 24.

11. The edito princeps (1471) of Ficino's translation is available in facsimile as *Mercurii Trismegisti Liber de Potestate et Sapientia Dei: Pimander* (Florence: Studio Per Edizioni Scelte, 1989). The classic study of the emergence of Renaissance hermeticism is Frances Yates, *Giordano Bruno and the Hermetic Tradition* (Chicago: University of Chicago Press, 1964).

12. [Lodovico Lazzarelli], "Diffinitiones Asclepii Hermetis trismegisti discipuli ad Ammonem regem per ludovicum lazarellum ad patrem suum Johannem ay. ad latinum e greco traducte . . . ," in Symphorien Champier, *Liber de quadruplici vita Theologia Asclepij hermetis trismegisti discipuli cum commentariis eiusdem domini Simphoriani* (Lyon, 1507). Modern edition by C. Vasoli in E. Castelli, ed., *Umanesimo e esoterismo* (Padua: CEDAM, 1960), 251–259.

13. [Lodovico Lazzarelli], "Ludovici Lazarelli Septempedani Poetae Christiani ad divum Ferdinandum Ar. Siciliae Regem De Summa Hominis Dignitate Dialogus qui inscribitur Via Christi et Crater Hermetis," modern edition with annotated translation in Wouter J. Hanegraaff and Ruud M. Bouthoorn, *Lodovico Lazzarelli (1447–1500): The Hermetic Writings and Related Documents* (Phoenix, Ariz.: Medieval and Renaissance Texts and Studies, 2005). The quotation is from *Crater Hermetis* 10.5.

14. Marsilio Ficino, *De Vita* II, 15. Translation in Marsilio Ficino, *Three Books on Life*, ed. and trans. Carol V. Kaske and John R. Clark (Binghamton, N.Y.: Medieval & Renaissance Texts & Studies in conjunction with the Renaissance Society of America, 1989), 211.

15. Ficino, *De Vita* II, 15; in Ficino, *Three Books on Life*, 209–211.

16. Ficino, *De Vita* II, 15; in Ficino, *Three Books on Life*, 211.

17. Giovanni Pico della Mirandola, Oratio "De hominis dignitatis," 3. Translated in Ernst Cassirer, Paul Oskar Kristeller, and John Herman Randall, eds., *The Renaissance Philosophy of Man* (Chicago and London: University of Chicago Press, 1948), 224–225.

18. Cornelius Agrippa, *De occulta philosophia libri tres*, II, 50. See critical edition by V. Perrone Compagni (Leiden: E. J. Brill, 1992), 373.

19. See discussion in Wouter J. Hanegraaff, "Lodovico Lazzarelli and the Hermetic Christ: At the Sources of Renaissance Hermetism," in Hanegraaff and Bouthoorn, *Lodovico Lazzarelli*.

20. On the relative importance of the occult sciences with respect to the ultimately superior truths of the Christian faith, see Marc van der Poel, *Cornelius Agrippa: The Humanist Theologian and His Declamations* (Leiden: Brill, 1997), Chapter 3.

21. George Perrigo Conger, *Theories of Macrocosms and Microcosms in the History of Philosophy* (New York: Columbia University Press, 1922), 27–28.

22. See George Boas, "Macrocosm and Microcosm," in Philip P. Wiener, ed., *Dictionary of the History of Ideas* (New York: Scribner, 1973), 129.

23. Manichaean Psalms 223, in C. R. C. Allberry, *A Manichaean Psalm-Book*, II (Stuttgart: W. Kohlhammer, 1938), Psalm 9, verses 5–7); Armenian Hermetic Defi-

nitions 9, 4, in J.-P. Mahé, *Hermès en Haute-Egypte* II (Québec: Presses de l'Université Laval, 1982), 393; NHC II, 138, 16–18, in Robinson, ed., *Nag Hammadi Library,* 201.

24. Zosimos of Panopolis, "Mémoires authentiques" X, 2, in Zosime de Panopolis, *Mémoires authentiques,* ed. Michèle Mertens, in *Les alchimistes grecs* IV.1 (Paris: Les Belles Lettres, 1995), 35–36.

25. Carl Gustav Jung, "The Idea of Redemption in Alchemy," in Stanley Dell, ed., *The Integration of the Personality* (New York: Farrar and Rinehart, 1939), 210.

26. See discussion in Lawrence M. Principe and William R. Newman, "Some Problems with the Historiography of Alchemy," in William R. Newman and Anthony Grafton, eds., *Secrets of Nature: Astrology and Alchemy in Early Modern Europe* (Cambridge, Mass.: MIT Press, 2001), 401–408.

27. Principe and Newman, "Some Problems with the Historiography of Alchemy," 406.

28. See Wouter J. Hanegraaff, *New Age Religion and Western Culture: Esotericism in the Mirror of Secular Thought* (Leiden: Brill, 1996), 496–513; and Principe and Newman, "Some Problems with the Historiography of Alchemy," 385–431.

29. Principe and Newman, "Some Problems with the Historiography of Alchemy," 399.

30. See Antoine Faivre, "The Theosophical Current: A Periodization," in Faivre, *Theosophy, Imagination, Tradition: Studies in Western Esotericism* (Albany: State University of New York Press, 2000), 3–48.

31. The literature on Paracelsus is vast. For a brilliant short introduction, see Alexandre Koyré, "Paracelse," in *Mystiques, spirituels, alchimistes du XVIe siècle allemand* (Paris: Gallimard, 1971), 75–129.

32. See the excellent analyses in Pierre Deghaye, *La naissance de Dieu, ou la doctrine de Jacob Boehme* (Paris: Albin Michel, 1985).

33. Jacob Böhme, *Mysterium Magnum,* XVIII, 2.

34. Cf. Boudewijn Koole, *Man en vrouw zijn een: De androgynie in het Christendom, in het bijzonder bij Jacob Boehme* (Utrecht: Hes, 1986), 69–71.

35. See Pierre Deghaye, "Jacob Boehme and His Followers," in Antoine Faivre and Jacob Needleman, eds., *Modern Esoteric Spirituality* (New York: Crossroad, 1992), 241: "It is the devil who denies the body. The devil is an idealist."

36. Jacob Böhme, *Morgen-Röthe im Aufgangk,* Chapter 3 in Jacob Böhme, *Werke,* ed. Ferdinand van Ingen (Frankfurt am Main: Deutscher Klassiker Verlag, 1997), 68.

37. Friedrich Christoph Oetinger, "Leib," in *Biblisches und Emblematisches Wörterbuch,* ed. Gerhard Schäfer et al. (Berlin and New York: Walter de Gruyter, 1999), 1: 223.

38. See, for example, Paola Mayer, *Jena Romanticism and its Appropriation of Jacob Böhme: Theosophy, Hagiography, Literature* (Montreal: McGill-Queen's University Press, 1999); and several contributions to Antoine Faivre and Rolf Christian Zimmermann, eds., *Epochen der Naturmystik: Hermetische Tradition im wissenschaftlichen Fortschritt* (Berlin: Erich Schmidt, 1979).

39. I will refer to the relatively accessible Reclam edition: Justinus Kerner, *Die Seherin von Prevorst: Eröffnungen über das inner Leben des Menschen und über das Hereinragen einer Geisterwelt in die unsere* (1829; reprint, Leipzig: Reclam, 1846). About Kerner and the Seeress, see also Wouter J. Hanegraaff, "A Woman Alone: The

Beatification of Friederike Hauffe, *née* Wanner (1801–1829)," in Anne-Marie Korte, ed., *Women and Miracle Stories: A Multidisciplinary Exploration* (Leiden: Brill, 2001), 211–249; and the longer German version, Wouter J. Hanegraaff, "Versuch über Friederike Hauffe: Zum Verhältnis zwischen Lebensgeschichte und Mythos der 'Seherin von Prevorst,' " *Suevica: Beiträge zur Schwäbischen Literatur- und Geistesgeschichte* 8 (1999–2000): 17–45 and 9 (2001–2002), 233–276. See also the recent study by Bettina Gruber, *Die Seherin von Prevorst: Romantischer Okkultismus als Religion, Wissenschaft und Literatur* (Paderborn: Ferdinand Schöningh, 2000).

40. Heinrich Straumann, *Justinus Kerner und der Okkultismus in der Deutschen Romantik* (Horgen-Zurich: Verlag der Münster-Presse, 1928), 84.

41. Justinus Kerner, letter to Ludwig Uhland, November 26, 1812, in *Justinus Kerners Briefwechsel mit seinen Freunden* (Stuttgart and Leipzig: Theobald Kerner, 1897), 1: 340–342.

42. Ibid.

43. Justinus Kerner, letter to Tafel, n.d., quoted in Lee B. Jennings, "Probleme um Kerners 'Seherin von Prevorst,' " *Antaios* 10 (1968–1969), 135.

44. Kerner, *Die Seherin von Prevorst*, 225.

45. Ibid., 228–229.

46. Ibid., 229.

47. See discussion in Hanegraaff, "A Woman Alone" and "Versuch über Friederike Hauffe."

48. Kerner, *Die Seherin von Prevorst*, 227.

49. Ibid.

50. Ibid.

51. Ibid., 228.

52. J. Görres, "Einleitung," in *Heinrich Suso's, genannt Amandus, Leben und Schriften* (Regensburg, 1829), esp. xc–xciv. Görres describes the circles in terms of a mystical astronomy: "Just as . . . that which happens in heavenly space is a transparent image and testimony of that which is accomplished in the stillness of the mystery between God and the soul; thus, in the realm of life, the phenomena which tend to accompany clairvoyance in the somnambulic state testify in their own way to that higher commerce, by transposing in a peculiar way the types, forms and laws of the external physical heaven onto the internal spiritual heaven" (lxxxiv–lxxxv). He makes much of Friederike's statement that she could only gaze into the center of the *Gnadensonne* but could not penetrate it; this, he claims, is what distinguishes the somnambulic clairvoyants from the true saints (xciii).

53. See discussion in Hanegraaff, "A Woman Alone" and "Versuch über Friederike Hauffe."

54. Kerner, *Die Seherin von Prevorst*, 232.

55. "*nichts Ungewöhnliches, sondern schon oft . . . Vorgefallenes, in der Natur gegründetes, durchaus Wunderloses*"; Kerner, *Die Seherin von Prevorst*, 73.

56. See the famous book by Catherine Crowe, *The Night-Side of Nature; or, Ghosts and Ghost-Seers* (1848; facs. repr., Wellingborough: The Aquarian Press, 1986).

57. See Henri F. Ellenberger, *The Discovery of the Unconscious: The History and Evolution of Dynamic Psychiatry* (New York: Basic Books, 1970).

58. See Hanegraaff, *New Age Religion and Western Culture*, 482–513.

59. See Hanegraaff, *New Age Religion and Western Culture,* 439–441, with reference to R. Laurence Moore's observations about the implicit materialism of spiritualism (*In Search of White Crows: Spiritualism, Parapsychology, and American Culture* [New York: Oxford University Press, 1977], 23–24) and the case of Andrew Jackson Davis as discussed by Catherine Albanese, "On the Matter of Spirit: Andrew Jackson Davis and the Marriage of God and Nature," *Journal of the American Academy of Religion* 60, no. 1 (1992): 1–17.

SACRED (AND SECULAR) SELF-FASHIONING: ESALEN AND THE AMERICAN TRANSFORMATION OF YOGA

Catherine L. Albanese

In what follows, I offer a broad-gauged retrospective on selected figures and moments in the history of American yoga and the role of Esalen in that history as a culture broker from the late 1960s. The plot goes something like this. Americans moved from a thorough revulsion, in the early and middle years of the nineteenth century, toward anything remotely yogic (and this among the most liberal elites) to a cautious acceptance (again among the most liberal elites; i.e., Theosophists) of certain aspects of meditation yoga, although there was continued disdain for hatha (i.e., physical) yoga. In the twentieth century, the theosophical legacy combined with certain aspects of New Thought and growing interest in other aspects of tantra to create a new and American yogic product. This American yoga more and more came to value the physical as a route to the transcendent. Along the way, it began to pay attention to the all-but-overlooked language of the Self in earlier American transcriptions of the Atman-Brahman equation, and by the early and middle twentieth century, American yoga gave fuller—though still limited—acknowledgment of the Self.

In the cultural revolution that the late 1960s brought—in the emergence of Esalen, the human potential movement, and the New Age—the Self began to wobble out of its exalted metaphysical orbit and to make better and better friends with an expanded ego-based self that trailed behind it a prior American history of Theosophy and New Thought. Emerging from all of that came what may be called the enlightened body-self. American yoga became a thorough celebration of the healthy body that was also sensual, sexual, and beautiful. It simultaneously became a celebration of the Self to which Americans could return for sustenance, consciousness, and bliss in introspective and meditative moments.

TRANSCENDENTAL TRANSCRIPTS

In the American beginning was the Oversoul.[1] In his well-known essay on the theme in 1841, Ralph Waldo Emerson announced the Transcendental message: "Man is a stream whose source is hidden. Our being is descending into us from we know not whence." He told readers that the soul circumscribed all things and that it abolished time and space. An energy, he said, descended into "individual life" only on condition of "entire possession," and in a visionary declaration he proclaimed infinite human possibility. "The soul gives itself alone, original, and pure, to the Lonely, Original and Pure, who on that condition, gladly inhabits, leads, and speaks through it. . . . Behold, it saith, I am born into the great, the universal mind. . . . More and more the surges of everlasting nature enter into me, and I become public and human in my regards and actions. So come I to live in thoughts, and act with energies which are immortal." The person so lived by the Oversoul would "cease from what is base and frivolous in his life, and be content with all places and with any service he can render."[2]

Emerson's forthright declaration of American mysticism is interesting for a number of reasons. As Frederic Ives Carpenter long ago showed, it originated not in Asian sources but in Western Neoplatonism with its idea of a World Soul in which all discrete and individual souls are joined.[3] Although by 1861, at least one entry in Emerson's journal in language strikingly reminiscent of the Oversoul would invoke "Hindoo theology" and its goal of restoring "that bond by which their own self (atman) was linked to the Eternal *Self* (paramatman)," the language of the Self was not to be found in the earlier Emerson.[4] It was Souls, not Selves, that Emerson affirmed, and—even though he already knew that Atman equaled Brahman—his rhetorical choices were Western. If a grand inflation of the individual soul ran through the Emersonian statement, the call was still one to asceticism (cease from the "base and frivolous"), nonattachment (be content wherever you are), and nonpreferential service (give any service you can). Peace and tranquility, more than radical transformation, characterized Emerson's vision of the soul in union with the Oversoul.

Emerson's younger friend, the second-generation Transcendentalist Henry David Thoreau, seems at first glance more promising in making the explicit yogic connections that later Americans would come to accept as Hindu (and Americanized) gospel. There is at least one tantalizing letter, written in 1849, in which Thoreau invoked yoga, and by the time he lived at Walden Pond and wrote about his sojourn there, he had immersed himself in Asian classics.[5] Thoreau's language in *Walden* was a veritable catalog of his reading, and he knew all about the "conscious penance" of the Brahmins of India, "sitting exposed to four fires and looking in the face of the sun; or hanging suspended with their heads downward, over flames" and in other astonishing positions (which he found not more astonishing than the "lives of quiet desperation" led by his fellow Americans). More affirmatively, later in the text he quoted a "Hindoo philosopher" on how the soul, with the help of a " 'holy teacher,' " finally " 'knows itself to be *Brahme*.' " Nor is it difficult to find an evocation of meditation yoga in Thoreau's well-known account of how he spent his days at the pond: "In the morning," he wrote, he bathed his "intellect in the stupendous and cosmogonal philosophy of the Bhagvat Geeta." After he put his book down, he went to his well for water. What followed next was reverie, or meditation, or mysticism. "There," he remembered, he would "meet the servant of the Brahmin, priest of Brahma and Vishnu and Indra, who still sits in his temple on the Ganges reading the Vedas, or dwells at the root of a tree with his crust and water jug. I meet his servant come to draw water for his master, and our buckets as it were grate together in the same well. The pure Walden water is mingled with the sacred water of the Ganges." For Thoreau, the message was clear.

The old Puritan covenant of works and the "conscious penance" of the Brahmins had both disappeared in a new and more persuasive vision. "I realized what the Orientals mean by contemplation and the forsaking of works."[6]

For all that, the complex texture of Thoreau's literary work and his thinking in general make it overambitious to call him fully a yogi. In the specific case of *Walden,* it needs to be emphasized that the Hindu references interspersed through the substantial text exist side by side with a plethora of literary allusions to Western, Islamic, and East Asian texts. Thoreau read voraciously and apparently forgot little. His work was an awesome and encyclopedic record of his intellectual and spiritual project, and to elevate one set of references above the others hints of twenty-first-century concerns and does not make good critical sense. Like all complex thinkers, Thoreau expressed considerable ambivalence about religious and philosophical wisdom and where it lay; there was a tensile quality to his Asia. Still more, if Thoreau celebrated Asia, in the end he pruned it for planting in the domestic soil of Concord, Massachusetts, grafting it to Puritan-Calvinist roots. Asia knew the bliss of the contemplative life and was "infinitely wise," but it was also "infinitely stagnant." As Arthur Versluis has argued, Thoreau's views were "essentially Unitarian," and Harvard moral philosophy had shaped his spirituality in abiding ways.[7]

Walden was first published in 1854; a year later, Lydia Maria Child, the sister of Transcendentalist minister Convers Francis and a notable author in her own right, was publishing her huge three-volume *Progress of Religious Ideas, through Successive Ages.*[8] The first comprehensive American account of comparative religions (outside of Hannah Adams's more limited 1817 *Dictionary of All Religions*),[9] Child's work was intended, as she wrote in the preface, to treat "all religions with reverence." Its index was innocent of references to the Atman or to yoga, and the most germane references in its opening chapter on "Hindostan, or India," were to "Brahm." "Brahm" was for Child the "one invisible God," the "invisible Supreme Being," one with Nature, and evidence of "Hindoo" pantheism. "They believe," she wrote, "that all life, whether in essence or form, proceeds constantly from Brahm."[10] In this context, Child told of the union of the soul with the divine, at least in the case of the Brahmin who turned his back to society to become the classic hermetic forest dweller, confiding to readers that "he must renounce his family, give up every species of property, sleep on the ground, and annihilate his body by such self-torments as ingenuity can devise. By this process he may finally attain absorption into the Divine Soul, which is the great object of devotional efforts among the Hindoos."[11] The message for Child was clear, and it was a works-based righteousness of asceticism—not the sensual delight of the self finding its Self—that ruled her Hindu mystic.

There was no Atman or yoga, either, in the index references of James Freeman Clarke, the Transcendentalist (Unitarian) minister who published *Ten Great Religions* sixteen years later in 1871. Nor was his message uncritical: "An ultra, one-sided idealism is the central tendency of the Hindoo mind. The God of Brahmanism is an intelligence, absorbed in the rest of profound contemplation. The good man of this religion is he who withdraws from an evil world into abstract thought."[12] Thus, the first problem of Hindu spirituality was the lack of a service orientation on the part of the yogi (or, for Clarke, simply the "Hindoo" contemplative). The second—and, from the rhetoric, worse—problem was the extreme asceticism and the denigration of this world that accompanied the Hindu seeker. Clarke's existential horror was consummate:

> They torture themselves with self-inflicted torments; for the body is the great enemy of the soul's salvation, and they must beat it down by ascetic mortifications. . . . In one part of India, therefore, devotees are swinging on hooks in honor of Siva, hanging themselves by the feet, head downwards over a fire, rolling on a bed of prickly thorns, jumping on a couch filled with sharp knives, boring holes in their tongues, and sticking their bodies full of pins and needles, or perhaps holding the arms over the head till they stiffen in that position.[13]

While some beat their flesh into submission (which evoked the Catholic Middle Ages), perhaps worst of all for Clarke was the third problem. "Meantime in other places whole regions are given over to sensual indulgences, and companies of abandoned women are connected with different temples and consecrate their gains to the support of their worship."[14] Tantra on stage, we may surmise.

Clearly, members of the Transcendental circle were bringing Asia to American notice—or at least to the notice of the Americans who were reading their texts and, especially in Emerson's case, hearing them speak.

But it was an Asia that, for all the admiration that Emerson and Thoreau in particular evinced, got mixed marks and was ultimately found wanting. It is significant that Child titled her work *The Progress of Religious Ideas*. Over the accounts of Asia hovered romantic notions of progress toward the Good and the Better and hovered, too, the doctrine of evolution in incipient form. This was hardly Darwinism yet, except perhaps in the case of Clarke: *The Origin of Species* did not appear until 1858. But as early as the first (1836) edition of his little book *Nature*, Emerson prefaced his introduction with an epigraph declaring that "striving to be man, the worm / Mounts through all the spires of form."[15] Here was Lamarckian evolution, with its insistence that all life forms were continuous, that they had arisen gradually over ages, and that characteristics acquired because of need were passed on to progeny. As for humans, so for their religions. The Christian faith stood at the pinnacle of the world's spiritual traditions, and the Transcendentalists, for all their Asiatic tours, knew that home ground was best ground. Failures of servanthood, extreme asceticism, and—at least for Clarke—an equally extreme libertinism marred South Asian spirituality. In the horrified descriptions of yogis hanging head downward over fires and in other excruciating postures, we can read, perhaps, the early warning reports on the dangerous asanas of hatha yoga. Meanwhile, we may surmise in general, the Brahm who spent his existence contemplating his own navel was not the Brahm in whose company mid-nineteenth-century Americans felt particularly comfortable.

THEOSOPHY, YOGA, AND THE LATE NINETEENTH CENTURY

If there were few full-time yogis in Transcendental forests, we may turn to the post–Civil War Theosophical Society with some sense of expectation that matters will be different. The name of Helena Blavatsky (1831–1891) carries a certain metaphysical weight, and part of it, we can say at least in a broad sense, is yogic. With Henry Steel Olcott and William Q. Judge, Blavatsky founded the Theosophical Society in New York City in 1875, initially as a spiritualist reform movement.[16] By 1878, however, Blavatsky and Olcott were turning east to Asia and had set sail for India. Meanwhile, a series of huge works by Blavatsky—*Isis Unveiled*

(1877), *The Secret Doctrine* (1888), and *The Key to Theosophy* (1889)—used South Asian classics as a major part of a complex theological synthesis that provided, for Theosophists, an intricate roadmap to mark their spiritual path.[17]

Blavatsky's earliest classic, *Isis Unveiled,* already demonstrated her immersion in South Asian sources. She clearly knew the Atman and knew it in Indian terms as the Self. More than that, she displayed considerable enthusiasm for yogis, whom she portrayed as spiritual athletes who readily performed miracles and generally evidenced awesome physical and psychological prowess. In the face of typical criticism of yogis as "obscene ascetics" who shocked Western sensibilities by going naked, she warmly defended them.[18] By the time she wrote *The Secret Doctrine,* Blavatsky was calling yoga itself "mystic meditation" and the source of "Supreme Wisdom," preferring raja yoga—which she identified with the classical system ascribed to Patanjali as well as with two other schools—as the "best and simplest." She continued to be fascinated by the siddhi powers, the esoteric abilities that demonstrated supernormal control of physical and psychological reality. Even so, the world of hatha yoga—the physical yoga to ready the body for meditative practice—was an alien and uninviting realm for Blavatsky. She saw it as a "lower" form and linked it to "torture and self-maceration"—language that echoes, surely, earlier reports of yogis hanging downward over fires. Moreover, even pranayama, or control of the breath, belonged, for Blavatsky, to the "lower Yoga." "The *Hatha* so called," she warned, "was and still is discountenanced by the Arhats. It is injurious to the health and alone can never develop into Raj Yoga."[19]

Blavatsky's *Key to Theosophy* offered readers the clearest explication of her distinctive esoteric reading of the Atman, now transposed from South Asia to function as part of her eclectic and synthetic theological edifice. In a schema of seven bodies in which only the first one was fully physical, she identified the "Atma" as the seventh and highest metaphysical body, "one with the Absolute, as its radiation." She thought that the "Atma-Buddhi" was not to be identified with the Universal World Soul of ancient Greek mystical philosophy, but she clearly—if provisionally—saw the Atma(n) as the Higher Self, "inseparable from its one and absolute *Meta*-Spirit as the sunbeam is inseparable from sunlight." And it is significant that she declared the Atma, "the inseparable ray of the Universal and ONE SELF," to be the "God *above,* more than within, us."[20]

The same year that Blavatsky published her *Key to Theosophy,* William Q. Judge (1851–1896) published his esoteric reading of the *Yoga Sutras* traditionally attributed to Patanjali. Using an English translation produced in Bombay in 1885 by Tookeram Tatya, an Indian member of the Theosophical Society, Judge emphasized the distinction between hatha and raja yoga already adumbrated by Blavatsky.[21] His preface clearly explained the difference between the two and warned readers of the dangers of hatha yoga, quoting from the words of Henry Steel Olcott in the earlier Bombay edition. Hatha yoga would establish health and train the will, wrote Olcott, but "the processes prescribed to arrive at this end are so difficult that only a few resolute souls go through all the stages of its practice, while many have failed and died in the attempt. It is therefore strongly denounced by all the philosophers." Minimizing allusions to "postures" (the asanas) in the *Yoga Sutras,* Judge went on to laud raja yoga, which, he said, was "certainly spiritual." Hatha was distinctly not. Instead, it resulted in "psychic development at the delay or expense of the spiritual nature." When the Patanjali text itself announced, in translation, "A posture assumed by a Yogee must be steady and pleasant," Judge was quick to explain that the "postures" of the various yogic systems were "not absolutely essential to the successful pursuit of the practice of concentration and attainment of its ultimate fruits." More than that, he found them "only possible for Hindus" who had practiced them from childhood and who knew their physiological effects. Still, Judge was fairly complacent about the dangers: "These last named practices and results may allure the Western student, but from our knowledge of inherent racial difficulties there is not much fear that many will persist in them."[22]

What appealed to a late-nineteenth-century Anglo-American about the *Yoga Sutras,* we can guess, was the moral inscription that the text wrote over yogic practice. The Patanjali yogi developed such qualities as "harmlessness and kindness," "veracity," "abstinence from theft," "continence," the elimination of "covetousness," and similar virtues along the way to the proverbial flight of the Alone to the Alone. There was no discourse of the Self in this rendering, no prevailing language that Atman *was* Brahman, but instead a translation that hailed the "Isolation" of the soul. Judge was quick to explain that the translated text did not mean "that a man is isolated from his fellows, becoming cold and dead, but only that the Soul is isolated or freed from the bondage of matter and desire."[23] His anti-isolationist reading accorded with readings by later translators, but the reasons for Judge's caveat were neither textual nor linguistic. For him, instead, theosophical (and Christian) brotherhood had become Hindu righteousness. Beyond that, in the original *Yoga Sutras* there were the tantalizing allusions to the siddhi powers. The accomplished yogi, for example, could "move his body from one place to another with the quickness of thought, to extend the operations of his senses beyond the trammels of place or the obstructions of matter, and to alter any natural object from one form to another." Judge remained ambivalent about what he understood as these exploits of "Will." He was clearly fascinated, but he worried over the inextricable bond, for most, between will and desire, and he seemed grateful, or at least relieved, at the circumspection of the Patanjali text.[24]

Judge's work elicited at least one (fairly negative) review in *The New York Times,* suggesting some awareness of yoga, however minimal, among American readers ("those who love to be muddled may be safely recommended this little book").[25] Even further, by the 1890s Theosophists were apparently exempting pranayama (yogic breathing) from their strictures against hatha yoga—different from Blavatsky, who had found both to be "lower." Rama Prasad published *Nature's Finer Forces* from a series of articles that had previously appeared in *The Theosophist*—in what may have been, as J. Gordon Melton has suggested, "the first book to explain and advocate the practice of yoga."[26] It is significant that Prasad included with the "The Science of Breath" chapters on "Evolution," "The Mind," and "The Manifestations of Psychic Force," themes that at once evoke the preoccupations of the theosophical world and point the way toward a later American history of yoga.[27]

Theosophical interest in meditation yoga would continue under the rubric of raja yoga. Judge's successor as the head of the Theosophical Society in America (the American branch of the Theosophical Society that, with Judge, had broken away from the international organization) was Katherine Tingley (1847–1929), whose "applied Theosophy" at Point Loma, California, became a showcase for raja yoga. But it was a raja yoga decidedly changed, even from the moral transformation that was already part of the Judge reading. Tingley used "raja yoga" as a new descriptive term for the work of socializing children that she carried forward in her experimental school at the utopian Point Loma colony. Tingley's Raja Yoga School opened in 1900, including American and Cuban children, and from the first it aimed at creating a "pure moral atmosphere" for its (resident) students. Reading, especially of newspapers and magazines, was censored; daily silence was observed; sexual activity (i.e., masturbation) was severely proscribed; and physical activities—but not hatha yoga— were encouraged. Since the body housed the "spiritual Ego," hygiene and physical health were preoccupations. As W. Michael Ashcraft has summarized, Point Loma raja yoga meant "a lifestyle of faculty coordination, uniting all of the faculties to achieve spiritual and moral maturity."[28]

In the case of purely meditation yoga, the strongest impetus to growing public awareness came from Swami Vivekananda, founder of the Vedanta Society, who had come to the United States for the World's Parliament of Religions in Chicago in 1893 and stayed thereafter to tour and lecture. Vivekananda wrote four books on the different branches of yoga— karma (the yoga of works), bhakti (the yoga of devotion), jnana (the yoga of knowledge), and raja (the yoga of meditation). The first three accorded with the classical tradition. The last was the yoga that Theosophists had identified with Patanjali although it was not named in the *Yoga Sutras*. In this context, the book that Vivekananda produced under the title *Raja-Yoga* sold out in a matter of months in 1896 and was ready for a new edition by November. As its publishing success already suggested and as Elizabeth De Michelis has argued, his reconfiguration of the *Yoga Sutras* in *Raja-Yoga* both reflected and augmented an emerging spirituality significantly different from Indian classical spiritual teaching. Vivekananda, in his late-nineteenth-century moment, had become a major conversation partner in a new yogic discourse, epitomizing in his personal history the revolving doors that were already connecting East with West with East again in British India.[29]

Where was hatha yoga in all of this? To be sure, there was no separate work from Vivekananda on it, but even so public awareness had apparently begun. For example, by 1893 at least one spoof on "A Western Yoga" had appeared in the columns of the *New York Times*.[30] Still for all that, as the heyday of early Theosophy faded and the World's Parliament became inscribed in the halls of memory, the American experience of yoga remained guarded and ambivalent. Meditation yoga signaled exoticism and the promise of something that was spiritually more. It also fed, as in the rhetorical choices of Vivekananda, into evolving discourses of the mind and its powers—point to which I shall return below—and it presaged, as well, a "scientific" perspective that could address religio-philosophical themes and practices rationally and pragmatically. At the cutting edge of this discourse, the yogic practice of pranayama, which Vivekananda and Prasad before him had cited approvingly, had begun to bring some idealizing American devotees of religious liberalism back to their senses, back to their bodies.

THE MYSTERIES OF YOGI RAMACHARAKA

Given this nineteenth-century history and its ambivalences—given the tortured bodies of its yogis hanging upside down—how did hatha yoga come to prevail as the preferred American yogic practice? Likewise, how did it incorporate into its discourse and practice the translated language of the Self in union with the universe—and, in the American context, the (lowercase) self and selves? Against the backdrop of hatha yoga's ascendancy, what, in general, happened to forms of meditation yoga? Any satisfactory answer to this series of questions must begin with the recognition that the route to the enlightened body-self and its metaphysical entourage on American shores was circuitous. That acknowledged, however, the *American* teachers pointing toward an American yogic future were there, and they supplied important hints of what was to come. J. Gordon Melton has identified two such early-twentieth-century teachers in William Walker Atkinson and Pierre Bernard, both of them proponents of hatha who located it in a larger yogic context.[31] What is intriguing about the pair is that between them they introduced the major themes that, I argue, have come to characterize American yoga and that were much later, in the second half of the century, valorized by the work of the Esalen Institute.

William Walker Atkinson (1862–1932), who had a business background, was drawn to the American metaphysical tradition and became a leading New Thought author. He apparently moved to Chicago around the beginning of the twentieth century and from there produced a prodigious set of titles, one after another, book after book. As they are reproduced in the online library catalog of the University of California, they clearly display Atkinson's preoccupation with a series of themes. They speak of subconscious and superconscious planes of the mind, of the powers of mind and thought, of the attainability of health and success, of the exercise of will and its effects in the American pragmatic version of psychic forces. Here was New Thought in its brashest, least christianized and God-dependent version; here was the rationalist—the noetic—tradition that Gary Ward Materra has distinguished from the more affective and socially concerned version of New Thought taught by Emma Curtis Hopkins and her students.[32] Readers of these books, however, likely did not know that Atkinson was also the author of another series of works on yoga under a pseudonym designed to suggest their South Asian provenance. From 1902, as Yogi Ramacharaka, Atkinson produced a different set of titles. Along with books on "Yogi philosophy and Oriental mysticism," by 1904 he had published *Hatha Yoga; or, The Yoga Philosophy of Physical Well-Being* and by a year later the related *Science of Breath*, followed the next year by *A Series of Lessons in Raja Yoga* and *The Science of Psychic Healing*.[33] Apparently, Atkinson wrote from experience. Gordon Melton tells us that he "became an accomplished student of yoga, so much so that his books circulated and were well received in India."[34]

Ramacharaka's titles already suggest a theosophical interest in raja yoga and siddhi powers, along with pranayama. Linked to Atkinson's New Thought themes—with, in his case, their theosophical tilt toward ideas of magical and occult powers of mind—the conceptual frame is not hard to decipher. Ramacharaka cited and quoted from Mabel Collins's theosophical devotional classic *Light on the Path* in his work on raja yoga, and his general teaching throughout was theosophical.[35] Each human being was composed of a series of five hierarchical planes from the lowest, which was vegetative, through to the instinctive, the intellectual, the intuitive, and finally the plane of Cosmic Knowing. According to the "Yogi philosophy," even the "atoms of matter" had "life and an elementary manifestation of mind," while at the highest level "the higher regions of the mind, while belonging to the individual, and a part of himself, are so far above his ordinary consciousness that to all intents and purposes messages from them are as orders from another and higher soul." Still, there were the "confining sheaths"—an evocation of the lower bodies of which Blavatsky had written—and the "Higher Self" had to do the best that it could. If one could reach the cosmic plane, the fortunate individual would be "able to see fully, plainly and completely that there is One Great Life underlying all the countless forms and shapes of manifestation." Separateness, however, was " 'the working fiction of the universe.' " In this context, mental healing was but the restoration of "normal conditions" on the vegetative plane, so that this level of consciousness could "do its work without the hindrance of adverse conscious thought."[36]

With this anthropology as backdrop, Yogi Ramacharaka conceived the work of yogic adepts to be to awaken their consciousness of the "Real Self," a process that, he explained, the yogi masters taught in two steps—the "Consciousness of the I," with a life not dependent on the body; and the "Consciousness of the 'I AM,' " which was identified with the "Universal Life." Always, though, before one sought mastery of the secrets of the universe outside, one "should master the Universe within—the Kingdom of the Self." In the world within could be found "that wonderful thing, the Will," which was "but faintly understood by those ignorant of the Yogi Philosophy—the Power of the Ego—its birthright from the Absolute." There were Emersonian echoes in the allusion to Will (Emerson's Transcendental gospel *Nature* in 1836 had announced its power) and in Ramacharaka's instructions about distinguishing between the "I" and the "Not I." But the "Real Self of Man" was "the Divine Spark sent forth from the Sacred Flame." It was the "Child of the Divine Parent. . . . Immortal—Eternal—Indestructible—Invincible." For Ramacharaka, in the progression that was raja yoga, the Real Self, "setting aside first this, and then that . . . finally discards all of the 'Not I' leaving the Real Self free and delivered from its bondage to its appendages." "Then it returns to the discarded appendages, and makes use of them."[37]

The Ramacharaka-Atkinson synthesis was smooth and seamless. Here was Theosophy yoked to the ancient texts of India in their recent and Westernized transmission and yoked as well to an American celebration of will and control. The Higher Self and the ego self played in not-too-distant fields, ready to join forces, ready to enhance the waking, everyday existence of the body in which they dwelled. For what was decidedly new with Ramacharaka's American yoga was the body. His works on hatha, the breath, and psychic healing were companion books that pointed toward the enhancement of the high self through enhancement of its earthly residence.

Given all of this, the claims that Yogi Ramacharaka makes for hatha yoga seem, from a yogic perspective, strikingly spare, and his description of the asanas suggests instead their continuity with simple calisthenics. If his books went to India, as Melton reported, we have to wonder who was reading them. Meanwhile, in America, in the context of late-century and new-century worry regarding "overcivilization" and Theodore Roosevelt's widely influential celebration of *The Strenuous Life* (1901), a new moral crusade was championing bodily vigor, direct action, and experience over the learning that could be gleaned from books. The natural environment, far from the corruption and debilitating ethos of cities, became the object of cultus. By 1903, *Outlook* magazine was describing nature as the "middle ground between God and man" and the "playground of the soul." Camping and scouting would institutionalize these sentiments as physical training assumed new ascendancy as part of moral education.[38] At the same time, natural hygiene and physical culture—older nineteenth-century currents in the health reform movement—had joined forces to lead into the gymnasium. Calisthenics were in, and they held the promise of glowing health for those who would be zealous. Will power became equated with muscle power and, in a culture characterized by the language of "muscular Christianity," became a force for public and private good order. "The identification of morality with muscularity was to grow as an article of hygienic faith through the final third of the [nineteenth] century and the Progressive years," wrote James C. Whorton in his landmark study *Crusaders for Fitness*. "The arena would become congested with competing programs of health building."[39]

Ramacharaka was a thorough child of his times. "Hatha yoga," he wrote, "is that branch of the Yoga philosophy which deals with the physical body—its care—its well being—its health—its strengths—and all that tends to keep it in its natural and normal state of health." It could appeal to American denizens of the "strenuous life" because it was "first, nature; second, *nature*, and last NATURE." "By all means," Ramacharaka encouraged readers, "apply the nature test to all theories of this kind—our own included—and if they do not square with nature, discard them." Not a "doctor book," his work was instead concerned with "the Healthy Man—its main purpose to help people conform to the standard of the normal man."[40] The asanas that followed were listed as "yogi physical exercises," and, to be sure, they were generally active and aerobic. They did not resemble the classical postures that have been identified with hatha yoga. "Swing back the hands until the arms stand out straight. . . . The arms should be swung with a rapid movement, and with animation and life. Do not go to sleep over the work, or rather play."[41]

What did this yogic workout have to do with the meditative and mystical pursuit that characterized raja yoga? Ramacharaka's answer was fairly trite and perfunctory. The body was "necessary" for human "manifestation and growth"; it was the "Temple of the Spirit"; its care and development constituted a "worthy task" since an "unhealthy and imperfectly developed physical body" would obstruct the proper functioning of the mind. The "instrument" could not be "used to the best advantage by its master, the Spirit." The closest Ramacharaka came to later and standard explanations regarding the quieting of the body to prepare it for meditation and the acknowledged alteration of consciousness that came from certain yogic asanas—inversions and forward bends, for example—was his appeal to instrumentalism. The body was the instrument for the "real part" of a person "in the work of Soul growth." The yogic devotee would "feel as proud [of his body] as does the master violinist of the Stradivarius which responds almost with intelligence to the touch of his bow."[42]

More than that, Ramacharaka was at pains to separate his teaching from the American knowledge of yoga that we have already met in Transcendentalist and theosophical circles. "In India," explained Ramacharaka, "there exists a horde of ignorant mendicants of the lower fakir class, who pose as Hatha Yogis, but who have not the slightest conception of the underlying principles of that branch of Yoga." They engaged in "tricks," he confided to his audience, such as reversing the peristaltic action of their intestines to eject items introduced into the colon from "the gullet." "Rank frauds or self-deluded fanatics," these people were "akin to the class of fanatics in India . . . who refuse to wash the body, for religious reasons;

or who sit with up-lifted arm until it is withered; or who allow their finger nails to grow until they pierce their hands; or who sit so still that their birds build nests in their hair; or who perform other ridiculous feats, in order to pose as 'holy men.' "[43]

Yogi Ramacharaka did tell readers that they needed to "throw some mind" into their hatha yoga, and there was also a tantalizing discussion, surrounded by late-Victorian caveats and veiled allusions, of "transmuting reproductive energy" through pranayama (raising energy from the sexual organs at the base of the spine to the crown of the head to be used in meditation). In essence, however, Ramacharaka/Atkinson had communicated a yoga of Will and self-effort, of self-construction that called on a Higher (divine) Self to achieve enhanced ego goals. In so doing, he had effectively linked the language and intent of New Thought to that of Theosophy. He had also succeeded in joining hatha yoga, at least in his hatha yoga book, to raja and other forms of yoga as a venerable and respected branch. But the enlightened body-self was more a devotee of the strenuous life than of the bliss of yogic connection. A brisk "yogi bath" and body rub were fitting partners to the active asanas of Ramacharaka's yogic world. The chapters in his text point toward natural hygiene and physical culture and toward the mantra that characterized the devotees of the health building movement—a sound mind in a sound body.[44]

THE TANTRA OF PIERRE BERNARD AND THEOS BARNARD

Enter, in New York City, the tantric master. Pierre Bernard (1875–1955) probably came from a middle-class California family with interests in Eastern religion, although he left a trail of assumed names, including that of Iowan Peter Coon or Coons. He apparently traveled to India with an interest in "curing diseases of mind and body" and learned hatha and tantra yoga at first hand in Kashmir and Bengal. When he returned, purportedly with the title "Shastri" acquired for his knowledge of comparative religion, his attraction to metaphysical themes led him to San Francisco, where he conducted an academy dedicated to hypnosis until the 1906 earthquake. Around this time, Bernard founded his "Tantrik" order and published the first and only issue of his *International Journal of the Tantrik Order in America: Vira Sadhana.* By 1910, he was in New York City, where he called himself Dr. Pierre Arnold Bernard and opened the New York Sanskrit College. According to reports, hatha yoga was taught on the first floor, while upstairs, tantric initiates were ushered into deeper secrets. Dogged by sex scandals and hounded by the press as Oom the Omnipotent, he was apparently as flamboyant as the name suggests, reportedly sitting enthroned in the upstairs room before his wealthy initiates and receiving their worshipful adulation. His wife, Blanche deVries, was also a student, an "Oriental" dancer, and a teacher of hatha yoga. She taught, too, it was said, a softer form of tantrism than her husband's more provocative version.[45]

Yet there was telling evidence that Bernard was a serious student of South Asian yogic themes. By 1924, he had purchased a 70-acre estate in Nyack, New York, which became a colony for his elite and socially well-placed devotees. Here he located his impressive library, described by the Web site devoted to him as the "finest collection of Sanskrit works (original texts, manuscripts and translations) in the United States at the time, containing approximately 7,000 volumes on the subjects of philosophy, ethics, psychology, education and metaphysics as well as much collateral material on physiology, medicine and related sciences." Students flocked to Nyack, and Asian teachers visited. Eventually, Bernard purchased more property in the area, and he also opened a series of tantric centers in Cleveland, Philadelphia, Chicago, and New York City as well as a men's camp for tantra on Long Island. Unlike Atkinson-Ramacharaka, who seemed rarely to have an unpublished thought, Bernard left little in writing. Nevertheless, as Gordon Melton estimates, his work in shaping American yoga was "immense."[46] This work looked to the human body as aesthetic and pleasurable in ways that went beyond the more muscular approach of the natural hygiene movement and the traditional tantrism of India. As Bernard announced in the lone issue of his journal, "The trained imagination no longer worships before the shrines of churches, pagodas and mosques or there would be blaspheming the greatest, grandest and most sublime temple in the universe, the miracle of miracles, the human body." In the specific case of hatha yoga, we gain a few clues to the substance and direction of Bernard's work through his journal's stylized illustration of an "American tantrik in the practice of his yoga." Here the American yogi sits in padmasana (lotus), spine erect, with hands held in esoteric mudras or hand gestures. Evidently, too, Bernard knew about inversions and was practicing headstands, at least, at Nyack, invoking the "Art of Reversion" and enjoining students to "reverse your circulation, not once but several times a day."[47]

Bernard's legacy was in part continued in the master's thesis written by his anthropologist nephew Theos Bernard (d. 1948) in the early 1940s at Columbia University. Published as *Hatha Yoga: The Report of a Personal Experience* (1950), this work boasted thirty-seven full-page glossy black-and-white plates, including a frontispiece—photographs of a male yogi in classical hatha yoga postures.[48] In the first American work to include such representations, readers could see, among others, padmasana (lotus), sarvangasana (shoulder stand), halasana (the plough—a shoulder-stand variation), pascimotanasana (seated forward bend), bhujangasana (cobra), sirsasana (headstand), and a series of other asanas familiar to twenty-first-century students of yoga. Bernard's published bibliography, divided with scholarly correctness into primary and secondary sources, was instructive. In addition to, among primary sources, the Patanjali *Yoga Sutras,* the *Hatha Yoga Pradipika,* the *Gheranda Samhita,* and the *Siva Samhita,* the bibliography of secondary works listed, tellingly, a number by the popular and controversial Arthur Avalon. These included the well-known *The Serpent Power*—a major conduit for Western knowledge of tantrism and kundalini, the mysterious and sexually charged energy, coiled like a serpent at the base of the spine, that could be drawn to the crown of the head to bring samadhi, the ecstasy of the self contemplating its Self.[49] Secondary sources also listed works by the mysticizing scholar of Tibetan lore W. Y. Evans-Wentz and by Sir John Woodroffe (as distinct from Arthur Avalon). One work, by V. G. Rele, was titled provocatively enough *The Mysterious Kundalini,* and several—S. Sundaram's *Yoga Physical Culture,* Yogi Vithaldas's *The Yoga System of Health,* and Shri Yogendra's *Yoga Personal Hygiene*—pointed unmistakably toward hatha.[50] There will be more to say about Shri Yogendra, who would make his way to the United States and exert significant influence in the nation.

What concerns me here, however, is the substance and tenor of the Bernard text. Theos Bernard did not offer distanced learning acquired from his reading and his uncle's influence. On the contrary, and like his uncle, he went to India, and he went native. "When I went to India, I did not present myself as an academic research student, trying to probe into the intimacies of ancient cultural patterns; instead, I became a disciple." Beyond that, he understood the hatha yoga he was presenting to readers as thoroughly tantric. Hatha yoga, he explained to readers, was predicated centrally on the control of the breath, and he went on to link the term "hatha" itself to "the flowing of breath in the right nostril, called the 'sun breath', and the flowing of breath in the left nostril, called the 'moon breath'." Hatha yoga meant the union of these two breaths to "induce a mental condition called samadhi." "This," he went on to assure readers, "is not an imaginary or mythical state, though it is explained by myths, but is an actual condition that can be subjectively experienced and objectively observed." How did yogis reach this condition? The answer lay in purification of the body and the physical techniques of yoga—intended "to make dynamic a latent force in the body called Kundalini." Kundalini yoga led in turn to laya yoga, in which the "single aim" was "stilling the mind," while finally the mind's complete subjection, understood as the "Royal Road," was raja yoga. This, of course, was the scheme laid out by the formidable Arthur Avalon, whom Bernard identified, according to the conventional wisdom, with Sir John Woodroffe. Thus, following Avalon, he told readers that "all these forms are often classified under the general heading Tantrik Yoga, since they represent the practical discipline based on tantrik philosophy."[51]

What Bernard described thereafter in this very personal account was surely startling from the Western point of view—seeming almost to confirm the long-ago Transcendentalist descriptions of yogic excess but inverting them to celebrate the physical feats he was eventually able to perform. He held three-hour headstands, and he practiced a series of kriyas ("actions" or, as he called them, "duties") recommended in the *Hatha Yoga Pradipika*, including the purificatory dhauti karma in which he swallowed a three-foot length of cloth to cleanse his digestive tract. The text progressed through detailed instructions for pranayama and body locks (mudras, bandhas), disclosing yogic secrets and quoting (translated) texts generously along the way. There were practices of listening to internal sound and seeing inner light; there was a candle exercise—staring into its light to create a retinal afterimage; and in a three-month retreat to gain samadhi, there were a series of other rigorous purifications, pranayama, and hatha yoga exercises. At the end came an initiatory ceremony to induce the awakening of kundalini, although Bernard's teacher warned him that no ceremony could actually achieve that goal.[52]

If Bernard had, in fact, discovered tantra, it was a tantra that in practice operated far differently from all reports of his uncle's earlier tantrism and from what would emerge in the growing tantric movement that surfaced at Esalen and in the New Age in general during the late 1960s and beyond. Bernard's "Tantrik philosophy" and practice meant rigorous asceticism, flight from the world, totalitarian dedication, and various inscriptions on the body that looked remarkably similar to those that had been written off with disgust and revulsion in nineteenth-century accounts of yoga. The Self that Bernard could find through the awakened kundalini and samadhi seemed a far cry from the softer, kinder, ego-friendlier Self that later emerged as the enhanced body-self of the human potential movement and the American practice of yoga. At the same time, Pierre Bernard and Theos Bernard, along with William Walker Atkinson/Yogi Ramacharaka, had set some important directions for an American yogic future. Here siddhi powers had become Will Power; the world was Will and (health-building and/or ascetic) Desire; Will could succeed, and Desire could find fulfillment; the body could be liberated into a state of never-dreamed health and well-being; even if attained through harshness and asceticism, there was a (disciplined and discipline-producing) pleasure that surpassed all knowledge in this body's pleasure; and Will, Desire, Health, and Pleasure could all lead into the highest spiritual realities that humans might experience and receive. Best of all, in the American mode, humans could achieve all of this for and in themselves.

THE AMERICAN MISSIONS OF SHRI YOGENDRA AND PARAMAHANSA YOGANANDA

That acknowledged, just as in the earlier heyday of Vivekananda, Americans did not always need to work alone, with just books as teachers, in their private yogic quests. Nor did they need to travel, like Theos Bernard, to South Asia for wisdom and its practical application (although, to be sure, they increasingly would do so). Even before the 1965 change in the immigration law—which brought more Asians and more elite Asians to the nation—the East was coming to the West. Yogic teachers were bringing saving knowledge to American disciples. During his research stay in India in 1937, the younger Bernard had made his way to the Yoga Institute of Bombay where one Shri Yogendra taught his "scientific" yoga—the man whom Melton credits with initiating the scientific approach and with being "largely responsible for the revival and spread of hatha yoga in the twentieth century."[53] Now Shri Yogendra would come to other American seekers. A disciple of Paramahansa Madhavadasaji of Malsar, Shri Yogendra (born in 1897 as Manibhai Haribhai Desai) returned to the householder life after a several-year sojourn with his guru, marrying instead of becoming a renunciate and swami. What he had learned from his teacher, especially, was the study and practice of hatha yoga, and he would thereafter work to put it on an academic footing and to establish its scientific basis. In this context, according to his biographer, Yogendra came to America at the end of 1919 with the aim of "popularizing yoga." He went back to India less than five years later, intending to return to the United States but thwarted by the restrictive immigration legislation of 1924. Still, he had managed to found his Yoga Institute at Santa Cruz, California, and he had written four works on yoga.[54]

We glean some sense of Yogendra's teaching from these works, and in general they resonate more with the natural hygiene–physical culture orientation of Yogi Ramacharaka than with the tantric ambience of the Bernards. Yogendra's yoga was based on the *Hatha Yoga Pradipika,* and that text's concern for purification, which we have already seen in the yogic experiment of Theos Bernard, became for Yogendra a question of health and hygiene. "Even the civilized society has been sick, to a more or less extent, *throughout history,*" he would later write in *Why Yoga,* "because human civilization and culture did not fully succeed in weeding out the grass roots of savage inherited potentials." He was thoroughly committed to the science that grounded the health-building enterprise; he worked with medical professionals in New York; and he knew such natural health celebrities as Bernarr Macfadden, Benedict Lust, and John Harvey Kellogg. Still, the science he preached was a science of the spiritual. Hatha yoga would put its students "in the direct touch with the Reality (of objects on which they contemplate)." Besides, the physical body that demanded the rigorous discipline of natural hygiene was but one of a series of bodies. In the textual tradition of South Asia and in the language that Theosophists were continuing to invoke, he could tell that "yoga recognizes more subtle bodies or sheaths . . . than one."[55]

Shri Yogendra was a new type of Asian teacher. Neither an ancient chanter of texts nor a renunciate hidden away for years in Himalayan hills, like Vivekananda, he was already partially a Westerner before he ever came to the United States. Growing up in British India, matriculating—before he met his guru—at St. Xavier's College in Bombay, translating the yogic message into a scientific argot, linking his religio-philosophical views to those of Plotinus and Henri Bergson, Shri Yogendra was a blended product of East and West.[56] It is too simple to say that East (Yogendra) met West (Americans) in the United States in the 1920s. More complexly, East-West met West, and the West that got met was already textually in touch with a series of Asian sources and had even, in a few cases, sent its progeny traveling to sit at the feet of South Asian masters. Twenty-first-century language is peppered with references to globalization and transnationalism. Already, in the early twentieth century, and earlier in the case of Vivekananda, we can see the contact of cultures and their transformation.

Culture contact and transformation were even more thoroughly the case for the celebrated Bengali Paramahansa Yogananda (1893–1952), who came to America in 1920 to attend, as India's delegate, the International Congress of Religious Liberals in Boston. Afterward he remained to lecture and teach on the East Coast and then to establish the headquarters of the Self-Realization Fellowship, which he had founded in 1920, in Los Angeles. It is in Yogananda, as the name he chose for his American organization already suggests, that we get a conscious language of the Self to refer to the Atman and its long-hailed union with Brahman. But this acknowledgment should not be overdrawn, despite the organizational title. Yogananda's language of the Self was hardly incessant, and, indeed, he spoke as much, or more, of the Christ within. Born as Mukunda Lal Ghosh in Gorakhpur in northeastern India, close to the Himalayas, Yogananda—like his guru Sri Yukteswar Giri and his guru's guru (who was also his father's guru) Lahiri Mahasaya—was a Westernized Hindu long before he ever made his way to the West Coast of the United States. His father had been a railroad official, and the younger Ghosh's attempts to run away to the Himalayas were thwarted and disdained. When, in 1910, Mukunda Ghosh met and came under the tutelage of Sri Yukteswar, he was urged by his guru to attend Calcutta University. He did, and he graduated in 1915. It was only thereafter that he took formal vows as a swami and renunciate.

Yogananda's *Autobiography of a Yogi* (1946) is an important document in constructing any account of what happened to Yogananda, yoga, and its Americanized form. A complex and enormously skillful hybrid of traditional Indic elements, combinative Hindu-Western culture in India, and self-fashioning and self-posturing meant to appeal to American readers even as Yogananda drew them into an alternate world, the autobiography provides clues to an important transition time for American yoga. For simplicity's sake, we can identify two simultaneous streams that ran through its pages. On the one side, there was the appeal to marvel and miracle, to the siddhi powers that were part of the yogic tradition that Yogananda represented. Here was the mysterious Mahavatar Babaji, hailed by Yogananda as the founding guru from which his lineage descended. This Babaji was hundreds of years old, materialized and dematerialized at will (and in so doing supplied indirect insight into the possible sources of Madame Blavatsky's Mahatmas), and had appeared to Yogananda to commission him to spread his kriya yoga to the West. On the other side, there was a running barrage of footnotes that contained a series of Christian gospel references and theological points regarding Christ, a copious supply of quotations from Ralph Waldo Emerson, and a steady commentary on what Yogananda considered cutting-edge science of the period to establish the scientific credentials of yoga.[57]

Indeed, what Paramahansa Yogananda stressed about kriya yoga was its unequaled utility as a "scientific" path to the attainment of samadhi, the highest state of yogic realization—with exact and practical details revealed only after an initiatory period in the Self-Realization Fellowship. The "science" of this yoga, however, smacked of the mysterious kundalini power already admired by Theosophists. "The scientific method teaches a process enabling us to draw to our *central part*—spine and brain—the life current distributed throughout the organs and other parts of our body. The process consists of magnetizing the spinal column and the brain, which contain the seven main centers, with the result that the distributed life electricity is drawn back to the original centers of discharge and is experienced in the form of light. In this state the spiritual Self can consciously free itself from its bodily and mental distractions."[58]

More than that, kriya yoga flourished, for Yogananda, in a context in which the physical body became active and energized. In 1918, he had opened a school for boys in Ranchi, a town in Bihar, some 200 miles from Calcutta. Here students were taught not only yoga meditation but also what Yogananda called "a unique system of health and physical development, *Yogoda*," the principles of which he believed he had discovered two years earlier. "Realizing that man's body is like an electric battery," he wrote, "I reasoned that it could be recharged with energy through the direct agency of the human will."[59] All of this language of energy and electricity hints of a tantric quotient, perhaps disguised for an American audience, perhaps already reinvented in India in a Westernized Hindu milieu. In fact, as for the fabled Pierre Bernard and for a string of Hindu gurus to the West, Yogananda now comes with a sex scandal attached to his name, since an elderly miner from Oregon has claimed to be his son. Reportedly, Yogananda had had a series of relationships with women despite his celibate swami vows.[60] Be that as it may, what Yogananda had done was to bring tantric themes in touch with an American language of science that circled New Thought and theosophical themes and that coexisted comfortably with liberal versions of Christianity. The kundalini had met the Self, and the Self was discovered to be the living Christ presence within.

NEW TEACHERS, NEW TEACHINGS, AND THE NEW YOGA OF ESALEN

After Yogendra and Yogananda, a series of yogic teachers—of hatha yoga and meditation yoga and both of them combined—came and went in the American yogic world. Kriya yoga itself fractured into a series of competing forms and teachers. As for others, there is not space here to tarry further on leading names, although a series do come to mind—Indra Devi (Eugenie Petersen), who was healed in India by Krishnamacharya and studied with him; Yogi Gupta, who was a follower of Swami Sivananda Saraswati, founder of the Divine Life Society; Swami Satchidananda, likewise a popularizer of Sivananda's "integral yoga"; and Richard Hittleman, who authored numerous popular books and introduced hatha yoga to television in the 1960s. Meanwhile, with the publication of B.K.S. Iyengar's *Light on Yoga,* which became the sacred text of the hatha yoga world, his visits to America, and the ambitious worldwide certification process for Iyengar teachers, a canon was emerging.[61] Along the way, yoga got feminized, and women became the prevailing producers and consumers of yogic asanas. In meditation yoga, likewise, divine mothers and female spiritual teachers proliferated—and kundalini formed their general message. Against the backdrop of the civil rights movement, the Vietnam War, second-wave feminism, and rising ethnic consciousness among a series of groups, more and more non–Asian Americans were turning east and refashioning what they found in new forms of spirituality in the New Age movement and beyond.

Among meditation yoga teachers, Maharishi Mahesh Yogi achieved celebrity status during the 1960s when, discovered by the Beatles, he taught the simple silent mantra practice that he called Transcendental Meditation. It is significant that it came trailing behind it promises not of samadhi but of lowered blood pressure, increased intelligence, relief from stress, and reduction of crime in locales inhabited by a critical mass of meditators.[62] By the 1970s, in turn, Swami Muktananda was visiting the United States, preaching the good news of a "meditation revolution." His American disciples in Siddha Yoga practiced and, under his successor Swami Chidvilasananda (Gurumayi), rationalized and domesticated a form of tantric yoga. Important here, Muktananda's message was one of interior consciousness and bliss, of the divinity of the Self that echoed, in stronger, more insistent language, the earlier teaching of the Self-Realization Fellowship. "Honor your Self, worship your Self, meditate on your Self," Muktananda enjoined. "God dwells within you as you."[63] Still further, at South Fallsburg, New York, in Muktananda's American ashram, hatha yoga was in. Between them, the Maharishi and Muktananda spelled out for devotees the new Americanized version of ancient India—a world bathed in spiritual consciousness and bliss that also had become a pleasure dome and abode of this-worldly good health, good fortune, and thorough enjoyment.

As we survey this late-twentieth-century spiritual landscape, arguably we obscure more than we inform if we pronounce this transformed American yoga clearly and simply a form of Indian tantrism. It is true that if we single out hatha yoga, scholars of yogic India have pointed unmistakably to its tantric origins.[64] As practiced in twentieth- and twenty-first-century America, however, it would be overly simple to call hatha yoga a tantric practice. Nor, despite the popularity of kundalini in numerous contexts, can meditation forms of yoga prevalent in New Age spirituality be described, in uncontested ways, as tantric. But the enlightened body-self functions at the center of both hatha and meditation yogas, and this is the place to think through the role of Esalen in advancing that body-self's trajectory into an American future. Not that Esalen was sole initiator or operator on the American yogic stage or that it single-handedly brought the Self to the self in a body of bliss. We know too much now about the pervasiveness of subtly (and decidedly transformed) tantric themes in this emerging American yogic spirituality to settle for so easy an explanation.[65] I argue, however, that Esalen did act as an important culture broker, a model of certain religio-cultural themes, and a broadcaster of the new-enlightenment message of the Self/self and its embodied blissfulness. Esalen gave the word to many Americans who otherwise might not have heard the news—or, at least, not heard it so clearly and authoritatively.

One obvious—and productive—way to tackle this Esalen presence and role in American yogic self-fashioning is through the persona and practice of Sri Aurobindo (1872–1950). Walter Truett Anderson tells how Esalen cofounder Michael Murphy first encountered Aurobindo at Stanford University, where he read the huge and formidable *Life Divine* as a result of his philosophy class under Frederic Spiegelberg and began to meditate. As Jeffrey Kripal noted in his chapter in the present volume, Murphy experienced a metanoia, a spiritual conversion that turned his life around and led him to drop out of Stanford for a quarter to study at the American Academy of Asian Studies in San Francisco and return to the university thereafter to study religion and philosophy. So profound was the influence of Aurobindo on Murphy that, in 1956, he traveled to Pondicherry, a French colonial city in India, where 1,500 devotees of the guru were living under the direction of Mirra Alfassa Richard (1878–1973), the "Mother," at his ashram. Murphy remained for sixteen months, meditating for eight hours a day (not a requirement) and participating in the life of the community. He liked its "spiritual sports" (i.e., its sports program), we are told, and its freedom regarding daily schedules. But he thought he saw a form of cultism among the devotees—what Anderson calls the "almost idolatrous reverence for the works of Aurobindo and the daily pronouncements of the Mother"—and he never became a total Aurobindian.[66]

Who was this Sri Aurobindo whose ghost still haunted the Pondicherry ashram through the adulation of his devotees? Born as Aurobindo Acroyd Ghose in Calcutta, the Bengali Aurobindo was, like Yogendra and Yogananda, the child of Westernized parents; his father, in fact, was a Western-style physician. Only English was spoken in the parental home, and Aurobindo was educated at Western schools throughout. He was brought to England at the age of seven or so and remained there for the next thirteen years, the last two of them at King's College, Cambridge. When he returned to India, he became a professor and educator but also a passionate leader in the growing independence movement. His politics brought him a national reputation until, in 1908, he was arrested by the British and thrown in jail for seditious activity. During this period of solitary imprisonment, Aurobindo began to practice the meditation yoga he had earlier learned in a new and more serious way. He also began to study the great classics of South Asian spirituality, among them the Bhagavad Gita and the Upanishads. By 1910, released from prison with an acquittal but still hounded by authorities for his nationalist activities, he followed inner guidance and ended up in French territory in Pondicherry. There his political activism fell away, his message grew more spiritual, and he became the head of an ashram. He wrote prolifically on philosophical and spiritual themes. After 1914, when Mirra Alfassa Richard joined him as a spiritual partner, the "Mother"—as devotees called her—came to be associated in the work, continuing it alone for many years after his death.[67]

Aurobindo's "integral yoga," which he developed at the ashram, was in fact what might be described as a "right-handed" tantric system—that is, one in which no deliberate or intentional transgressive activity was enjoined or practiced but in which the material world was valued positively and affirmed. Here, instead of the asceticism that separated body from spirit, the two were united. Yoga moved the practitioner into spirit, only to return with clarity, bliss, and empowerment to transform the everyday world. The result, however, was hardly existence in a lotusland of pleasured absorption. Rather, the world was the place where the eternal Brahman rediscovered its body and being, and evolution dominated the Aurobindian vision. He introduced *The Life Divine,* for example, by declaring that the "animal" was "a living laboratory in which Nature has . . . worked out man." It is significant that he added, "Man himself may well be a thinking and living laboratory in whom and with whose conscious co-operation she wills to work out the superman, the god." Aurobindo's yoga was meant to bring "a divine creation here on earth," as Georges van Vrekhem wrote, "a divine species, as the successor of the present human being." Here was the Self reveling in its earthly self. And for devotees, here embodying that exalted Self and self were Aurobindo and the Mother—twin avatars to bring in the Kingdom of God, "making possible the appearance of a new species on our planet" and playing an "active and even decisive role in world history." As van Vrekhem summarized:

> In the view of Sri Aurobindo and the Mother, the Earth is an evolutionary field in which the mental being we call human must be succeeded by a supramental being just as man has been preceded by a whole series of inframental beings. Man is a transitional creature. For every material, terrestrial embodiment of a new evolutionary gradation, a direct intervention of the Divine in his creation is required. Such an embodiment—this time a complete, double-poled Avatar—were the Mother and Sri Aurobindo.[68]

What did the vision mean in practice? At Pondicherry, and later at Auroville, the aspiring planetary community that Richard established in 1968, women and men were treated equally and moved freely, ignoring Indian social conventions in the process. Meanwhile, at Pondicherry, Richard—like Yogananda at Ranchi—founded a nontraditional school that aimed to teach its students self-reflection. More than that, self-reflection meant physical culture, and in the Playground—an important center—there were gymnastics and bars, boxing and horse-vaulting, and hatha yoga. The girls on the grounds wore shorts. The body had its "mind," the cells had theirs, and so did hard, seemingly intractable matter.[69]

This, of course, gets us ahead of Michael Murphy's story. But Murphy caught the vision, and the "spiritual sports" he enjoyed at Pondicherry take on a new aura in light of the evolutionary tantric metaphysics of the Aurobindian synthesis. Murphy would reject the notion of the avatars. Like a good American—an American cultural vision of perfectionism and divinization pervaded the culture from the nineteenth century—he would celebrate the God within and the God embodied. And, as Kripal argues in his chapter in this volume, in the democratic ethos of Murphy's American culture could be found a major departure from the religious culture of India. In America, there was space for the Self and self without the trappings of the guru. Thus, when the Esalen Institute opened its doors in 1962, it took to heart its mission of exploring the "human potential"—a phrase that former *Look* magazine senior editor George Leonard, Esalen's vice-president and later its president, would reiterate again and again. To the point here, Esalen understood the human potential to reside in the enlightened body-self. Its bodywork brigade, its lush beachside ceremonies of nudity and hot tub, its evolving humanistic and transpersonal psychologies that pushed at micro-adjustments of the self-in-relation, its social vision of one interconnected, interracial, and interethnic world—all of these must be read, from Murphy's side, as a selection and partial translation of the Aurobindonian charter.

So there was India on Big Sur shores. But there was also an enormous legacy from an American past and as large a presence from an evolving American yogic culture. Esalen inherited Transcendentalist idealism with its Oversoul gone Indic, and it absorbed an abiding theosophical bequest carried forward subtly in a longing for Asia and an older evolutionary vision. It felt the old-style newness in New Thought, although it never named the movement, embracing Will and Desire, health and positive thinking, wealth and metaphysics. It placed its own American swamis and gurus on its roster of faculty—with names such as Fritz Perls and Abraham Maslow, Baba Ram Das and Timothy Leary, James Pike and William Schutz, Starhawk and Alan Watts, Paul Tillich and Aldous Huxley.

But Esalen did not stop there. If it seemed to be a giant sea sponge absorbing American culture, its twin talents for synthesis and celebrity made it the purveyor of a new American yoga, one that summarized past and present but went on to broadcast it to willing takers. The media helped enormously, and so did Esalen's continuing educational programs, crafted for a new clientele in weekend or five-day bytes that could be inserted into workday worlds. If the plot of this account is how the enlightened body-self came to be, it is also how it came to full recognition and form in an Esalen-infused American culture. Esalen Self-fashioning taught a cross-section of Americans, and it led them to an enhanced ego-self, to this world, to their realization as new American Gods and Goddesses who walked a transformed earth. Esalen led them to a Shangri-La in which sacred merged with secular, yogic inversions subverted religion-as-usual, and peace and pleasure came to this world amid the meditative bliss. The message may seem overly simple in this early twenty-first-century time in which war and terror continually rehearse for us the horrors of what humans can do to other humans and, in the process, to themselves. Yet the message is there and will not soon go away. To deny the long pathway to the consciousness and bliss of the enlightened body-self in this transformed American experience of yoga is as bad as to deny the complex and morally ambiguous world in which it finds itself.[70]

Notes

1. This may be an overstatement (see J. P. Rao Rayapati, *Early American Interest in Vedanta: Pre-Emersonian Interest in Vedic Literature and Vedantic Philosophy* [New York: Asia Publishing House, 1973]). Yet arguably it is only with Emerson and later Transcendentalists that knowledge of South Asian beliefs builds on a pervasive and well-integrated religio-philosophical synthesis that already exists—achieves what might be called a critical American transposition—and is articulated authoritatively and publicly. As Rayapati assesses, "Vedic literature was read in early America mainly out of an interest in the curious" (ix).

2. Ralph Waldo Emerson, "The Over-Soul," in Ralph Waldo Emerson, *The Collected Works of Ralph Waldo Emerson,* vol. 2, *Essays: First Series,* ed. Joseph Slater et al. (Cambridge: Harvard University Press, Belknap Press, 1979), 159, 162, 171, 174–175.

3. See Frederic Ives Carpenter, *Emerson and Asia* (Cambridge, Mass.: Harvard University Press, 1930), esp. 75–78, where he demonstrates clearly that Asia entered the Emersonian equation as a corroborating, not first, voice.

4. See Ralph Waldo Emerson, *The Complete Works of Ralph Waldo Emerson*, ed. Edward Waldo Emerson (Boston: Houghton, Mifflin, 1903–1906), 6: 426n (emphasis in original). See also Carpenter, *Emerson and Asia*, 123, where after "(paramatman)," he interpolates in square brackets "[i.e., Over-Soul]." In so doing, Carpenter echoes Emerson's son and editor Edward Waldo Emerson, who precedes his quotation from Emerson's 1861 journal entry with a discussion that links it to the Oversoul (Emerson, *Complete Works*, 6: 425n).

5. William Harding and Carl Bode, eds., *The Correspondence of Henry David Thoreau* (New York: New York University Press, 1958), 251, quoted in Carl T. Jackson, *The Oriental Religions and American Thought: Nineteenth-Century Explorations* (Westport, Conn.: Greenwood Press, 1981), 65. Arthur E. Christy long ago acknowledged the Transcendentalist's yogic consciousness in *The Orient in American Transcendentalism: A Study of Emerson, Thoreau, and Alcott* (1932; reprint, New York: Octagon Books, 1963), 199.

6. Henry D. Thoreau, *Walden*, ed., J. Lyndon Shanley, (Princeton, N.J.: Princeton University Press, 1971), 4, 8, 96 (emphasis in original), 298, 112.

7. Henry D. Thoreau, *A Week on the Concord and Merrimack Rivers*, ed. Carl F. Hovde, William L. Howarth, and Elizabeth Hall Witherell (Princeton, N.J.: Princeton University Press, 1980), 136; Arthur Versluis, *American Transcendentalism and Asian Religions* (New York: Oxford University Press, 1993), 84. For Unitarian moralism, see Daniel Walker Howe, *The Unitarian Conscience: Harvard Moral Philosophy, 1805–1861* (Cambridge, Mass.: Harvard University Press, 1970). And for an essentially Christianizing reading of Thoreau, see William J. Wolf, *Thoreau: Mystic, Prophet, Ecologist* (Philadelphia: Pilgrim Press, 1974).

8. Lydia Maria Child, *The Progress of Religious Ideas, through Successive Ages*, 3 vols. (New York: Francis, 1855).

9. Hannah Adams, *A Dictionary of All Religions and Religious Denominations, Jewish, Heathen, Mahometan, and Christian, Ancient and Modern* (New York: James Eastburn, and Boston: Cummings and Hilliard, 1817).

10. Quotations are from the following edition of Child's work: Lydia Maria Child, *The Progress of Religious Ideas, through Successive Ages*, 4th ed. (New York: James Miller, 1855), 1: viii, 10–11. For the index, see 3: 465–478.

11. Ibid., 1: 23.

12. James Freeman Clarke, *Ten Great Religions: An Essay in Comparative Theology*, 34th ed. (1871; reprint, Boston: Houghton, Mifflin, 1895), 519–528, 83.

13. Ibid.

14. Ibid.

15. Ralph Waldo Emerson, *Nature* (1836), in Emerson, *Collected Works*, vol. 1, *Nature, Addresses, and Lectures* (Cambridge, Mass.: Harvard University Press, Belknap Press, 1971), 7.

16. For the Theosophical Society as a spiritualist reform movement, see Stephen Prothero, "From Spiritualism to Theosophy: 'Uplifting' a Democratic Tradition," *Religion and American Culture: A Journal of Interpretation* 3, no. 2 (Summer 1993): 197–216. See also Stephen Prothero, *The White Buddhist: The Asian Odyssey of Henry Steel Olcott* (Bloomington: Indiana University Press, 1996), 38–61.

17. H. P. Blavatsky, *Isis Unveiled: A Master-Key to the Mysteries of Ancient and Modern Science and Theology* (New York: J. W. Bouton, 1877); H. P. Blavatsky, *The*

Secret Doctrine: The Synthesis of Science, Religion, and Philosophy (London: Theosophical Publishing Company, and New York: William Q. Judge, 1888); H. P. Blavatsky, *The Key to Theosophy* (London: Theosophical Publishing Company and New York: William Q. Judge, 1889).

18. H. P. Blavatsky, *Isis Unveiled: A Master-Key to the Mysteries of Ancient and Modern Science and Theology* (1877; reprint, Los Angeles: Theosophy Company, 1975), 2: 565, 612, 620, 346.

19. H. P. Blavatsky, *The Secret Doctrine: The Synthesis of Science, Religion, and Philosophy* (1888; reprint, Los Angeles: Theosophy Company, 1974), 1: 43, 132, 158, 293; 2: 296; 1: 47, 95 (emphasis in original).

20. H. P. Blavatsky, *The Key to Theosophy: An Abridgement*, ed. Joy Mills (Wheaton, Ill.: Theosophical Publishing, Quest Book, 1972), 56, 63, 74, 81, 83 (emphasis in original).

21. William Q. Judge, assisted by James Henderson Connelly, *The Yoga Aphorisms of Patanjali: An Interpretation* (New York: Path, 1889). My information on the translator—unlisted in the 1973 copy I have used (see the next note)—comes from the *New York Times,* June 10, 1889, p. 3, col. 1.

22. William Q. Judge, *The Yoga Aphorisms of Patanjali* (1889; reprint, Los Angeles: Theosophy Company, 1973), viii–ix, 33–34, ix.

23. Ibid., 30–31, 61, xvi.

24. Ibid., 57, xiv–xv.

25. *New York Times,* June 10, 1889, p. 3, col. 1.

26. J. Gordon Melton, "Yoga," in J. Gordon Melton with Jerome Clark and Aidan A. Kelly, eds., *New Age Encyclopedia* (Detroit: Gale Research, 1990), 502. I am very much indebted to Melton's essay for my own construction of the late-nineteenth-century and early-twentieth-century history of American yoga.

27. Rama Prasad, *Nature's Finer Forces: The Science of Breath and the Philosophy of the Tattvas* (1894; reprint, [Whitefish, Mont.]: Kessinger Publishing 1997).

28. See W. Michael Ashcraft, *The Dawn of the New Cycle: Point Loma Theosophists and American Culture* (Knoxville: University of Tennessee Press, 2002), 85–107, 95, 102. I am indebted to Sarah Whedon for bringing this work to my attention.

29. See Swami Vivekananda, *The Complete Works of Swami Vivekananda, Mayavati Memorial Edition,* 14th ed. (Calcutta: Advaita Ashrama, 1973); Elizabeth De Michelis, *A History of Modern Yoga: Patanjali and Western Esotericism* (London and New York: Continuum, 2004), esp. 119–126, 124-125. I am grateful to David White for information on the absence of raja yoga from the *Yoga Sutras.*

30. *New York Times,* October 15, 1893, p. 22.

31. Melton, "Yoga," 502.

32. Gary Ward Materra, "Women in Early New Thought: Lives and Theology in Transition from the Civil War to World War I" (Ph.D. diss., University of California, Santa Barbara, 1997).

33. Yogi Ramacharaka, *Advanced Course in Yogi Philosophy and Oriental Occultism* (Chicago: Yogi Publication Society, 1905); Yogi Ramacharaka, *Hatha Yoga; or, The Yogi Philosophy of Physical Well-Being* (Chicago: Yogi Publication Society, 1904); Yogi Ramacharaka, *Science of Breath: A Complete Manual of the Oriental Breathing Philosophy of Physical, Mental, Psychic, and Spiritual Development* (Chicago: Yogi Publication Society, 1905); Yogi Ramacharaka, *A Series of Lessons in Raja Yoga* (Chicago: Yogi Pub-

lication Society, 1906); Yogi Ramacharaka, *The Science of Psychic Healing* (Chicago: Yogi Publication Society, 1906).

34. Melton, "Yoga," 502.

35. Mabel Collins, *Light on the Path: A Treatise Written for the Personal Use of Those Who Are Ignorant of the Eastern Wisdom, and Who Desire to Enter within Its Influence* (Boston: Cupples, Upham and Company, 1886). Collins was a novelist and the coeditor of the London theosophical journal *Lucifer,* and—after first claiming Helena Blavatsky's Mahatma Koot Hoomi or another Hindu adept as author—she subsequently declared that she merely wrote down the words of the treatise as she saw them "written on the walls of a place I visit spiritually." See Sylvia Cranston, *HPB: The Extraordinary Life and Influence of Helena Blavatsky, Founder of the Modern Theosophical Movement* (New York: G. P. Putnam's Sons, 1994), 371; and Alvin Boyd Kuhn, *Theosophy: A Modern Revival of Ancient Wisdom* (New York: Henry Holt, 1930), 301.

36. Yogi Ramacharaka, *A Series of Lessons in Raja Yoga* (Chicago: Yogi Publication Society, 1906), 197–198, 216–218, 202.

37. Ibid., vi, 1–3. For the Emersonianism, see Emerson, *Nature*, 23–29, 42–43, 8.

38. Theodore Roosevelt, *The Strenuous Life: Essays and Addresses* (New York: Century Company, 1901); "Back to Nature," *Outlook* 74 (June 8, 1993): 305–306, quoted in Clifford Putney, *Muscular Christianity: Manhood and Sports in Protestant America, 1880–1920* (Cambridge, Mass.: Harvard University Press, 2001), 35 (see 33–39 for a useful general discussion of these themes).

39. James C. Whorton, *Crusaders for Fitness: The History of American Health Reformers* (Princeton, N.J.: Princeton University Press, 1982), 281–282.

40. Yogi Ramacharaka, *Hatha Yoga; or, The Yogi Philosophy of Physical Well-Being* (Chicago: Yogi Publication Society, 1904), 9–10, 11, 13.

41. Ibid., 195 (emphasis in original).

42. Ibid., 17–18.

43. Ibid., 11–13.

44. Ibid., 232–233, 211–213.

45. My account of Bernard's life is based on J. Gordon Melton, "Pierre Bernard," in Melton, Clark, and Kelley, eds., *New Age Encyclopedia,* 64–65; Hugh B. Urban, "The Omnipotent Oom: Tantra and Its Impact on Modern Western Esotericism," *Esoterica* 3 (2001): 218–259, available online at http.//www.esoteric.msu.edu/VolumeIII/HTML/Oom.html; n.a., "The Library of Pierre Arnold Bernard," available online at http://www.vanderbilt.edu/-stringer/library.htm. For an account that emphasizes Arnold's sexual transgressiveness, see also Hugh B. Urban, "*Magia Sexualis*: Sex, Secrecy, and Liberation in Modern Western Esotericism," *Journal of the American Academy of Religion* 72, no. 3 (2004): 715–723.

46. "The Library of Pierre Arnold Bernard"; Melton, "Pierre Bernard," 65. So far as I can tell, Bernard's published writing seems confined to the single issue of his journal.

47. On the differences between American and traditional Indian tantra, see Urban, "Omnipotent Oom," esp. 34–38; Pierre Arnold Bernard, *International Journal of the Tantrik Order in America,* quoted in Urban, "Omnipotent Oom"; Charles Boswell, "The Great Fuss and Fume over the Omnipotent Oom," *True: The Man's Magazine,*

January 1965, 86. According to Richard Tarnas, Ida Rolf—a favorite at Esalen with her well-known Rolfing bodywork technique—was Bernard's student.

48. Theos Bernard, *Hatha Yoga: The Report of a Personal Experience* (London and New York: Rider, 1950).

49. Arthur Avalon, *The Serpent Power*, trans. with introduction and commentary (Madras: Ganesh, 1927). As Jeffrey Kripal discussed this matter in his conference paper (and I am indebted to him for this information), Arthur Avalon was a composite—not merely a pseudonym for Sir John Woodroffe as long thought, but a collaboration of Woodroffe and one Atul Behari Ghosh, a Bengali and tantric scholar. See Kathleen Taylor, *Sir John Woodroffe, Tantra, and Bengal: "An Indian Soul in a European Body?"* (Richmond, Surrey: Curzon Press, 2001).

50. See Bernard, *Hatha Yoga*, 97–99.

51. Ibid., ix, 15.

52. Ibid., 35, 75–96.

53. J. Gordon Melton, "Shri Yogendra," in Melton, Clark, and Kelly, eds., *New Age Encyclopedia*, 511.

54. See the hagiographic biography by Vijayadev Yogendra in *Shri Yogendra: The Householder Yogi* (Santa Cruz: Yoga Institute, 1977), esp. 56. Vijayadev Yogendra states that the Yoga Institute was founded at Bear Mountain, near Tuxedo Park, New York, in 1920 (*Shri Yogendra*, 64), and, indeed Shri Yogendra did work in New York for a time. But Shri Yogendra himself identifies Santa Cruz as the place where he founded the American Yoga Institute. See Shri Yogendra, *Yoga Asanas Simplified*, 7th ed. (Bombay: Yoga Institute, 1958), 10.

55. Shri Yogendra, *Why Yoga* (Santa Cruz: Yoga Institute, 1976), 20 (emphasis in original), 53, 51; Melton, "Yoga," 503.

56. See Melton, "Shri Yogendra," 511; Yogendra, *Why Yoga*, 54.

57. For the classic description (for the uninitiated), see Paramahansa Yogananda, *Autobiography of a Yogi* (1946; reprint, Los Angeles: Self-Realization Fellowship, 1998).

58. Ibid., esp. 275–286; Paramahansa Yogananda, *The Science of Religion*, rev. and exp. ed. (1924; reprint, Los Angeles: Self-Realization Fellowship, 2001), 67 (emphasis in original).

59. Yogananda, *Autobiography of a Yogi*, 288–289 (emphasis in original).

60. See Carter Phipps, "In Search of Babaji," *What Is Enlightenment?* (Spring/Summer 2002): 85. Phipps cites an interview with Marshall Govindan as well as an investigative report in the *New Times* of Los Angeles.

61. B.K.S. Iyengar, *Light on Yoga* (New York: Schocken Books, 1966).

62. On the Maharishi, see Catherine L. Albanese, *America: Religions and Religion*, 3rd ed. (Belmont, Calif.: Wadsworth, 1999), 306–307.

63. See Douglas Renfrew Brooks et al., *Meditation Revolution: A History and Theology of the Siddha Yoga Lineage* (South Fallsburg, N.Y.: Agama Press, 1997), esp. the introduction by Brooks, xix–xli, xxxvii; and for the most responsible and believable account of Muktananda's tantra, see Sarah Caldwell, "The Heart of the Secret: A Personal and Scholarly Encounter with Shakta Tantrism in Siddha Yoga," *Nova Religio* 5, no. 1 (October 2001): 9–51.

64. See David Gordon White, *The Alchemical Body: Siddha Traditions in Medieval India* (Chicago: University of Chicago Press, 1996), 140–142; and Georg Feuer-

stein, *The Yoga Tradition: Its History, Literature, Philosophy, and Practice* (Prescott, Ariz.: Hohm Press, 2001), 382–387.

65. See, for example, Urban, "Omnipotent Oom," 34–38.

66. Walter Truett Anderson, *The Upstart Spring: Esalen and the American Awakening* (Reading, Mass.: Addison-Wesley, 1983), 27–31. *The Life Divine* was first published serially from 1914 to 1919 in Sri Aurobindo's periodical the *Arya.* It was thereafter revised and enlarged in 1939–1940 and appeared in an American single-volume edition in 1949. See Sri Aurobindo, *The Life Divine* (Twin Lakes, Wis.: Lotus Press, 2000). This edition is 1,154 pages long (!).

67. The most serviceable short biography of Aurobindo is Peter Heehs, *Sri Aurobindo: A Brief Biography* (1989; reprint, Delhi: Oxford University Press, 1997).

68. Aurobindo, *Life Divine,* 8; Georges van Vrekhem, *Beyond the Human Species: The Life and Work of Sri Aurobindo and the Mother* (St. Paul: Paragon House, 1998), 128, 215, 295.

69. Ibid., 304–306; see George Leonard, *Walking on the Edge of the World: A Memoir of the Sixties and Beyond* (Boston: Houghton Mifflin, 1988), esp. 107–248.

70. Many thanks are due to Michael Cox for his research assistance.

NOTES ON THE PREHISTORY OF THE HUMAN POTENTIAL MOVEMENT: THE VEDANTA SOCIETY AND GERALD HEARD'S TRABUCO COLLEGE

Timothy Miller

From its beginning in 1962, the Esalen Institute has been known as, among other things, a meeting ground between East and West—"something of a center-point for the translation of Asian religions into American culture," as Jeffrey Kripal has put it.[1] Some of the foundations for that reputation are fairly well known to those with at least a cursory familiarity with Esalen's history and programs. That Esalen cofounders Michael Murphy and Richard Price were influenced—one might say inspired—by Frederic Spiegelberg at Stanford University; that they became involved with the nascent American Academy of Asian Studies, where they came into contact with other Asianists, including Alan Watts; that Esalen early on presented workshops and seminars that promoted East-West encounter: those things are familiar parts of the record. But history is a complex tapestry of influences, and in the case of Esalen those influences go beyond Spiegelberg and Watts and the Academy of Asian Studies. This chapter seeks to bring to light another part of the

Asian-American encounter that helped make Esalen what it finally became.

Walter Truett Anderson, in his history of Esalen, provides a brief but intriguing glimpse of one group of persons who helped Murphy and Price as they worked to refine their vision of what would become Esalen: Aldous Huxley, Gerald Heard, Christopher Isherwood, and others who were, in Anderson's words, "members of the sizable circle of Southern California students of Buddhist and Hindu philosophy."[2] Particularly important, in Anderson's account, was Gerald Heard, a close friend of Huxley's who had himself founded a center that in many ways portended Esalen. Heard's proto-Esalen (about which more presently) had closed in 1947 after just five years of operation, but Heard maintained a passionate interest in human growth, human potential, for the rest of his life. Here is Anderson's depiction of Heard's passion as experienced by Murphy and Price in 1961, when they were trying to put their plan together:

> Huxley had so diffidently advocated a research project, had so hesitantly suggested its revolutionary possibilities. He thought something of that sort *might* happen. Heard thought it *had* to happen. Mankind, he believed, was at the turning point and could be saved from destruction only by a great leap, a new vision. There would have to be a psychological revolution, and, yes, there would have to be institutions to serve it. He had written of the need for "gymnasia for the mind" and in the 1940s had launched his own version in Southern California, a spiritual/educational center called Trabuco College. It had failed, but Heard remained irrepressibly optimistic about the prospects for new undertakings, new horizons, vast evolutionary transformations. He was a man of limitless energies, a brilliant and tireless talker. He welcomed the two young visitors, and they had a long conversation, a stunning four-hour exploration of evolutionary theory, biology, theology, philosophy. They spoke of many things, all connected to Heard's vision of a huge transformation of the human species that was, he was sure, trying to take place.
>
> Murphy and Price came away from the meeting feeling—as people who entered into conversation with Gerald Heard had often felt—a slight buzzing in the head, a certain overloading of the mental circuits. Yet it had been an invigorating and positive experience. Until then their project had been tinged with uncertainty, with a maybe-it-will-work-out-and-maybe-it-won't sort of doubtfulness that naturally accompanies thoughts of risky new ventures into the unknown. But Heard's enthusiasm, his sense of a cosmic mandate, changed all that. Murphy and Price were now both filled with a new sense of urgent conviction about their project: it *would* happen. It seemed to them, that day, that it had to happen.[3]

In a more recent conversation with me, Murphy confirmed Heard's influence on him and said that forty-two years later he still had vivid memories of that pivotal four-hour conversation. Heard's vision of the possibilities for the evolution of human nature and his wedding of the evolutionary to the mystical parts of the human psyche made a powerful impact on Murphy. Just as Huxley's language about human potentialities helped shape the philosophy that would drive Esalen, Heard's insights into the human mind and passion for centers where spiritual and moral evolution could be fostered helped round out the founding vision. So perhaps Heard could be called the catalyst of Esalen: Murphy and Price came away from that day with Heard "absolutely on fire," as Murphy put it, and firmly determined to found the Esalen Institute.[4]

This chapter will sketch the milieu in which Heard, Huxley, and others had been immersed some two or three decades before the founding of Esalen. My hope is to make it clear that alternative religiosity as it developed in southern California in the first half of the twentieth century was an important source of the Esalen work and indeed of the larger human potential movement in whose development Esalen played such a pivotal role.

Some of the history I am relating here is that of the Vedanta Society, the first form of what is commonly known as "Hinduism" to take root in American soil. Although many are well acquainted with the general outlines, at least, of the Vedanta story, for the sake of those who are not I will provide a few brief pieces of background.

The American part of the story begins with the World's Parliament of Religions in Chicago in 1893. The Parliament, part of the Chicago World's Fair of that year, attracted an unprecedentedly wide range of delegates and speakers, from James Cardinal Gibbons, the leading Catholic prelate in America, to an obscure Indian named Swami Vivekananda. From his first address Vivekananda was a sensation. Exuding charisma, he smashed stereotypes about Indian religion, declaring, for example, that polytheism did not exist there and that the Indian use of images did not constitute what westerners deemed the abomination of idolatry. Vivekananda's Hinduism was that of the Ramakrishna Mission, which was peaceful, expansive, all-tolerant, and given to works of charity. The swami did not condemn any religion but welcomed them all in the human race's universal pursuit of truth. His youthful good looks and striking attire further helped him carry the day in Chicago.

In the end, Vivekananda's most notable achievement may have been his establishment of the first Hindu organization in the United States that attracted western members. After the Parliament he stayed in the U.S. for several years, putting in place the foundations of the Vedanta Society. In his wake came several other swamis from the Ramakrishna Mission, who expanded Vivekananda's work and attracted yet more western followers.[5]

The strand of the Vedanta Society's work that had the most direct implications for the eventual founding of Esalen involved the development of monasteries and retreat centers. The seeds of Vedanta communities were scattered as early as 1895, when Vivekananda assembled a group of female disciples at the Thousand Islands on the St. Lawrence River in upstate New York for intensive spiritual teaching and the participants began to feel that they should live communally, sharing the work of daily living and immersing themselves in the life of the spirit. Vivekananda himself returned to India before any permanent monastery had been opened, but before he left a series of assistants and successors had begun to arrive, including Swami Turiyananda, who in 1900 opened a 160-acre retreat called Shanti Ashrama in California. Shanti (meaning "peace"), the land for which had been donated by a new Vedantist, was a remote and austere place, fifty miles from a railroad or market and a lengthy stagecoach ride from San Jose. Residents lived in tents and had to dig a well to get water. The hardships of Shanti undoubtedly helped define its relatively short life span, which amounted to a decade or so.[6] By then, however, new developments in the larger Vedanta movement provided more-convenient sanctuary.

In 1906, the first Vedanta temple in San Francisco was opened, and as had been the case with earlier Vedantists, some of the earnest seekers sought a more intense religious immersion than simple Temple membership would afford. In response to their requests, another swami, Trigunatita, opened a monastery for male members on the top floor of the new temple, a wonderfully exotic structure that had survived the great earthquake and fire just after it was constructed and that remains in place today. Soon a separate convent was opened in a rented house nearby for female adherents.

Again the ideal of getting back to the land and opening a communal center removed from urban life beckoned, and soon Trigunatita purchased a tract of around 200 acres near Concord, across San Francisco Bay. The development plan involved what today would be called a land trust, with the Vedanta Society retaining twenty-five acres for common use and the balance sold to members as homestead lots. The plan was tremendously ambitious, calling for a temple, a library, a hospital, a retirement center, and an orphanage in addition to the private homes. Adequate financial support, however, was not forthcoming, so the dream outstripped reality. In 1915, Trigunatita was assassinated by a deranged former student, and his death effectively meant the end of both the urban and the rural monastic communities (although a few monks continued to live, and still do, in the 1906 temple in San Francisco).[7]

In the years of Trigunatita's work, a similar project, Vedanta Ashrama, was opened at West Cornwall, Connecticut, in 1907; it survived until 1919. Back on the West Coast the Vedantist communal vision would languish until 1923, when Swami Paramananda, who had emerged as most influential swami after the departure of Vivekananda, purchased 135 acres at La Crescenta, outside Pasadena, where he established the Ananda Ashrama. Finally the Vedanta movement had a community with staying power; Ananda Ashrama has functioned over its eighty-two years as a major Vedanta center. It has facilities for meditation and personal spiritual work and it hosts public lectures and other programs. True to the vision of the Ramakrishna Mission, the community built a Temple of the Universal Spirit that was available for worship by persons of any and all religious persuasions. Ananda Ashrama achieved a solid financial footing through the development of several cottage industries and attracted a wide range of visitors.

Meanwhile, additional centers were established—Abhedananda Acres (named for yet another of the swamis) in the Antelope Valley north of Los Angeles, also in 1923, and then others.[8] By the 1920s, in short, the Vedanta Society had established on American soil several spiritual institutions that functioned both as monasteries and retreat centers. Eventually, similar Asian-inspired religious communal centers founded under other auspices than those of the Vedanta Society began to operate as well.

The exotic religious traditions of India did not appeal to the great majority of Americans, obviously. But they did find pockets of interest here and there, typically attracting well-educated, intellectually adventuresome people. One such pocket of interest was a group of Hollywood writers and intellectuals, of whom the best known was Aldous Huxley. A new swami, Swami Prabhavananda, moved to Los Angeles from Portland in 1929 and began to develop a Vedanta center in Hollywood. Although the move was regarded as unfriendly by the existing Vedantists of Los Angeles, who saw the new swami's work as a kind of turf invasion that threatened the local dominance of their own Swami Paramananda, eventually Prabhavananda attracted Huxley as well as his colleagues Christopher Isherwood and Gerald Heard to his congregation. The three literati were prominent enough that their presence led many others to the Hollywood center, and the Vedanta Society of Southern California, as it is now known, has been a leading arm of the Vedanta movement ever since.[9]

Of the literary lions of the Hollywood Vedanta center, it was Gerald Heard who had the most to do with the road to Esalen. Heard was born in London, of Irish ancestry, in 1886 and was educated at Cambridge. He studied theology, planning to follow his father into the Church of England priesthood, but he was never ordained. He did retain a profound and enduring interest in spiritual matters, however; one early manifestation of that fascination was his work as an official of the Society for Psychical Research in London. His spiritual interests continued to inform his career as writer, philosopher, and public speaker, but those interests were so wide-ranging that his essence is hard to delineate. Like Huxley, he was, for example, an early explorer of the mysteries of LSD, which had an effect on his spiritual outlook; as Alan Watts commented later about the Heard-Huxley acid experiments, "In my conversations with them I noticed a marked change of spiritual attitude. To put it briefly, they had ceased to be Manicheans."[10] Heard, incidentally, was involved with some early LSD research in which the chemical was used as an experimental treatment for alcoholism, and had a good friendship with Bill Wilson, cofounder of Alcoholics Anonymous, who took LSD and highly valued the experience.[11]

Heard was a well-known British intellectual by the 1920s, editor of a notable journal called *The Realist,* a BBC science commentator, and a prize-winning philosopher. Over his lifetime he wrote thirty-nine books, including several well-regarded philosophical and historical treatises such as *The Social Substance of Religion,*[12] *The Source of Civilization,*[13] and *The Five Ages of Man.*[14] Some of his works, including several books and a number of articles in the leading Protestant weekly *The Christian Century,* were outwardly Christian in orientation, with titles such as *The Code of Christ: An Interpretation of the Beatitudes*[15] and *The Creed of Christ: An Interpretation of the Lord's Prayer.*[16] But his spiritual passion was far too wide-ranging to be contained by a single historical tradition. A reader picking up a copy of *The Eternal Gospel,* for example, might have been expecting a Christian treatise but quickly was told that "[t]he Eternal Gospel has always been known to all mankind, though with varying explicitness" and that "it is that element owing to which [all] religions are great and enduring," a perspective essentially identical to that of the Vedanta swamis.[17] Heard, incidentally, also wrote several mysteries and works of fantasy under his birth initials H. F. Heard (for Henry Fitz-Gerald Heard), including such memorable titles as *The Great Fog and Other Weird Tales*[18] and *Doppelgangers: An Episode of the Fourth, the Psychological, Revolution, 1997.*[19] One of his novels, *A Taste for Honey,*[20] was later, with considerable artistic license, turned into a 1966 movie called *The Deadly Bees,* the first in the killer-bees genre, and a nonfiction work entitled *Is Another World Watching? The Riddle of the Flying Saucers*[21] was one of the first UFO books.

Gerald Heard and his close friend Aldous Huxley came to the United States in 1937. Heard had been offered a chair in historical anthropology at Duke University, but he decided after a single term that university life was not for him, and he left for southern California, where in 1939 he encountered Prabhavananda and immersed himself in the study of Vedanta, finally becoming a formal disciple of the swami in 1941.[22] Among other things, he devoted his literary talents to the movement, coediting, with Prabhavananda, the Vedanta Society's journal, *Voice of India,* from 1939 to 1941 and providing editorial advice and articles for it for years afterward.

By then he was well on his way to founding what would become a pioneering incubator of the human potential movement, Trabuco College—not a college in the sense of a traditional educational institution, but a center for a *collegium,* or community.[23] (Perhaps Heard's choice of the name "college" reflected that of Black Mountain College, which Heard and Huxley reportedly visited in 1937. Black Mountain was a college in the traditional sense in that it undertook the education of post–high school students, but it was relatively unstructured, communal, democratic, and thoroughly experimental in its approach to just about everything.[24]) The looming specter of World War II had planted in Heard, a devout pacifist, an apocalyptic sense of the direction of human society. His prospectus for Trabuco—written, reportedly, with some input from Huxley[25]—eloquently conveys his despair over the direction of things: "Humanity is failing. We are starving—many of us physically, all of us spiritually—in the midst of plenty. Our shame and our failure are being blatantly advertised, every minute of every day, by the crash of explosives and the flare of burning towns. We admit this. We are not proud of our handiwork. We know that we have, somehow, taken the wrong road."[26] And why was it all happening? The war, he argued, was the product of a civilization undermined by "diseased egotism and individualism—the fundamental appeal to greed and fear as the two sole compelling motives of man."[27] Humanity, Heard believed, stood at a crossroads: it needed vital transformation or it would die. The kinds of problem-solving usually favored in our secular society were not true answers:

> To the majority of the men of good-will, 'the way out' means chiefly social reconstruction, the general acceptance of some new political or economic faith, or a further attempt to erect an international organisation with which to curb the rival ambitions of nations. Admittedly all this work is valuable, but does it go to the heart of the evil? Can the statesman, the economist, the engineers, the architects, the social workers guarantee us against another and more terrible international breakdown within the next twenty years? They cannot, for the will to destruction is within ourselves. Rebuilding the cities and bringing vitamins to the survivors is only a repair job. Readjustment of our economics, however drastic, the reframing of our code of international behavior, however enlightened, will not change our hearts.[28]

And what was his formula for the necessary transformation of our consciousness? Heard believed that an entire "new race" of spiritual leaders could be created through disciplined religious immersion and that the new race could lead humankind in a wonderfully constructive direction, in contrast to the destruction of war then so evident. But the path would be difficult to locate and even more difficult to follow:

> It is very old, and narrow, and difficult to find. It is the way of humility and of self-discipline and re-education. It is the way back to God. We have to educate ourselves to discard our old values, for they were false. We have to learn that God is the only Reality, and that the whole visible world is real only in so far as He constantly sustains it. Behind those words is more than just 'another formula.' Behind them lies the live, intense, unutterable vivid Truth—a truth which can only be apprehended through a slow hard lifetime of study, prayer and disciplined, ascetic living.[29]

In response to that need, Heard wrote, Trabuco

> aspires to a type of community which will, we hope, become fairly common, both in this country and in Europe, in the years to come. It is un-denominational, and its doors are open to both men and women. It is not intended to be a place of withdrawal from the world—quite the reverse. But its founding trustees believe that only through change of individual character can there be any real apprehension of God's nature and will, and a lasting change in civilisation or humanity. Self-education comes first. And such an education necessitates three things:
>
> a. *Research.* The enormous mass of existing literature, from many countries and ages, on techniques of prayer, ways of self-integration and methods of psycho-physical development must be re-examined and re-interpreted in modern language to meet contemporary needs.
>
> b. *Experiment.* We must test out these techniques and determine which are the most applicable and convenient.
>
> c. *Practice.* Having chosen the particular techniques best adapted to our individual needs, we must proceed to make them part of our daily living.
>
> The founders do not regard themselves as possessed of any special message or esoteric "revelation." Trabuco begins its work in a spirit of humble and open-minded enquiry. There are no "prophets" among us. We all start from the beginning, bringing nothing but our need for God and our trust in His Grace, without which search for Him is vain.
>
> Trabuco hopes to grow, spiritually and organically, as the growth of its members progresses. Our ultimate structure may well be a modern version of the medieval university. There will be the students, whose whole concern must necessarily be self-education; the "masters," who are sufficiently advanced in their own self-education to be able to instruct and assist the students; and the "doctors," who are sufficiently qualified to be able to go out into the world and teach. Trabuco aims to become a new kind of missionary college, combining the world-wide concern and zeal of the old missionary work with the psychological and social knowledge of the present day.[30]

The community was to be spiritual, but without a sectarian basis. Heard had recently been immersed in the Vedanta version of Hinduism, but his background was Western Christian, and he was steeped in the literature of the Christian mystics and monastics. As one visitor put it, Heard "made a specialty of comparative religions, and with that incomparable erudition which brought biology, anthropology, and a host of other academic disciplines into the picture as well, quoted the Sufis [and] Hasidim, as well as Buddhist and Taoist ideas."[31] Moreover, Heard did not promulgate any rigid party line. Students were freely allowed their own points of view:

> Lunch was served in the large refectory. As we lined both sides of the long tables, Gerald sat in a large chair on the raised portion at the far end of the hall, reading to us from some elevating book. On those days when he happened to choose a Mahayana or Zen reading and Sister [Dhammadinna, a Theravada nun] disagreed with it, she could be heard whispering loudly to her neighbor, "What rot!" She had visited Japan and had a poor opinion of the purity and orthodoxy of the Zen monks.[32]

Organizationally, Heard planned to establish a core group of resident members who would constitute a small unpaid staff serving seekers who would come for limited terms, thus being "of service to maladjusted younger men and women prepared to submit to a regime whose strict discipline and fixed hours may help them regain full control of themselves and return to a more integrated life in the world."[33]

The gathering storm of World War II did more than just give Heard a sense of urgency about the development of the human potential. Wartime restrictions on the purchase of building materials were already imminent, so Heard had to scurry to build his new campus. Raising funds from sources that seem to have included his own inheritance (he came from an upper-class family) and probably included gifts from the wealthy, largely female, patrons who had funded many other Vedanta-related projects,[34] he purchased several hundred acres of isolated rolling ranchland in Trabuco Canyon about sixty miles southwest of Los Angeles, some twenty miles inland from Laguna Beach. Although suburbia is sprawling into the area today, in the 1940s the setting of the Trabuco campus was serene, in the middle of miles of forest, orchards, and grazing land, twenty miles from the nearest store. Development occurred quickly, and the buildings of the College were finished by 1942. One resident provided the following description of the institution's setting and facilities:

> On a clear day, as we told every cloudy day's visitor, you could see the Pacific Ocean, lying 17 miles to the west, over the valleys and lower hills in superb display. Built like a monastery, true; yet it was not built *as* one, exactly. Gerald Heard and his friends had garnered the funds to create this handsome pile of brick and tile in the Italian fashion. It sprawled from the water reservoir at the top of a long slope to the dormitory at its bottom, the whole structure exposed to a magnificent overlook of sky, cloud, valley and farm, distant roads and a spot of sea. The old engraved bell, nearly two feet in diameter in a modest tower and the hexagonal chapel, original and controversial, as well as the oversize bricks, were features of true distinctiveness.[35]

Just how many people participated in the austere life of Trabuco is unclear, and in any event the number varied, naturally. The buildings were reportedly designed to hold thirty (or perhaps as many as fifty) residents, and one observer at the beginning of 1946 reported that about twenty were there then,[36] although a slightly smaller number—one to two dozen—seems to have been more typical.[37] Perhaps the numbers were small because casual and affluent southern Californians were not attracted to the discipline and austerity of daily life at Trabuco. Although Heard's spirituality was eclectic, with a goodly Hindu component, his prescription for monastic life seems to have come straight from the asceticism of the Benedictine tradition. Laurence Veysey details the spirit of self-denial thus:

> Austerities included a near-total absence of heat and (for wartime reasons) of electricity. More than this, it was understood that no physical pleasures were supposed to be enjoyed by the residents, even eating. Meals were deliberately sparse and colorless, beyond mere vegetarianism. To prove her zeal, one woman ate mud. Even nature worship was discouraged as a distraction from pursuit of the Divine. In a remarkable round windowless building called the Oratory, whose interior was always kept completely dark, the members spent three hour-long periods of silent meditation daily.[38]

On the other hand, there was also high tea every afternoon.

The monastic restrictions did impose a requirement of celibacy, even for married couples who visited Trabuco together. That may have had as much to do with Heard's outlook as it did with monastic necessity; Heard was a homosexual who never came to grips with his sexual orientation and developed a strong disdain for any kind of sexual activity. In any event, the rule was considered excessive by some would-be Trabucans and seems to have helped hold down membership in the community. In some cases it backfired, as when Felix Greene, who had overseen the construction of Trabuco, and Elena Lindeman, a stalwart member, developed a romantic relationship, soon married, and thus departed.

Detailed accounts of daily life at Trabuco are few. Despite Heard's desire to emphasize independent spiritual work by each resident individual, he ended up being the de facto spiritual and temporal leader and was a major factor in the creation of the powerful intellectual and spiritual energy that infused Trabuco. "The intellectual treats were tremendous, and the zeal for making spiritual progress was intense," a former participant reminisced years later.[39] One visitor to the community recalled the scene at the daily informal breakfast:

> Gerald would sit on a high stool for his [breakfast], beaming down upon his little flock of students and coming out with those bursts of insight and arcane memorabilia which made up his style and his identity. A few of those gems have stayed with me all the years since, e.g., "Nicholas of Cusa said, 'God is beyond the contradiction of contraries.'" I thought then and think now, how profound that was and how Vedantic. Another day he told the story of the Sufi saint Al-Hallaj, who ran through the street crying, "I am He" and subsequently was decapitated. "The moral," said Gerald, "is that even if you know it, don't go about shouting it to others."[40]

Twice daily Heard gave lengthy "seminars," and individuals were expected to meditate three hours each day in the Oratory. Heard himself meditated six hours per day, a practice he observed for much of his life. A manual work requirement further added structure to the day's activities; sex roles were fairly traditional, with women doing most of the cooking and men doing the outdoor work. Nevertheless, the participants in the community had a good deal of time for their own pursuits, which were diverse. In 1945, it was reported, the three avowed focal points of work at Trabuco were "the study and practice of mysticism, high-level experimentation with ESP, [and] rest and recuperation for tired religious workers."[41] Aldous Huxley is said to have written *The Perennial Philosophy*, generally considered one of his most important books, in significant part at Trabuco.[42] Heard himself wrote several books there.

For several years the community went about its spiritual work. One resident member later described it as "a miniature revival of the Transcendentalist spirit of Brook Farm" and even as the crucible of what we now call postmodernism.[43] But Trabuco College never attracted the expected and needed core of long-term members and suffered from Heard's leadership style. A natural leader he was not: his human relations and communications were often awkward; his emotional torments were too real to suppress. Maria Huxley, Aldous's wife, was sharply critical in writing about him, after Trabuco's breakup, to her son Matthew:

> There is no doubt that Gerald really made a mess of the whole thing, chiefly by having favourites and then dropping them to take up another and so often making the dropped favourite despair of everything and leave Trabuco and God; forgetting that God and Gerald were not the same thing. . . . It transpired that Gerald was even more of an autocrat that we had thought; and more self-satisfied too. . . . Poor Gerald, I suppose.[44]

But even had Heard's style been different, Trabuco might not have survived. By and large its residents were intellectuals whose sincere desire for spiritual solitude did not erase their mental vitality and their involvement in the hectic culture of Southern California. The pieces of the puzzle, in short, did not fit perfectly together.

Heard clung to the vision for five years but eventually became discouraged, especially at the failure of the community to attract permanent residents. At the close of World War II, he hoped that Trabuco's pacifist reputation would attract conscientious objectors and disillusioned soldiers, and a few of them did materialize, but as with the others they tended to stay for a little while and then move on. Heard also tired of the physical demands of maintaining an extensive piece of real estate. By 1947, he had had enough of his communitarian experiment, and he shuttered it, telling friends that it was the will of God that it close.

Heard moved back to Los Angeles and let the property be used as a school for children, which soon incurred debts and itself closed. He resumed his career as a writer and lecturer and finally died in Santa Monica in 1971.[45]

At this point, I would like to interrupt my narrative to argue for just a moment with Walter Truett Anderson, from whose work this chapter takes its beginning point. In his discussion of the important conversation that Michael Murphy and Richard Price had with Gerald Heard in 1961, he simply says of Trabuco College, "It had failed."[46] That language is used over and over with regard to intentional communities that have closed. The Shakers, who are tenuously still alive after well over 200 years of communal life, are going to have that said about them just as soon as their last community in Maine closes. Some, in fact, would say that Shakerism failed long ago, when it began to suffer steep declines in membership. Someday Esalen will close, and it will probably then be said to have failed. I, however, find that language regrettable. A limited lifespan is not a failure. Am I a failure as a college teacher because my students eventually leave the university or for that matter because I am going to die someday? As I was preparing this chapter and doing a Web search for any tidbits on Trabuco College that had earlier escaped my notice, I came across a short piece by one Swami Yogeshananda, who has spent much of his life as a Ramakrishna Order monk and writer; it turns out that what started him on his spiritual path was a two-week stay at Trabuco.[47] Communities and spiritual movements and human potential centers make important contributions to the progress of the human race, and the fact that they eventually close down, as all human institutions do, does not inherently mean that they have failed. The Trabuco campus has been a center for spiritual life and growth for over sixty years. It is the site of an ongoing monastery. Several books and other pieces of literature were written there. Many persons earnestly seeking meaning were exposed to the wisdom and erudition of Gerald Heard and Aldous Huxley at Trabuco. Is Trabuco College a failure because in its original organizational configuration it operated for only five years? I cannot see that Trabuco failed at all; its positive influence on those who benefited from their experience there continues to resonate through our society, and even the physical facility serves an important spiritual purpose.

But to return to the main story: two years after the community closed, when it was clearer than ever that the experiment was over and that no other fitting plans for the campus were forthcoming, Heard donated the property to the Vedanta Society. Under its new auspices, the institution reopened as the Ramakrishna Monastery in September 1949.

The physical facility was ideal for its new purpose. As one monk in the first group to move in wrote, "Terra cotta everywhere. Long corridors of brick, matching tiles overhead. What better complement could there be to the ochre of the sannyasin's robes, dipped in the red earth? Fire—it was the color of fire, symbolic of the transience of earthly things: fire, in which the monk's body would finally shred and crumble on the pyre."[48] For more than half a century it has functioned as an all-male monastery (women have separate monastic facilities elsewhere within the Vedanta movement). Although the monastic life seems to be more structured than that envisioned by Heard, Vedanta has always been an open-minded and flexible movement, and variations in personal quests are still respected. The seeker today is advised that

> To some extent, each person's spiritual path will be different and is worked out in consultation with the Head of the Center. The Four Yogas—Karma Yoga, Bhakti Yoga, Jnana Yoga, and Raja Yoga—are blended in a combination suitable to each person's temperament. In our lives we try to work with concentration yet detachment, worship, work, and pray with devotion to God; study and contemplate the scriptures and affirm our true nature; and spend time each day in meditation.[49]

Just how long the monastery will endure remains a bit of an open question. It has never had more than a handful of members, and its land base has diminished. In the 1970s, needing to cut its property-tax bill, the Vedanta Society of Southern California donated all but forty acres of the once-extensive property to Orange County for use as a park. Now development is at the monastery's doorstep. Although plans to put 705 mobile homes on adjacent land fizzled some years ago, in November 2002 the Orange County Board of Supervisors approved plans for the construction there of some 283 homes, some of which would look directly down into the monastery grounds, and then in January 2003 they approved two more nearby projects totaling 162 new homes. The developers behind the first project, known as Saddleback Meadows, plan to level the hill that has largely protected the monastery from visual intrusion by earlier housing developments; to do so, they will need to keep heavy machines at work for three years, moving 9.3 million cubic yards of earth. Moreover, the other two projects, Saddle Creek and Saddle Crest, would destroy 492 mature oak trees, and all three of the projects pose a threat to already-polluted waterways in the area.[50]

Farewell, monastic tranquility. The monks at Ramakrishna Monastery have actively entered the legal and political battle against the developments. As one of them, Wil Devine, commented, "When you fight a battle, you can do it out of anger or out of love. These real estate developers, I have nothing personally against them. They are part and parcel of God in different forms. But I have to fight them just the same. It's my dharmic responsibility."[51]

At any rate, for the moment, at least, the Ramakrishna Monastery endures, and so do several other monastic centers under Vedanta auspices. That they have a kinship with the Esalen Institute many might find surprising, but the path of human evolution moves in unexpected directions.

I will close by noting that the connection between Esalen and the Hollywood-based spiritually inquisitive intellectuals continued once the Institute was started. Heard was there lecturing soon after Esalen opened, in the fall of 1962. In November 1963 he spent a month in residence, and he was there when Huxley died on November 22, participating in the vigil that Esalen held for Huxley. In the meantime Huxley and Isherwood had been to Esalen as well. But that is another later story.

If there is a final point here, it is the simple central point of the study of history: human events do not occur in vacuums. We live in a vast, interconnected web of ideas, people, places, and events. Esalen, like every other human undertaking, had a historical context from which it arose. As long as people seek to discern the meaning of life we will have Esalen—or wish we did.

NOTES

1. "An Interview with Dr. Jeffrey Kripal," *Tolle Et Lege: Religious Studies at Rice* [University] 1, no. 1 (2002): [2].

2. Walter Truett Anderson, *The Upstart Spring: Esalen and the American Awakening* (Reading, Mass.: Addison-Wesley, 1983), 57.

3. Ibid., 12–13.

4. Michael Murphy, telephone interview, January 8, 2003. For a more detailed account of the Heard-Murphy-Price encounter, see Michael Murphy, "Totally on Fire," on the official Gerald Heard website, http://www.geraldheard.com (accessed December 9, 2003).

5. On Vivekananda and the World's Parliament of Religions, see the works of Carl T. Jackson: *The Oriental Religions and American Thought: Nineteenth-Century*

Explorations (Westport, Conn.: Greenwood, 1981), 243–261, and *Vedanta for the West* (Bloomington: Indiana University Press, 1994), passim.

6. For a description of life at Shanti Ashrama and the problems posed by its location, see Swami Atulananda, *With the Swamis in America and India* (Calcutta: Advaita Ashrama, 1988), 61–79.

7. See Swami Gambhirananda, *History of the Ramakrishna Math and Mission* (Calcutta: Advaita Ashrama, 1957), 181.

8. An overview of the development of Abhedananda Acres is provided by Laurence Veysey, *The Communal Experience: Anarchist and Mystical Communities in Twentieth-Century America* (Chicago: University of Chicago Press, 1973), 266–270.

9. Several works provide elements of the history of the Vedanta movement. See *Vedanta in Southern California: An Illustrated Guide to the Vedanta Society* (Hollywood: Vedanta Press, 1956); Jackson, *Vedanta for the West*; Sara Ann Levinsky, *A Bridge of Dreams: The Story of Paramananda, a Modern Mystic-and His Ideal of All-Conquering Love* (West Stockbridge, Mass.: Inner Traditions/Lindisfarne Press, 1984).

10. Alan Watts, *In My Own Way: An Autobiography, 1915–1965* (New York: Pantheon, 1972), 342.

11. Huston Smith, *Cleansing the Doors of Perception: The Religious Significance of Entheogenic Plants and Chemicals* (New York: Tarcher/Putnam, 2000), 129. One Web site on the history of AA says that Heard administered Wilson's first LSD experience; see http://silkworth.net/aahistory_names/namesh.html (accessed December 9, 2003).

12. Gerald Heard, *The Social Substance of Religion: An Essay on the Evolution of Religion* (London: G. Allen and Unwin, 1931).

13. Gerald Heard, *The Source of Civilization* (London: J. Cape, 1935).

14. Gerald Heard, *The Five Ages of Man: The Psychology of Human History* (New York: Julian Press, 1963).

15. Gerald Heard, *The Code of Christ: An Interpretation of the Beatitudes* (New York and London: Harper and Brothers, 1941).

16. Gerald Heard, *The Creed of Christ: An Interpretation of the Lord's Prayer* (New York and London: Harper and Brothers, 1940).

17. Gerald Heard, *The Eternal Gospel* (New York: Harper and Brothers, 1946), 5, 6.

18. Gerald Heard, *The Great Fog and Other Weird Tales* (London: Cassell and Company, 1947).

19. *Doppelgangers: An Episode of the Fourth, the Psychological, Revolution, 1997* (London: Cassell and Company, 1948).

20. Gerald Heard, *A Taste for Honey* (New York: Vanguard, 1941).

21. Gerald Heard, *Is Another World Watching? The Riddle of the Flying Saucers* (New York: Harper, 1951).

22. Basic biographical information on Heard is located on The Official Gerald Heard Website, available online at http://www.geraldheard.com (accessed December 9, 2003).

23. The ensuing description of Trabuco College and the social and philosophical observations that propelled Heard to establish it is based on my earlier research on the subject; see Timothy Miller, *The Quest for Utopia in Twentieth-Century America* (Syracuse: Syracuse University Press, 1998), 1: 185–188.

24. The report of the Heard-Huxley visit to Black Mountain College comes

from a University of Utah student project on the history of Black Mountain. I have not been able to verify it independently, but it is certainly plausible: Heard was not far from Black Mountain during his short sojourn at Duke University in 1937, and he was always interested in cultural alternatives. See Katherine Reynolds, "Black Mountain, Meteor among Mavericks," available online at http://www.blackmountain college.org/bmcref/reynolds.html (accessed December 9, 2003).

25. See Veysey, *Communal Experience,* 271.

26. [Gerald Heard], "Trabuco" (prospectus), manuscript, Huxley Collection, University of California at Los Angeles library system. I appreciate the assistance of Daryl Ann Dutton Cody, who located the manuscript and, faced by a no-photocopying stipulation placed on it at the time of its deposit at UCLA, copied it out for me in longhand.

27. Gerald Heard, *The Third Morality* (London: Cassell and Co., 1937), 314.

28. Heard, "Trabuco."

29. Ibid.

30. Ibid.

31. Swami Yogeshananda, "Trabuco College Tryout," available online at http://www.geraldheard.com/recollections.htm (accessed December 9, 2003).

32. Ibid.

33. Heard, "Trabuco."

34. Veysey says that a large legacy was important to the basic funding of Trabuco (*Communal Experience,* 271). Jay Michael Barrie, Heard's longtime personal secretary, also mentions Heard's inheritance as financially vital. (See Jay Michael Barrie, "Who Is Gerald Heard?" on the Gerald Heard website, http://www.geraldheard.com/index.htm.) Other writers simply mention gifts by various supporters, which would conform to the pattern of generous giving that funded many Vedanta Society projects. Clearly a substantial amount of money was involved, given the large tract of land that was purchased and the fact that several good buildings were erected.

35. Swami Yogeshananda, *Six Lighted Windows: Memories of Swamis in the West* (Hollywood: Vedanta Press, 1997), 51.

36. Anne Fremantle, "Heard Melodies," *Commonweal* 43, no. 15 (January 25, 1946): 385.

37. One to two dozen is the figure given by Barrie in "Who Is Gerald Heard?"

38. Veysey, *Communal Experience,* 271.

39. Joseph Franklin Griggs, M.D., "A Review of My Spiritual Search," posted on an Internet discussion forum at http://www.show-control.com/txt/joes.txt (accessed December 9, 2003).

40. Yogeshananda, "Trabuco College Tryout."

41. Yogeshananda, *Six Lighted Windows,* 51.

42. Aldous Huxley, *The Perennial Philosophy* (New York: Harper and Brothers, 1945).

43. John E. Whiteford Boyle, *Of the Same Root: Heaven, Earth, and I* (Washington, D.C.: Academy of Independent Scholars/Foreign Services Research Institute, 1990), inside front cover.

44. Quoted by Sybille Bedford, *Aldous Huxley: A Biography* (New York: Alfred A. Knopf and Harper and Row, 1975), 463.

45. Some unattributed details pertaining to the life of Gerald Heard and the

history of Trabuco College come from Veysey, *Communal Experience,* 270–278. Other information is from the Gerald Heard Web site at http://www.geraldheard.com.

46. Anderson, *Upstart Spring,* 12.

47. See Yogeshananda, "Trabuco College Tryout."

48. Yogeshananda, *Six Lighted Windows,* 51. The second chapter of this book, entitled "High above Hollywood and Vine" (pp. 35–88), contains several passing vignettes of life at the facility in its Ramakrishna Monastery phase.

49. From the Ramakrishna Monastery Web site, http://www.vedanta.org/mon 1/wim.html (accessed December 2002).

50. "California Monks Wage Fight on Developers," *New York Times,* February 4, 2003, A16; Matt Coker, "Hillside Strangers: Trabuco Canyon Monks Brace for Major Changes to Their Quiet Lives," *Orange County Weekly* 8, no. 15 (December 13–19, 2002), available online at http://www.ocweekly.com/ink/03/15/cover-coker .php.

51. Quoted in "California Monks Wage Fight on Developers."

READING AUROBINDO FROM STANFORD TO PONDICHERRY: MICHAEL MURPHY AND THE TANTRIC TRANSMISSION (1950–1957)

Jeffrey J. Kripal

Few people today seem to have heard of Anquetil-Duperron or Sir William Jones or what they set out to accomplish in India in the eighteenth century, but they have drastically altered our ways of thinking nonetheless. Why, then, is the fact generally unknown? . . . The truth is that, in seizing upon the treasures of the poor Orient, critics have grasped only superficial influences that conceal the real issues, which concern the destinies of the intellect and the soul . . .

So many prophets of doom cry out to our age of a world near its end that it feels itself susceptible to what has never moved it before. Now is the time to present to our age a phenomenon completely interwoven with its substance . . . the birth of an integral humanism, a crucial, unprecedented chapter in the history of civilizations.

—Raymond Schwab, *The Oriental Renaissance*, 1950

What is her scope when she harmonises with the dawns that shone out before and those that now must shine?

—Sri Aurobindo on Usha, the Vedic Goddess of the Dawn

Given Esalen's natural beauty and the deep streams of nature mysticism that have bubbled, rather like the hot sulfuric springs of the baths, through the grounds for so many centuries from the times of the Esselen Amerindians, it would be safe to assume that the initial inspirations for the place must all have been in some natural environment, perhaps a crashing beach or ancient forest stand or at least a sunset or something.

And that assumption would be quite wrong. In actual fact, one of the earliest and most important events in Esalen's prehistory occurred in a quintessentially academic setting—the university lecture hall. It was April, the spring quarter of 1950, the second day of classes to be exact, and a young Stanford sophomore and fraternity brother named Michael Murphy was sitting in the wrong classroom. It all began, in other words, with a bit of providential synchronicity or, if you prefer, with a scheduling mistake. The room was supposed to be the place for a social psychology class (Murphy had an early interest in psychology), but there had been a room change, and what the young Murphy was actually sitting in was Frederic Spiegelberg's popular Comparative Religion course. The course was so popular that Spiegelberg needed a large auditorium to hold all those who showed up the first day, hence the last-minute room switch. "I'm just going to stay here and listen to the guy," Murphy thought to himself. This would turn out to be one of the most important decisions of his life.[1]

Frederic Spiegelberg (1896–1994) was Professor of Indian Culture and Thought in the Department of Asiatic Studies at Stanford. He came from a wealthy aristocratic German family, one of a generation of talented German theologians and intellectuals who had fled Hitler's Germany for safe haven in the American university system.[2] The great Protestant theologian Paul Tillich was his close friend. Tillich, however, had the dubious honor of appearing at the top of Hitler's hit list, hence his early flight from Nazi fascism in the early 30s. Spiegelberg would take over his friend's courses in 1933, leading a Pauline study trip around Asia Minor, but by 1937 things were much worse and he too was fleeing the country for a series of teaching stints at Columbia, Berkeley, and eventually Stanford, where Murphy met him that spring.

Spiegelberg was intensely interested in the meeting of East and West and believed that immense cultural transformations awaited the world just around the corner. He had edited *The Bible of the World*, an early perennialist source reader, and in 1949 had traveled to India, taking *darshana* (a kind of sacramental "seeing") with the great South Indian mystic and Advaita Vedantin, Ramana Maharshi, and the famous Bengali saint and philosopher of East-West synthesis, Sri Aurobindo (1872–1950), at Pondicherry, a French colony on the southeast coast to which Aurobindo had fled from the British as a young revolutionary and freedom fighter. There Spiegelberg spent two weeks living in Aurobindo's ashram. Murphy has noted that although Spiegelberg was never as influenced by Aurobindo as he was and in fact could be quite critical of the ashram, particularly for its sexual puritanism and the authoritarian style of the Mother, Aurobindo's spiritual partner and successor, Spiegelberg had nevertheless received some kind of spontaneous *diksha,* or initiation, from the Indian guru and was somehow able to transmit this charismatic energy in his lectures. Spiegelberg dedicated a book "To Sri Aurobindo for having X-rayed the author for five seconds lasting an eternity and for thereby calling forth the atman within as the only reality which he notices in any visitor."[3] Clearly, *something* happened.

Although never a great scholar or writer by temperament, Spiegelberg was an astonishing lecturer with a true poetic flare. His spiritual sensibilities were always deeply humanistic, essentially philosophical, and impressively cosmopolitan. He spoke of what he called "the mystery of Being" as the true essence of religion. He expressed his horror of all religious partisanship and dogmatism and wrote of what he liked to call "the religion of no religion."[4] In this same skeptical-humanistic mysticism of Being, he faithfully read Rilke in German every day, loved Plotinus in the original Greek, and read his Heidegger in the original German. (They had been classmates back in Germany.)

Spiegelberg's Comparative Religion course in the spring of 1950 very much reflected this Indian trip, an Aurobindonian East-West synthesis, and Spiegelberg's own profound perennialist and poetic commitments. The course began with the ancient Hindu scriptures, the Vedas and Upanishads; moved on from there to Buddhism, Saint Paul, and Plotinus; and ended with the Hindu mystic Sri Ramakrishna as the exemplar of the unity of world religions and Sri Aurobindo as the philosopher of the future. Looking back on the experience, Murphy has no doubt that the course was designed to be crowned by Aurobindo and what Spiegelberg considered to be one of the greatest works of twentieth-century philosophy, Aurobindo's *The Life Divine*. During the course, Spiegelberg formally announced the death of Ramana Maharshi. The following fall, again in class, he would announce the death of Aurobindo himself. It was an era of endings.

And beginnings. Murphy, it turns out, was hooked from the very first lectures on the Vedas and Upanishads. To this day, he considers Spiegelberg to have been the "number one door opener" into that realm of the metaphysical, the mystical, and the psychical that would define the rest of his own eventful life. Spiegelberg's course was a kind of initiatory event for him. From an Indian perspective, Spiegelberg was the guru, the course was the teaching, and a single potent Sanskrit word functioned as the initiatory mantra: "Brahman." The moment Murphy heard the charismatic Spiegelberg utter this single sonic word, his entire world changed. He knew that "it was all over." Something had changed, something deep and real. "Wake up!" Spiegelberg shouted to his class. "The Brahman is the Atman" ("The Absolute is the Self"). Here is how Spiegelberg remembered the event forty-three years later:

> In my lecture, I spoke the term "Brahman" with what one might call fullness of inflection, aided by the tremendous acoustics of the hall. Unbeknownst to me, this young Michael Murphy sat in the back, amidst the Hindi reverberation, wondering what strangeness he had happened upon. Some time later Michael paid a visit to my office to meet me, saying his life had not been the same since that moment. I offered my condolences, but he said, no, it was all to the good, and could he please study philosophy and religion at my direction for the rest of his academic career?[5]

The impact, in other words, was both immediate and gradual. It would take about nine months for everything in the young Murphy's life to change.

Or evolve. This was not, after all, the first religious thought Michael Murphy had ever been moved by. Even as an adolescent, around fourteen or fifteen, he had begun to develop what he calls an emanationist worldview through his reading and adolescent thoughts. Even then, he had begun to realize that one cannot really cure a neurosis; the best one can do is transform it into something else, what he would later call, drawing on the yogic and Tantric traditions, a *siddhi*, or "superpower." But that would come later. At fifteen, he may have been an aspiring Neoplatonist, but he was also still a good Episcopalian, an altar boy no less. Each summer he would go off to church camp and return with the conviction that he wanted to become a priest, only to be dissuaded by his family. Some time between his freshman and sophomore year at Stanford, however, he formally broke with the family faith. By his own account, an exposure to Darwinian evolution in a college class was the "knock-out punch," the final intellectual crisis that spelled the end of his adolescent faith.

But a resolution of the crisis was not long in coming. Toward the end of that first spring class, Spiegelberg suggested to the whole class that they read Aurobindo's *The Life Divine*. Murphy began reading the immense 1,100-page tome immediately. The shocks of recognition and inspiration were intense, like a "fire burning underground," as he puts it. But such fires did not burst into the surface immediately. That would take time.

Murphy went home for summer and played a great deal of golf. His younger brother, Dennis, was the first to notice that his brother seemed to be meditating as he played and bestowed on him a humorous description that would prove to be wildly accurate: Mike, in Dennis's jibe, was a "golfing yogi." Toward the end of the summer, Murphy went on his usual summer retreat, this time to a Jesuit center. The religious anomalies of the situation did not go unnoticed. Fathers Ryan and Cavanaugh, the Jesuit retreat directors, asked Murphy to stand up before the group at the end of the three-day retreat: "We want you to behold Mr. Michael Murphy. This man is an Episcopalian. Behold him!" "Yes, but I'm also a Hindu," the young Murphy quipped back. "A Hindu-Episcopalian named Murphy!" exclaimed the fathers, as the room burst into affectionate laughter. Anyone who has spent a single day with Murphy since could immediately recognize any number of familiar patterns here: Irish humor, social charm, and religious synthesis, all with a certain Hindu accent.

That next fall, Murphy, now a junior, enrolled in Spiegelberg's Indian Philosophy course and met Duncan Bazemore, who would go on to specialize in Aurobindo's thought and become a professor of philosophy, and Rob Crist. Crist had organized a study group led by a handsome and extremely charismatic Walt Page, an older graduate student who would interpret the history of philosophy for the small group. Murphy became suspicious of a kind of cult-like atmosphere that quickly built up around Page (who years later would kill himself), but he was also learning a great deal, and there was something truly infectious about the study group. It was then that the underground fires broke through. About this same time, Murphy had lost himself in *The Life Divine,* as Spiegelberg was explaining to his students in more detail what he had only sketched out in the previous class. Samkhya, Vedanta, and Tantra: one by one, he led them through the different systems of Indian philosophy. Later Murphy would describe his reading of *The Life Divine* in the context of these larger intellectual adventures as the "big climax" in which "it all came together" for him. Other thinkers and texts—Ramana Maharshi, Ramakrishna, Plotinus, and the western esotericists—were part of his growing mystical canon, and indeed the canon continues to grow to this day, but there was something special, something foundational, about *The Life Divine.*

The winter quarter saw Murphy quitting his fraternity, dropping out of his pre-med track, and taking a private but formal religious vow. Inspired by both Spiegelberg and Aurobindo, he had in essence converted to a new, spiritually conceived, evolutionary worldview. Accordingly, he made a vow to both himself and the divine by Lake Lagunitas on January 15th, 1951, near the Stanford campus, to dedicate the rest of his life to this Aurobindonian vision of an evolving human supernature.

At this point he was also giving more and more of himself to meditation and reading. Not everyone, however, was edified by this impressive transformation in the presence of Professor Spiegelberg. Murphy's own father, for example, was less than amused. Indeed, worried that his son would abandon a successful career track for what he no doubt thought of as Eastern cults, he "threatened to do something about Spiegelberg." The philosophers at the university would have been equally happy to see the charismatic Indologist go. As one university administrator explained to Murphy at that time, "Parents want their children to learn about these things, not become excited and passionate about them." Education was one thing; conversion quite another. Father or no, however, the young Murphy had been converted, and he was determined to persist in his newfound vocation.

In the late 1940s, a wealthy gentleman by the name of Louis Gains-borough donated some money to help found the American Academy of Asian Studies in San Francisco. He asked Spiegelberg to be its first Director of Studies. The two of them then approached Alan Watts to teach there. Watts, who eventually became the new institution's dean, would later describe Spiegelberg as the "*de facto* mastermind of the project."[6] Also teaching at the new Academy was a Bengali philosopher by the name of Haridas Chaudhuri. Spiegelberg had asked K. D. Sethna, an eminent Parsi intellectual and poet who had lived at the ashram, to join his faculty, but Sethna had just begun editing and publishing *Mother India* (a newspaper) and so did not want to leave India. Instead, Sethna proposed Haridas Chaudhuri, a young academic star from Calcutta University. Chaudhuri had taken *darshana* with Aurobindo many times and had adopted his philosophy as a new form of Vedanta that he called *purnadvaita*, literally "complete (*purna*) nondualism (*advaita*)."[7]

Toward the end of the winter quarter of 1951, Spiegelberg set up a table on the Stanford campus to recruit students for this new educational venture. According to the oral legend advanced repeatedly by Spiegelberg himself, Michael Murphy was the first to sign up. He immediately dropped out of Stanford for a quarter to attend the Academy that spring. Dick Price would also soon attend.[8] Spiegelberg, Chaudhuri, and Watts held colloquia every other Friday night in a Pacific Heights mansion they had been given for their work. At this time, Murphy was also consulting Chaudhuri on spiritual matters, as both shared a deep interest in *siddhis*, those "superpowers" that are said to develop spontaneously during certain stages of yogic practice.[9]

After a summer of playing catch-up, Murphy was back at Stanford the next fall and graduated on schedule in June of 1952. After taking some more classes at the American Academy of Asian Studies, he joined the army and was assigned various duties that he managed to transform into de facto retreat sessions. He spent most of his time reading and meditating or playing baseball, basketball, and golf. He would get up before reveille and meditate in chapel; he returned there in the evenings.

After his discharge from the army in January 1955, he began a doctorate at Stanford in the philosophy department. Things did not work out, to say the least. The professors of philosophy, now more or less dominated by analytic philosophy, were not well disposed to Murphy's mystical interests, and, even more tellingly, Murphy began to manifest serious neurotic symptoms. These he read as meaningful signs and abandoned the program to do what he had long wanted to do anyway: travel to India. Such a trip a few years earlier would have cost the young man his relationship with his father. Murphy's father had more or less told him that if he took this route, there would be no reason to come home again. But his father had changed as well. During his army service Murphy received, unasked, a large check in the mail with a note from his father that said, in effect, "Son, if you want to go to India now, here is something to help out." Encouraged by both this paternal blessing and this real financial help, he set off in April of 1956 for the other side of the world. On his way, ever the avid golfer, he stopped over in Scotland to play a round on the immortal links of St. Andrews. It was this pilgrimage and this round of golf that would become fictionalized in Murphy's popular mystical-realism novel, *Golf in the Kingdom*, long a favorite of professional and amateur golfers.

Although Sri Aurobindo was now dead, having passed away in 1950 shortly after Independence, the Mother, a French woman born Mirra Alfassa who had moved to Pondicherry and become Aurobindo's spiritual partner and successor, was still very much alive and active. Murphy stayed for about sixteen months (from June of 1956 to October of 1957), meditating, reading, organizing a softball team, and observing, with some concern, the deep ambiguities of communal life that these traditional hierarchical systems inevitably produce on the ground. The spiritual monarchies of Asian gurus, as we have repeatedly learned over the last forty years, do not always do well with democratic values such as radical individualism, human equality, gender justice, and the freedom of critical expression. Long before the American guru scandals of the 70s, 80s, and 90s, Murphy was worrying about similar problems. When he returned to the States and helped found Esalen, he and Dick Price would make sure that institutional principles were in place to prevent similar things from happening there. Such events, of course, happened anyway, but, thanks to the principles Price and Murphy put in place early on, no single teacher ever actually "captured the flag"; that is, no single individual or religious doctrine ever got to define what Esalen would be.

One way to tease out the Indian and American strands of Esalen would be to compare its operating principles and history to that of Aurobindo's ashram and Auroville, the utopian city founded by the Mother in Pondicherry. The differences, I would suggest, are indeed profound. They derive from the deep structural differences that American individualism and egalitarianism and ancient Indian caste hierarchy produce in human consciousness and social behavior, along with the different ways that the religious and the secular are legally defined in the two societies.[10] The place of the body and the expression of human sexuality in the two cultures are also dramatically different. Although there is certainly plenty of sex in Auroville, it is prohibited in the ashram, where a complete commitment to yoga is believed to require a celibate lifestyle. Seen in this comparative light, Esalen appears as a quintessentially American phenomenon, immeasurably enriched but never finally defined or limited by its Indian influences.

Still, cultural differences aside, there was something *there* in Pondicherry, something tangibly present and potent that Murphy could literally feel with a kind of sixth sense. When he was finally allowed, for example, to meditate in Aurobindo's apartment, he lost consciousness almost immediately. So powerful was this contemplative experience that he could speculate in F. W. H. Myers's terms that the room was a kind of "phantasmo-genetic center," or, in Rupert Sheldrake's later terms, that the Master's long decades of spiritual practice had created in effect a kind of "morphic field" in that holy room. In a pattern that would become definitive in the American experience of these Asian spiritualities, serious ethical reservations about the authoritarian nature of the guru-disciple relationship could go hand in hand with profound mystical experiences of the guru's occult presence and power.

READING *THE LIFE DIVINE* AS A TRANSMISSION EVENT

What did Murphy read when he lost himself in Aurobindo's *The Life Divine* that spring, summer, and fall of 1950? And what inspired him so in that room in Pondicherry, sending him into a blissful state of deep meditative absorption? What in the text saved him from his evolutionary crisis and inspired him to make a religious vow that he has kept to this very day?

The first thing that we need in order to appreciate Michael Murphy's reading of *The Life Divine* from Stanford to Pondicherry is a model of writing, reading, and understanding that is essentially hermeneutical and, potentially at least, mystical. That is, we need to recognize that the act of reading, far from being simply a mechanical exercise of vocabulary and grammar, is in fact an immeasurably complex psychic event in which two horizons of meaning—in this case an Indian and an American one—are "fused" in a mysterious process that we do not, and perhaps cannot, fully understand. Elsewhere, I have referred to a "hermeneutical mysticism" in the life and work of twentieth-century scholars of mysticism; that is, a disciplined practice of reading, writing, and interpreting through which intellectuals come to experience the religious dimensions of the texts they study, dimensions that somehow crystallize or linguistically embody the forms of consciousness of their original authors. In effect, a kind of initiatory transmission sometimes occurs between the subject and object of study to the point where terms such as "subject" and "object" cease to have much meaning.[11] And this, of course, is a classically mystical epistemological structure.

Certainly such a process, down to its metaphor of the fused horizons, drawn from the German philosopher Hans-Georg Gadamer, finds solid support in *The Life Divine* itself. Indeed, the very first epigram of the very first page announces a beautiful Vedic-Gadamerian fusion of past and present in the image of the goddess of the dawn, Usha: "What is her scope when she harmonises with the dawns that shone out before and those that now must shine?"[12] Aurobindo returns to the same image a bit later to argue for the necessity of a new language of the Spirit: "[A]s with all knowledge, old expression has to be replaced to a certain extent by new expression suited to a later mentality and old light has to merge itself into new light as dawn succeeds dawn."[13]

Aurobindo also operates with an understanding of language and inspiration that is essentially mystical. He can thus write about "ideas and images metaphysical and yet living and concrete,—images which might be taken by the pure Reason as figures and symbols but are more than

that and mean more to the intuitive vision and feeling, for they are realities of a dynamic spiritual experience."[14] Granted, spiritual truths can
be rendered in abstract formulas (and Aurobindo's text is as abstract and
formal as any), "but there is another side of truth which belongs to the
spiritual or mystic vision and without that inner vision of realities the abstract formulation of them is insufficiently alive, incomplete."[15] The text,
in other words, embodies the experiences of the author, and these can be
somehow communicated to the appropriately sensitive and intuitive
reader.

We must, I think, recognize a similar hermeneutical mysticism in
Murphy's lifelong interaction with Aurobindo's text. Michael Murphy did
not read *The Life Divine*. The text read him. Forever after, he would live
in its metaphysical world, and, just as important, it would take on a new
life and a new form in his. Put differently, each *translated* the other into
another mode of being, a new fusion of horizons, a new Dawn.

LITERARY FEATURES OF THE TEXT

But how? Let me begin with the text as a text; that is, with a few of
its more important literary features. The most obvious feature of the text,
and no doubt its most important if least appreciated, is the simple fact
that it was originally conceived and written entirely *in English*. Granted,
it is filled with Sanskrit words and an occasional brief Sanskrit footnote,
but for the most part this is an English document, not a Bengali or
Sanskrit one, and this has profound consequences for how we read and
understand it. In effect, the text is *already* a kind of cultural and metaphysical fusion or translation.

Take, for example, the crucial category of "the integral" in Aurobindo's English thought. Aurobindo writes of "integral philosophy," "integral yoga," "integral consciousness," "integral spirituality," and so on. By
such phrases, he seems to have in mind a complex system of grades or
dimensions that need to be kept in balance—in modern parlance, a kind
of holistic ecosystem. He can thus reject both the traditional Indic forms
of world-denying renunciation and asceticism, as we find for example in
the Buddha's nihilistic[16] nirvana or Sankara's Advaita Vedanta with its

reading of the world as an "illusion" (*maya*) and the superficial materialism of western science as important half-truths that must be integrated into a larger, more encompassing truth—namely, his "integral philosophy." The body and material life, it turns out, are not illusions to sublate on the road to the Absolute; they are "integral" manifestations of the Real whose welfare and occult significance must be respected and further transmuted on the spiritual path.

Now although such specific meanings of the integral find echoes or analogies in some forms of Indian political philosophy and religious thought, for the most part they are foreign to classical Indic thought, at least in their present Aurobindonian forms. This should not surprise us. These, after all, are western English categories, not traditional Sanskrit ones. Hence when Haridas Chaudhuri, one of Aurobindo's most important interpreters, attempts to explain Aurobindo's philosophical system with a Sanskrit neologism, *purnadvaita*, literally full or complete (*purna*) nondualism (*advaita*), what he appears to be doing is translating an original English idea *back* into a Sanskrit term where it did not originate and that cannot fully support it. *Purna* is certainly scriptural, but it does not generally carry the meanings that "integral" does in Aurobindo's thought. On a quite literal level, in the ancient Sanskrit Vedas, the term can refer to the fluid status of a ritual ladle ("full") or, in the Upanishads, to an ontological substratum from which names and forms (*namarupa*) emerge and back into which they are subsumed.[17] In later Indian thought, for example, in Ramakrishna's theological reflections on different kinds of *avataras*, a *purna-avatara*, or "full incarnation," is distinguished from a "partial" one (*amsa* or *kala*) within a kind of mathematical theology of fractions: here "full" means "added up" or "total," but certainly not "integral" in Aurobindo's sense. Indeed, in no case with which I am familiar is there any notion of integralism in the sense that one finds in such abundance in Aurobindo's English thought. Granted, *purna* can carry a sense of "emergence," and Aurobindo is clear that what evolves out of the Absolute is somehow preexistent in it (which is certainly faithful to the Sanskrit *purna*), but Aurobindo's passionate call for the nurturance of all levels of the human being and Nature is, it seems to me, much more indebted to western biological and psychological thought than Sanskrit philosophy, whether this is acknowledged or not (and it is usually not).

This is not to argue, however, that Aurobindo derived his system entirely from western thought. This would be going entirely too far, for even when he employs a term such as "evolution," Aurobindo is clearly not using it the way most western thinkers would (with the important exceptions of thinkers such as Teilhard de Chardin or Henri Bergson). Rather, he has hermeneutically fused ancient Indian monism with modern Western thought to come up with a third realm of meaning, a realm in which the Indian and the mystical is clearly privileged over the western and scientific modes of thought within a discourse that foreshadows the later "mysticism of science" works of such (Esalen-related) authors as Fritjof Capra and Gary Zukav. Consider, for example, the following passage:

> It is so that the ancient and eternal truth of Vedanta receives into itself and illumines, justifies and shows us all the meaning of the modern and phenomenal truth of evolution in the universe. And it is so only that this modern truth of evolution which is the old truth of the Universal developing itself successively in Time, seen opaquely through the study of Force and matter, can find its own full sense and justification,—by illuminating itself with the Light of the ancient and eternal truth still preserved for us in the Vedantic scriptures. To this mutual self-discovery and self-illumination by the fusion of the old Eastern and the new Western knowledge the thought of the world is already turning.[18]

Put differently, Aurobindo's thought would have been *literally* impossible in either Sanskrit or English alone; it only makes sense, it only exists, as a creative hierarchical fusion of the two linguistic and cultural worlds. Aurobindo, in other words, is already an East-West hybrid, a kind of mystical union of India and the West, and his English text filled with Sanskrit categories is a rather obvious witness to this.[19] Catherine Albanese has made a similar case for influential yogic authors of the twentieth century in her chapter in this volume. The English writings of Aurobindo certainly fit comfortably in this same model.

Which is another way of saying that Aurobindo's English and the influence of western thought on his thinking need to be honored as linguistic features that are central, not peripheral, to his system. Part of the rhetorical problem here—and this is the second literary feature of the text that I would like to highlight—is Aurobindo's almost complete failure to cite his western sources. He is perfectly happy citing Vedic and Indic philosophical sources, but he almost never cites a western author, even when it seems obvious that he is drawing on one: Nietzsche (the philosopher's Übermensch floats somewhere behind Aurobindo's "Superman" and "Supermind"), Kant,[20] Einstein,[21] and, of course, Darwin all seem to be present here, but oddly there is virtually no mention of their names. In one of his rare nods to a western thinker, Aurobindo can appreciatively and insightfully incorporate "the new method of psycho-analysis" into his discussion of dreams, but he declines to name Freud in the process.[22] Even more tellingly, despite the absolutely central, if creative, use of the Darwinian concept of evolution, there are precious few instances of Darwin's name in the thousand-plus-page text, and then mostly as a dismissive adjective.[23] Similarly, I detect the profound influence of Frederic Myers and his notion of the subliminal self, which Aurobindo explicitly distinguishes from the psychoanalytic subconscious,[24] throughout the text but not a single reference to the British psychical researcher. One section on the subliminal kinship of the genius, the mystic, and a kind of automatic writing reads like a outline of a few chapters from Myers's *Human Personality and the Survival of Bodily Death*.[25] To be fair, Aurobindo does occasionally cite a western author. Plato, Shakespeare, and Heraclitus are all mentioned by name.[26] He also fails to name an Indian physicist whose work he approvingly cites.[27] We should, of course, not expect modern referencing styles in an early twentieth-century spiritual writer, and it is certainly likely that he lacked the physical books to reference anyway at his ashram, but one must still wonder about Aurobindo's failure to mention even the names of intellectual influences on him. It is almost as if real influences do not exist as such, as if their names need to be erased from the record.

This kind of nonreferencing strategy leaves the (false) impression that Aurobindo is originating the entirety of his text within a kind of revelation-out-of-nowhere, when in fact what is actually happening is a creative merging of western scientific, philosophical, and psychological theory and Indian philosophical thought and yogic practice. There is, in other words, a kind of dissimulation going on here that needs to questioned and reflected on. Perhaps such a pattern is an expression of the text's colonial context and its attempted reversal of the power flow. Put politically, truth cannot flow from West to East, for that is also the direction of colonialism. Truth must come from India, not Nietzsche's Germany or, worse yet, Darwin's England. In this model, the colonial context of the text has submerged its profound, and profoundly creative, English-Sanskrit hybrid nature.

Third, and finally, I am also deeply struck by the text's incredible abstractness, by its long complicated sentences, its architectonic scholastic structure, and its almost total lack of reference to emotion or the physical body. There is something strangely disembodied about the whole thing: lots of talk about material nature and the body as an abstract entity, even a few pages on love, but no real bodies, desires, or organs appear here, much less an embrace, a kiss, a child, or a tear. None at least that I can see. I am reminded here of Spiegelberg's charge of an unnecessary and unhealthy sexual repression in the ashram community. Certainly this text could do little to challenge such an observation. Such a feature also marks it as standing in sharp contrast to the later somatic practices and sensual literature of Esalen.

READING *THE LIFE DIVINE* AS A TANTRIC EVENT

It is also important to point out that Aurobindo's system of thought is fundamentally a Tantric system, not necessarily in the fashion that he would have understood or used that adjective, but in the sense in which Indologists use it today. Catherine Albanese has suggested the same (with important qualifications) in her chapter in this volume. I would like to return to this Tantric thesis again here. Consider, for example, the work of David Gordon White, the doyen of American Tantric studies, who uses the term to describe a broad pan-Asian worldview or metaphysic spanning such local traditions as Hindu Tantra, Tibetan Vajrayana Buddhism, Chinese Taoism, and Japanese Zen Buddhism.[28] All manifest for White the basic doctrinal features of "Tantra," which he defines as follows:

> Tantra is the Asian body of beliefs and practices which, working from the principle that the universe we experience is nothing other than the concrete manifestation of the divine energy of the godhead that creates and maintains

that universe, seeks to ritually appropriate and channel that energy, within the human microcosm, in creative and emancipatory ways.[29]

Equally appropriate for our purposes, however, is the definition of the French Indologist André Padoux. Tantra, for Padoux, is

> an attempt to place *kama*, desire, in every sense of the word, in the service of liberation . . . not to sacrifice this world for liberation's sake, but to re-instate it, in varying ways, within the perspective of salvation. This use of *kama* and of all aspects of this world to gain both worldly and supernatural enjoyments (*bhukti*) and powers (*siddhis*), and to obtain liberation in this life (*jivanmukti*), implies a particular attitude on the part of the Tantric adept toward the cosmos, whereby he feels integrated within an all-embracing system of micro-macrocosmic correlations.[30]

Now what is so striking to the historian of religions is the fact that either of these classical western definitions of Asian systems of "Tantra" could easily function as a metaphysical approximation of "Esalen," particularly as the latter phenomenon has been conceived and envisioned by Michael Murphy and his Aurobindonian readings. These classical Tantric emphases on the religious capacities of the human body, on a monistically structured universe as the manifestation of divine energies and processes, on the mystical uses of erotic desire and its hydraulic sublimations, on the desirability and centrality of psychical powers, and on a type of radically altered consciousness in this life and this world—these are *all* the precise features of Murphy's literary and comparative corpus and of much of Esalen's history. Holiness—both in "Tantra" and "Esalen"—is not some ascetic retreat from the world but a search for wholeness in and as the embodied world, now thoroughly spiritualized through the nondual philosophical vision and mystico-erotic potentials of the human body. The one doctrinal feature, moreover, that clearly distinguishes traditional Hindu Tantra from Esalen is precisely that feature that Aurobindo himself added—the temporal and progressive metaphysic of evolution.

From a purely lexical standpoint, it must be admitted that we have to be very careful about calling Aurobindo's system a form of Tantra. He would have likely described it as a form of Vedanta, but one that rejects the *maya-vada* or illusion doctrine of Advaita Vedanta. As a simple illustration of this lexical problem, consider the fact that the index to *The Life Divine* lists only four references to "Tantra" or "Tantrik" in the entire text. On the rare occasion when Aurobindo uses the word as a textual designation ("the Tantras"), what he clearly has in mind is what Murphy will later call a science of the supernormal that needs to be embodied within forms of sustained practice. Indeed, this is Aurobindo's exact understanding of what the Tantras were all about. "The remarkable system of the Tantras," Aurobindo tells us toward the end of the text, was "not only a many-sided science of the supernormal[31] but supplied the basis of the occult elements of religion and even developed a great and powerful system of spiritual discipline and self-realization. For the highest occultism is that which discovers the secret movements and dynamic supernormal possibilities of Mind and Life and Spirit and uses them in their native force or by an applied process for the greater effectivity of our mental, vital and spiritual being."[32]

There are, moreover, good historical reasons that can help explain why Aurobindo would have avoided any explicit alliance with the Tantras. We must never forget that he was writing in a political context and time period in which the terms "Tantra" and "Tantric" carried overwhelmingly pejorative meanings, and Murphy himself is clear that these same categories still evinced reactions of deep ambivalence and cultural embarrassment from Bengalis at the ashram in the 50s. Simply because we lack the centrality of the term "Tantra" in his text, then, does not mean that we cannot or should not use the term in our own precise ways; it simply means that Aurobindo chose not to do so for his own perfectly sensible and very defensible historical and cultural reasons.

What, then, constitutes what I am calling the "Tantric" features of Aurobindo's system of thought? I would list the following six features of *The Life Divine:*

• The Bengali Tantric lineage or prehistory of the text

• The dialectical nature of Reality often expressed within a gendered symbolism of Purusha-Prakriti ("Man/Spirit-Woman/Nature"), Father-Mother, or God-Goddess

• Aurobindo's understanding of desire as something that needs to be satisfied on the level of the infinite rather than repressed on the level of human life

- Aurobindo's explicit rejection of all "liberation" or "extinguishing" models of salvation

- The subtle alchemy of the divine human body and the stated hope for an earthly immortality with a consequent divinization of Matter itself as a real manifestation of the Divine

- An emphasis on psychical abilities as signs of the human being's greater nature within the subliminal mind or, more radically still, the Supermind

A few words about each of these six features are necessary here to make my point.

The Bengali Prehistory. Without going into the details of Aurobindo's biography,[33] it is fruitful to point out that Aurobindo was writing and thinking within a Bengali milieu suffused with Tantric cultural patterns, ritual practices, and doctrinal traditions. Indeed, although he was clearly upset by the fact and desired to counter these same Tantric traditions, Aurobindo's Bengali predecessor, Swami Vivekananda (1862–1902), was explicit in his conviction that "[t]hese Vamachara sects [radical "left-handed" Tantric groups that engaged in sexual yoga] are honey-combing our society in Bengal. . . . You who are of Bengal know it. The Bengali Shastras [Scriptures] are the Vamachara Tantras."[34] As if to confirm Vivekananda's observations, minus his angry polemics, numerous scholars have observed that early Vajrayana Buddhists, Nath Siddhas, Shakta Tantrikas, Vaishnava Sahajiyas, Bauls, and Kartabhajas all flourished in the Bengali region as intimate features of the religious landscape, helping in the process to forge the Bengali language into one of the richest in Tantric histories and connotations. Historians of the language often cite a classically Tantric Buddhist document, the Caryapadas, as the first recognizable Bengali text, and cultural historians such as Shashibhushan Dasgupta have studied these "obscure religious cults" as a unique window into the history of the language and its literature.[35] It would thus be surprising indeed if a text such as Aurobindo's, even in English, were *not* suffused with Tantric echoes and shadows, if not actual sounds and lights.

A Tantric Bipolar Ontology. But the strongest evidence for the text's Tantric nature does not lie in such a historical context. It lies in the actual doctrinal content of *The Life Divine* itself. Abstractly put, that content is

consistently and rigorously determined by a dialectical ontology that identifies Reality as bipolar and bisexual (or androgynous). Aurobindo invokes
numerous binarisms to express this dialectical nature: the One and the
Many, the Transcendent and the Immanent, Consciousness and Energy,
Spirit and Nature, Being and Becoming, Father and Mother. But his
vision is always the same: the ultimate Reality that is Sacchidananda
(Being-Consciousness-Bliss) is best understood as a bipolar, dialectical
process within which neither pole can be effaced, denied, or renounced.
This bipolar Reality, moreover, is often expressed in classical Indian terms
drawn from Samkhya philosophy (Purusha/Prakriti or "Man-Spirit/
Woman-Nature"), Advaita Vedanta (Nirguna/Saguna Brahman), or
Shakta Tantra (Shiva/Shakti). In a Tantric register, "[w]e must accept the
double fact," Aurobindo writes, "admit both Shiva and Kali and seek to
know what is this measureless Movement in Time and Space with regard
to that timeless and spaceless pure Existence."[36]

Of immense significance for a gender analysis of his ontology, it is
the "male" or Spirit pole that is often given ultimate dominance in *The
Life Divine,* and here Aurobindo stands against "the Tantriks," who are
(in)famous for privileging the energies and illusions of the Goddess over
the infinite existence of the God.[37] In this same vein, Consciousness/
Spirit/God is commonly referred to as "He" in Aurobindo's text, even as
Energy/Nature/Goddess is given an important, if usually secondary, place
as "She." After hundreds of pages of this sort of thing, one begins to
suspect that Aurobindo—perhaps unknowingly—has slipped in a specific
historical construction of gender as an ontological absolute. He has, in
effect, confused the sexual assumptions of his own Bengali culture with
the metaphysical nature of the entire universe.

Divinizing Desire and Delight. In another classically Tantric move,
Aurobindo insists that desire is not something to be repressed or, worse
yet, extinguished (a code word in his text meant to evoke the nirvana of
Buddhism), as it is essentially divine: "Desire is the lever by which the
divine Life-principle effects its end of self-affirmation in the universe and
the attempt to extinguish it in the interests of inertia is a denial of the
divine Life-principle, a Will-not-to-be which is necessarily ignorance."[38]
Desire rather is to be sublimated and fulfilled in the Infinite: "Desire too
can only cease rightly by becoming the desire of the infinite and satisfying

itself with a supernal fulfillment and an infinite satisfaction in the all-possessing bliss of the Infinite."[39] Not surprisingly, drawing on the Vedantic trinity of *saccidananda*, one of the three highest terms Aurobindo can give the nature of Reality is that of a capitalized Delight (*ananda*).

Refusing the Refusal for the Complete Affirmation. Still within this same Tantric affirmation, Aurobindo rejects what he calls the "refusal of the ascetic" in the very first pages of the text. A bit later he will criticize "the pessimistic and illusionist philosophies,"[40] almost certainly a reference to "the Nihil of the Buddhists"[41] and to Advaita Vedanta's famous dismissal of the phenomenal world as *maya*, a word that can be variously translated as "illusion," "magical trick," or "perceptual mistake." *Maya* he can describe as "an inexplicable paradox and a fixed yet floating nightmare of conscious existence which could neither be classed as an illusion nor as a reality."[42] Such experiences may often be necessary to the Spirit's struggling freedom, but they are also dangerous and ultimately false half-truths on the road to the greater ontological syntheses of the Supermind. What really worries Aurobindo is that the seductive experience of the pure Self or soul might become the grounds for a rejection of the phenomenal world.[43] Indeed, he worries out loud that "this revolt of Spirit against Matter" has "dominated increasingly the Indian mind" to the point where for millennia now, "all have lived in the shadow of the great Refusal."[44] Aurobindo blames the origins of this "perilous" move on Buddhism, which first disturbed "the balance of the old Aryan world."[45]

Similarly, and even more radically, Aurobindo denies any cyclical notion that human life is merely "a subordinate circumstance in a divine play or Lila, a play which consists in a continual revolution through unending cycles of pleasure and suffering without any higher hope in the Lila itself or any issue from it except the occasional escape of a few from time to time out of their bondage to this ignorance."[46] This, of course, is the quite traditional ascetic model of *moksha*, or traditional Indian "liberation" from the cycle of birth and death (*samsara*). Aurobindo flatly rejects all of this as "that ruthless and disastrous view of God's workings" that denies the essential evolutionary potentials of human beings.[47] Instead, he writes that we must seek "the fulfilled existence which will eventually solve all this complex problem created by the partial affirmation emerging out of the total denial; and it must needs solve it in the only possible way, by the complete affirmation fulfilling all that was secretly there contained in potentiality[48] and intended in fact of evolution behind the mask of the great denial."[49] In short, evolution intends an integrated wholeness, not an ascetic denial of that which has evolved.

The Alchemy of the Divine Body. Something that is often overlooked about Tantric traditions in South Asia is their intimate connection to the practice of alchemy and its attempt to transfigure the human body into an immortal divine one, often through hydraulic techniques of sublimation involving the sexual fluids.[50] Aurobindo, writing well within this tradition, argues for something similar, if in a decidedly less sexual register. This is certainly one of his boldest moves: the claim that the human body, like the human mind, possesses its own subliminal and occult dimensions,[51] that these are intended to emerge gradually through the evolutionary process, and that they are linked to such traditional psychical abilities as hypnotic suggestion, mind reading, precognition, and clairvoyance. If "man be the inhabitant of terrestrial existence through whom that transformation of mental into the supermental can at last be operated, is it not possible that he may develop, as well as a divine mind and a divine life, also a divine body?"[52] The Supermind and the Superman will thus also possess what we might call a Superbody. Certainly we should not stop at "our present limited conceptions of human potentiality," Aurobindo argues, since "[t]here are, quite certainly, other states even of Matter itself; there is undoubtedly an ascending series of the divine gradations of substance; there is the possibility of the material being transfiguring itself through the acceptation of a higher law than its own which is yet its own because it is always there latent and potential in its own secrecies."[53] Hence the writer can imagine "a physical working of divine life in the human frame and even the evolution upon earth of something that we may call a divinely human body."[54]

Superpowers for the Superman. In the meantime, it is the *siddhis*, or superpowers, so prominent in the Tantric traditions of South Asia, that offer us a glimpse of this alchemical superbody and its emergent potentialities. Aurobindo can thus write of "psychic" or "supernormal" phenomena that derive from "an occult subtle physical energy."[55] We are also told that "our life energies while we live are continually mixing with the energies of other beings" and that "there is a constant dissolution and dispersion and a reconstruction effected by the shock of mind upon mind with a constant interchange and fusion of elements."[56] Similarly, "there are also senses which are superphysical [that] can bring us into contact with other realities."[57] Here he draws on "new-born forms of scientific research" into telepathy and other similar phenomena (perhaps a reference to the psychical researches of Myers and his London Society for Psychical Research) whose evidence "cannot long be resisted except by minds shut up in the brilliant shell of the past."[58] Along these same lines, Aurobindo invokes the psychological technique of hypnosis and its anesthetic uses to help us see how pain and suffering are relative to specific forms of consciousness and can be effectively transcended.[59] In all of this, Aurobindo is greatly aided by his epistemology and his conviction that the brain is the product, not the producer, of Consciousness. The latter is essentially transcendent, using the physical brain as a kind of receptor.[60] To use a later analogy that such Esalen-related authors as Stanislav Grof will employ to describe a very similar model of consciousness, again in a distinctly Hindu Tantric language,[61] consciousness can be thought of as a kind of TV signal that is certainly congruent to the neurophysiology of the brain (as the latter has evolved to "pick up" this consciousness), but in no way can this "signal" be reduced to its human "receptor." One can no more find consciousness in the brain than one can find, say, the tiny cast of a popular sitcom inside a TV set.

There is much more that could be said here, particularly with reference to the communal *Sitz im Leben,* or life-context, of the reception of *The Life Divine* within the Pondicherry community, a life-context ordered around the esoteric, and essentially Tantric, relationship of Aurobindo and the Mother. But this would take us well outside the text itself and into the immense biographical literature that surrounds such an important question. I mention the relationship here only to reiterate my earlier point about the Bengali-Tantric context of *The Life Divine:* Aurobindo and the Mother reproduced on a communal level a bipolar Tantric theology that had been enacted many times before in Bengali history, with Ramakrishna and Sharada Devi being perhaps the most famous example. We need not speculate about the unlikely sexual dimensions of their relationship, nor need we deny that it symbolically reversed the sexual politics of colonialism with an Indian Male husbanding a western Female,[62] in order to recognize that the bipolar Tantric structure of the tradition demanded both a Father and a Mother, both a Shiva and a Shakti. Whereas *The Life Divine* set out this Tantric ontology within an elaborate thousand-plus-page metaphysical argument, Aurobindo and the Mother literally embodied it within their mystical community. Textual structure, social form, and human relationship thus all mirrored one another within a shared Tantric worldview.

LATER ASIAN AND TANTRIC STRANDS

When we turn to the figures and literature of Esalen, we can see that many of these same Tantric features carry over, if almost always in a democratically transformed or transmuted state. We could begin, for example, with the remarkable speculations of Wilhelm Reich, which have been so formative to the somatic practices of Esalen. Reich's sexual ontology and his mature concept of the orgone, an essentially erotic life energy with clear conceptual connections to both sexual mysticism and psychoanalysis, could easily be approached as a kind of western Tantra.

It is also a well-known fact, of course, that both founders of Esalen were deeply influenced by Asian religions. Dick Price was inspired by Alan Watts, who was himself profoundly indebted to Tantric models of sexuality and spirituality.[63] Price was particularly attracted not so much to Watts's unique brand of "Beat Zen" but to a particular type of Theravada Buddhism. Embodying a very nonpersonal approach to the sacred, Price was drawn to traditions that expressed a similar philosophy, such as Chinese Taoism (often itself infused with Tantric strands), and shied away from those that expressed belief in a personal God, such as his mother's Christianity, his father's Judaism, or his cofounder's Aurobindonian philosophy with its place for personal devotion to a guru or a god. Price was also convinced that he had been some type of monk in a previous life, probably a Buddhist one, and during one of his psychotic episodes he seriously entertained taking the bodhisattva vow of Mahayana Buddhism. The Buddhist dimensions of Dick Price, in other words, were hardly superficial. They ran very deep and determined much of his personality and religious convictions.

In this same Buddhist spirit, Price meditated regularly and would later work to integrate these Asian influences into his Gestalt practice, a practice which innumerable witnesses perceived to be a deeply spiritual exercise for both Price and those he so directly engaged in Gestalt therapy, a psychological tradition partly informed by Zen Buddhism and its emphasis on authentic consciousness in the here and now. (Perhaps inspired by Fritz Perls's patriarchal presence and Jewish background, Esalen figures sometimes jokingly called Gestalt "Zen Judaism.") Later in his life, Price also briefly engaged in—to the great befuddlement and consternation of many of his closest friends and associates—a devotional relationship with Bhagwan Rajneesh, the famous Hindu Tantric "sex guru" who combined western psychological techniques such as Gestalt therapy and Asian contemplative traditions to shock his devotees into enlightenment.

Price would soon abandon this path after witnessing the ethical excesses and physical violence of Rajneesh's community in Pune, India, but his commitment to some type of meditative practice and his deep attraction to Asia remained constants throughout his adult life at Esalen.[64] Although Price's Rajneesh episode has puzzled many a friend and observer, it makes more than a little sense once placed in the larger textual and metaphysical history of Esalen as mapped out briefly here: Tantra, after all, whether Hindu, Buddhist, or Taoist,[65] is something that resurfaces remarkably often in Esalen's history, sometimes quite dramatically, as in Price's devotion to Rajneesh. Dick Price's temporary and seemingly "inexplicable" devotion to a Hindu Tantric guru, in other words, was—for whatever else it happened to be—expressing something deep and important about Esalen's original inspiration and metaphysical logic. In the end, it is not inexplicable at all. It is Tantric.

The Tantric influences, of course, are even more dramatic in the life and work of Michael Murphy. Central to Murphy's corpus is a lifelong interest in what the Indian traditions call the *siddhis*, those psychic "powers" or supernormal "capacities" or "attributes" that are said to develop along the spiritual path that are commonly said to function as distractions or obstacles on the way to the absolute. In other words, most Indic traditions, with the very important exception of many of the Tantric traditions,[66] take a decidedly ambiguous, if not to say condemning, attitude toward such powers. Although routinely criticized in the literature, they are nevertheless imputed to innumerable admired and/or feared practicing Tantrikas, who are believed to use them for their own and others' personal gain. Following Aurobindo and Myers, Murphy departs considerably from the South Asian traditions here in his insistence that these *siddhis* are not distractions on the path but significant signs of an evolving human supernature. These are not nefarious powers to reject; they are human potentials to nurture and develop, even evolutionary buds that, once comparatively organized and interpreted across human history, signal "the future of the body."

Murphy explores this same evolutionary alchemy imaginatively in his mystical-realism novels *Golf in the Kingdom* (1975), *Jacob Atabet* (1977), *The End of Ordinary History* (1982), and *The Kingdom of Shivas Irons* (1997). In a more comparative and analytical vein, he maps it again in his magnum opus, *The Future of the Body* (1992), an 800-page collection and comparative analysis of psychic powers, saintly charisms, and "miraculous" physical feats recorded in the world's religious, popular, and scientific literatures, a text whose historical influences and methodology Ann Taves has explored for us in her chapter in this volume.

But Murphy is certainly not alone here with his Tantric interests. Anyone familiar with South Asian Tantric traditions knows that mind-altering drugs are commonly used to induce religious states within these subcultures and that goddesses, particularly the goddess Kali, are consistent theological features of these same traditions. Here too Esalen and the Hindu Tantra converge, this time in psychoanalysis and one of its most psychedelic (literally, "mind-manifesting") moments; that is, the work of Stanislav Grof, the Czech-born psychiatrist who abandoned his early Freudian worldview after a series of LSD researches shattered any possibility that he could remain within the Master's materialist and scientistic assumptions. Grof lived and taught at Esalen for fourteen years. His publications are many and diverse, and he continues to publish into the present, but his thorough, if profoundly ill-timed, *LSD Psychotherapy* (1980) can be approached as one of his most extensive and developed statements. It can also be read as a profoundly "Tantric" document.[67]

Freud speculated that mystical experiences of oneness stemmed back to fusion experiences between the newborn infant and the mother. Later theorists radicalized this idea by extending it back into prenatal existence, a kind of *regressus ad uterum,* or "return to the womb." Grof develops this idea even further, locating a whole series of what he calls "basic perinatal matrices" around the clinical experience of birth and the intrauterine life of the infant, all creatively relived (and no doubt reinterpreted) within the LSD experience. There are four such basic perinatal matrices: BPM I, II, III, and IV, described respectively as "Primal Union with Mother," "Antagonism with Mother," "Synergism with Mother," and "Separation from Mother." All of this flows out of Grof's conviction that there exist astonishing parallels between the patterns seen under LSD and the clinical stages of delivery. Grof's entire Basic Perinatal Matrix model, in other words, is centered on the infant's experience of the Mother, her womb (which is also, of course, a sexual organ), and the trauma of the birth experience—structurally speaking, it is a maternal mysticism, similar to much of Tantric spirituality. Add to this the consistent appearance of Kali in his texts (usually in a Jungian mode as the Great or Terrible Mother); the essentially Hindu-perennialist nature of Grof's Cosmic Void evident in such later works as *The Cosmic Game*; the nondual metaphysics that he works with; the many explicit Tantric *yantras* (ritual geometric diagrams used in Tantric meditation), authors, and deities in his texts; and the central place that sexuality plays in his conclusions, and one begins to see that there is something profoundly Tantric about his thought. We thus arrive finally at a type of mystical psychoanalysis that dramatically confirms the findings of classical psychoanalysis (even as it also relativizes them), sexualizes spiritual states in a Tantric fashion, and concludes, after thousands of experiments with workshop participants, with a nondual Hindu worldview that is fundamentally Tantric in nature and function. Psychoanalysis has morphed into a kind of western Tantra, and, in the process, the Tantra has been enriched by an encounter with psychoanalysis and LSD.

Reich, Price, Watts, Murphy, and Grof: we could, of course, go on for some time with many more examples, but the point is made, I hope, that a distinct Tantric transmission can be detected in Esalen's history and literature. How might we explain this?

Doctrinally and historically speaking, what seems to have been at work at Esalen, and perhaps in American culture's interaction with Asian thought as a whole over the last forty years, is an increasing American emphasis on and cultural attraction to Hindu, Buddhist, and Taoist Tantra, that deep dimension of Asian religious thought that, as we have seen above, attempts to unite the spirit and the body through often sexualized imagery and practice in a simultaneous quest for both sensual enjoyment (*bhukti*) and religious liberation (*mukti*). Although the term "Tantra" has certainly not been dominant at Esalen (just as it is rare in Aurobindo's *The Life Divine*), it can be argued that a distinctly "Tantric" causal energy (*shakti*) has been transmitted to Esalen, partly through the Aurobindonian readings, mystical and psychic experiences, and metaphysical visions of Michael Murphy and partly through the broader erotic, psychedelic, and religiously pluralistic "openings" of the 60s and 70s. The ontological "joy" of Esalen is thus also the onto-erotic "bliss" (*ananda*) of Tantra.

If one prefers a more structural and less religious language, we could also speak of a certain countercultural "echo" or "harmony" at work in the phenomenon of Esalen, one resonating between the American counter-culture and the ancient Asian countercultures historically expressed as "Tantra." In effect, the American counterculture, with its radically egali-tarian and individualist values, acted as the cultural "receptor" of the Tan-tric influences from Asia, determining in large part which features of the Asian traditions would be assimilated and which would be ignored or rejected.[68] What contemporary scholars of Hinduism, Buddhism, and Taoism today call Tantra constitutes one of the many contemplative, yo-gic, and philosophical legacies that have been transmitted and transmuted into American culture through Esalen.

THE TRUTH OF A JOKE

Murphy has said repeatedly that *The Life Divine* put it all together for him. But he has also repeatedly joked that despite forty years of eager suggestions and begging, he has in fact never managed to convince a single person at Esalen to read it. Like most jokes, this is most likely a mis-chievous exaggeration that nevertheless holds an important truth. It was this same joke that originally got me thinking about Aurobindo and Es-alen, and it was Murphy's implicit dare, if you will, that inspired me to write this chapter: "I'll be the first to read the text through," I thought to myself in a moment of narcissistic hubris. Then I realized that Murphy was certainly exaggerating a bit here. But these reading obsessions of mine, I suspect, are not at all the point of the quip. I take the joke now as something quite different, as a founder's slightly frustrated wish that things had worked out a bit differently; in this case, that Esalen had developed into something a bit closer to his own original Aurobindonian vision. The fact is that it did not. The joke, then, captures beautifully a certain inevitable tension between a founder's ideal desire and the institution's actual history, between religious vision and social reality. Once again, it bears repeating: the Aurobindonian Tantric charisma has been transmitted through Murphy and institutionalized at Esalen in ways that both preserve and transform its energies into something else.

Ironically, into something more, well, "integral."[69] As Murphy notes, he eventually learned to see Esalen's growth away from his original vision as something organic, natural, and necessary. Perhaps he did not necessarily intend to direct the resources of the Institute toward educational and health reform, Soviet-American relations, and the growing perils of environmental degradation, but there they were, and so they addressed them, worked through them, and helped change them together. The integral thrust of Esalen, it turns out, always working in tandem with the deeper currents of American culture and politics, had its own independent logic and life. Employing a Tantric term that he first learned from Spiegelberg, Murphy can thus describe Esalen as a kind of *sphota*, a seed-like sonic "swelling" or flash that originates an entire universe. Yes, there were certain things he once disliked but now appreciates, and there are others that only disgust him still more now (like Will Schutz having Gestalt participants pee in their pants). But if everything is the divine unfolding, then who is to say that even these were not necessary, were not part of the unfolding? If all is really One, just where do you draw the line? Can you even draw one?

I am finally struck here by the earliest pamphlets that were issued to announce the beginnings of the Esalen Institute and its seminars. Murphy has spoken about how intent he was on designing these early brochures with Peter Bailley as symbolic statements of Esalen's cultural and cognitive syntheses, particularly along the polar axes of East/West, ancient/modern, and spiritual/scientific. From the fall of 1962 through the winter of 1965, the green, orange, and red brochures are dominated by a single iconic image that morphs slightly from year to year but nevertheless remains

Fig 4.1. Second Esalen Pamphlet (1963). Designed by Michael Murphy and Peter Bailley. Property of Esalen archives.

obviously consistent: a line drawing of a lotus, no doubt meant to suggest traditional Hindu and Buddhist notions of enlightenment as something pristine and pure that nevertheless arises out of the fertile mud (see Figure 4.1). Perhaps also significant here are the facts that the name "Aurobindo" translates literally as "lotus" and that a very similar lotus is featured on the logo of the Aurobindo Ashram and in all of its publications. Consciously or unconsciously, then, there is a very definite symbolic association being set up here between the founding of Esalen and the lotus teachings of Sri Aurobindo. Although never made explicit, the lotuses of these early Esalen brochures also signal a clear Indic subtext. As we have seen above, that Indic subtext was also a distinctly Tantric one.[70] Its blossoms would never quite develop in the ways that Murphy may have intended (much less the way Aurobindo might have wished), but it was there nonetheless, blooming in and drawing nourishment from the fertile loam and hot-spring waters of the early 60s American counterculture in ways that we are only beginning to understand and appreciate.

Notes

1. The narrative of this section relies on conversations I had with Michael Murphy on November 20, 2002.

2. For a brief but insightful synopsis of Spiegelberg's life and an interview, see Keith Thompson, "The Astonishment of Being," *The Esalen Catalog,* September 1993–February 1994, 4–7.

3. Frederic Spiegelberg, *Spiritual Practices of India,* introduction by Alan W. Watts (New York: Citadel Press, 1962), xx.

4. See especially Frederic Spiegelberg, *The Religion of No-Religion* (Stanford, Calif.: Delkin, 1948).

5. Quoted in Thompson, "The Astonishment of Being," 7. I am not certain why the word "Hindi" is used here; I suspect it is a typo or a simple mistake, as the noun or nominal adjective "Hindi" (referring to an Indian vernacular language) is often confused with the noun or nominal adjective "Hindu" (referring to a follower or feature of Hinduism). In any case, "Hindu" or, better still, "Sanskrit" would be more correct here.

6. Alan Watts, *In My Own Way* (New York: Vintage, 1972), 285.

7. There is some debate about what actually happened here. Chaudhuri came to believe that Aurobindo had selected him, but according to a signed declaration from Sethna himself, this was in fact not the case. ("Note on Haridus Chauduri's appointment as conveyed by K.D. Sethna [Amal Kiran] to Minna Paladino, his PA, on February 8, 2005," Aurobindo Ashram Archives). My thanks to Peter Heetis for this note. For a brief synopsis of his system, see Chaudhuri's "The Integral Philosophy of Sri Aurobindo," in Haridas Chaudhuri and Frederic Spiegelberg, eds., *The Integral Philosophy of Sri Aurobindo* (London: George Allen and Unwin, 1960).

8. Despite the dynamic presence of individuals such as Spiegelberg, Watts, and Chaudhuri, the original institution did not last long, particularly after Gainsborough experienced some business losses and had to withdraw his financial support. The doors were finally shut in the mid-60s. Chaudhuri, however, was determined to continue and founded the California Institute of Asian Studies in 1968, which for the next six years functioned as the educational wing of the Cultural Integration Fellowship, which Chaudhuri and his wife, Bina, had founded. Chaudhuri himself died in 1975, but his dream lived on and in 1981 was reestablished as the California Institute of Integral Studies (CIIS). For two brief synopses of this history, see "Esalen and the American Academy of Asian Studies" at www.well.com/user/davidu/esalen.html and "History" at www.ciis.edu/catalog/aboutinstitute.html.

9. In one of those synchronistic moments that define the meanings of a life attuned to such patterns, on the very day Chaudhuri died in 1975 Murphy received from his friend a long list of yogic powers that he had researched and organized at Murphy's request (Murphy was at that point writing his supernatural novel on such powers, *Jacob Atabet*, and needed some help with their classical formulations in Sanskrit and Bengali lore).

10. For an insightful study of Auroville, particularly around the secular/religious theme, see Robert N. Minor, *The Religious, The Spiritual, and the Secular: Auroville and Secular India* (Albany: State University of New York Press, 1999).

11. Jeffrey J. Kripal, *Roads of Excess, Palaces of Wisdom: Eroticism and Reflexivity in the Study of Mysticism* (Chicago: University of Chicago Press, 2001).

12. Sri Aurobindo, *The Life Divine* (Twin Lakes, Wis.: Lotus Press, 1990), 5; henceforth *LD*.

13. *LD*, 74–75.

14. Ibid., 374.

15. Ibid.

16. Aurobindo explicitly described nirvana as a kind of "Nihil" (*LD*, 84).

17. I am indebted to Laurie Patton for these philological details.

18. *LD*, 124.

19. This fusion took some fascinating turns in the same century. The ten *avataras* of classical Hinduism, for example, (beginning with the fish and the boar and ending with Kalki, the apocalyptic warrior) were sometimes said to foreshadow Darwinian evolution. It is mythology, not just ontogeny that recapitulates phylogeny here!

20. *LD*, 69, 83, 180, 312.

21. Ibid., 377–379.

22. Ibid., 441–443.

23. See ibid., 62, 213–214.

24. "The real subconscious is a nether diminished consciousness close to the Inconscient; the subliminal is a consciousness larger than our surface existence. But both belong to the inner realm of our being of which our surface is unaware, so both are jumbled together in our common conception and parlance" (Ibid., 237n6).

25. Ibid., 290–293, 226.

26. Ibid., 315, 315, and 300, respectively.

27. Ibid., 193.

28. David Gordon White, "Introduction," in *The Practice of Tantra: A Reader* (Princeton, N.J.: Princeton University Press, 2000), 8.

29. White, "Introduction," 9.

30. Quoted by White in ibid., 8. In the background of Padoux's discussion is Madeleine Biardeau's discussion of Tantra in her *Hinduism: An Anthropology of a Civilization* (Delhi: Oxford University Press, 1994).

31. Aurobindo's common use of the adjective "supernormal" may be another example of his unacknowledged borrowing from a western author, in this case Frederic Myers, whom the *Oxford English Dictionary* cites as the second author of the term (Michael Murphy, personal communication, February 27, 2003). I realize, of course, that it is possible that two authors could have come up with the same term independently, but Aurobindo's demonstrated and obvious familiarity with psychical research

and his long residence and education in Myers's England renders a borrowing scenario far more likely. In any case, the same term would become central to Murphy's later corpus and the general mystical vocabulary of Esalen.

32. *LD*, 911.

33. For these, see especially Peter Heehs, *Sri Aurobindo: A Brief Biography* (New Delhi: Oxford University Press, 1989).

34. Quoted in Mahendranath Gupta, *Sri-Sri-Ramakrsna-Kathamrta*, 31st ed. (Calcutta: Kathamrita Bhaban, 1987), 5: 181.

35. Shashibhushan Dasgupta, *Obscure Religious Cults* (1946; reprint, Calcutta: Firma KLM Private, 1976).

36. *LD*, 88.

37. Ibid., 93. It should be pointed out that this is not always the case in the collected works of Aurobindo, who often, in classical Tantric style, understood Reality as the Divine Mother and so privileged the feminine over the masculine.

38. *LD*, 209.

39. Ibid.

40. Ibid., 126.

41. Ibid., 84.

42. Ibid., 126.

43. Ibid., 28.

44. Ibid.

45. Ibid.

46. Ibid., 404.

47. Ibid. Here, I think, we have one of the most dramatic examples of a western linear model of time and progression replacing an ancient and quite traditional Indian cyclical model. Aurobindo may present such a move as traditional and even "Vedantic," but it is in fact neither.

48. It is often said that Aldous Huxley was the first to coin the expression "human potential" as "human potentialities," but in fact similar phrases are common in *The Life Divine,* a text which often reads like an Esalen tract. Aurobindo can write, for example, of "the integral development of our many-sided potentialities" (*LD*, 230). For a sampling of other occurrences of the term, see 64, 99, 122, 223, 266, 273, 285, and 911.

49. Ibid., 226.

50. For the definitive study of this linkage and the erotics of Indian alchemy, see David Gordon White, *The Alchemical Body: Siddha Traditions in Medieval India* (Chicago: University of Chicago Press, 1996); and *Kiss of the Yogini: "Tantric Sex" in Its South Asian Contexts* (Chicago: University of Chicago Press, 2003).

51. *LD*, 275.

52. Ibid., 266.

53. Ibid.

54. Ibid., 269.

55. Ibid., 241.

56. Ibid., 216.

57. Ibid., 23; cf. 71.

58. Ibid., 23.

59. Ibid., 116–117.

60. Ibid., 95.

61. Stanislav Grof, *The Cosmic Game: Explorations of the Frontiers of Human Consciousness* (Albany: State University of New York Press, 1998).

62. As any number of writers have noted, beginning with the famous Orientalist critique by Edward Said, the usual gender patterns of British colonialism spoke of India as a Woman that needed to be civilized or domesticated by British Man. In the process, Indian males were routinely feminized and seen as weak and incapable of self-government. Drawing on this same discourse, Ashis Nandy has insightfully noted that Aurobindo's relationship with the French woman Mirra Richard reversed the colonial discourse and its sexual politics. See his *The Intimate Enemy: Loss and Recovery of Self under Colonialism* (New Delhi: Oxford University Press, 1983).

63. One of the earliest essays "assigned" at Esalen, for example, was Watts's "Spirituality and Sensuality," from his *This Is It* (New York: Macmillan, 1960), a little book that was listed as recommended reading in the very first Esalen brochure. Watts's writings are suffused with a general but sophisticated Tantric sensibility of the unity of sexuality and spirituality. See especially his *Nature, Man and Woman* (New York: Pantheon, 1958).

64. The previous two paragraphs are drawn largely from an interview with Barclay James Erickson (October 26, 2003, Esalen Institute).

65. For the mystico-erotic practices of Chinese Taoism, see especially Douglas Wile, *Art of the Bedchamber: The Chinese Sexual Yoga Classics Including Women's Solo Meditation Texts* (Albany: State University of New York Press, 1992).

66. For an erudite discussion of these *siddhis* and their often-sexualized expression in medieval Indian Tantric culture, see White, *Kiss of the Yogini.*

67. Stanislav Grof, *LSD Psychotherapy: Exploring the Frontiers of the Hidden Mind* (Sarasota: Multidisciplinary Association for Psychedelic Studies, 2001). As Grof himself notes, this book could not have been released at a worse time (ibid., 11). Widespread and irresponsible drug abuse combined with a sensationalizing media and an increasingly hostile political environment threatened to sink the entire subject into oblivion.

68. I am indebted to conversations with Catherine Albanese for this metaphor of the cultural receptor.

69. These final two paragraphs are based loosely on a telephone conversation with Murphy (February 27, 2003).

70. I am reminded here of the Tibetan double *vajra* of *dorje* that mysteriously appears on the first-edition hardcover of Swami Nikhilananda's *The Gospel of Sri Ramakrishna* (New York: Ramakrishna-Vivekananda Center, 1942), as if to signal a secret, even unconscious, Tantric subtext to that tradition as well. The encircling *kundalini* serpent of the Ramakrishna Order's logo, which appears on the spine, can be read with the same Tantric hermeneutic.

THE ONLY WAY OUT IS IN:

THE LIFE OF RICHARD PRICE

Barclay James Erickson

On a bright, sunny, humid August morning in 1957, a somewhat dazed young man with a puffy but strikingly handsome face was shuffling down the street in Hartford, Connecticut. He had just climbed over a high wall in order to make his escape from one of the most expensive mental hospitals in the United States: the Institute for Living. Figuring out how to escape from the hospital had not been difficult. He knew, however, that in his overweight, physically weakened condition he simply was not capable of climbing over the hospital wall. First, he had needed to get himself in better condition, despite what they were doing to him.

To begin with, he learned how to "cheek" the Thorazine they were giving him rather than swallowing it, and that had helped his condition quite a bit. But the electroshock treatments were taking a collective physical and mental toll. The treatments themselves felt like getting smashed really hard in football or boxing and getting knocked out cold, then waking up not knowing who or where you were. After a few days he would recover, but he had gaps in his memory that he knew might never be filled in. It was the insulin shock treatments, however, that were the worst. They would knock him out, too, putting him into a hypoglycemic coma. He would wake up, unable to move, feeling like his body had been filled with cement. The only thing he could do to get some relief, once they gave him sugared orange juice and he could move again, was to continuously walk the hospital halls, drinking copious amounts of water. Largely because of the insulin shock treatments, he had ballooned from 145 pounds to 240. After the first fifty treatments he began to wonder how many more it would take to kill him. He thought he'd come very close to dying a couple of times already and he knew people did die from these treatments. Feeling desperate, he had made up his mind that escape was his only option. They would not let him exercise at the Institute for Living, despite the fact that he had been a champion high school and college athlete. But he had done his best to get in better shape and he had finally lost enough weight to make it over the wall.

As he walked down the street in Hartford a single thought repeated itself over and over in his mind: Now what? He realized that he really did not have an answer. The first person to really notice him was a bum on the street. He'd said hello and the bum had asked him to sit down. It was a warm day and it felt better to be sitting in the shade than walking without a destination or a plan. He'd figured out pretty quickly he could trust the bum and told him all about his family and how they had tricked him into the hospital, had him committed, and then had his marriage annulled. There had been nothing he could do to stop them. His father, the executive vice-president of Sears & Roebuck, had never been able to stand up to his mother, so her demands that he be hospitalized at the Institute and that his marriage be annulled were carried out. It was an enormous price to pay for not living up to his mother's view of what he could and should be.

Eventually he and the bum talked about what he should do now. Their talk drove home the realization that he was still too incapacitated to make good his escape. In the end, the bum loaned him a dime to call his father. The young man realized that the only way out of this horrible no-win situation was to go back into the hospital. He made the call and told his father he had escaped but could not possibly make it in the world in his present condition. He also told his father what they had been doing to him and pleaded for his father to intercede for him at the hospital in order to stop the devastating shock treatments and get him off the locked ward so he could begin to recover his health.

The young man's father did what his son asked. When he returned to the hospital he was placed in an open ward. Three months later, on

Thanksgiving Day in 1957, he gained his release. In early 1962, a little more than four years after his release from the Institute for Living, Dick Price, together with his friend Michael Murphy, would become the co-founders of Esalen Institute.

Dick Price was born in Chicago, Illinois, on October 12, 1930. His birth, as was that of his twin brother Bobby, was by Caesarean section. His immediate family circle consisted of his parents, Herman and Audrey Price, and a sister, Joan, who had been born almost two years before the twins.

The young Price family faced a major crisis in 1933 following a series of traumatic events. Dick's sister Joan described 1933 as "a truly horrible year for the family."[1] In January, Joan, who had suffered ongoing medical problems dating from her premature birth, contracted ethmoiditis. She had to undergo surgery, and she came very close to dying. Her illness lingered and she needed another surgical procedure later that year. Then, in the fall, Bobby fell suddenly and very seriously ill. The family pediatrician, Dr. Peacock, was out of town at the time. Bobby's sudden illness, actually acute appendicitis, was misdiagnosed by the doctor who was covering Dr. Peacock's practice. Bobby's appendix burst, causing peritonitis. An emergency operation to save his life was unsuccessful, and Bobby died.

It is hard to calculate the impact of an infant's death on a young family. Dick felt that as a child he was left very much alone in handling the impact of his twin brother's death. Dick's loneliness was compounded by his mother's dismissal of a nurse to whom he was attached within months of Bobby's death.[2] Joan was old enough to understand that Bobby was never coming back. Dick, however, was only three and was too young to understand the finality of Bobby's death. Joan remembers that for months, Dick kept looking for Bobby whenever they went to places where the boys had played together. In Gestalt sessions that Dick did with his wife Chris in his adult years, it was clear that "at some place in him, he held his mom, both of them [his parents], but more his mom, responsible for Bobby's death."[3] Dick came to believe that "the appendix was about toxicity, there was just too much toxicity."[4]

Bobby's death also engendered a division in parental alignment toward the children. Dick came to be identified as being more under Audrey's parental influence and control, while Joan became more aligned with Herman. According to Joan, Audrey became "much more possessive with regard to Dick than to me, because she had turned Dick in her own mind into a kind of mirror image of herself and her views."[5] Herman seems to have withdrawn from the family into his business life after Bobby's death and "could never bear to hear Bobby's name spoken."[6]

Bobby's death, according to Joan, "affected not only Dick, but also served to emphasize the differences in my parents' characters."[7] From reports of those who knew him, Herman emerges as a charismatic figure, universally liked in the greater Price family and by his business associates. He was a strikingly handsome, warm, intelligent, and highly focused man who possessed a tremendous work ethic, qualities that enabled him to rise from a being a poor, non-English-speaking Lithuanian immigrant to a position at the top echelon of Sears & Roebuck. Herman had abandoned his mother's adherence to Orthodox Judaism and did not attend religious services. Orthodox Judaism simply did not make sense to Herman or his brothers in the context of their new circumstances. He remained very close to his brothers, who also lived and worked in the Chicago area, and spent a considerable amount of his time pursuing business interests. He maintained an active social life aligned with his business interests as a member of both the Brynmore Country Club and the Standard Club of Chicago.

Herman Price was the product of "a strong, domineering mother and married a woman who became a strong, domineering wife and mother in turn."[8] Dick's sister Joan observed that Herman was often unable to withstand his wife Audrey's insistence on the absolute rightness of her point of view and preferred to give in rather than fight with her. At the beginning of a family history, Joan Price wrote: "The recurring pattern of strong woman—passive man is obvious in what follows."[9]

Audrey, in contrast to her husband, emerges as a figure that was universally disliked in the greater Price family. She is described as having been strong, hard, strict, rigid, cold, superstitious, overprotective, possessive, jealous, crazy, domineering, and controlling. A maternal cousin told Joan that "Audrey is a tyrant, just like Grandmother."[10] Audrey and her mother-in-law are said to have "truly hated" each other.[11] Dick's second wife, Chris Price, commented that the Prices were "a family in which the mother was the dominant force, period."[12]

In 1941, when Dick was ten, the family moved from their high-rise "penthouse" apartment near Lake Shore Drive in Chicago to 138 Winnetka Avenue in Kenilworth, an affluent Chicago suburb. The Price's new home was located only a short walk from New Trier High School, a school that had received significant attention as one of the best in the country. The move enabled Joan to begin high school at New Trier. Because Kenilworth did not allow the selling of property to Jewish families, Audrey instructed her children not to tell anyone that the family was Jewish. In Kenilworth, Audrey wanted the family to join the Episcopalian church, so Dick and Joan were baptized. Joan recalls that she "avoided this religious training as much as I could, but Dick attended regularly, carried the flag at services, and took confirmation classes."[13] Joan is not sure how much Dick's participation reflected any genuine personal beliefs. His attendance may simply have been a reflection of the need to accommodate his mother's wishes. Audrey wanted the family to fit into the anti-Semitic neighborhood in which they now lived.[14]

In Kenilworth, Dick started participating in athletics, eventually going for the football and wrestling teams. Dick was not very big, but he was very tough and very scrappy. His football coach once told him: "Pound for pound I get more out of you than anyone, Price."[15] Sports became an avenue that supported Dick's need to establish an identity for himself outside the confines of his family. Dick told his friend Leonard Bearne that though he did not fully realize it at the time, he was very, very angry when he was young and that in wrestling he discovered an outlet in which he could fully express his anger, using absolutely all his physical and mental resources.[16] Wrestling became a real passion for Dick. He was a dominant high school wrestler who placed second in his weight class at the Illinois State Wrestling Championships.

Dick graduated from New Trier High School in 1948. Although there was considerable peer pressure to attend either Harvard or Yale, Dick chose Stanford. Stanford's relative informality appealed to him, and as he acknowledged, "I probably wanted to get as far away from my family as possible."[17] Leaving home must have felt like a liberating escape from the ruling power of his mother's authority and from a father Dick had come to regard as absent, uninterested, and uncaring.

In the fall of 1948, Dick moved to California and started classes at Stanford University. He enjoyed the new sense of personal and social freedom that college life afforded him. His family may not have given him the kind of emotional support he had needed, but his parents had always been very generous materially and financially. Dick started college with a new Studebaker and a bank account tied to his father's that automatically kept his balance at $1,000 irrespective of expenditures.

It was expected that he would complete college, serve some time in the military, and then pursue a career in business. To quote Dick:

> My father had grown from an immigrant to a top executive. So, in some way, a little oedipal perhaps, O.K., my role in life was to beat what he was doing. So I had some image growing up that to consider myself a success I would have to be something like the president of U.S. Steel, right, or president of General Motors.[18]

Dick went to Stanford assuming that he would major in business. Since the school did not offer an undergraduate business major, Dick began his college career studying economics, a subject that did not sustain any lasting interest for him. A beginning psychology course, however, sparked his interest, and he changed his major to psychology.

As Dick's interest in psychology solidified, he became a more serious student, maintaining a 4.0 grade point average. He also developed a new career plan, one he hoped could extricate him from the status-seeking type of life he associated with his parents and was expected to follow. His new plan was to go to graduate school in psychology, become a psychologist, and eventually work as a professor or be trained as an analyst. He obtained his B.A. in Psychology from Stanford in 1952 and applied to Harvard University's newly created graduate program in social relations. He was accepted and began Harvard that fall. As Dick describes his interests at the time:

> I wasn't interested in being an experimental psychologist. I was interested in, you know if I had to label it in any way, in being a kind of anthropologist in mental health and illness . . . and it seemed to be a department where this might be possible to pursue.[19]

Harvard proved to be a huge disappointment for Dick. He had the naïve hope that the department of social relations would be more socially enlightened and less hierarchical than Stanford's psychology department with its focus on experimental psychology, rats, and questionnaires. Instead, his initial course of study at Harvard directly focused on experimental psychology. He also found the department to be hierarchical, authoritarian, and filled with academic bickering. Toward the end of his first year, Dick wrote an examination that used the material he was learning to criticize what the department was doing. As a result, he received a C, which was effectively a failing grade. Dick had never before received any grade less than an A in psychology. Exacerbating the whole experience was the fact that "I knew this was the best examination I'd ever written."[20] Personologist Henry Murray (1938) was the only professor in the department who showed any interest in helping and supporting Dick, and he feared that he had made lasting enemies out of two very powerful professors in the department, Jerome Bruner and Richard Soloman.

In the summer of 1953, he decided to leave Harvard. "By that time," according to Dick, "I wasn't in really good shape, mentally myself."[21] He had been studying very hard at Harvard and had been ignoring the physical exercise regime that had been so important to him in high school and at Stanford. He had also become very isolated socially. He was discovering that he simply could not live on a diet of academic discipline alone. He told his parents he was going to transfer to either Stanford or the University of California at Berkeley (Cal) and left for California.

When Dick arrived in California, he stayed at Stanford for a few months at his old fraternity house, enjoying the peace and quiet afforded by the summer break. In the fall, Dick registered for some courses at Cal, including a course taught by a visiting professor, Carl Rogers, from the University of Chicago. Dick had read all of Rogers's books, and they had struck a very positive chord in him. The course, however, left him unimpressed with Rogers's actual work.

Feeling somewhat adrift, Dick decided to accept an army commission as a psychological tester. The Korean War, however, was winding down and his commission fell through. He then decided to join the air force and take advantage of opportunities that existed there for psychology majors. He did his basic training in 1954 at Lackland Air Force Base. At first, Dick enjoyed his air force experience:

In a way it was really a good experience, I was so cluttered in my head, I didn't know what I was doing, really. I no longer seemed to have the ability, the strength, a certain type of strength, to kind of put emotion and everything else aside and really concentrate on books, which seemed to be what the academic life was about.[22]

Instead of working in the field of psychology as he had hoped, Dick was given a job doing obsolete gunnery research. To Dick, it soon became "a little like Harvard, I didn't get along too well with the people who were running it."[23]

Eventually Dick was able to obtain a transfer to Parks Air Force Base in Pleasanton, California, where he took a position as a teacher of recruits. It was good duty. His schedule was two days on (night duty for twelve to fourteen hours) followed by two days off. This meant he could go back to school, as both Cal and Stanford were only a half-hour's drive from Pleasanton.

In the spring of 1955, Dick started taking some courses at Stanford. One of the courses was taught by Frederic Spiegelberg, a popular, highly regarded professor at Stanford who was teaching a course on the Bhagavad Gita. In his own words, "For the first time, I began thinking there was something in religion; it was more than a system of deceit and enforcement of social rules."[24] At Spiegelberg's suggestion, he went to the Vedanta Society to hear a lecture by Swami Shokananda. He was very impressed. Spiegelberg also recommended Alan Watts's lectures to his students. Dick went and was "immensely impressed; it was like nothing I'd ever touched into."[25] He found a vitality in Watts that profoundly affected him, and he began taking courses at the Academy of Asian Studies, where Watts was the principal teacher. He even took a room at the Academy and began to spend time in San Francisco studying Buddhism, meditating, and observing the burgeoning Beat scene with which Watts was inextricably linked. Beat scene luminaries such as Gary Snyder, Jack Kerouac, Allen Ginsberg, and Lawrence Ferlinghetti all attended Watts's lectures.

He also began to hang out at The Place, an as-yet-unknown North Beach nightspot where he could get a pitcher of beer and usually find someone interesting to talk to. At the time, he had passing acquaintances with both Snyder and Ginsberg. At The Place, he watched the transformation of the Beat scene as it burst into the spotlight and onto the national scene, seemingly coinciding with and mirroring his own growth and the felt senses of excitement and expansion that accompanied it.

Experiences he was having in his meditation practice were also feeding Dick's excitement and expansiveness. At the Asian Academy he studied the writing of Thera Nyanaponika,[26] a Buddhist Vipassana meditation teacher, incorporating what he was learning into his growing meditation practice.[27] Dick began having some intense spiritual experiences, some of which excited him and some that were more disconcerting. Sensing that he needed some guidance, he went to his teachers at the Asian Academy and asked them what he should do. Unfortunately, the knowledge of his teachers at the Academy was more intellectual than experiential; they simply could not help him. He felt that the only people who could really relate to his actual experiences were people who were involved in the Beat scene such as Gary Snyder.

In December of 1955, a friend, Gia-fu Feng, came by the Academy to have dinner with Dick and introduce him to a woman he had brought along. Her name was Bonnie. She was a very attractive dancer who, like Dick, had grown up Chicago. At the time, Dick was toying with the idea of becoming a Buddhist monk. Thoughts of a long-term relationship or marriage were a very long way from his mind. There had not been much of an example that would induce him to value marriage; as he put it, he did "not [see] anything that was outside of this role-playing, status-seeking type of life" that he associated with the marriage of his parents and the marriages in the circle of friends he grew up with in Kenilworth. As a result, he recognized that he had "a tremendous approach-avoidance thing with women."[28]

As he was eating dinner with Gia-fu and Bonnie, he heard a commanding voice that said: "There is your wife." Dick looked up to see if anyone else in the room had heard the voice. He even remembered arguing subvocally with the voice, saying something like: "Don't be ridiculous, I'm happy with the way my life is now."[29] Within a few months, however, Dick would marry Bonnie.

Dick and Bonnie were married at the Soto Zen Temple in San Francisco in a ceremony performed by the Reverend Tobasi in February 1956.

The ceremony was conducted in Japanese with an English translator. The bridesmaid was Black, the best man Japanese, and the guests were ethnically and culturally quite mixed. "To me," said Dick, "it was one of the deepest aesthetic experiences I'd ever had . . . opening up to sound and music and the scene of all the mixture of Whites and Blacks and Orientals."[30]

Dick's parents, to say the very least, did not share his view of the wedding. The guests certainly were not what his mother considered to be the "right people." He was later able to admit that part of him was deliberately shocking his parents and that he had been determined to marry in spite of their objections. Part of the reason, no doubt, was to symbolically and emphatically state his independence from his parents' views and values with a kind of euphoric belief, buoyed by his current energetic state, that he might actually be able to be free from them. As Dick described his experience at the wedding:

> My experience was very much like, hey, you know there's another me, that's somehow vaster and greater, that I can't quite trust, that's running the conscious Dick and there is the conscious Dick up at the altar being married by Reverend Tobasi.[31]

After his parents left for Chicago, Dick and Bonnie drove down the coast to Ensenada, Mexico, and then north into the Sierra Nevada Mountains in California. Dick recalled barely being able to contain his energetic state on the long drive. When they got back to San Francisco, they moved into an apartment together. He now split his time between Bonnie and their life together, his job at the air force base, the Asian Academy, and the North Beach scene. His high energetic state made all his activities possible; he was now getting by on two hours of sleep a night.

Things were beginning to go very fast for Dick. He was experiencing an upwelling of energy that he was barely able to contain. He was not having any problems at the air base, largely due to the fact that his sergeant, a close friend, was covering for him. Dick only had to show up once every two weeks to pick up his paycheck. In his own words: "At the time, especially with almost Bonnie catalyzing this, I started to go crazier and crazier. But in a way for me it was just this immense expansion and excitement which I was having trouble containing."[32]

On one of Dick's visits to North Beach, the tremendous state of internal energy he was riding burst through any attempt at restraint. As Esalen chronicler Walter Truett Anderson described:

> Finally, one night in a bar in North Beach, all the energy came to a head. He felt a tremendous opening-up inside himself, like a glorious dawn. The place he was in had a fireplace, and he thought it would be appropriate for them to light a fire there, in celebration of this great and mysterious event. "Light the fire," he kept saying; "light the fire."[33]

Instead of lighting a celebratory fire, the bartender called the authorities and six very large San Francisco policemen handcuffed Dick and wrestled him into a paddy wagon.

Initially, he was taken to Letterman's Army Hospital in San Francisco. After a few days, he was transferred to a hospital at Parks Air Force Base, where he was stationed. At Parks, he was given a few electroshock treatments and an occasional dose of Thorazine, but in general he was appreciative of the way he was treated there. While hospitalized, he attempted to sort through the powerful upwelling of unconscious material that kept coming through him at the time. As Dick described: "For three months I was going through all sorts of experiences, some of which I remember, some of which I don't." One was a regression through history in which Dick felt that he was leaping through a series of past lives. Before this experience, he considered past lives to be a superstition, although transmigration had been treated seriously at the Asian Academy. Of particular importance to him was when the procession of lives came to a stop, "coming to a life that was some type of monk" who spent his time in meditation.[34]

Other experiences in the hospital Dick labeled as "more characteristically schizophrenic, experiences like feeling a kind of an early shut-up in my genitals." He recognized that some of what he was going through was an attempt to come to terms with his early psychosexual development, on which there had been a "lot of restrictions." He felt the experiences he was having were an "organismic" attempt to restore his life energy in a way that would allow it to flow freely rather than having to remain bottled up and restricted. His childhood memories of having to contain so much fear and rage at unmet needs that he was never allowed to express had been vividly awakened. He felt that his childhood had been one filled with his mother's rage, and it engendered an immense sense of fear and anxiety in him: "[T]he ambience was always this immense rage, do anything wrong and 'vroom.'" While in the hospital he also had what could be termed from a Buddhist perspective "mini satori," or small enlightenment experiences.[35]

After about three months at the military hospital, there was a major shift in his experience. In his words:

> I was in a balanced, fine energetic space and I remember my feeling was one of gratitude . . . to the nature of things and to my own nature. . . . I was still a little volatile but I was no longer in the super excited state but in kind of a balanced state, in a state that in some way I felt washed clean.[36]

He had come through an experience that he would later term a "transitional psychosis" and was ready to get back to his life and his marriage.[37] The air force was planning to release him from the hospital and give him an honorable discharge despite the fact that he had another year and a half of his enlistment to serve. His preference was to "get out as soon as I could and my discharge was forthcoming and this would have been in September of 1956. I wanted to stay on the coast; I didn't want to go back into the family situation."[38]

Dick's discharge from the hospital at Parks Air Force Base never came. Instead, he was notified that he was being transferred to another hospital. His father, exerting his political influence through a "high-level contact in Washington," had secured Dick's transfer to an air force hospital in Illinois located some fifteen miles from the family home in Kenilworth.[39]

After his hospitalization, Dick "had a sense," according to Chris Price, "that even there [with his parents], there was new possibility. . . . So when they came and said 'trust us,' from that place I could forgive and we could start fresh,' and then it happened."[40] The "it" that Chris is referring to was a whole series of duplicitous events perpetrated by his parents that resulted in his involuntary commitment to the Institute for Living.

First, his wife Bonnie moved into the Price home in Kenilworth. Things did not go well between Bonnie and her mother-in-law. One weekend when Dick came home from the hospital, Dick's mother told him that she had gone into Bonnie's room and found some of her letters. She had read those letters and had discovered material that convinced her Bonnie was unfit to be his wife. In answer to what must have been a maddening repetition of many childhood experiences of his mother's toxic invasiveness, Dick, "blew up."[41] For the first time in his life, Dick openly expressed his anger and rage against his mother's intrusiveness. He had allowed himself to be open and vulnerable, and he had been met with terrible betrayal.

Dick immediately moved Bonnie out of the Price household, reported back to the hospital, and made inquiries about getting his discharge. He knew it was time to get out of Chicago and out from under his family's control. He wanted to go back to California. Dick could have simply left with Bonnie, but he knew if he did so before the air force officially discharged him, he would be considered to be AWOL and subject to military discipline. What he did not know was that he had already been discharged and was free to leave.[42]

Shortly thereafter, Dick's father came to visit the hospital and took him out for an expensive lunch. During lunch he told Dick about a highly recommended private hospital on the East Coast, the Institute for Living, insisting that he go there for a few months.

> "What if I don't want to go?" he asked. The question was a challenge, an expression of barely contained anger, and his father knew it. The conflict was out in the open, and the older man was ready for it. "If you don't want to go," he said harshly, "then, I'll commit you." It was kind of ironic in a way: Price's father had never taken that much interest in him, never showed much emotion, even anger. Price had always regretted that and wished he had a real father. Now, at last, he had one.[43]

Dick agreed to a compromise. He would go to the Institute for Living on a voluntary basis for three months. Herman was really acting at the insistence of his wife. As Dick's sister Joan remembers the circumstances surrounding the event:

> Her habit of seizing on an idea and her insistence on having her own way explained the decision about the Institute. It had received a great deal of publicity and she kept demanding that Dick go there. Both my parents were devastated by Dick's condition; both behaved as they had for their entire marriage. Mother saw only her point of view, was convinced she was absolutely right, and Dad was unable to withstand her.[44]

Dick Price entered the Institute for Living on December 7, 1956, a day of infamy in his life. Dick spent his first weeks in locked, smoke-filled, crowded hospital rooms, unable to exercise or go outside. Nominally under the care of some of the best psychiatrists in the country, he received no treatment of any kind except for drugs designed to keep him manageable. Given his voluntary status, Dick could, at least theoretically, sign himself out of the hospital and, following a ten-day waiting period, be released. When he did so, the Institute notified his father, who had him committed under the psychiatric diagnosis of paranoid schizophrenia.[45] Making a terrible situation even worse, as soon as he was legally committed, his parents had his marriage to Bonnie annulled.

Now the hospital had an interest in treating him. Over the next nine months Dick received fifty-nine insulin shock treatments, ten electroshock treatments, and frequent large doses of Thorazine. He came to regard the Institute for Living as little more than a "private prison"[46] in which he was "effectively tortured."[47] He knew, however, that the only viable course of action was to accommodate, or in Anderson's words, "to be a very good boy, take whatever they handed him, and hope that sooner or later they would let him out."[48] However, as time dragged on and being a good boy did not work, Dick began to seriously fear for his life. When he realized, after his escape in August 1957, that he was too debilitated to successfully make it in the world, Dick called his father with a dime from the bum who had befriended him. As Chris Price remembers:

> He clearly told me that when he called his dad with that dime, he said to his dad "They've made me so ill, I literally have to recover my health. I'm not well enough to come out into a job or anything. . . . I'm not even asking for you to get me out, now. . . . I can't stay out, I may have escaped but I can't just go out there. I'm sick, now. I'm going to go back but I want you to get me on an open ward so I can regain my health. . . . I'm literally debilitated."[49]

Dick returned to the hospital, was placed on the open ward, and began the long, slow process of recovery. Three months later, on Thanksgiving Day 1957, Dick was released from the hospital after a stay that was just short of a year. He had paid a very high price for deviating from the plan his parents had for him. The lesson was simple: conform or be punished. Dick took the only option; he conformed. He moved back in with his parents and took a job at Price Brothers, working for his uncle Louis as an assistant purchasing agent.

Working for his uncle was dull, but it allowed him to bide time and demonstrate his sanity to his parents, something he needed to do if he was going to avoid their long reach in the future. After three long years of working for his uncle, he learned that Gia-fu Feng and some old friends were starting a cooperative in San Francisco. It was called the East-West House. Dick decided it was time go back to California and restart a life that could be more authentically his own. His parents did not try to stop him. In May of 1960, Dick got on a plane in Chicago that was bound for California.

How might Dick's hospitalization and the events that culminated in Dick's feeling "newborn" at the North Beach bar be understood? Dick was acutely aware that his excessive, barely containable mental and physical energy had been the major precipitating factor in his hospitalization. He had been experiencing what was essentially a manic state of mind. Indeed, if Dick were to be hospitalized today for those events, I think he would be diagnosed as having a manic episode. As contemporary psychological theorists Atwood, Orange, and Stolorow have commented:

> A pervasively important meaning of mania is that it may express a kind of protest against annihilating accommodation to agendas and roles that are not authentically the person's own. It thus provides a transitory restoration of a sense of agency and authenticity, by disrupting the "borrowed cohesion" . . . of an identity based in compliance with others' agenda. The reason this restoration can only be transitory and is always so destructive is that the manic protest is a bursting of familiar patterns but in the absence of any psychological organization that can constitute an alternative. The classic diagnostic signs defining the manic state can thus be understood as manifestations of this active breaking out of a surrendered life into chaotic freedom.[50]

Dick still had not fully recovered from his hospitalization and was in a great deal of physical discomfort, which he attributed to the insulin shock treatments. There were also deep feelings of having been betrayed by his family and a growing sense of grief and feelings of rage about his hospitalization. His intention now "was to find a place where people who were going through the type of experience I had could simply get better treatment and to utilize whatever I might find."[51] In San Francisco, he had made a connection with fellow Stanford classmate Mike Murphy (they had not really known each other at Stanford), and the two of them ended up living next door to each other at the Cultural Integration Fellowship, Haridas Chaudhuri's meditation center on Fulton Street.

The two young men certainly had much in common. Both were thirty-year-old, handsome Stanford graduates who hailed from prosperous families. In addition, they were athletes, had spent time in the military, were graduate school dropouts, and had been strongly shaped by the teachings of Eastern philosophic traditions and meditation practices. Common teachers they had studied with and were influenced by included Frederic Spiegelberg, Haridas Chaudhuri, and Alan Watts. Perhaps most important was that they shared "breakout" experiences, both of which occurred in 1956, leading to a rejection of the expectations placed upon them by their families and by society. For Dick, the "breakout" ultimately led to his hospitalization at the Institute for Living. For Mike, the need to escape the "straitjacket" he felt himself to be in led to his leaving Stanford and going to India for a stay in Aurobindo's ashram,[52] an event that Jeffrey Kripal's chapter in this volume explores in some detail. When Mike Murphy quit a job because his employer wanted him to work full time, he invited Dick down to his family's property in Big Sur to see if the two of them might try living there.

They loaded their possessions in a borrowed old Jeep pickup and drove down the coast from San Francisco. Their destination was Big Sur Hot Springs, a small fledgling resort motel owned by Mike's grandmother, Vinnie Murphy. Their intention was to take up residence and investigate the possibility of starting some kind of conference center on site.

One of Dick's hopes for their new project was that it would eventually become the kind of place that could offer help to people who were going through difficult psychological experiences. As Dick recalled:

[Mike] mentioned that his grandmother had this place in the country. I had been talking to a friend who was a psychiatrist who had himself been hospitalized. He had gone into psychiatry and we had talked about finding a place that would be more than the ordinary mental hospital. Michael's interest wasn't specifically in this area. He had spent over a year at the Aurobindo Ashram in India and his interests were more contemplative and intellectual. So we had originally talked about taking over the place as a conference center that would in some way apply itself to a range of interests: meditation, religion, particular experiences, whether religious or psychotic.[53]

They officially took over the property in October 1961, cofounded the actual business that would become Esalen Institute in early 1962, and held their first seminars that same year. They were equal partners in the venture. Mike's family owned the property and Dick provided the needed capital. He had $17,000 in stock, jointly owned by his father, which could provide the security for a $10,000 loan needed to capitalize their project. Dick, with some trepidation, asked his father to release his share of the stock. He was staking out a new territory of hope and autonomy in his life and must have been keenly aware of the catastrophic consequences of his last foray into freedom. His father agreed, however, and the loan was secured. Their new venture was now ready to begin in earnest. Though it started slowly, it would progressively gain momentum through the next decade. In Dick's own words:

> We had started with the connections we had, through people like Alan Watts, and begun to set up programs. I think one of the first programs— it was probably early in 1962—was Alan Watts. Alan did his own program from his own mailing list. At that time we tended to use people who had their own followings, their own mailing lists, their own programs, and we would just provide the place as a conference center for them. Then gradually, I think the following year, we began to get out our own catalogue and formed Esalen as a separate entity. Before that we were running Big Sur Hot Springs, Incorporated, and then we started running weekends. We gradually got a few five-day programs, and we were running it for just "drop-in traffic." Then gradually—I think by 1967—we took the Big Sur Hot Springs sign down and put the Esalen sign up and attempted to make the whole place a conference center. The big turning points were the people who came in residence here, primarily Fritz Perls, in 1964, Virginia Satir about the same time, Will Schutz in 1967.[54]

A natural division of labor emerged that befitted differences in Mike's and Dick's temperaments. Mike, who possessed the more charismatic, affable, and outgoing personality, took the more visible entrepreneurial role, lining up the leaders and working at publicizing the seminars. Dick took charge of the administration of the place itself, a less visible but equally vital role that better suited his preference for remaining in the background and out of the spotlight: making reservations, housing and feeding the guests, keeping the books, and paying the staff and seminar leaders. Busy with the running of the place (he did not take a day off for the first eight years) and still in recovery mode, he would drop in and out of the seminars and workshops when he had free time, hoping to find something useful for himself.

Differences in temperament would take the cofounders in very different directions as Esalen developed. Mike was always restless and sometimes a little uncomfortable in Big Sur. As a child, he often felt like he had been dragged down the coast on vacations when he would have preferred playing baseball or golfing with his friends in Salinas. In his role as the institution's principle spokesperson, he gained a degree of fame as Esalen's emissary, representative, and public persona. Murphy was in high demand as the national media began to cover the Institute's activities in the mid-1960s, and as a result, he was often away from Big Sur.

Dick, on the other hand, felt completely at home in Big Sur. Unlike Mike, Dick did not put himself in the public view, did not make speeches, did not go to conventions, and did not like giving interviews to the media. Dick openly expressed his "appreciation that Mike was willing to do that because I had no way that I would want to do that. I think he was much better at that than I could have been." As far as Dick was concerned, his and Mike's relationship "worked out wonderfully."[55] As everyone on the staff knew, from the earliest days to my era of involvement in the mid-1970s and beyond, the quickest way out of Esalen was to complain to Dick about Mike or vice versa. Through all the difficulties of Esalen's early years, the two founders never had a major disagreement or dispute between themselves.

Esalen had a very permissive bohemian atmosphere in its early days, and Dick, like many of the staff, had quite a few short-term relationships. One of Dick's liaisons, with a woman named Ilene Gregori, resulted in a son, David, though by the time David was born the relationship was long over. It was not Dick's choice to have a child and, according to David, he "wasn't in a place where he was able to be a parent." This, however, changed over time, especially after Dick's second marriage to Christine

Stewart and the birth of their daughter Jenny. According to David, Dick "was really there when I was older" giving "support for me to be whatever I would want."[56]

Through the 1960s, Dick still felt he was in recovery from his stay at the Institute for Living. He was still in some physical pain and he also had an intense semiconstant state of restless internal energy that was at times very hard to manage. How much Dick suffered and how hard he worked on himself to maintain his psychological equilibrium was not fully appreciated by most of the people around him. Dick's three central practices were sports, Buddhism, and Gestalt. When agitated, he would often turn to one or a combination of these practices in order to help modulate his psychological state. Strenuous physical exercise, daylong hikes on the steep trails of the Ventana Wilderness, yoga, meditation, bodywork, soaking in the baths, the use of psychedelics, and Gestalt work were the techniques Dick used for self-regulation and the tools he recommended for people working through their own psychological "states" or "experiences."

From its very inception, Esalen began to confront the issue of mental illness and how it was being defined and treated in the United States. One of Esalen's first seminars in the fall of 1962, led by Dick's old Stanford professor Gregory Bateson and Joe K. Adams, was entitled "Individual and Cultural Definitions of Reality."[57] Many more seminars addressing mental illness were to follow. By the mid-1960s, an alternative view of severe mental illness was beginning to emerge in this country, and Esalen was one of the main forums supporting it. Perhaps the most eloquent spokesperson of the alternative view was the English psychiatrist R. D. Laing, who wrote about the possible value of psychotic experience. Sometimes, according to Laing, psychosis was a "potentially *natural* process that we do not allow to happen."[58] He also proposed the possibility that "[m]adness need not be all breakdown. It may also be breakthrough. It is potentially liberation and renewal as well as enslavement and existential death."[59] Both Michael Murphy and Dick Price were admirers of Laing's work, and they invited him to teach at Esalen in 1967.

In the interest of further promoting Laing's ideas in the United States, Dick also invited the young up-and-coming National Institute of Mental Health (NIMH) researcher Julian Silverman to Esalen. Dick wanted Esalen to sponsor a project in which psychiatric patients would be treated

Fig 5.1. Richard Price (1967). Photo by Sterling Doughty.

along the same lines that Laing had developed at Kingsley Hall in London, where psychiatric patients were given support rather than drugs or shock treatments and were allowed to work through psychotic episodes at their own pace. Dick and Julian cooperated in developing what came to be known as the Agnews Project, a double-blind study cosponsored by the NIMH in which two groups of schizophrenic patients at Agnews Hospital (near San Jose) would be treated humanely with one group receiving drugs (phenothiazines) and the other a placebo. The results of the double-blind study, which included a three-year follow-up, provided solid evidence that schizophrenic patients who were treated humanely and without drugs showed more long-term clinical improvement, better overall functioning in the community after discharge, and lower rates of rehospitalization than patients taking medication.[60]

Dick hoped that the Agnews Project would eventually lead to an accepted mainstream alternative to the way severe mental illness was being treated in the United States. Dick's actual involvement in the project, however, was quite limited. The first limiting factor was Dick's all-consuming job as Esalen's director. The second was the fact that Dick suffered another psychotic episode in early 1969 just as the project was getting under way.

Dick's life in the late 1960s was incredibly intense. Murphy had left Big Sur to live in San Francisco in 1967, leaving Dick to run the growing complexity of Esalen's Big Sur operations largely by himself. He still had not taken a vacation since Esalen opened. Jeanie McGowan, a woman Dick loved and with whom he had lived for two years, had recently broken up with him and the pain of their breakup lingered.[61] His personal work and Gestalt training with Fritz Perls—precipitated by his breakup with Jeanie—were ongoing. His psychedelic "voyaging" (principally with LSD) also occupied a considerable amount of his free time. The mass media had discovered Esalen, and the media spotlight, gaining in intensity, demanded the time and attention of both cofounders. The hippie movement, which Esalen had actually helped create, was in full swing with people living in the hills all around Esalen, in local communes and in various illegal encampments, especially during the summer months. Esalen's residential program, a yearlong, all-out effort to explore new regions of human experience by resident "psychonauts" using "meditation, encounter, sensory awareness, creativity, movement, emotional expression, inner imagery, dream work, and peak-experience training" was in full operation with Will Schutz firmly ensconced as its primary leader and encounter therapy as its central discipline.[62] Finally, the strong personalities and rather large egos of a few Esalen leaders then living on the same small, isolated property fueled an endless game of "capture the flag," the shorthand term Mike and Dick used to describe the struggles for control of Esalen. These struggles came to be epitomized by, but certainly not limited to, the legendary battles between Fritz Perls and Will Schutz and their respective followers.

In late 1968, amid all the intensity, Dick's father came for one of his rare visits to Big Sur, the last visit before his death the following year. Dick and his father had an unusual exchange, one in which Herman actually told his son about his life and the violence he had witnessed as a young Jewish boy in czarist-controlled Lithuania. After Herman left, Dick slowly began to go crazy. He knew he was drifting into a "second psychosis."[63] This time he took precautions, attempting to ensure that he would not be hospitalized and that his parents would not find out what was happening.

Arrangements were made for Dick to stay on a remote property near Plaskett Ridge, south of Esalen. There it was hoped that Dick could work through the episode on his own, without psychiatric "interference."[64] When it became evident that the episode would not end quickly, Dick was brought back to Esalen. After a short stay, he moved to his friend Jan Brewer's property in Sycamore Canyon, a place Dick used as a refuge that was known by his intimate friends as the "blowout center." After several months without getting noticeably better, there was a growing feeling by those taking care of Dick that he was beyond their help. Jack Downing, a psychiatrist and close personal friend of Dick's, eventually took responsibility for having him hospitalized at Agnews, where he spent about ten days before being released. He was housed on a ward at the hospital adjacent to the one that would soon be used for the Agnews Project that he had been so instrumental in creating.[65]

After his discharge from Agnews, he traveled to Canada with Julian Silverman to take part in Fritz Perls's first Gestalt training session at his new center, the Gestalt Institute of Canada on Lake Cowichan in British Colombia. He was able to work on the things that had precipitated his psychosis. At the close of the training, Fritz Perls pronounced that Dick was "recovered" and was ready to start leading Gestalt groups and trainings at Esalen.

How is Dick's 1969 "psychotic episode" to be understood? He did not talk about his second psychotic episode with his friends and cohorts to the same extent that he talked about the first, and little detail about his actual experience at the time is known. His friend Penny Vieregge provided a glimpse into his actual experience when she described the "incredible fragility" in Dick at the time, "like fine, fine, porcelain. . . . I wanted to put on kid gloves and be there in case the shattering came."[66]

He came to believe that he was, in fact, several legendarily powerful historical figures. The two figures most often mentioned were Alexander the Great and Napoleon Bonaparte. Dick told his wife Chris:

> He would go in and out of awareness when he was his state, still being completely out there but not having any recall and having a sense of coming to. So he would tell the funny story about coming to, finding himself striding up and down the 12-foot dinner table at Jan's being Pontius Pilate or somebody while everybody was eating. . . . [H]e said he was on a historical trajectory. . . . So the way I heard it, it was Alexander, Rasputin, and when he reached Napoleon, he said forget it.[67]

Though some might find this story humorous, I think there is a deeper meaning contained in becoming a powerful historic figure, who, as in the case of Dick being Alexander, announced that he "had more kingdoms to conquer."[68] Viewed from the outside, Dick's experience of becoming powerful historical figures seems to confirm a delusional break from the putative real world. From a perspective that includes Dick's unique subjective world, however, becoming a figure like Alexander or Napoleon perhaps concretized a symbolic conquering or retaking of the territory surrendered in psychological usurpation and accommodation, powerfully reasserting a sense of personal agency and autonomy in which the vulnerability associated with its loss is reduced to a bare speck on the experiential horizon.

After Dick's recovery from his second break, he began to put more and more of his energy into his Gestalt work. He led Gestalt seminars at Esalen, ran Gestalt training programs, and worked as a Gestalt facilitator with Esalen's visitors and staff. Dick also continued to champion the rights of mental patients and was known to extend himself to anyone in the greater Esalen community who was in psychological difficulty. Dick had been through a great deal at this point in his life, and he had much to offer people experiencing acute psychological distress. Although Esalen was never used on a consistent basis for helping people through acute psychological states, Dick supported many people who were going through those experiences at Esalen that "otherwise," by his own recognition "would have been locked up."[69] In a characteristically humorous acknowledgment of what Dick had been able to accomplish at Esalen in this regard, Michael Murphy was known to say: "Esalen is Price's revenge on mental hospitals."[70]

Both because of, and in spite of, his painful experiences in mental hospitals, Dick embarked on a lifelong journey of intense personal exploration. For Dick, the only way out was his continual work on what lay within. Dick relentlessly scanned the spiritual-psychological horizon and was willing to embrace, at least for a while, a remarkable array of adventurous explorations "along the psychological-spiritual front" that drifted through Esalen.[71] Dick's searching also included sojourns outside of Esalen. The two prime examples were his participation in Oscar Ichazo's Arica One training in New York in 1971 and a trip to Poona, India, to study at Bhagwan Rajneesh's ashram in the late 1970s. Both Oscar Ichazo and Rajneesh held out a promise Dick found subjectively appealing. They both claimed to be enlightened. They both offered a combination of psychological, spiritual, and physical practices that Dick had, for years, been attempting to synthesize himself. They both engaged Dick's longings for an idealizable teacher, at least for a while. Both, however, tried to use Dick and his position as cofounder of Esalen for their own proselytizing purposes. In the end, what Dick found most troubling with both Arica and Rajneesh was that

> [e]verything you do that is at variance with the company line, is an ego. So you're already categorized, there is no way to come back at it, the only way to come back at it is quit. Which I did, both at the Arica training, and with Rajneesh.[72]

Both Arica and Rajneesh had delegitimized and pathologized the experiential truth of what Dick had been witness to by denying the authoritarian dimensions of what was being done. This denial was a repetition of a very old, powerful subjective danger for Dick—the attempt to reject his subjective reality and replace it with an external authority using coercive means.

What Dick found to be beneficial in his explorations of many forms of psychotherapy, personal growth, and spiritual practice were utilized both personally and in his burgeoning form of gestalt therapy that he called "gestalt practice." What he found to be coercive or demeaning, he personally, and often publicly, rejected. Dick's maxim for Esalen became "maximum availability, minimal coercion." Dick's concern with coercion was a distinctive, recurrent subjective theme that became a guiding personal philosophy that served a self-reparative function by delegitimizing external determinations of the validity of personal, subjective experience.

As Mike Murphy remembers, Dick Price "came into his own gradually in the 1970s."[73] One of the major contributing factors was his second marriage, to Christine Stewart. Dick met Chris in February of 1971 when she came to attend a Gestalt and Rolfing workshop that Dick co-led with Hector Prestera. Chris returned to Esalen in the fall of 1971, and she and Dick became romantically involved. In October of 1972, Chris came to live at Esalen permanently. The couple married in February of 1974 and had a daughter named Jennifer late that same year.

Dick's marriage to Chris and the birth of his daughter had a profoundly positive impact on his life, something everyone who knew Dick is in agreement about. As Dick's friend John Heider commented: "Really, when Chris came into his life, it was transformative."[74] Seymour Carter, another of Dick's close friends, was even more emphatic:

> He was so deeply scarred, it was clear to me he needed a love and then Chris came into his life. Chris turned out to be a gift from heaven in the sense that she was a very beautiful woman, loved Dick unrestrainedly, was a nurturing mother, a warm person, all those things that, if I were analyzing the things and ingredients, he needed in his life. I felt the friendships he established, the peer group, and then bonding with Chris took him out of his incredibly encapsulated isolation. I would say that Chris was the ingredient he needed; everything else was preliminary.[75]

Dick's relationship with Jenny was also transformative, eventually helping to take much of the sting out of his painful past. As Chris commented:

> He certainly had been through incredibly bitter and hard feeling periods; Seymour calls it stuck, that's one way to say it. It was a long siege between

him and the past. I don't think he was in that state his last couple of years. A lot happened when Jenny was born; it made a difference and it kept making a difference. . . . Dick reworked a lot just from being a dad.[76]

I think that Dick's marriage and his relationship with his daughter Jenny enabled Dick to begin to feel a sense of satisfaction with this life and to begin to trust that life had the potential to truly be satisfying.

Another avenue that was transformative for Dick was the development, together with Chris, of his own form of gestalt work called "gestalt practice." Dick started leading gestalt groups and trainings at Esalen in 1970 at his mentor Fritz Perls's suggestion and with his full permission. Though their work was similar in many ways, Dick came to emphasize slightly different aspects of experience as he transformed what he had assimilated from his mentor into a style more befitting his personal phenomenology.

Dick specifically chose the term "gestalt practice" in order to separate what he did from more traditional forms of psychotherapy, including Fritz's occasionally authoritative doctor/patient gestalt therapy paradigm. In Gestalt practice:

> The authority to make choices remains with what we call the initiator. It's quite different from patient/therapist roles. The initiator designates an active role, while the word "patient" implies, at least to me, someone who lies back and is acted on. The role of the doctor is, for me, one who acts. Therapy is active. So this isn't therapy; it's a practice. This isn't something the therapist does to a patient. It's what two people in complementary roles do together.[77]

Dick was a very body-based person, and he put direct focus on the body in his gestalt work by paying attention to breath and bodily sensations. His concept of "basic practice," which he defined as "becoming established in body and breath," was the way he began many of his gestalt sessions and a place to return to, if needed, for grounding throughout his sessions.

> Basic Practice is attention to breath, to movement, to kinesthetic sensations, to sensations in the body—feeling state, emotion, thought, image. And what's important again is a mode of present-centered contact, which doesn't judge what is brought to that.[78]

Dick's gestalt work became his central practice, a practice that was strongly aligned with his long-standing interests in Buddhism and meditation. Unlike Fritz Perls's theatrical gestalt style, Dick's gestalt work was much more meditative, focusing primarily on the quality of awareness brought to moment-to-moment experience. As Dick was fond of saying: "Coming out with something is secondary to making contact with whatever is, with clarity, and making it real and present." As many people, including myself, observed, in doing gestalt, Dick was also doing an ongoing spiritual practice that served both him and the people he worked with. Dick's spiritual-experiential depth was, at least at times, quite palpable in the room when he conducted gestalt sessions. I think it was the direct experience of a spiritual dimension of consciousness combined with his deep interest in other people, in who they were without any need to shape them to fit his world or into commonsense notions of what could be "real" or "true," that engendered such profound feelings of acceptance in the people Dick worked with.

Through the public exposure of his gestalt work, Dick became a role model for many different people that came through Esalen in the late 1970s and early 1980s. As someone who had gone through some of the most challenging psychological experiences one could possibly encounter, Dick sanctioned others at Esalen to live a life of intense psychological and spiritual exploration. For many psychiatric survivors, Dick became a much-needed role model for what was possible, for what one could dare hope to attain or achieve: a successful, satisfying, independent life without the use of mind-numbing medications. For psychotherapists, especially gestalt therapists, Dick became someone to watch, learn from, and emulate. Dick's gestalt practice represented a real alternative to Fritz Perls's legendary abrasive style. As psychologist and psychoanalyst Arnold Bernstein observed: "I simply thought that he had taken the sting out of Perls' methodology. . . . He took the gestalt model and placed it in a different philosophical context than the psychiatric one Fritz came from; he humanized it."[79]

On November 24, 1985, following a few days of intermittent rain, Dick decided to take advantage of a break in the weather and take a quick hike up Hot Springs Canyon. His destination was "the source," the site where Esalen's water supply is taken from Hot Springs Creek. Dick did not plan to be gone long as he had business meetings scheduled that afternoon. It was a hike, however, from which Dick was never to return.

A devastating forest fire in the hills behind Esalen the previous summer had left Hot Springs Canyon starkly bare of vegetation. In the fire's aftermath, rocks had been rolling down the hillside, breaking Esalen's water line. With the advent of the rainy season, silt and sediment flowed into the creek, clogging up the catch basin and cutting off Esalen's water supply. Dick, who hiked up the canyon regularly, routinely checked the water line and the catch basin at "the source."

On that fateful Sunday, the steep, bare, rain-soaked hillsides of Hot Springs Canyon allowed a boulder about the size of a small car to slip from its perch high above "the source" and begin what would quickly become a leaping, bounding path toward the canyon bottom. The boulder split apart when it hit the creek bottom and one of the pieces hit Dick in the head, breaking his neck. From what those who found Dick's body could tell, he must have been surprised by the very loud noise of the large boulder crashing downhill through the vegetation. His body was found in a seated position in the shallow water running back toward Hot Springs Creek from the overflow channel of the catch basin. The topmost of the three boards that formed the dam for the catch basin had been removed. That board was found under Dick's body. The lower two boards were smashed and broken by the piece of the falling boulder that had killed Dick. He had undoubtedly been in the process of cleaning the silt from the catch basin when he became aware of the sound of the falling boulder as is crashed through the trees near the bottom of the canyon, ending in a loud shattering din as it hit the creek bottom and exploded into fragments. Within a split second, Dick was stuck by one of those fragments. He died instantly.

That evening, when Dick still had not returned from his hike, searchers were sent up the canyon to look for him. They found his body and brought him back down to his residence at the "Little House." Dick's death, coming so suddenly and unexpectedly, devastated the greater Esalen community.

My last memory of Dick is looking at his body, lying in state on his bed, framed by a background of bushes in the window behind him, bushes that were all bearing bright red fruit. I remember feeling that I was in trouble, many of my friends were in trouble, Esalen was in trouble, and especially Dick's wife Chris and his daughter Jenny were in trouble, but I did not have the sense that Dick was in any trouble at all. There was a profound tone of peace and completion in the room that morning. It was as if Dick's lifework had been completed and all was well in his world. It was a feeling I will always remember.

Like every human being, Dick Price had to confront both painful and rewarding life experiences and carried unconscious residues from them. His particular life history is poignant and filled with some very painful events but one that is ultimately redemptive. Dick suffered immensely, first at the hands of his mother's invasive, intrusive control and later in psychiatric hospitals where he was subjected to dehumanizing so-called treatments. As a result of those experiences, Dick carried a heavy burden of grievances against his family, grievances that were never, perhaps, completely healed and that impacted his ability to form and sustain essential relationships. Dick's real legacy, however, was his gestalt work. In that work, he was able to help alleviate the suffering of countless others. Through his pain and suffering, Dick learned how to function as a powerfully validating other in the lives of many people. In so doing, Dick literally became for others what he was never able to find someone to fully be for himself. As Dick's wife Chris said: "He gave what he wanted, which is like the rest of us, I think."[80]

Dick Price was a remarkable man. Despite his being more than a little crazy at times, he was one of the sanest men I have ever met. In a very personal way, he taught me the value of accepting and working with my imperfections and limitations rather than striving to overcome them. Dick served as an example, for many people, of someone who was doing good in the world. As Dick's friend Leonard Bearne put it:

> But I think the meaning of Dick to me is that he has been and always will be a symbol of what a person can do to accomplish good in a very kind of understated, low key way. And I think that Dick tried to do good on a lot of different levels and in a lot of different ways, and he largely succeeded.[81]

In the 1960s and 1970s, egocentric gurus and often tyrannical, manipulative group leaders were plentiful on the human potential scene, something Dick Price and Mike Murphy knew only too well. By personal example, Dick provided an alternative. He was someone who was extremely humble, who was very unpretentious, and who above all deeply wanted to do the right thing. This was true from the very beginnings of Esalen until the time of his death in 1985. Dick's longtime friend, fellow Esalen group leader and author John Heider, remembered what Dick meant to him in the following way:

> I would put him in the category of great influential men I have known, or men and women. I would say that he was one of the least corrupt of them. He was one of the most earnest, about simply being about what he was about. That is to say, he wasn't interested in money, he wasn't interested in fame. Maybe he was interested in enlightenment, as you've suggested. He was just about what he was about, that's how I make sense out of him. Very non-corrupt.[82]

Dick was a teacher and a mentor for me. I feel lucky to have known him, and for that I will always be grateful. He left this world much too prematurely, unexpectedly, and suddenly. As many of his students and friends have expressed in various ways, so much of what Dick wanted Esalen to be and to contribute to the world has proved unsustainable without his ongoing presence. It is a reminder of how truly fragile the things of this world are. W. B. Yeats attempted to express these very sentiments in his poem "Gratitude to the Unknown Instructors":

> What they undertook to do
> They brought to pass;
> All things hang like a drop of dew
> Upon a blade of grass.[83]

Notes

1. Joan Price, "Family" (unpublished manuscript, 2002), 4.
2. Chris Price, interview with Eric Erickson, January 7, 2002, digital recording, Part 1. In author's possession.
3. Ibid.
4. Chris Price, interview with Eric Erickson, January 7, 2002, digital recording, Part 2. In author's possession.
5. Price, "Family," 6.
6. Price, "Family", 4.

7. Ibid., 4.

8. Ibid., 3.

9. Ibid., 1.

10. Ibid., 3.

11. Ibid., 2.

12. Chris Price, interview with Eric Erickson, January 7, 2002, digital recording, Part 1. In author's possession.

13. Price, "Family," 8.

14. Ibid.

15. Chris Price, interview with Eric Erickson, January 7, 2002, digital recording, Part 1. In author's possession.

16. Leonard Bearne, interview with Eric Erickson, September 2, 2001, digital recording. In author's possession.

17. Dick Price, sound recording of interview with W. T. Anderson, undated [cassette tape A1830/CS A], Walter Truett Anderson Collection, Department of Special Collections, Davidson Library, University of California, Santa Barbara.

18. Dick Price, sound recording of interview with W. T. Anderson, December 19, 1976 [cassette recording A1831/CS B], Walter Truett Anderson Collection, Department of Special Collections, Davidson Library, University of California, Santa Barbara.

19. Ibid.

20. Ibid.

21. Ibid.

22. Ibid.

23. Ibid.

24. Ibid.

25. Ibid.

26. Thera Nyanaponika, *The Heart of Buddhist Meditation* (London: Rider, 1962).

27. Chris Price, interview with Eric Erickson, January 7, 2002, digital recording, Part 2. In author's possession.

28. Dick Price, sound recording of interview with W. T. Anderson, December 19, 1976.

29. Ibid.

30. Ibid.

31. Ibid.

32. Ibid.

33. Walter Truett Anderson, *The Upstart Spring: Esalen and the American Awakening* (Menlo Park, Calif.: Addison-Wesley, 1983), 39.

34. Dick Price, sound recording of interview with W. T. Anderson, December 19, 1976.

35. Ibid.

36. Ibid.

37. Dick Price, sound recording of interview with W. T. Anderson, December 12, 1982 [cassette recording A1835/CS A], Walter Truett Anderson Collection, Department of Special Collections, Davidson Library, University of California, Santa Barbara.

38. Dick Price, sound recording of interview with W. T. Anderson, December 19, 1976.

39. Anderson, *Upstart Spring*, 40.

40. Chris Price, interview with Eric Erickson, January 7, 2002, digital recording, Part 2. In author's possession.

41. Anderson, *Upstart Spring*, 40.

42. Ibid., 41.

43. Ibid.

44. Joan Price, "Family," 8.

45. Anderson, *Upstart Spring*, 40.

46. C. Tomkins, "New Paradigms," *The New Yorker*, January 5, 1976, 35.

47. David Price, interview with Eric Erickson, May 30, 2002, digital recording. In author's possession.

48. Anderson, *Upstart Spring*, 42.

49. Chris Price, interview with Eric Erickson, January 7, 2002, digital recording, Part 2. In author's possession.

50. G. E. Atwood, D. M. Orange, and R. D. Stolorow, "Shattered Worlds/Psychotic States: A Post-Cartesian View of the Experience of Personal Annihilation," paper presented at the spring meeting of the Institute for Contemporary Psychoanalysis, Los Angeles, California, 2001, p. 17.

51. W. Hudson, ["An Interview with Dick Price"], *The Esalen Catalog, January–June 2001* (Big Sur, Calif.: Esalen Institute, 2001), 5.

52. Michael Murphy, sound recording of interview with W. T. Anderson, 1977 [Cassette Recording A1824/CS A], Walter Truett Anderson Collection, Department of Special Collections, Davidson Library, University of California, Santa Barbara.

53. Hudson, ["An Interview with Dick Price"], 5.

54. Ibid., 6.

55. Dick Price, sound recording of interview with W. T. Anderson, December 12, 1982.

56. David Price, interview with Eric Erickson, December 20, 2001, digital recording. In author's possession.

57. Anderson, *Upstart Spring*.

58. R. D. Laing, *The Politics of Experience* (New York: Ballantine Books, 1967), 124.

59. Ibid., 133.

60. Dick Price, sound recording of interview with W. T. Anderson, June 14, 1981 [cassette recording A1833/CS A], Walter Truett Anderson Collection, Department of Special Collections, Davidson Library, University of California, Santa Barbara.

61. Dick Price, sound recording of interview with W. T. Anderson, December 12, 1982.

62. Anderson, *Upstart Spring*, 122.

63. Hudson, *Esalen Catalog*, 6.

64. Dick Price, sound recording of interview with W. T. Anderson, December 12, 1982.

65. Julian Silverman, interview with Eric Erickson, February 23, 1994, cassette recording. In author's possession.

66. P. Vieregge, interview with Eric Erickson, August 30, 2001, digital recording. In author's possession.

67. Chris Price, interview with Eric Erickson, March 6, 2002, digital recording. In author's possession.

68. George Leonard and Michael Murphy, interview with Eric Erickson, December 17, 2001, digital recording. In author's possession.

69. Dick Price, sound recording of interview with W. T. Anderson, December 12, 1982.

70. Tomkins, "New Paradigms," 35.

71. Anderson, *Upstart Spring*, 302.

72. Dick Price, sound recording of interview with W. T. Anderson, undated [cassette recording A1830/CS B], Walter Truett Anderson Collection, Department of Special Collections, Davidson Library, University of California, Santa Barbara.

73. George Leonard and Michael Murphy, interview with Eric Erickson, December 17, 2001, digital recording. In author's possession.

74. John Heider, telephone interview with Eric Erickson, January 23, 2002.

75. Seymour Carter, interview with Eric Erickson, August 8, 2001, digital recording. In author's possession.

76. Chris Price, interview with Eric Erickson, January 7, 2002, digital recording, Part 1. In author's possession.

77. Hudson, *Esalen Catalog*, 7.

78. Ibid., 4.

79. Arnold Bernstein, interview with Eric Erickson, August 8, 2001, digital recording. In author's possession.

80. Chris Price, interview with Eric Erickson, March 6, 2002, digital recording. In author's possession.

81. Leonard Bearne, interview with Eric Erickson, September 2, 2001, digital recording. In author's possession.

82. John Heider, telephone interview with Eric Erickson, January 23, 2002.

83. W. B. Yeats, "Gratitude to the Unknown Instructors," in R. J. Finneran, ed., *The Collected Works of W. B. Yeats*, vol. I, *The Poems Revised* (New York: Macmillan, 1983), 243.

SPIRIT AND SHADOW: ESALEN
AND THE GESTALT MODEL

Gordon Wheeler

WESTERN CULTURE AT MID-CENTURY:
CONTEXT AND CRISIS

The dawn of the twentieth century, as has often been observed, brought the high-water mark of something we may call, particularly in its Anglo/American inflection, the "high Victorian synthesis." This was that optimistic and fiercely self-confident worldview that held that Western European civilization was the vanguard of a new departure in human history, a permanent if sometimes bumpy upward arc of progress marked by the enormous advances of the past few centuries in science and technology, which were themselves now nearly complete. Along with this came the growth and spread of individual rights and expression. All of these features together were both the vehicles and the finest flowers of the culture. This arc, which was now of some 500 years' duration in Europe (some said 1,000), was already well on the way to completion of the liberal reform of Western society itself, without the need of any deep disturbance to the present structure of that world. A hundred years without a major war in Europe meant that war itself was becoming a thing of the past. Poverty and disease would soon follow. History was progress; "the West" was its harbinger and vehicle. And both the new historicism of the nineteenth century and science itself (including the new current of Darwinism) confirmed these obvious truths.

This world was pluralistic, of course, like all worlds. Doubters and dissent existed, from Marxists/Socialists to Freud to the suffragists, and in retrospect we may see some of the more easily caricatured features of the age as uneasy accommodations to the rapid pace of change of the previous 200 years and the disquieting intercultural contacts of European imperialism. Still, to a great extent, even these reformers and revolutionaries drank deeply at the same well of cultural superiority and self-confidence, offering only a different program for the realization of the inevitable progress to come (Freud, for example, liked to picture himself as a conquistador in the dark continent of the Unconscious, and Kipling, who cautioned against hubris, was himself one of the Empire's greatest champions). Meanwhile, through the engine of enlightened imperialism, the institutions, attitudes, and prosperity of Europe and its cultural off-spring, the United States (often pictured as Rome to Europe's Greece), would naturally, inevitably spread over the rest of the globe.

By 1950, of course, all of this ebullient complacent edifice was shattered, a casualty, like so many others, of the nightmares and waking horrors of the previous few decades. In its place was a cultural landscape of deep psychic contradictions and experiential rifts: on the one hand, an upbeat official optimism, the "return to normalcy" yet again, this time with a new consumerist vengeance, and, on the other, in the shadows a dark foreboding, civil defense exercises all the more alarming for their manifest naiveté, amid dream imagery of mushroom clouds. Church attendance was up against a steady undercurrent of mid-century existentialist despair. It was the "age of conformity" and the birth of the Beat generation. The body was denied, while *Playboy* was the publishing sensation of the decade. The demise of the Left and the end of class warfare were proclaimed, while the search was on for the "enemy within" and the Cold War only seemed to grow hotter from day to day.

And so it went. There seemed literally to be no end to the sharp polarizations and "false dichotomies" of the day (to use Gestalt writer Paul Goodman's term[1]), which now were offered, as deep cultural polarities always are, as the basic and stable categories of existence itself: masculine/feminine, black/white, American/un-American (a telling neologism), normal/abnormal, straight/gay (these last terms themselves, of course, were not yet in use, the times being far from any such relaxed colloquialisms on so destabilizing a subject). And then along with these came all the older, even more entrenched, categories of the cultural tradition: mind/body, body/soul, intellect/emotion (both were distrusted now as being equally disturbing to the status quo), and civilized/primitive (a Victorian favorite, but dating back at least to the Greeks and containing the deeper polarity of us/them), together with newer (or newly inflected) ones such as facts/values, science/art, science/religion, progress/tradition, East/West, self/society (a particularly tricky opposition in a culture both fiercely individualistic and deeply conformist), and, of course, conscious/unconscious. All the perennial Christian themes still obtained as well: good/evil, damned/saved, religious/infidel, here/hereafter, and so on. To this familiar catalog Goodman now also appended, even more subversively, those of adult/child, work/play, poetry/prose, man/animal, disciplined/lazy, spontaneous/deliberate, and, most tellingly of all, desire/despair.[2]

This too was a world easily (and often) caricatured, then and since, but in the main these landscape features and background contours were amply confirmed at the time (and since) by numerous contemporary observers, ranging from novelists such as J. D. Salinger and Philip Roth to scholars and social critics such as David Riesman (*The Lonely Crowd*) and Paul Goodman himself, whose 1961 indictment of "the organized system," *Growing Up Absurd*, was to become a bible of the next generation in the quite different landscape of the 1960s.[3] To be sure, this world too was pluralistic, yet it seemed that dissent itself had a different status now from its place in the eras immediately before and after. Whereas social and political outliers (at least high-status ones) in an earlier, more self-assured age such as Oscar Wilde or even the revolutionary Prince Peter Kropotkin in tsarist Russia (a strong influence on Goodman's social anarchism) sometimes seemed to have to go well out of their way to get themselves persecuted, dissidents now seemed to face no such difficulty, as victims of the time such as Alan Turing, Wilhelm Reich, Ethel Rosenberg, or the many targets of McCarthyism and the House Un-American Activities Committee could attest.

It is surely no accident either that so many of these cultural features are themselves the hallmarks and clinical criteria of what is now known, both clinically and popularly, as PTSD (post-traumatic stress disorder), the reaction, now seemingly on a mass level, to unassimilable psychic assault and trauma.[4] These included repression and dissociation themselves, chronic fear of the body (especially the sexual body), desensitization and denial, a generalized dulling of affect and intolerance of strong passion, compulsive activity, conformism and mistrust of difference, fear of conflict, discomfort with both stillness and excitement, and a consequent generalized simplification of thought, especially around charged themes or situations, together with a nagging vulnerability to depression and despair. In the extreme, this fear of difference and destabilization can amount to paranoid ideation and behavior, the frantic detection of impurities and enemies everywhere, with the projection of evil designs onto presumed enemies, who in the extreme case must be preemptively destroyed. If the definition of trauma is stress that cannot be integrated, then the reaction, individually and socially, may be a kind of vicious circle, as the chronic avoidance of new stress only leads to steadily less tolerance for difference, challenge, or stress itself. The self, or by analogy here the social body, moves to protect itself from being overwhelmed and dissolution by trying to limit experience itself, both internally and externally. The result is the kind of "as-if" life remarked on by Sartre and others and a compromise in capacity for creativity, flexibility, passion, and any real satisfaction in living.

Indeed, the stresses and traumas of the previous half-century did seem to defy integration. This tragic litany is now sadly familiar: the pointless sacrifice of a generation in the trenches of the First World War, followed immediately by the revolutions and civil wars of Europe, worldwide depression, the rise of Nazism and other fascisms, the terrible disillusionment (to the Left) of the Soviet gulag, and then renewed war itself, truly on a world level this time with its mass firebombing of civilians, the advent of atomic weapons (and their prompt use on civilian populations), and then finally, shatteringly to the Western psyche and self-concept, the revelation at the end of the war of the full horrors of the camps.

The last two of these nightmares, Hiroshima and Auschwitz, in particular seemed to lie outside all human capacity for integration—and all the more so if they were held up together so that each set off and underscored the horror of the other (not surprisingly, they seldom were held up together in this way). For if we human beings now had it in our hands to wipe out all the advances and achievements of the past millennium, if not indeed life itself on the planet, it was hard to know where to look for any assurance within ourselves that we would shrink from *using* that power. The chilling effect of the Holocaust on the postwar world had been to collapse what Jung called "the projective theory of evil," that fond illusion, so characteristic of the period just prior to this one, that savagery and cruelty had finally been "cured" by the advances of Western culture and were now safely contained in some faraway, probably dark-skinned "other," quite remote from our enlightened neighborhood, where moral constraints were firmly in place.[5] This illusion was now obviously untenable. On the contrary, it now seemed that there was nothing after all in our inherent human nature—and worse still, nothing in our supposedly enlightened Western civilization—to suggest that there were any limits at all to our human capacity for cruelty and wanton evil (over a million *children* had been killed in the Shoah, after all, and not as "collateral damage" but as targeted, intentional murders, while the Holocaust itself had been a major, perhaps crippling diversion from the German military project of hegemony on the Continent). Taken together in this unbearably clear way, any full reading of the facts seemed to counsel only panic or despair.

The United States of course had emerged as the only true "winner" of the Second World War, not just largely unscathed but even industrially and militarily enhanced and heir to both the European and Japanese empires and spheres of influence. But what kind of world had been inherited? If the old idea of American "exceptionalism" was much invoked now as an apology for empire, that exceptional status itself, and the whole structure of denial it was built on, began to seem dangerously fragile, everywhere beset by threats as vague as "negativism," as pervasive as "infiltration," or as sharp as the subversive promptings of one's own body.

Most of this is now commonplace and has been much written about (and filmed), however difficult it may be to convey fully, another fifty years on, to those too young now to have known that postwar world at first hand. Fully appreciated or not, however, the importance of setting this scene here is crucial, as it was this world, marked as it was by deep cleavages of mind and spirit and struggling to contain and deny a profound sense of cultural failure, that would be both context and occasion for the founding of two of the most remarkable, rehabilitative, and alternative projects of those times. One was the Esalen Institute in Big Sur California in 1962, the brainchild of two Stanford graduate-school dropouts, Michael Murphy and Richard Price, both in search in different ways of something they could not find (because it was simply unavailable) in the mainstream culture. The other was the Gestalt model of psychotherapy, first articulated by Frederick (Fritz) Perls and Paul Goodman, growing out of the leftist intellectual and émigré circles of New York City in the early postwar period and then spreading progressively across the country, to arrive and take root at Esalen in the person of Perls himself soon after its founding. From that time, in addition to its wider influence in the popular and clinical culture, the Gestalt approach would continue to color (and be colored by) the development of the Institute over the next several decades.

Each of these projects, both separately and through their interaction, would go on to have profound formative effects on the mainstream culture they set out to "counter," deconstruct, and reform. In both cases, these effects were to be out of all proportion to the seeming size of the two enterprises or even perhaps to the expectations of their respective founders. In the process, each affected the other profoundly as well, both creatively and expansively at first and then for a time perhaps in a more constricting way, as each seemed to succumb to its own (and the other's) shadow, both losing some part of their creative edge and direction in the 1980s (even as each of them was also breaking new ground in this period in areas at first outside the sphere of their interaction). When both went on to recover impetus and full creative energy in the years after that decade, it was as leaders but also as beneficiaries of a larger cultural shift in the wider world, the mainstream feeding back to the countercultural world now, in company with many of the allied movements and institutions that each of these two had helped to spawn directly or indirectly.

In retrospect, the two projects seem utterly fated to meet and conjoin, so similar were many of their founding assumptions, their aspirations, their deconstructive spirit, and their unexamined shadows. Each was in its own way fundamentally and sincerely optimistic about the human condition, contrasting sharply with the forced, hollow cheer (and nagging underlying nihilism) of the day. But at the same time, each rejected equally sharply the old failed programs, goals, and assumptions of the previous prewar synthesis. Each of them promised, on slightly different but overlapping grounds, a radically new understanding of human nature and with it new energy and a new basis for hope about the human race, the planet, and the future of both.

Even their approaches to their specific agendas were similar: each was founded with the idea of integrating (or reintegrating) an extensive roster of the "neurotic splits" (Goodman's term again) and projections of the culture, both past and present. At the same time, each project contained, in retrospect, some unexamined splits and shadows of its own. These too were largely overlapping, and some of them were coextensive with deeper blind spots of Western culture itself. Finally, for all their similarities of vision and shadow, each did contain a germinal idea the other needed in order to reach its own full potential.

The story of the creative interaction between these two countercultural projects reflects and sheds light on some of the key cultural themes and dynamics of the past half-century in the West, beginning with the postwar age of conformism characterized above, continuing into the subsequent period of protest and cultural/political reform, and moving on into the 1980s, a time of considerable retreat and regression from the humanistic and progressivist agenda of the previous two decades. The story of their recovery and renewal from this retreat serves to illuminate a profound cultural sea change in the wider culture, one still very much ongoing on in our own times. Both Esalen and the Gestalt movement, in common with many other allied projects this time, are part of the leading edge of this change. The interaction between the two projects—the one having now achieved an international profile and the other a worldwide movement, both still alternative—is supporting and influencing the creative development of each partner.

To understand all this—the genesis and growth of each project, the burgeoning and excitement of each in the early period, the partial stasis that seemed to mark both enterprises for a time, and finally the capacity each has found in a return to its own germinal assumptions to transcend that stasis and renew growth—we need to look at both projects from the inside in terms of the founding vision and ground assumptions of each and in terms of the dynamic relation of each of these alternative projects to the cultural mainstream each has influenced so profoundly over the intervening years. And then too, we need to understand the shadow that each of these fertile deconstructive projects failed for a time to deconstruct and how that process has undergone revision and renewal and has led to renewed growth in new directions. The examination of these last themes will bring us right up to the present and the shifts going on today at Esalen, in the realm of Gestalt and other psychotherapy and related movements, and in the wider world.

THE GESTALT MODEL: CONSTRUCTION AND EVOLUTION

Gestalt, most succinctly stated, is the psychology of constructivism. That is, the model grows out of the foundational insight that our experiential world is not and cannot be *given* to us, all prepackaged and organized in any direct, representational, or camera-like way (the old assumption known in philosophy as "representational" or "naive" realism) without need of organization or interpretation. Rather, we *construct* that world—often on the fly, as it were, and in the pressures of the living moment—out of some dynamic synthesis of our own past experience and beliefs, attentional habits and capacities, expectations, present felt needs, future intentions, cultural and dispositional screens, *and* present conditions and stimuli (but even these are screened, selected, and pruned through our own neurological and experiential filters). In other words, there are no "pure data." Perception itself is an act of interpretation, rendering sense data (itself selected and interpreted) into useable whole units, or gestalts, of imaginal pictures, narratives, and other sequences.

The elements of perception, that is, are not isolated stimulus/response units out there but are themselves already organized wholes, which then serve to mediate emotion, cognition, behavior, and other experience alike. We construct both experience and meaning (which are structurally the same or at least lie on a continuum of elaboration) and then use those

constructed wholes of understanding predictively and evaluatively to perceive and deal with the resources and challenges of our shared world.

Exactly *how* we do this was studied brilliantly and extensively in lab
research through the first half of the past century. This work is only now
being sweepingly confirmed by the new technologies of brain imaging.[6]
Where James and others had already noted that selective attention had to
be the key to resolving what he called the "blooming, buzzing confusion"
of (potential) sense data,[7] the early Gestalt research movement set out to
flesh out and explicate the dynamics of that attentional process itself. So
foundational and revolutionary was this body of work that there really is
no psychology today that is not essentially Gestalt in nature and premises.[8]
The role of expectation in perception, the emotional basis of cognition,
the inseparability of mind and body, the futility of trying to consider
behavior apart from intention and context, the way meaning-making con-
trols perception and behavior, the problem-solving nature of perceptual
process itself, the primacy of relationship in living process and individual
development, the way brain, mind, emotion, action, and belief become
tightly integrated in experiential/behavioral schemas which tend to unfold
as whole sequences—all these things are now both taken for granted and
well-grounded in research. And all of these conclusions and more come
directly out of Gestalt lab and social research.[9]

Fritz Perls and Paul Goodman were not the first to see the immediate
applications of this work to psychotherapy,[10] but their groundbreaking
1951 text *Gestalt Therapy: Excitement and Growth in the Human Personality* gave us the first full theoretical exposition of the method. In their
hands, the model emphasized especially the articulation of self-experience,
experiment, profound respect for the individual as creator of her own
meanings, authentic therapeutic relationship, rejection of externally imposed authority, and a wide reclaiming of lost parts of the self (especially
body feeling, spontaneity, creativity, and strong emotion and affective expression, specifically including both aggression and sexuality), all of it
grounded in a deep faith in each person's innate striving for growth and
wholeness. All these themes are still vitally present in Gestalt work today.

It is worth noting again that all these major themes—the primacy of
emotion, the grounding of experience in embodiment, the quest for meaning, the centrality of relationship, the authoritativeness of self-experience,

the validation of self-expression, the key role of desire in human process, and the reclamation and celebration of erotic passion—were deeply problematic in the American culture of the times. And more than that, each of them tended to be held in a way that was split off from everyday awareness and life to a degree and in a manner that is difficult to appreciate today. It was not, of course, that people did not have all these feelings, register body sensations, reflect on and construct meanings, or feel erotic and other passions, though, to be sure, some of these sensations and processes might actually have been muted by the fact of a nonreceptive cultural surround. Rather, it was that many of these experiences might be held apart from the rest of life and experience and thus remain less than fully explored for want of an active and articulated social discourse for that exploration. In any case, what remained from all this splitting was the familiar identity sanctioned by the mainstream cultural voices of the times: conformist, materialist/consumerist, conservative in style and affect, risk averse, and in general deeply distrustful of the realms of body, emotions, sex, and the passions in general.

In place of all this, the founders of the Gestalt therapy model would build their approach, theoretically and methodologically, around the reclamation of desire and aggression themselves, the very energies that Freud had posed as the dangerous dark side of human nature and the irreducible antagonists of civilization and social order (this was, of course, the later, gloomier Freud, the Freud of *Civilization and Its Discontents* who was far more pessimistic about the human prospect after the pointless spectacle of the First World War, which seemed to be an expression of destructiveness for its own sake).[11] Paul Goodman, the principal author and theoretician of the new model, was himself deeply versed in the Freudian model and cultural Freudianism, as were most leftist intellectuals of the times, even those, such as Sartre, of a manifestly Marxist/anti-Freudian bent. But Goodman drew his inspiration from the earlier, sunnier Freud, who had once proclaimed the analyst to be the "ally of the Id" against a repressive culture before thinking better of such a radical subversion under the shadows of the First World War, the resurgence of anti-Semitism in Europe, and perhaps the vehemence of some of his own early critics.[12] And Goodman's own therapy had been originally with Alexander Lowen, a student of Wilhelm Reich and a founder of bioenergetic therapy, with its emphasis on embodiment and cathartic bodily release.[13]

Moreover, Goodman was a serious social activist and a philosophical anarchist, by which he understood chiefly the proposition that human beings left to themselves can be trusted to build spontaneously far more humane, cooperative, and life-affirming social networks and institutions than any a central authority might provide. When not interfered with, communities, like individuals in the Gestalt perspective, have a self-regulating or "organismic" capacity, exactly like the capacity of the un-hampered organism to meet its animal needs (eating, excreting, and sex and the like) without external regulation.[14] "Man" ([sic]—not just the language but the erotic imagery of Goodman's writing is always heavily gender-inflected) is an animal, to be sure, but above all a social animal. This is Darwin much tempered by Kropotkin's cooperative evolution (1908) as well as by Dewey and the American pragmatists, with their strong echoes of the great American Romantic/individualist tradition of both Emerson and Twain. This was individualism, to be sure, but it was an individualism based in an instinctively moral communitarianism that was far from the social-Darwinist "survival of the strongest" individualist flavor of Nietzsche and Freud.

Central to all this and indeed the engine and the genius of Goodman's notions of spontaneous, "organismic" self-regulation, both individually and relationally/politically, is always *eros,* or desire. This is not the dark and Oedipal libido of Freud's vision, rapacious and imperialistic in nature, ready at least metaphorically (or was it literally?) to murder the father so as to possess the mother with fierce and startlingly precocious genitality. Rather, Goodman, who was both bisexual himself (today he might be better called polyamorous) and a fierce proponent of the sexual rights of children and adolescents, saw the crux of and the key to a new vision of human nature in *eros,* away from the heavy authoritarian (if resolutely meliorist) systems of psychoanalysis and behaviorism but equally far again from the old conformist/imperialist synthesis of the prewar world. Not our human nature, but oppressive social institutions were to blame for the perilous, paralyzed state of the world of the day. Goodman's Gestalt, that is, was deeply political at its core, in contrast, as we shall see, to the inflection of his coauthor, Fritz Perls. Where they agreed was that the way out led forward, not back, in the direction of less social control, not more. For Goodman, this route would always pass through a radical re-affirmation of the truth and health and finally the political reliability of our fundamental social-animal nature, our inborn relational/political *eros,* which was not our downfall but rather our one possible path to the salvation of a dying world.

Here we see Goodman's most radical theoretical departure from Freud and the key to what he hoped to get for his purposes out of the Gestalt tradition in psychology: the reassessment and repositioning of desire in human relationships and process. Indeed, so seamlessly integrated was this reevaluation as the basis of a program for therapeutic and social change that it is easy to overlook how radically it revises the mainstream Western tradition and challenges much of the East as well. Not only is the entire course of Western culture (and not just Freud and his fellow Victorians), from Plato through the entire Christian tradition to Descartes and beyond, marked by a deep suspiciousness if not wholesale condemnation of desire, and especially of embodied desire, but the East as well has had puritanisms of its own that have tended to relegate desire and attachment to the status of enemies of spiritual progress or enlightenment. Ecstatic voices and minority traditions have, of course, existed in both great cultural lineages (though even here, condemnation of sexuality and the body has often been a feature), but they have never predominated in the mainstream of either lineage, sex being inherently subversive of institutions of power, as Goodman himself liked to point out (indeed, that is what he *valued* about sex, among other things).[15]

In Gestalt psychology, Goodman saw essentially three things that would serve him in this project. First was this reclamation of desire itself. Second was a basis for grounding this program in a coherent theory of human cognitive/emotional/ behavioral process. Indeed, as he would retell the Gestalt narrative, *eros* became the key to the whole process, the "Id of the situation"[16] that was the *elán vital* driving the formation of gestalts (itself the very essence of human perception and experience). In other words, it was desire itself that defined life, not struggle or spirit or some other ultimate goal. If this was existentialism (and it was), it was existentialism with a particular American/communitarian flavor, both embodied and instinctively relational and without its continental undertones of *inherent* alienation on the shores of an existence where we find no natural belonging. And if it was Freudianism (and it was), it was likewise Freud without the dark side, liberated from his reductive, Social Darwinist, biomechanical pessimism about the inherent conflict between individual nature and human society.

What Gestalt was telling us, Goodman argued, was that without desire there simply was no life at all, and that that process itself, the unfolding and completion of gestalts of perception, action, and meaning, moving toward goal and closure, was the life cycle of particular desires themselves. If a germ of this idea could be found in early Freud (and certainly in Reich[17]), that germ now produced more than the mere assertions that had marked Freud's biological reductionism. In essence, a psychological *how* was now added to the picture. Freud's fatal flaw, according to Goodman, had always been not his clinical insights but rather an "inadequate theory of awareness"; that is, an unfortunate grounding in mechanistic/associationist psychology, as opposed to Gestalt process and cognitive psychology.

Second, Goodman looked to Gestalt as a basis for reintegrating the whole panoply of repressive splits and exaggerated polarizations of the culture. The Gestalt model of perception and cognition was itself fundamentally holistic. If the subject was interacting with a whole field of perceptive experience, actively and synthetically integrating wholes of understanding and meaning, then the idea of holding some parts of experience outside that process would define repression itself. In other words, the whole idea of splitting off, say, body experience or emotions from intellect, sexual or aggressive impulse from social life, or, for that matter, politics from personal relations and the life of feelings and the body would reflect dysfunction at the deepest level of awareness process itself. Such a person would be in no position to make sound choices and judgments in any of those areas because his/her opinions would be literally false and of no value (this of course is one of the malicious pleasures of all clinical psychology, as Goodman himself noted: one's critics and opponents are not just wrong, but pathologically wrong).[18] Freud had, of course, already pointed out much the same thing, but his argument was essentially only by clinical speculation and inference. Here once again, Gestalt would provide a true theoretical, psychological rationale for insights Freud himself could only assert.

Moreover, if embodiment is the fundamental condition of being alive and desire is always in essence embodied desire felt and registered in the whole organism, then why should not body itself be a kind of ultimate authority of whether something is good or not? Man, Goodman insisted, is always a social/psychological *animal,* making connection and meaning out of a reality that is only perceived physically. Again, this is what the Gestalt model is telling us. Therefore, once more, to exclude body from the picture leaves us in no position to work, make art, or live an inter-personal or political life creatively and freely. Rather, the person with diminished body experience would be merely a political automaton subject to programmed control by the system, just as one could see on all sides merely by looking at the society and the world of the times. Again, it was not, after all, our animal nature and spontaneous impulses that were the problem, as in the later Freud; rather, the threat both to survival and to full living came from trying to split ourselves off from that nature. In other words, in the return to embodied desire lay the key to politics at every level from local to global and thus the answer to the cloud hanging over the future of humanity itself.

Third, and equally radical in practical terms, in Gestalt—and partic-ularly in this idea of the embodied basis of perception and meaning—Goodman saw the chance to articulate a psychotherapy without authority, a new attitude for the therapist freed of the heavy Freudian mortmain of the analyst as expert/judge pronouncing on what was and was not an acceptable sublimation of passion, both in degree and in object choice. Freud's way led only backward to the repressions and oppressions of the past, which were replicated, not dissolved, on the couch—and thus to everything that had landed us in a world that was both deadening and deadly and poised to blow itself up ("Make love not war" would be a completely logical slogan of this new program). Rather, this therapy would consist of a dialogic engagement of equals, each of them striving to be authentically present, a phrase by which Goodman understood chiefly a mutually free expression of felt experience and awareness, beginning with body awareness and without any censorship of impulse, desire, or passion on the part of either participant (Freud too had called for "free association," the relaxation of self-censorship, but in the service of revealing hidden secrets of the past and not in the exercise of real passions in the real encounter of the moment).

The therapist, to be sure, was presumed to be farther along in this project of authenticity: thus, the therapy would focus on the various inhibitions, distortions, and blocks in the patient along the road from sensation to full awareness and desire, to full expression of that passionate impulse in the "here and now" (as well as its accomplishment, right then and there, as in a full venting of anger or tears, or at least the positioning of the patient on a better, more practiced and aware basis for that accomplishment in some other setting—as with a larger life ambition, say, or sex itself).[19] As for accomplishment, Goodman was not beyond turning to other members in a group setting and appealing directly for an amorous assignation for the desirous patient, while for the attractive young man with libidinous curiosity an adventure of a different kind might well await with the therapist himself at some other time or even right in the next break.[20]

In other words, the therapist would analyze only *process*, not content. It was the full, clear, energized realization of "the gestalt" that was sought, not an externally imposed judgment about the particular content of the desire, which was the individual's own responsibility. To guide the therapist (or the self-help client reading the book) in this "gestalt analysis," Goodman then went on to catalog a brief nosology of "resistances" that might typically distort or block healthy "contact," as the healthy gestalt-formation process was called. The goal was to move "organismically" through the rise of desire to action and arrive at the goal state and the natural release of energy, which was then followed by a period of retreat and the arousal of a new awareness, need, or desire (again, the imagery is drawn from a traditionally "masculine" sexuality). The parallels here to Freudian libido theory and defense mechanisms are strong (several terms are on both canonical lists). But the difference is that in Freud, and particularly in Anna Freud's classic *The Ego and the Mechanisms of Defense*, the therapeutic goal was to soften the harshness of the defenses just a bit but still to use them to contain the inevitable instinct-anxiety and rechannel otherwise dangerous energies,[21] whereas here the idea was to confront and dissolve all inhibitions and distortions toward a full natural expression of "organismic impulse."[22]

Eros thus untrammeled, Goodman assures us, would not lead us to a Nietzschean (or Freudian) nightmare of berserker rampage or chaos unrestrained. Those horrors were rather the consequence of *not* giving free reign to the natural energies of aggression and desire. Problems and conflicts would, of course, arise, perhaps physical aggression or even murder, but none of it would reach the horrifying levels of the mechanized impersonal destruction that we saw everywhere around us and that depended on the kind of out-of-touch, disembodied, chronically half-mobilized human being who was the product of modern statism and constituted the modern neurosis.[23] Liberation and free self-expression, not central design, would save the world.

Of course, there was at least one flaw in this program, even in its own terms. By proposing such a canon of "resistances" to full "contact," Goodman *was* placing the therapist in the position of authority and judge—the very thing he set out not to do. In place of the dialogic engagement of equals he envisioned—exploring, arguing, perhaps laughing and weeping together, perhaps exchanging physical tenderness, all along the way to a fuller awareness of desire and its vicissitudes—such a therapy might, in less relational hands, easily lend itself to a reductive and authoritarian caricature, just as so much Freudian therapy had done, in which the therapist confined him/herself to safe and shaming pronouncements about the blocks and failures in the client's process. (Erv Polster, Goodman and Perls's student and probably the most prominent Gestalt trainer of the second generation, would much later term this retreat to authority "reintroducing the couch").[24] Indeed, in the view of many observers, this is just what did tend to happen for over a generation, following the lead of Fritz Perls, the cofounder of the method and the man who would bring Gestalt therapy to Esalen and from there champion and represent it to a much wider world.[25]

Meanwhile, Perls had taken something rather different from the Gestalt psychology model, which he likewise saw as a vehicle for the advancement of his own therapeutic agenda. In contrast to Goodman's grand and radical project of reevaluating and recentering desire, Perls's aim with the Gestalt method was, at least originally, more modest. By his own account,[26] Perls was no reader, and he absorbed ideas more by osmosis than by study.[27] What he did see in Gestalt's constructivist vision of human process as the formation and dissolution of wholes of cognition/emotion was the basis for his own program of rescuing aggression from the limbo of Freud's later twin-instinct theory (that is, Eros *and* Thanatos, sex and death, in place of just libido alone) in which aggression was equated with the "death instinct."[28] For did it not require self-assertion, which is aggressive energy, to construct these wholes of meaning and action? And did not every whole so constructed then eventually need to be dissolved or destructured to make way for new growth and larger or at least fresh understanding? Here Perls joined Goodman in drawing on Reich's character theory, in which essentially any fixed pattern of personality tends to be seen as pathological, a rigidification in the service of containing anxiety. The body, of course, carries these fixities as body armor, but by the same token it also betrays them.[29] Thus, Gestalt therapy's emphasis on the telling or revealing gesture: the denial of anger, say, accompanied by a clinched fist or of erotic feeling, together with an open and suggestive pelvic posture or a closed, constricted one. And as in Freud, the display or the denial of the affect the patient was "accused" of could serve equally as evidence that the analyst was "right." This was what many people found so maddening or shaming—in any case, disempowering—about psychotherapy. It was also what Goodman hoped to get away from, yet managed to replicate in the new method.

Perls's first (and only) theoretical work had centered around this project of rehabilitating aggression from its bad odor in the later Freud.[30] Freud was essentially right in all his theorizing, Perls wrote from exile in South Africa in the early years of the war, *except* that he overlooked the importance of oral aggression as an "instinct" in its own right along with libido and "Thanatos." This aggression, unlike the other kind, was essential and life-affirming, corresponding in development to dentition in the infant and thus to the transition from infantile helplessness and passivity, or mere sucking, to real chewing, or the active destructuring of the food. Thus, "oral aggression" was associated with autonomy, self-determination, and the maturing drive to "chew" everything taken in, thereby mastering it and rendering it one's own, as opposed to "swallowing it whole." Thus, there could be "oral resistances" in addition to the "anal resistances" of classic theory: all of these are various kinds of failure to attack the stuff of life aggressively and so lead to a chronic passivity and avoidance of self-responsibility. Introjection, for example, was the classic case and pro- totype for all the others: the infant *introjects* the milk passively. The toothling bites (and thereby causes a rupture with the mother, predating the one the father would impose at a later age, in Oedipal theory). This may seem to reflect a fantastic unfamiliarity (in a father with two small children at the time) with the aggressivity of suckling infants. Nonethe- less, for Perls the image remained emblematic for the "transition from 'other-supports' to 'self-supports,'" which he would equate with mature development itself.[31]

In practice, this meant a therapy, in Perls's hands, in which aggression was always celebrated as a return to embodied, energized, and "self- responsible" life. Isadore From, an early patient who was later a prominent Gestalt trainer, tells of once hurling a heavy glass ashtray in a rage at Fritz Perls during a session. He missed, but Perls merely murmured, "Gut, gut."[32] Aggression was being disinhibited, that was the main thing. Richer and more passionate living would surely be the result.

In retrospect now, the tensions between Goodman's and Perls's un- derstandings of the import and potential of the Gestalt model seem both fundamental and not completely reconcilable. In the context of the times, though—the world of the 1950s evoked above, followed by a period of heady rejection of much of that world—it was the overlap that counted, the common agenda of challenging the iron fist of social control in art, politics, the bedroom, in the therapeutic hour. It was in this spirit that Perls brought Gestalt to Esalen in 1965, and it was the showcase Esalen provided that catapulted Gestalt into the popular imagination in its Perl- sian version, which emphasized unrestrained individual expression and autonomy over relationship, interdependence, and political engagement. Both Gestalt and Esalen would suffer for a time from this reduction of the model to only the first come-to-your-senses phase of its potential, which Goodman had presented more as a preparatory or recovery stage on the way to the rest of the agenda: "to create a new world" together.[33] But this reduction was of course syntonic with the wider culture of the times and thus may be seen as the limit, for a time, of the deconstructive use of the model to reform that wider culture. Today, in a different time, the rest of that agenda can be seen more clearly to the benefit of the fuller realization of both projects, Gestalt and Esalen alike.

GESTALT AT ESALEN

The founding notion of the Esalen Institute, in the slightly later words of longtime Esalen president George Leonard, was always the idea that "the world doesn't have to be the way it is."[34] This is of course a notion shared by all revolutionaries and reformers in one way or another, but what was more unusual in the Esalen project was its open-ended agenda. In the words of cofounder Michael Murphy, the vision was "to create a space for everything that was excluded from the academy."[35] As a quick glance back at the above sketch of some of the dichotomies and shadows of the culture of the times will confirm, this was a large agenda indeed. Embodiment and sexuality, spiritual experience, alternative psychotherapies, consciousness itself, the philosophical implications of quantum physics, shamanic studies, alternative healing traditions, countercultural art and music (much of it soon to become mainstream), race relations, environmental concerns (not yet known as "ecology"), cross-cultural initiatives (leading eventually to the new political form of citizen, or track-two, diplomacy)—all this and much, much more was off the page of the mainstream culture in 1962, and all of it and more would be explored, incubated, nurtured, and developed at Esalen over the next decades, leading in many cases to influential shifts and movements in that wider mainstream itself. All this is amply documented in this volume and elsewhere and, as such, constitutes the story of Esalen as a (counter)-cultural institution in its own right over the ensuing four decades and continuing today.

Certain features of the story, however, are set off or clarified in a new way by consideration of the mutual influences between Esalen and the Gestalt model from the beginning and down through these years, and it is these that interest us here. This discussion begins with consideration of some principal ways Esalen and Gestalt were *not* alike in certain of their fundamental thrusts and concerns. This in turn leads to what each of them had, and has, to offer to the other, and how that mutual enrichment has led, and continues to lead, to an expansion of vision of each project. Finally, consideration of that expanded vision sheds light in turn on the central cultural assumptions that neither project was at first able to see deconstructively: the Western individualistic self-model itself, its rich gifts, and its sharp limitations, all of which are crucial to the next stage of the unfolding of both these projects and indeed to the cultural transition underway today on a global level.

To begin with, Esalen itself was always fundamentally more in spirit than a smorgasbord menu of richly diverse practices, explorations, topics, and concerns. Transcending this eclecticism, contextualizing it and to a degree unifying it, was the vision of "the integral"—simply put, the notion, so deeply shared with the Gestalt movement, that we had split off and lost whole dimensions of our human potential so that we possessed either limited or no access to them at all or these shadow poles of human experience and functioning were held in a way that was cut off from the rest of our experience to stultifying and even life-threatening effect. Thus there was from the beginning at Esalen the unifying idea of a *conversation* (Murphy himself has often invoked the idea of Plato's or Ficino's academy), an integrative space where any part of the human experience could enter into open discourse with any other part.

Naturally, these cross-disciplinary exchanges (in many cases with disciplines that were themselves as yet undefined, for want of this kind of conversational space) tended from the first to zero right in on the central splits of the culture: mind/body was an early and persistent theme, soon to be followed by the related topic mind/spirit, and then the even more subversive discourse, *body*/spirit, with its inherently deconstructive effects on Western and Eastern cultures alike. This then led naturally to the opening of a space for traditional and alternative healing traditions (and new methods), which were themselves if anything even more taboo in the academic/scientific discourse of Western medicine of the day. It was then very much in Murphy's integrative spirit to open these conversations to (the more open-minded members of) the mainstream medical profession as well, both in workshop explorations and in a series of invitational conferences on these topics in the 1980s. The well-known result was the development of what we know today as complementary medicine, the common experience of patients today, who are not surprised to hear their neurologist or dermatologist recommend acupuncture or their cardiologist recommend meditation and stress reduction techniques or their oncologist recommend all of the above plus group psychotherapy—all of them with "hard" studies to back up their recommendations (but of course, such studies themselves, in the way of mainstream science, *follow* on the opening of such a discourse rather than precede it).

This is merely one example of many illustrating the pulse of the integrative spirit in action, the nature of a countercultural institution at its best in relation to the mainstream culture it counters, and the methodology of Esalen's vision of an open space for integral inquiry. The key word here is "integral"—again, the idea that human experience is potentially unitary, that we are at an essential level unified with, not separate from, our world, and that the foliation and then reweaving of new parts of that experience is an evolutionary process, resulting in the generation of novelty and new forms; that is, the unfolding of human potential. In all this we can see the deep influence on Murphy, in particular, of the tradition of the Indian philosopher-saint Sri Aurobindo, to whose ashram Murphy had repaired for an extended time in the early 1950s, more or less in flight from the strictures of academic philosophy (remember, this was an age in which any "spiritual" experience was deeply pathologized) and in quest of something he could not yet name but must have in some sense intuited.

In the Cambridge-educated, intensely political Aurobindo (who had recently died, so that the two never actually met), Murphy found a figure who was himself already an apostle of "the integral" in his life as well as in his philosophy. Part of Aurobindo's signal contribution as a student of both the Eastern and Western traditions was to give a certain Darwinian flavor, at least, to the Vedantic and other Eastern traditions of the story of humanity and the universe as the evolutionary unfolding of Spirit (Goethe, Hegel, and the rest of the German Romantic tradition of course also come to mind here, as Aurobindo himself was well aware and as Jeffrey Kripal reminds us in his chapter in this volume).[36] Far from being hostile to Western science and philosophy, Aurobindo's perspective offered a way of contextualizing those traditions, incorporating them into a vision that was cosmic and yet progressive, spiritual and yet activist in the world, as Aurobindo himself had been (it was Aurobindo, in anticipation of Gandhi, who had first moved the political conversation in colonial India from home rule to independence and who had been jailed for his pains).

At its best, this was a perspective the Gestalt model was prepared to join and to support with its constructivist participatory psychological system. In the holistic existentialist-inflected version of Gestalt that had been pioneered by Lewin and then articulated by Goodman, everything begins with a *whole, unified field*. Awareness, the resolution of that field into figure/ground, is the assertion of a point of view in/on that field, but (and this nuance would be crucial) *by a knower who is not just "in" the field but actually "of" it*. The boundary, that is, between knower and known, between organism and environment (to take Goodman's favorite, animal-flavored terminology) is only a provisional and fluctuating dynamic phenomenon, not a real place, much less an essence of the person. It is easy to see how such a perspective lends itself to seeing cosmic or mystical states and experiences as just one more possible inflection of that dynamic, no more and no less inherently valid, healthy, and usable than our more familiar, everyday Western state of experiencing ourselves as in some way detached from our surroundings, which we are operating in and on.[37]

This was the theory, and certainly this perspective, if not its consequences for spiritual experience, is articulated at times by Goodman in *Gestalt Therapy* and elsewhere. However, it was Perls, not Goodman, who brought Gestalt to Esalen and from there to its status, for a time, as *the* psychotherapeutic modality of the "new age." And if Goodman, very much steeped himself in the deep individualism of both the American Emersonian tradition and continental existentialism (both of which seemed to offer a much-needed subversion of the fascisms and statisms of the day), was ambivalent about this matter of self-dissolution and loss of self-definition, Perls for his part showed no such ambivalence: he was squarely against it. Goodman, after all, had employed the term "egotism" in his catalog of "resistances" to the full process of "contact" (egotism was defined as the inability finally to let go, to *lose* oneself in the act, the moment, the other, a sort of sustained orgasmic state, deeply refreshing, which he equated with full contact). Perls, in his later writings and teaching about the dangers of inhibiting the contact process, never seemed to mention the term (this is not surprising, given his own emphasis, mentioned above, on independence and autonomy as the criteria of health). At the same time, both of them feared and pathologized the dynamic state of "confluence," which is likewise a kind of losing oneself in the other (Sartre's being-for-others comes to mind).[38] Both of them, moreover, generally equated "confluence" with "introjection," the passive swallowing of authority in abrogation of the self-responsibility on which both men pinned so much hope.

The result of this ambivalence in the model at Esalen was a complex set of interrelated paradoxes. On the one hand, Esalen was (and is) a community made up of some hundred or more long-term residents, another seventy-five or more extended-term interns, various other dependents and service providers, plus a rotating group of a hundred or so students or conference participants at any given time, amounting to an aggregate traffic of some 10,000 hardy souls per year. Definitely a community, if one structured in overlapping concentric circles of progressive degrees and lengths of involvement (individuals may pass from one category to another at various times, and many of the transient students are themselves old-timers who have been there before, in some cases going back years). And yet for many years at least—and here was part of the paradox—this community itself was founded on a kind of anticommunality, which was itself a part of the Gestalt legacy at Esalen, at least as Perls had represented and shaped it.

Perls himself was actually in residence as part of this community for only a few years at the end of the 1960s, but he left a legacy of process style and values that long permeated the Esalen culture, from the residential community to the workshops to many of the research initiatives. This legacy might be summed up in two key themes, which amount to injunctions: remember the body, and take responsibility for yourself. These are indeed valuable lessons, and, again, refreshing and revitalizing in that deadening postwar landscape in ways probably impossible to appreciate fully today for those who were not there. What was missing in this legacy, however, was Goodman's perspective, which was that these injunctions themselves were only intended to clear the way for the resumption of full human functioning, which would always be (spontaneously—this was the essence of Goodman's anarchistic faith) the resumption of the natural contact arc of relationship, community, politics, an arc which Goodman saw as having been broken by the dehumanizing terms of modern life. Perls was himself, of course, very much of the cultural Left, a product of his own youth in the ferment of Weimar Berlin, when psychoanalysis itself was still radical. And Perls remained in many ways a classical psychoanalyst to the end, pronouncing on other people's neuroses from a position of detached authority, for all that he turned around and faced an audience in a theatrical presentation of the work. But his interest in community remained essentially that: as an audience. It is significant that Perls finally left Esalen after a few years in search of a more compliant setting, unhappy with the Institute's refusal to let him, in Murphy's words, "capture the flag and run the show."[39]

In other words, if Gestalt seemed perfect for the 1960s as a call to return to the body and break the shackles of conformity, in Perls's particular inflection it was even more so for the 1970s and early 1980s, the period sometimes called (then and now) "the me generation," a time when the earlier bubble of naive enthusiasm for changing the political world had burst against the sharp resistance of "the system" and many people turned inward to "work on themselves" psychologically or (increasingly) spiritually. ("Change has to begin with yourself" went a compensatory shibboleth of the times; unfortunately, all too often it seemed to end with oneself as well.) Thus, the paradoxes mounted at Esalen and elsewhere: a psychotherapeutic model based on holism and contact that showed tendencies toward relationship and commitment phobia in the context of an intimate community founded on anticommunitarian individualism. Small wonder if both projects—Esalen and Gestalt itself—seemed at times stuck in those periods, torn between repeating the great moments of the 1960s and uncertain about where and how to go forward from here. At the same time, at a deeper level, each project still had something powerful to teach the other and, in teaching it, would recover its own essence and move forward with renewed focus and energy.

Meanwhile, separately and apart from their intense local embrace, both projects were looking outward to a larger world, plowing new ground that would yield new impetus and direction later on. For Esalen, apart from the world of alternative psychotherapy, bodywork, and healing, the 1980s was the flowering of an initiative that had begun some time before with the Murphys' first trip to the Soviet Union in the 1970s. This initiative, which represents one of the many and most public of Esalen's successful innovative projects (and a brilliant example of free space for exploration and conversation in action), was the Esalen American-Soviet Exchange Program, which began with the idea of hosting an encounter between Soviet and American astronauts (in other words, with an integral image of the whole earth, seen from outer space), soon proliferated to other professional and cultural exchanges, and helped spawn the new forms of citizen diplomacy and "track-two," or nongovernmental, diplomatic exchange. These forms in turn have, to put it plainly, changed our world from one of a monolithic (or dilithic) confrontation of superpowers to a pluralistic (and now chaotic) world in which NGOs are recognized as key to any international project of peacemaking and progress. In the process, once again, the entire project illustrates dramatically how alternative institutions (Esalen and, of course, many others) interact with and change their host cultures by incubating and midwifing explorations and new methods that initially find no reception in the institutions of the mainstream.

At the same time, the Gestalt model at other venues was going through a time of similar outreach and redefinition beyond the narrowly individualistic terms set by Perls (both Perls and Goodman had died at the beginning of the 1970s, Goodman at only sixty, by which time he had largely left the world of psychotherapy altogether in favor of more direct political engagement in the antiwar and other movements of the times). Gestalt itself by this time was loosely split into two overlapping yet competing schools. One, West Coast, or Perlsian, Gestalt, followed the more authoritarian, analytic, and sharply confrontive pattern Perls had set at Esalen, which was widely copied by a generation of his followers, there and abroad. The other, East Coast Gestalt, under the loose leadership of Goodman's and Perls's (and Laura Perls's) student Isadore From, was always somewhat more relational in focus and more intellectual and political in flavor. In the middle, in Cleveland, Ohio, was the largest Gestalt training center in the U.S. and indeed in the world, the Gestalt Institute of Cleveland, made up of students of all the founders, but with its own more interpersonal focus of psychotherapy as a relational encounter,[40] whole-group dynamics (growing directly out of the T-group movement pioneered by Gestaltist Kurt Lewin after the war[41]), and—a wholly new application—the use of Gestalt principles and methods in working with organizational dynamics and development at a large-systems level, also growing out of Lewin's work.[42]

Thus, by the end of the decade some of the most fertile new work growing out of both Esalen and the Gestalt movement was taking place outside Esalen itself in venues as distant as Moscow, Cleveland, and elsewhere. At the same time, by 1990 large parts of the initial agenda of both projects had achieved respectability and passed on into the mainstream. The result was both an enormous degree of impact and influence in the wider world (not always credited to its sources, of course) and a certain sense of a particular vein having been mined out and run its course. By the 1990s, revolutions that had begun and been fostered at Esalen—such as bodywork in psychotherapy, somatics as a field of study, the powerful new cultural forms of complementary medicine and citizen diplomacy discussed above, innovative early childhood education, experiential and lifelong education themselves, the study of the affective base of cognition, holistic approaches to health and healing, and of course the centrality of spiritual concerns in psychotherapy, among numerous others—were now well accepted and widely available in the culture and indeed throughout the world. Many of these were Gestalt themes as well, of course, to which we could add the transformation in mainstream psychotherapy over the previous generation, as dominant traditional schools (particularly the Freudian, behaviorist, and cognitive movements, which together accounted for the vast majority of practitioners in the U.S. and worldwide) one by one "discovered" the centrality of present-centered experience and authentic present relationship to the psychotherapeutic process.

At the same time, while the Gestalt revolution Perls and Goodman had jointly espoused to subvert and replace the disembodied, deeply conservative mainstream psychoanalysis of the times with something more energizing, enlivening, and permission-giving, had certainly succeeded (in concert with other reform therapies of the times), the specifically political agenda of Goodman's own vision had clearly not fared as well. Indeed, never had the two streams, psychotherapy and political action, seemed further apart: if it was completely normative to go to a psychotherapist by the 1990s, it seemed only increasingly aberrant to be deeply involved in politics. The two activities seemed to belong, just as many Marxists had insisted in an earlier day, to entirely different worldviews and different conceptions of human nature and purpose. If anything, psychotherapy (and for that matter, spiritual practice) often seemed to be now about what one did *instead* of "getting involved."[43] Why? What was the block in this period to trying at least to apply the manifest learnings about human organization, education, and experience to the increasingly desperate problems of political and economic organization in today's world?

One part of the complex answer to this urgent question lay in the terms of the problem itself, terms which take us beyond the differences between Perls's and Goodman's versions of Gestalt to underlying cultural assumptions about human nature and process themselves. The original terms of the Gestalt model, remember, were more radically holistic than their theatrical (and rather authoritarian) presentation by Perls or the diagnostic roster of "resistances" to contact (which is also suitable for analysis by an outside expert) offered by Goodman. In the original terms of the model, which derived from an attempt to understand the psychological processes themselves of perceiving and understanding, the analysis starts not with an "individual self" in the isolated monadic imagery of Western cultural tradition. Rather, the terms give necessary primacy to a relational field out of which a sense of self (and a sense of others) arises through a process of differentiation that is awareness itself (the very process Goodman called desire). This takes us back to the radical terms of Goodman's analysis of desire itself as synonymous with and definitional of existence. "Self," that is, does not and cannot precede or lie apart from relationship, as the Western cultural tradition has long insisted (even before the term "self" as a substantive came into general use in the seventeenth century).[44] Rather, *self arises, developmentally, existentially, and experimentally, out of and as part of a relational field,* which not only contextualizes but interpenetrates with the individual self. The three terms—self, desire, and relationship—are, if not exactly synonymous, then at least coterminous.

All this follows from a radical return to the terms of the Gestalt model itself and constitutes a deconstruction of the Western model of self to a degree that lay just outside even Goodman's grasp. This is the discourse and the thematizing of Gestalt theory and practice today in common with some allied movements in other schools, such as the inter-subjective movement in psychoanalysis,[45] and the transition from constructivism to social constructionism in social and cultural studies.[46] But here again, what Gestalt adds to these other approaches is a much more complete psychological model, encompassing emotion/cognition, the co-construction of meaning and experience, and the world of rela-tional/organizational process alike.

This, then, is what contemporary Gestalt offers to Esalen and to its wider audience as well. The effect is to erode the old distinction between "self" and "other" and, with it, the myth that either one can flourish without equal attention to the other. The potential implications of such a paradigm shift for both relationship and political action seem profound and are only now beginning to be explored.[47]

But if Esalen can gain from a basic shift in perspective on the nature of the self from a monadic view to one grounded in relationship and desire, Gestalt as well has something to learn from the founding vision of Esalen and, in particular, from its evolutionary focus and emphasis. Today, some forty years after Esalen's founding in the spirit and context of Aurobindo's notions about the evolution of consciousness, the topic of evolution is very much at the center of intellectual debate. This conver-sation itself is of course the contemporary form for the revival of a much older, deeper theme in philosophy and cultural studies, which had been dormant in the academy, to say the least, down through much of the twentieth century: the question of human nature. This question, long out of fashion (having been discredited and then tainted, seemingly, by its uses at the hands of the eugenicists[48] and then, of course, by the Nazis), was thrust back into view with the publication of Wilson's *Sociobiology* in 1975 and then kept there by the steady accumulation of new findings in the areas of genetics, cognitive neuroscience, and infant development in particular in the years since.

Today, it seems clear that the model that succeeds in capturing the evolutionary narrative will very likely be central to our cultural vision of what is possible in human affairs and society—that is, in our human potential—in the period to come. And that vision of what is possible will then set the limits, as ever, to our political, social, and economic imagination for that period. For some years now, Esalen, in yet another of its pioneering cross-disciplinary conversational initiatives, has sponsored an annual research conference on this topic, bringing together exponents of the material sciences (geneticists, neuroscientists, and cosmologists, among others), chaos and complexity theorists, philosophers of society and consciousness, developmental psychologists, and students of cultural evolution to explore this vision. In these conversations, both projects—Esalen and Gestalt—have a particular contribution to make. For Esalen, that particular contribution is the Aurobindonian perspective that our nature, our human potential, is itself evolutionary and constitutes the ongoing generation of new forms. Gestalt contributes a new understanding of the self beyond the monadic individualism of the post-Darwin period in evolutionary theory. In this view, which is deeply in accord with current findings and thinking in evolutionary theory and evolutionary psychology, our most fundamental nature, from the gene to the phenotype, is relational: either we establish a mutually supportive context, or we fail to achieve viability at every level. In this sense, Gestalt, whose figure/ground, distributive, holistic model of cognition is being confirmed every day by research in cognitive neuroscience and brain and mind models, is emerging now as the process model of evolutionary psychology itself.[49] That is, it is the Gestalt model, founded as it was in the attempt to offer a naturalistic, process description of how we go about coping with our world,[50] that offers us our best available psychological system for understanding the evolutionary processes of survival, cooperation, and growth.

Thus these two projects of an earlier countercultural moment find themselves once again at the center of a time of powerful cultural deconstruction and reorganization, a period of the emergence of some new world order, yet unclear, for which the ferment of the 1960s now seems only a prelude and a preparation. As always in moments of chaotic disequilibrium, the influence of small "germ crystals" may at times be disproportionately great, as the new order takes form around the template or creode of some organizing pattern of thought. Reenergized now by their ongoing cross-fertilization, Esalen and the Gestalt model together have a new contribution to offer to that emergent world in the form of a new self-story of who we are and what our destiny may be as a culture and as a species. In this new story, the gains and learning of the human potential movement of the past decades provide a foundation for the completion of that potential by applying those gains now to the urgent task at hand: the co-creation of a sustainable, livable world.

NOTES

1. Paul Goodman, *Novelty, Excitement and Growth,* vol. 2 of *Gestalt Therapy,* in Gordon Wheeler, ed., *Reading Paul Goodman: Gestalt for Our Times* (1951; reprint, Hillsdale, N.Y.: The Analytic Press/GestaltPress, 2004).

2. Ibid.

3. Paul Goodman, *Growing Up Absurd* (New York: Random House, 1961).

4. See especially Bessel A. van der Kolk, Alexander C. McFarlane, and Lars Weisaeth, eds., *Traumatic Stress: The Effects of Overwhelming Experience on Mind, Body, and Society* (New York: Guilford, 1996).

5. Joseph Campbell, *The Portable Jung* (New York: Viking, 1972).

6. See, for example, M. Wertheimer, "Experimentelle Studien über das Sehen von Bewegungen," *Zeitschrift für Psychologie* 61 (1925); Kurt Lewin, "Kriegslandschaft," *Zeitschrift Angewandter Psychologie* 12 (1918): 440–447; Kurt Lewin, "Vorsatz, Wille, und Bedürfnis," *Psychologische Forschung* 7 (1926): 330–385; Kurt Lewin, *A Dynamic Theory of Personality* (New York: McGraw-Hill, 1935).

7. William James, *Principles of Psychology* (1903; reprint, Cambridge, Mass.: Harvard University Press, 1983).

8. For a fuller discussion of this, see Gordon Wheeler, "Why Gestalt," in Gordon Wheeler and Stephanie Backman, eds., *On Intimate Ground: A Gestalt Approach to Working with Couples* (San Francisco: Jossey-Bass, 1994).

9. And note here that the field of group dynamics itself, the study of organizational processes on a group level, was founded on Gestalt premises by pioneering social psychologist and Gestaltist Kurt Lewin; see the latter's *Resolving Social Conflicts* (New York: Harper & Brothers, 1948).

10. See K. Koffka, *The Origins of Mind: An Introduction to Child Psychology,* trans. R. Ogden (New York: Harcourt, Brace, 1925), as well as the discussion in Gordon Wheeler, "Why Gestalt."

11. Sigmund Freud, *Civilization and Its Discontents* (1930; reprint, New York: Norton, 1961).

12. See Jeffrey Masson, *The Assault on Truth* (New York: Farrar, Straus, Giroux, 1984); and P. Roazen, *Freud and His Followers* (New York: Alfred A. Knopf, 1976).

13. Taylor Stoehr, *Here Now Next: Paul Goodman and the Origins of Gestalt Therapy* (San Francisco: Jossey-Bass/GestaltPress, 1994).

14. Goodman, *Novelty, Excitement and Growth.*

15. Paul Goodman, *Crazy Hope and Finite Experience: Final Essays of Paul Goodman,* ed. Taylor Stoehr (San Francisco: Jossey-Bass, 1994).

16. Goodman, *Novelty, Excitement and Growth.*

17. Wilhelm Reich, *Character Analysis* (New York: Farrar, Straus, Giroux, 1970).

18. Goodman, *Novelty, Excitement and Growth.*

19. Ibid.

20. Stoehr, *Here Now Next.* I am also indebted here to conversation with Edwin Nevis.

21. Anna Freud, *The Ego and the Mechanisms of Defense* (New York: International Universities Press, 1937).

22. Frederick Perls, Ralph F. Hefferline, and Paul Goodman, *Gestalt Therapy: Excitement and Growth in the Human Personality* (New York: Julian Press, 1951).

23. Goodman, *Novelty, Excitement and Growth.*

24. E. Polster, "Imprisoned in the Present," *The Gestalt Journal* 8, no. 1 (1985): 5–22.

25. For a discussion, see Gordon Wheeler, *Gestalt Reconsidered: A New Approach to Contact and Resistance* (New York: Gardner Press, 1991).

26. Frederick S. Perls, *In and Out the Garbage Pail* (Moab, Utah: Real People Press, 1969).

27. Wheeler, *Gestalt Reconsidered.*

28. Sigmund Freud, *The Ego and the Id* (1923; reprint, New York: Norton, 1960).

29. Reich, *Character Analysis.*

30. F. S. Perls, *Ego, Hunger & Aggression* (London: Allen & Unwin, 1947).

31. Perls, *In and Out the Garbage Pail.*

32. J. Wysong, *An Oral History of Gestalt Therapy* (Highland, N.Y.: Gestalt Journal Press, 1983).

33. For a discussion, see Stoehr, *Here Now Next.*

34. George Leonard, personal communication.

35. Michael Murphy, personal communication. Murphy has made much the same statement many times, in public addresses and in print.

36. Sri Aurobindo, *The Life Divine* (Berkeley, Calif.: Lotus Press, 1982). See also Robert McDermott, *The Essential Aurobindo* (New York: Steiner Books, 1979).

37. Gordon Wheeler, *Beyond Individualism: Toward a New Understanding of Self, Relationship, & Experience* (Hillsdale, N.J.: The Analytic Press/GestaltPress, 2000).

38. For a discussion, see ibid.

39. Michael Murphy, personal communication.

40. See E. Polster and M. Polster, *Gestalt Integrated* (New York: Brunner/Mazel, 1973); and J. Zinker, *Creative Process in Gestalt Therapy* (New York: Brunner/Mazel, 1977).

41. Lewin, *Resolving Social Conflicts.*

42. See also E. Nevis, *Organizational Consulting: A Gestalt Approach* (New York: Gardner Press, 1987).

43. James Hillman and M. Ventura, *We've Had 100 Years of Psychotherapy (and the World Is Getting Worse)* (New York: HarperCollins, 1992).

44. See Wheeler, *Beyond Individualism.*

45. R. Stolorov and G. Atwood, *Contexts of Being: The Intersubjective Foundations of Psychological Life* (Hillsdale, N.J.: The Analytic Press, 1992).

46. K. Gergen, *The Saturated Self* (New York: Basic Books, 1991).

47. See Wheeler, *Beyond Individualism*; Wheeler, "L'Age de la Complexité: Paul Goodman pour Notre Temps," *Gestalttherapie* XV, no. 2 (2003): 29–51; and Robert

G. Lee, *The Values of Connection: A Relational Approach to Ethics* (Hillsdale, N.J.: The Analytic Press/GestaltPress, 2004).

48. F. Galton, *Hereditary Intelligence* (London: Macmillan, 1869).

49. See, for example, K. Goldstein, *The Organism* (Boston: Macmillan, 1940); A. Damasio, *Descartes's Error: Emotion, Reason, and the Human Brain* (New York: Putnam, 1994); and Terrence W. Deacon, *The Symbolic Species: The Co-Evolution of Language and the Brain* (New York: Norton, 1997).

50. Kurt Lewin, "Vorsatz, Wille, und Bedürfnis," *Psychologische Forschung* 7 (1926): 330–385.

ESALEN AND THE CULTURAL

BOUNDARIES OF METALANGUAGE

Robert C. Fuller

When Richard Price and Michael Murphy opened the doors of Esalen in 1962, they probably anticipated that scholars would someday celebrate and assess their Institute's role in shaping American religion, psychology, and culture. Or at least they must have dreamed of it. Their plans were a bit vague, but they had confidence in their fundamental vision. They knew they were on the edge of the future. They believed they were at the forefront of a major leap forward in humanity's evolutionary development that would be both philosophical and cultural. All the elements needed to effect this evolutionary leap already existed. It would be Esalen's role to bring these otherwise disparate elements into close proximity and facilitate the creative combinations that would inevitably emerge.

Now, some forty years later, we are in a position to assess the cultural impact of Esalen's pioneering vision. While this vision may not (at least yet) have occasioned an evolutionary leap in most Americans' way of life, its influence has nonetheless been both pervasive and profound. Esalen has succeeded in bringing together otherwise disparate theories about humanity's untapped potentials. The many psychologists, philosophers, and theologians who have participated in Esalen's programs over the years have subsequently carried these theories to one of the largest subcultures in modern American life. Their books, seminars, college courses, and sermons have forged something along the lines of a new cultural community whose boundaries are quite unlike those of previous American subcultures (e.g., universities, churches). Persons from all walks of life believe they have changed their outlook on life. They now embrace a holistic vision of the human person, believing that the body, mind, and emotions are intimately connected. They acknowledge the transformative powers of such Eastern spiritual disciplines as yoga, Zen, and t'ai chi. They believe that the mind has untapped potentials which, in all probability, include extrasensory modes of perception such as clairvoyance and telepathy. Finally, they believe that a new paradigm is emerging that will revolutionize both our religious and scientific understandings of the universe and will draw attention to the causal forces capable of lifting humanity to the next stage in our evolutionary development. The most distinctive feature of this new paradigm is thus its articulation of a new language, a metalanguage, that reveals how our spiritual and scientific interests—far from being in opposition to one another—can be seen to be in perfect harmony.

The majority of those who will read this chapter will be familiar with the range of ideas that have been generated out of Murphy's and Price's founding vision. But such was not the case in 1962—particularly among those affiliated with the religious, academic, and therapeutic establishments in America. Murphy and Price were on the periphery of the American culture. If they were to pursue their vision, they would need to redraw existing cultural boundaries.

CULTURE AND THE LANGUAGE OF CAUSATION

In the early 1960s, most educated Americans subscribed to a cultural outlook, often referred to as "modernism," that was hardly sympathetic to the Esalen vision.[1] The modernist outlook has an abiding confidence in the goal of continuous secular progress. Modernism assumes that this progress not only is, but rightfully should be, directed by scientifically grounded technologies. It is thus not surprising that the era's psychological theorists exuded confidence in the powers of the rational ego—including its ability to devise a behavioral technology capable of imposing efficiency and control onto our otherwise unruly world. It is an irony that America's religious establishment also embraced this modernist outlook. True, biblical religion differed from science in that it also acknowledged the possibility of supernatural intervention. Yet mainstream religion viewed this supernatural influence as originating in a realm wholly beyond our natural universe. Religious beliefs therefore did not alter prevailing cultural understandings of how humans should go about their everyday lives. In 1962, religious faith was widely assumed to facilitate (rather than impede or call into question) successful adaptation to the prevailing cultural climate.

A culture's fundamental vision is most succinctly captured in its distinctive notion of causation. That is, every culture rests upon certain basic assumptions about the causal forces that affect human well-being. Beliefs concerning what constitutes a "real" cause thus go to the very heart of its normative vision. For example, a culture that recognizes the role of spirit possession in the etiology of illness will pattern the lives of its members differently than a culture that attributes illness to a virus or the repression of sexual desire. We might remind ourselves that Aristotle carefully distinguished between four different understandings of what constitutes a cause: the material cause (the substance of which it is made); the formal cause (the form of something or class to which it belongs); the efficient cause (the direct impetus of change); and the final cause (the intention, purpose, or goal of an action, which Aristotle described as "that for the sake of which" something happens). Modern science—including psychology—largely separated itself from philosophy and theology by concentrating on the material and efficient causes of an event (demanding, moreover, that such causal agents be discernible by the five physical senses or extensions of these senses).[2] The study of material and efficient causation fit nicely with the modernist cultural outlook and contributed to our progressive mastery of the natural and social environments.

Esalen found itself on the edge of the future because it championed an entirely new mode of causal explanation. What has distinguished Esalen over the years is less the specific topics featured in its programs than the distinctive notion of causality it brings to the discussion of these topics. Murphy and Price's founding vision focused squarely on the role of what might be called the "ultimate" or "metaphysical" cause that ontologically precedes the entire domain of physiological and environmental factors. Their conception of an ultimate cause affecting human life was bolder than the concept of an initial First Cause such as one might find in a deistic world view (which leaves the causal explanations of the natural sciences intact). Their vision postulated a far more radical interpenetration of physical and metaphysical spheres of causation. Such a vision is not, in the words of William James, intended to be

> a mere illumination of facts already elsewhere given . . . [but] a postulator of new *facts* as well. The world interpreted religiously is not the materialistic world over again, with an altered expression; it must have, over and above the altered expression, *a natural constitution* different at some point from that which a materialistic world would have. It must be such that different events can be expected in it, different conduct required.[3]

Esalen's cultural vision was grounded squarely in this conviction that the universe has a natural constitution different from that ordinarily depicted by the existing sciences. It was Esalen's cultural mission to help disseminate this understanding such that Americans might better understand what different events to expect and what different conduct they might engage in as they approach the edge of the future.

Esalen understood the metacause of growth and development in two related, but distinguishable ways: 1) as an immanent cosmic principle propelling "material" and "efficient" causes from within—a theory of causation that thus contains elements of Aristotle's notion of both "formal" and "final" causes; and 2) as more-than-physical energies that become efficient causes of their own by exerting causal force from without. It has been Esalen's task to function as a "university of metalanguage"—promoting broad inquiry into phenomena that reveal humanity's relationship to causal forces that go well beyond those recognized in the existing sciences. In doing so, however, Esalen located itself in ambiguous and uncharted cultural territory. It championed causal language that corresponded to neither the prevailing scientific nor religious establishments. Esalen was seeking to draw new cultural boundaries—an enterprise certain to infuriate at least as many as it would inspire.

THE SOURCES OF ESALEN'S METALANGUAGE

There were two principal sources of Esalen's metalanguage: the perennial philosophy espoused by Sri Aurobindo, Aldous Huxley, and others and the phenomenology of psychedelic experience. Initially, it was the perennial philosophy that informed Murphy's and Price's guiding vision. As Murphy has repeatedly explained over the years, he had "been influenced primarily by Sri Aurobindo, who saw human nature as part of cosmic evolution and participating in the awakening of the latent divinity in all things."[4] In his epic text *The Life Divine*, Aurobindo taught that the whole of biological evolution is in fact the progressive movement of existence toward spiritual union with God. The cosmos originated in the creative movement whereby the Absolute diffused itself into the material universe. The subsequent history of evolution has been the divine sport whereby matter has progressively evolved from predominantly material to predominantly spiritual forms. Thus, in the first stage of evolution, nothing but "matter" existed. Yet since the whole of reality—including so-called matter—is infused to varying degrees with Absolute Spirit, the gradual evolution of life from lower forms to higher forms is inevitable. In the second stage of evolution, life appeared, and in the third and current stage, mind or consciousness has emerged.

According to Aurobindo, the next step in evolution is bringing into existence a higher state of consciousness, or Supermind. Humanity therefore finds itself as the torchbearer of further cosmic evolution. It is our cosmic destiny to push beyond the mental to the supramental level of development. Just how this is to come about discloses the very heart of perennialist thinking as well as the distinctive vision of metacausality at the core of Esalen's cultural agenda. On the one hand, this next stage in cosmic evolution is to be achieved by the conscious efforts of humans (a causality from "below"). We can further our personal and collective development by identifying ourselves mentally with the Absolute—not only through reading and study, but also through entering more profound states of awareness such as is achieved in yoga meditation. Because our fundamental human nature is not ontologically limited to the material and mental levels, our ongoing spiritual development is assured. Our lawful movement toward higher levels of mental and spiritual attainment is, however, not solely the consequence of activities set into motion by us. Cosmic evolution proceeds both from below and from above. Absolute Spirit is continuously emanating causal energies into our universe. Supreme energy and bliss come down from above and meet the energy of a human being striving for wisdom. Thus, while human beings strive through spiritual disciplines such as yoga to ascend upward, higher energies also descend from above.

Aurobindo claimed that human consciousness exists at the vortex of the ascending and descending flow of cosmic energy. If we wish to further life's evolutionary surge we must personally learn "to go beyond the mind and the reason. The reason active in our waking consciousness is only a mediator between the subconscient [1] All that we come from in our evolution upwards and the superconscient[,] [2] All towards which we are impelled by that evolution."[5] Any science which restricts itself to the study of physiological or environmental causes misses the ultimate or metacause of all human becoming, which both "pushes from below" and "pulls from above." It is no surprise that Murphy and Price recognized a vague resonance between Aurobindo's cosmology and the views of select Western theorists. As Murphy explained, "What Aurobindo called yoga, what Abe Maslow called self-actualization, what Fritz Perls called organismic integrity, Assagioli called psychosynthesis. All these share basically the same idea—that there is a natural tendency toward development, toward unfoldment, that pervades the universe as well as the human sphere, and that our job is to get behind that and make it conscious."[6]

Murphy's exposure to Aurobindo's ideas proved life altering. They (along with Teilhard de Chardin's similar mystical vision of cosmic evolution) proved instrumental in prompting him to abandon his early interest in medicine and instead to pursue philosophy. While Aurobindo's cosmic vision was the first perennialist influence on Esalen's distinctive notion of causality, the institute soon became a melting pot for other metaphysical philosophies steeped in the perennial tradition. For example, the theosophically grounded ideas of such luminaries as Alan Watts, Jiddu Krishnamuti, and D. T. Suzuki were also prominently featured in early programs at Esalen. An even more influential source, however, was Aldous Huxley, who Price had heard lecture at Berkeley and who corresponded with Price and Murphy at a pivotal juncture in the early planning stages of Esalen, encouraging them to meet personally with his good friend Gerald Heard—a meeting destined to confirm Price and Murphy's confidence in the cultural significance of their vision (see Timothy Miller's chapter for more on the encounter with Heard).

From Huxley and Watts in the early days to Stanislav Grof today, Esalen's most noted and influential "gurus" have had a strong commitment to perennial philosophy.[7] There have, of course, been different versions of perennialism advanced by those close to Esalen.[8] Overall, however, Esalen has consistently provided a forum for those advocating core perennialist principles: 1) that Absolute Spirit is the fundamental essence of the universe in its entirety, including human nature; 2) that the physical universe is a result of a process of emanation or involution of Absolute Spirit, hence Spirit is ontologically prior to matter; 3) that consciousness is fundamental to existence and is not an epiphenomenon; 4) that reality is composed of different layers or levels of being that are hierarchically organized in the "Great Chain of Being"; 5) that there are important nonphysical energies emanating from these other layers or levels that can be tapped for the purpose of stimulating growth and becoming at the human level; 6) that certain altered states of consciousness bring humans into greater rapport with these other layers or levels. Together these principles imparted a distinctive notion of metacausation that directed Esalen's approach to such varied subjects as psychotherapy, education, evolutionary biology, and theoretical models in the natural sciences.

The last of these principles of perennial thought, the connection between altered states of consciousness and knowledge of "higher" levels of the universe, helps explain why the phenomenology of psychedelic experiences was the other principal source of Esalen's distinctive metalanguage. As Murphy has recently explained, "I was not [initially] impelled by any knowledge of or interest in psychedelics, but once we started, there it was."[9] A high percentage of those who were influential in Esalen's early days—Aldous Huxley, Gerald Heard, Humphry Osmond, Alan Watts, John Lilly, Michael Harner, Carlos Casteñeda, Claudio Naranjo, Ram Dass, and Timothy Leary—had strong connections with the psychedelic movement. In fact, the very first seminar ever held at Esalen, titled "Human Potentialities," was led by Jim Fadiman and Willis Harman, who were both at the time studying psychedelic drugs. It came to be accepted wisdom that psychedelics enable us to "enter other domains of consciousness," that they "open the mind and reveal that consciousness creates the world, that physical reality is created out of consciousness and not the opposite. . . . [revealing] that there are realms of tremendous transcendent understanding."[10]

The point here is that the phenomenology of psychedelic experience gave experiential credibility to new understandings of the natural constitution of the universe. Because psychedelic experiences often supported belief that consciousness creates the world, they also encouraged belief in the version of metacausation that postulated an immanent cosmic principle propelling "material" and "efficient" causes from within. And because they seemed to disclose multiple or alternate perspectives that disclose other transcendent realms, they also fostered belief in the version of metacausation that postulated more-than-physical energies that become efficient causes of their own by exerting causal force from without.

It is probably impossible to describe *the* phenomenology of psychedelic experience. Set (the person's belief structure, personality traits, and expectations concerning the experience) and setting (the immediate context or environment) play such an important role that some investigators conclude that all drug experiences can be exhaustively accounted for in cultural terms. Also important, of course, are the precise chemical properties and doses of the specific substances being ingested. Yet for all their potential variability, there are certain common features in the use of both "minor" psychedelics such as marijuana and "major" psychedelics such as mescaline or LSD. A commission appointed by the Canadian government to study the effects of marijuana offered a succinct inventory of those features of the lighter ranges of psychedelic experience that prompt new notions of causality:

> Happiness, increased conviviality, a feeling of enhanced interpersonal rapport and communication, heightened sensitivity to humour, free play of the imagination, unusual cognitive and ideational associations, a sense of extraordinary reality, a tendency to notice aspects of the environment of which one is normally unaware, enhanced visual imagery, an altered sense of time in which minutes may seem like hours, enrichment of sensory experiences, increased personal understanding and religious insight, mild excitement and energy.[11]

These experiential features combine to give individuals a sense of having stepped beyond their ordinary limits. Unleashing what the report calls "unusual cognitive and ideational associations," the use of even a mild psychedelic drug imparts a vivid sense that one is viewing aspects of the universe that elude our normal waking consciousness. William Novak's study of the role that marijuana has played in changing people's worldview amplifies this point. Novak wrote that "for some, marijuana has served as a teacher whose principal lesson has been that life holds multiple forms of reality."[12] Psychedelics provide an experiential introduction to these other forms—including the new understanding of causality they reveal.

The use of psychedelics—ranging from marijuana to mescaline and LSD—produces states that favor the "discovery" of the metacauses of human behavior. The destructuring of those structures of consciousness related to our perception of linear time or our ability to focus attention on separate or discrete sensory information simultaneously makes it possible for us to understand other forms of causation that are typically found in the natural sciences. As Eugene Taylor recently commented in a personal communication to me,

> psychedelic experience has often prompted persons to become interested in models of causality similar to the Buddhist principle of codependent origination because it explains exactly all the acid trips people took. Another answer might be the Hindu concept of kalpas—or mythic aeons—most prosaically expressed in their concentric notion of time. For example, the Hindi word for "day before yesterday,"—*aj kal*—is the same as the word for "day after tomorrow." Hence marijuana users end up becoming Transcendental Meditators, and those who use major psychedelics go into Japanese Zen, Theravada insight meditation, or Tibetan dzochen.[13]

Those influential in shaping Esalen's early vision tended to translate the contours of psychedelic experience into ontological claims that postulated forms of metacausation that ran directly counter to the prevailing cultural visions found in academic psychology or conventional Christian theology. George Leonard, for example, interpreted the fact that psychedelics provided him with new, multiple perspectives as proving the existence of "Another Reality."[14] Alan Watts also placed important ontological significance on the dissolution of the subject-object structure of the normal waking state. Watts argued that the very fact that normal cognitive boundaries dissolve during psychedelic experience is evidence that the very "reality" they purport to represent is itself an illusion.[15] Stanislav Grof, as we have already noted, also suggests that psychedelic experiences afford new glimpses of reality. He argues that the insights from psychedelic states indicate that "the universal process offers not only an infinite number of possibilities for becoming a separate individual, but also an equally rich and ingenious range of opportunities for dissolution of boundaries. . . . [T]his process dissolves all the boundaries and brings about a reunion with Absolute Consciousness."[16] All in all, then, the phenomenology of psychedelic experiences was argued to be sufficient evidence for overturning the "materialistic monism" of Western science. Whereas the materialistic worldview of Western science views consciousness as an epiphenomenon of material causes, psychedelic experiences "strongly suggest that the universe might be a creation of superior cosmic intelligence and consciousness an essential aspects of existence."[17]

Esalen's novel conceptions of causality were making it possible to bring entirely new perspectives to bear upon existing theories in such fields as biology, physics, psychology, and religion. Esalen was championing the need to consider metacauses in any explanation of developmental processes, growth, or wholeness-making activity. These new conceptions of causality were inimical to either orthodox science or orthodox theology in 1962; they challenged the basic assumptions upon which cultural modernism rested. Esalen therefore faced the daunting task of inventing ideas and experiences that would be sufficiently seductive to tempt persons to transgress established cultural boundaries.

INVENTING NEW CULTURAL SPACE

The very formation of Esalen expressed dissatisfaction with existing cultural boundaries. Its founders believed that neither science nor religion was succeeding at awakening the divinity within. Science, to its credit, was furnishing tremendous insight into the causal connections that influence human growth and development. However, science ignored the "ultimate" causes that will propel the next stage in cosmic evolution. Religion, meanwhile, proclaimed faith in the existence of ultimate causation yet considered it blasphemous for persons even to consider willfully availing themselves of extrahuman energy or wisdom.[18] So while science considered concern with metacausation to be lacking in intellectual rigor or credibility, religion considered it heretical. The kinds of concerns at the very heart of Esalen's founding vision were thus culturally taboo. For example, George Leonard noted that the eastern intellectual establishment had little sympathy for the thinking that deliberately transgressed time-honored boundaries separating religious and scientific conceptions of the world. "The good people of the Establishment," Leonard found, "are quite genial in honoring freedom of inquiry and expression. But only up to a certain boundary. Step across that boundary—which has to do with new categories, new ways of perceiving and ordering reality—and the geniality vanishes in the wink of an eye."[19]

It is hard to believe now, but in 1962 the word "spiritual" was not a part of common parlance (particularly among educated people). Esalen's earliest guests viewed the Institute's activities as vehicles for psychological exploration, personal growth, and a sense of cultural liberation—but few would have thought of, much less admit to, being engaged in something spiritual. Most of these guests would, however, have readily admitted to a vague but pervasive sense that something was lacking or incomplete in their lives. While they were for the most part successful in economic and social terms, Esalen's clientele were among the leading cohort of those who found themselves intellectually and emotionally restless, longing for something "more." It was Esalen's particular genius to mold this restlessness into spiritual curiosity and willingness to adopt a new cultural vision.

Esalen's 40-year history illuminates some of the innovative ways in which the era's social restlessness was transformed into a form of the "seeker spirituality" that Robert Wuthnow, Wade Clark Roof, Robert Ellwood, Catherine Albanese, and others have argued now characterizes the religious lives of up to 20 percent of the American population. Esalen succeeded in carving out new cultural territory by disseminating its vision of metacausality in a manner that completely bypassed the institutional practices of academic science and institutional religion. My principal argument is that Esalen successfully transformed cultural malaise into spiritual exploration by providing a metalanguage that relocated concern with biological and psychological development within the framework of cosmic evolution. But its effectiveness at doing so can scarcely be understood without considering at least four of the conduits along which Esalen transmitted this new cultural vision: 1) the sacred space of the Big Sur setting; 2) the offering of weekend retreats and short-term programs; 3) the inclusion of concern for the body as well as the mind; and 4) the ecstasy of altered states of consciousness.

Esalen—unlike most vehicles of countervailing cultural visions (e.g., lecture circuits, books, magazines)—occupied space. Sacred space. Space that naturally elicits receptivity and encourages something along the lines of what William Clebsch calls esthetic spirituality.[20] One is reminded of Paul Tillich's autobiographical reflections of a life "on the boundary" between the church and the academy, between philosophy and theology. Tillich observed that one of the most important influences on his life and work was his time along the seacoast. It provided him with a felt experience of the "infinite bordering on the finite [that] suited my inclination toward the boundary situation and supplied my imagination with a symbol that gave substance to my emotions and creativity to my thought." He went on to note that "the sea also supplied the imaginative element necessary for the doctrines of the Absolute as both ground and abyss of dynamic truth, and of the substance of religion as the thrust of the eternal into finitude."[21]

There is great debate among contemporary scholars of religion about whether space becomes sacred owing to certain ontological qualities adhering to a given locale (the Eliade camp) or due to the ritual activity and verbal constructions of those who use this space in sacred ways.[22] Whatever the resolution of that debate, Esalen's space has long been considered sacred. One frequent visitor to Esalen suggested to me that

> there is something about the place Esalen, the grounds, that gives it a special feel. I think it is something natural, some places evoke those feelings. Esalen Institute happens to be located there, but the sense of sacredness goes deeper than building, people, and organizations. Maybe it's part of natural religion in a Native American sense. If God is immanent, maybe God is more immanent in some places than in others, a great concentration, so to speak. I think this attracts people who are spiritually oriented but unchurched, and some of these people find this atmosphere a good setting for entheogens.[23]

Few other sources of contemporary unchurched spirituality are so associated with a specific location. Attending Esalen links one to a community that spans generations—a community including Native Americans, beatniks, literati, and countercultural rebels who have at this site deliberately violated the boundaries traditionally honored by mainstream American culture.

Weekend retreats and short-term programs were a second component of Esalen's ability to stake out new cultural territory outside the boundaries of existing institutions. These retreats and programs functioned as principal conduits of Esalen's founding vision. They should, in this sense, be viewed as the counterparts of the institutional mechanisms (e.g., seminaries, weekly sermons, ritual, Sunday schools, and devotional readings) through which America's denominational churches and synagogues have transmitted their distinctive cultural visions. Esalen's innovative programs exemplify the sharp difference between what Robert Wuthnow describes as "habitation spirituality" and "seeker spirituality."[24] For one, attendance and participation require a more self-conscious voluntary commitment. This includes taking responsibility for picking and choosing among different messages and themes. Participants are invited to attend not out of obligation to a demanding Heavenly Father but to contribute to their own growth and development. Thus, as sociologist Meredith McGuire has noted of such gatherings, "the 'journey' image is used frequently, for example to describe a weekend workshop or retreat—modern equivalents of popular religious pilgrimages. This kind of 'commitment,' I would argue, is particularly apt for late modern societies with their high degrees of pluralism, mobility and temporally limited social ties, communications, and voluntarism."[25] Attending Esalen's programs also had the effect of networking persons into a kind of experimental community. Attendees shared reading interests, and many of these titles were available in Esalen's bookstore. Esalen thus fostered connections of ideas and persons. To appreciate Esalen's influence on the recent history of American psychology and religion, then, is to appreciate how these connections functioned to promote a distinctive kind of spiritual thinking (as will be illustrated below in the case of Carl Rogers).

A third factor contributing to Esalen's ability to impart a new cultural vision was its attention to the body as a vehicle of spiritual growth. This in part grew out of the baths that very much defined the place and its ritual activities. The baths themselves help dissolve the feelings of boundaries at a personal and societal level—imparting a light mystical experience (perhaps along the lines of Grof's Basic Perinatal Matrix I). Concern for integrating the body into programs of growth and development was also central to Price's and Murphy's abiding interests. One facet of this concern for the body deserves special mention: it expressed in the most concrete way an insistence that spirituality was not about the afterlife or a place called heaven but was a mode of being in the world now. Esalen's eclectic offerings never strayed from this fundamental holism (and its demand that all beliefs and outlooks have a this-worldly pragmatism about them).

The emphasis upon altered states of consciousness (particularly the sustained presence and use of psychedelic drugs) was a fourth factor in Esalen's ability to engender a new cultural vision. The importance of the experiential contours of these altered states for promoting new under-standings of reality has been discussed earlier in this chapter. But it is also important to note that when Esalen opened its doors, there was almost no recognition that other states of consciousness were valuable to human well-being. By providing forums where various mind-body technologies could be discussed, Esalen helped change the intellectual and cultural views of these states. In this regard, it is important to note that Esalen was especially effective in forging a dialogue between Western psychology and Eastern meditation systems (something most of us take for granted now, but this was hardly the case in 1962). Esalen thus succeeded at locating the discussion of altered states in a decidedly spiritual, if not conventionally religious, context. Mysticism was now within the purview of seekers with no ties to biblically based theologies.

Esalen's genius, then, was its uncanny appreciation of the combina-tion of factors that together formed what Peter Berger calls the "plausibil-ity structures" capable of supporting a particular cultural vision. In Esalen's case this was a cultural vision predicated upon belief in the essentially spir-itual nature of all growth and development. The importance of this can not be overstated. In 1962, many educated persons were wholly disenfran-chised from biblical religion. The only vocabulary available to them in their professional lives was that of the secular sciences—a vocabulary fo-cused on the material and efficient causes of events in our lives. Esalen's many programs and workshops gradually incubated a new vocabulary that enabled these persons to reintroduce a spiritual dimension to their under-standing of biological and psychological development. This vocabulary of metacausation finally enabled these professionals to carve out a new cultural territory, the territory of being "spiritual, but not religious."

Documenting precisely how Esalen fostered this reintroduction of ultimate cause language into educated Americans' vocabularies is difficult. Esalen's principal function was to connect persons who might not otherwise interact with one another and to connect ideas from wholly disparate areas of scientific or cultural discourse. Esalen's influence on American psychology, religion, and culture must thus be traced through the history of these connections.

THE CASE OF CARL ROGERS

There is perhaps no better example of how Esalen connections helped create a new American culture of metalanguage than the life and thought of Carl Rogers. Like many of the pioneering figures in the history of American psychology, Rogers was raised in a very conservative Protestant family.[26] While pursuing graduate education in religion, however, Rogers came to a personal crossroads. His deep commitment to personal and intellectual freedom made it impossible for him to continue to profess Christian dogma. He made a radical break from his Christian past and instead undertook training in counseling psychology at Columbia University. From this point forward in his life he became fairly zealous in his attack upon all forms of conventional Christian belief and piety. And from this point forward he would look to the ultimate sources of human well-being within, rather than beyond, human experience.

Rogers was still fairly new to the psychological profession when he attracted national and even international attention as the originator of the client-centered approach to psychotherapy. Though Rogers personally radiated a certain mystic depth, he lacked a vocabulary that would include the consideration of an ultimate cause behind human growth and development. Rogers, of course, had rejected all theological language concerning divine providence or supernatural intervention. His theory instead appeared to embrace the material and efficient cause explanations that were alone deemed acceptable within academic psychology. Rogers marshaled certain experimental evidence to support his claim that every person has an innate biologically grounded impulse toward wholeness and self-actualization. This actualizing tendency is guided by what he termed the "organismic valuing process" that steers individuals toward growth-enhancing experiences. In sharp contrast to Christian theology that accounts for "the Fall" in terms of humanity's disobedience to the commands of a Heavenly Father, Rogers explained that all human misery stems from our tendency to ignore this organismic valuing process in favor of following the dictates of social convention. To Rogers, it followed that successful therapy requires only that the therapist provide a warm, accepting environment so that clients might drop their defensive masks and instead rediscover the full range or their own inner experience. Rogers found that his clients gradually learned to replace the values that society had programmed into them and to trust their impulses toward growth and discovery.

What is so fascinating about Rogers's thought is that in his late career he came to embrace the mystical element that he had been forced to abandon with his rejection of biblical theology. Indeed, slowly but surely Rogers embraced an "ultimate cause" language very similar to the perennial philosophy's notion of cosmic evolution. As Rogers wrote me in 1981, "[T]he notion that a divine force in life might be a struggling force, struggling to express itself through my life and yours, as well as through the physical universe, has always appealed to me." By his late career, Rogers had come into contact with a number of persons who helped him develop a vocabulary that enabled him to situate his psychological concept of the organismic valuing process within a larger metaphysical framework. Rogers ventured that some of his colleagues had suggested to him that the psychological processes he had observed in therapy were themselves grounded in deeper ontological and metaphysical structures. Rogers came to agree with these colleagues and wanted to push this line of thinking even further:

> Thus, when we provide a psychological climate that permits persons to be . . . we are tapping into a tendency which permeates all of organic life as a tendency to become all the complexity of which the organism is capable. And on an even larger scale, I believe we are *tuning in to a potent creative tendency which has formed the universe* . . . and perhaps we are touching the cutting edge of our ability to transcend ourselves, to create new and more spiritual directions in human evolution.[27]

Rogers's eagerness to pursue this cutting edge of our psychological ability to tune into the source of cosmic evolution spurred a newfound fascination with altered states of consciousness, precognition, telepathy, psychic healing, out-of-the-body experiences, trance channeling, and psychedelic experience. The fact that many of his professional contacts were exploring these topics in a scientific way suggested to him that we are "on the verge of discovering a new type of lawful order." It was Rogers's hope that increased knowledge about this lawful order would enable persons to get "in touch with, and grasp the meaning of, this evolutionary flow."[28] The new language Rogers had begun to appropriate had thus enabled him at long last to move beyond the narrow confines of both conventional science and conventional religion.

Most of Rogers's late-career interest in the metacauses of psychological growth can be found in two or three seminal essays.[29] What is striking about these essays is how they reveal the steps Rogers had traveled on his recent intellectual pilgrimage to the culture of metalanguage. He credits several well-known natural scientists (e.g., Albert Szent-Gyoergyi, Jonas Salk, Ilya Priogine, and Magohah Murayama) with helping him to understand scientific causation in a new light, particularly by helping him to recognize "the ever operating trend toward increased order and interrelated complexity evident at both the inorganic and the organic level." And, even more important, he credits seven other persons for helping him push his thinking about just how our individual minds might further participate in this larger formative tendency. All seven had Esalen connections:

• Stanislav Grof, whose studies convinced Rogers that in certain altered states of consciousness "persons feel they are in touch with, and grasp the meaning of this evolutionary flow."[30]

• George Leonard, who provided Rogers with "an almost ecstatic vision of the human species undertaking 'an awesome journey into a higher state of being,' a transformation he regards as inevitable."[31]

• Andrew Weil, who convinced Rogers that the future will belong to "stoned" thinking (i.e., intuitive thinking based on unconscious factors and altered states of consciousness).[32]

• Claudio Naranjo, for helping him to understand the possibility of a convergence between our individual consciousness and the "directional evolutionary process."[33]

• Thomas Hanna, who provided him a vision of "the wholeness of the pulsing, growing human soma—body and mind united—and to the new human mutants who are living that realization, leading us toward a new goal."[34]

• John Lilly, whose work on altered states of consciousness reinforced Rogers's view that in certain states we can become receptive "to a flood experience at a level far beyond that of everyday living."[35]

• Fritjof Capra, whose writings helped Rogers understand a new model for the natural sciences in which "the traditional concepts of space and time, of isolated objects, and of cause and effect lose their meaning . . . [and how] physics and Eastern mysticism are separate but complementary roads to the same knowledge, supplementing each other in providing a fuller understanding of the universe."[36]

It is difficult to identify Esalen's precise role in Rogers's late-career shift to a more overtly spiritual and metaphysical understanding of his life work. He had, of course, visited Esalen on multiple occasions and been moved by its sacred space. In his conversations with Michael Murphy, Rogers appeared deeply intrigued by what was going on at Esalen and tried to absorb as much as possible about what Esalen was offering in its conferences and programs. Like many intellectuals of his generation, Rogers first came to Esalen after having personally rejected organized religion and its language of supernatural intervention. What Rogers's connection with Esalen afforded him was contact with professionals immersed in the culture of metalanguage. This was a culture with which he was quite unfamiliar. Yet over time this language came to assist Rogers in his own journey, his own spiritual growth. Rogers's connections with Esalen spurred his adoption of a language of metacausation that convinced him that we are "on the verge of a great evolutionary-revolutionary leap."[37] This evolutionary leap was one that would enable persons to get "in touch with, and grasp the meaning of, this evolutionary flow"—precisely what

Price and Murphy had hoped to accomplish the day they first opened the doors of the Institute.

THE SIGNIFICANCE AND VIABILITY OF THE VISION

A culture based upon metalanguage renders the universe in a way quite unlike the modernist outlook that dominated American thought in the 1960s. It depicts the world in such a way that different events are expected, different behavior called for. We might, therefore, seek to assess the significance and viability of such a cultural vision. With precisely such a task in mind William James proposed that cultural visions ought to be assessed according to their immediate luminousness, philosophical reasonableness, and moral helpfulness.[38] The issue of the "immediate luminousness" of Esalen's culture of metalanguage would appear to be the most straightforward. While most of the new cultural visions spawned in the early 1960s advocated freedom from political repression, Esalen was advocating what Timothy Leary described as "freedom from the learned, cultural mind. The freedom to expand one's consciousness . . . to the joyous unity of what exists beyond."[39] Esalen unabashedly responded to the era's social anomie by focusing attention on the intrinsic joy of living in harmony with the metacauses of growth and development. Will Schutz's bestseller was aptly titled *Joy*. Alan Watts's "adventures in the chemistry of consciousness" was titled *The Joyous Cosmology*. In a 1966 lecture, George Leonard sought to awaken his Esalen audience to the fact that the heart of human nature is "pure and holy joy."[40] Michael Murphy, the "joyous mystic," as Sam Keen called him, believed that it was Esalen's special mission to expand people's awareness such they might tap into unexpected sources of this pure and holy joy.[41]

We might note that Esalen seemed to have two distinct visions of joy, corresponding to its two views of metacausation (i.e., the metacause of growth and development imparted into life through the immanent Absolute Spirit and the metacause of an influx of higher energies streaming into the human plane from above, as it were). Thus, for example, when Esalen initially embraced encounter groups, it did so largely guided by the first view of metacausation.[42] From the perspective of a cultural vision predicated upon metalanguage, encounter groups remove self-imposed barriers that prevent persons from living in joyous harmony with the ultimate causal power of all growth and development. Yet if I am correct in my argument that Esalen's major function was to promote meta-cause understandings of life, then many of the encounter groups that took place on Esalen's grounds were actually at the far periphery of Price and Murphy's cultural vision. That is, Esalen was expounding a cultural vision that envisioned far more than just freeing persons from cultural restraints. Its ultimate goal was enabling full participation in the progressive move-ment of Absolute Spirit. Not all of those who made presentations or led groups at Esalen shared this deeper vision. This helps explain why Mur-phy and Price were often hurt by the caricatures and criticisms of Esalen in the popular media. Esalen was commonly lampooned for fostering self-absorption and making self-enhancement an end in itself. For Murphy and Price—and for Esalen's cultural vision—the point and purpose of such exploration was always understood to be in the service of "awakening the divinity latent in all things."

Although Esalen promoted views equating joy with the removal of repressive cultural conditioning, it also equated it with the ecstatic expe-rience of receiving causal energies from above. Esalen's speakers and pro-grams have held out the imminent possibility of opening ourselves to the inflow of higher energies that automatically exert growth- and healing-promoting activity. In this sense, Esalen's conception of joy builds upon what William James called a "piece-meal" supernaturalism whereby ex-tramundane energies occasionally enter into and exert sanative effects within our natural universe. Seeking joy thus requires us to adopt a boldly metaphysical posture toward life and to cultivate altered states of con-sciousness conducive to ecstatic encounters with higher metaphysical en-ergies. The joy occasioned through such ecstatic encounters with more-than-physical reality should properly be deemed one of life's highest intrinsic values, regardless of whether it serves any further utilitarian pur-pose. Thus, on this count, Esalen's culture of metalanguage seems to have considerable significance in the recent history of American psychology and religion.

Second, we might attempt to measure the overall philosophical rea-sonableness of Esalen's theoretical contributions. By bringing the per-spective of metacausation (both in terms of an immanent cosmic principle and of more-than-physical causal energies) to psychological discussions, Esalen swayed American psychology from an exclusive emphasis on empirically verifiable "efficient" causes. Simply because many theories concerning metacausation do no not lend themselves to experimental validation does not in and of itself jeopardize their scientific legitimacy. We might distinguish between two types of evidence in scientific reasoning: procedural evidence (i.e., philosophical argumentation, consistency or coherence with observed phenomena, compatibility with agreed-upon or accepted knowledge, ability to generate a comprehensive worldview) and validating evidence (i.e., experimental validation of a theory's predicted relationship between cause and effect).[43] Many Esalen-connected humanistic and transpersonal theories (as with theories in geology, physical anthropology, and astrophysics) are built squarely upon impressive forms of procedural evidence. True, they are probably not amenable to the kinds of validating experimentation that theories focusing solely upon efficient causation enjoy. But, again, the absence of validating evidence is not in itself fatal for the construction of intellectually defensible theories.

Jorge Ferrer has recently offered a helpful critique of transpersonal theory (and by implication many Esalen-connected efforts to construct theories of metacausation). He notes that the metalanguage of perennialist philosophy fosters "a subtle devaluation of the material world as illusory."[44] A corollary of this is the tendency of metacausal theories to privilege various altered states of consciousness at the expense of the normal waking state of consciousness. A good many Esalen-connected theorists suggest that the normal waking state is illusory, yet they rarely say the same of the kinds of states that Stanislav Grof would call "holotropic." There is, furthermore, a tendency for metacausal theories to assume a correlation between alternative mental states and alternative realities. It would be far safer for those developing a new metalanguage to stay closer to the purview of empiricism and argue for the functional value—not the truth—of the states of consciousness and causal forces they seek to draw attention to.

Connected with the tendency of metalanguage to privilege some states and some causal forces over others is the tendency to sever discussions of metacauses from other contexts of human functioning. Even if there is an immanent principle of sacred power underlying our actualizing tendencies or under some conditions higher energies enter into and exert causal power within the human organism, this does not vitiate the need to consider the other causal forces impinging upon the human organism. Metalanguage is characteristically bereft of insights from evolutionary biology, sociobiology, and functionalist psychology; as a consequence, it is characteristically bereft of a full appreciation of the full range of causal influences and developmental schedules affecting human growth and development. Severed from these theoretical connections, the culture of metalanguage all too readily presents a dangerously superficial vision of human progress and envisions everything in the universe as subject to human volition.[45]

It is also important to assess the philosophical reasonableness of Esalen's contributions to recent American religious thought. From the outset, Esalen realized that metaphysics can only be as intellectually compelling as the physics upon which it is predicated. Toward this end Esalen has inquired broadly and deeply into the empirical conditions under which humanity finds itself aligned with the metacauses of growth and development. The result has been nothing short of revolutionary. As William James said almost 100 years ago, "Let empiricism once become associated with religion, as hitherto, through some strange misunderstanding, it has been associated with irreligion, and I believe that a new era of religion as well as philosophy will be ready to begin."[46] Esalen provided a forum for empirical inquiries into the metadimension of human experience. Interdisciplinary investigations of meditation, consciousness, paranormal phenomena, and integral practice all sidestepped materialistic science and conventional theology en route to mapping the metaphysical boundaries of human experience. And for this reason Esalen found itself at the cutting edge of the seeker style of spirituality that now informs as many as one in five adult Americans.

A third and final approach to assessing Esalen's contributions to American culture is in relationship to its moral helpfulness—the way its beliefs and practices have shaped human lives. All too often commentators have leapt to the easy observation that Esalen's spiritual and psychological teachings prompt persons to become self-absorbed, preoccupied with their own personal growth. Indeed, many Esalen-connected theorists have romanticized our biological nature and assumed a predetermined harmony between all organisms. As a result, many of these theorists have preached the facile gospel that liberation from cultural or biological restraints is a necessary and sufficient cause of healthy development.

These criticisms are well taken. Most stem from the failure to integrate theoretically the interaction between metacauses and the broader web of causal influences described by comparative biology, sociobiology, and functional psychology. Thus, these criticisms do not so much detract from Esalen's fundamental agenda as they point to important work that still lies ahead.

My principal thesis, however, is that nearly all of the criticisms traditionally leveled against Esalen miss the fundamental point that the Institute's focal concern has never been with self-exploration per se. Instead, the Institute's guiding mission has been the exploration of ways through which humans might better connect themselves with the metacauses of growth and development. For this reason, Esalen's labors must be judged by a very different criterion: the degree to which its labors have helped Americans free themselves from accustomed scientific or religious ways of thinking to affirm for themselves what Emerson called "an original relationship to the universe."

The metalanguage Esalen helped put into circulation over the past forty years has contributed to a new cultural and religious outlook distinguished by four defining traits. First, it encourages persons—in the words of the Buddha—to "be lamps unto themselves." Spiritual maturity requires taking responsibility for one's own beliefs. Esalen championed intellectual honesty and integrity at a time when America's churches appeared to equate religious faith with the acceptance of doctrines without consideration of their coherence with other known truths. The language of metacausation it helped put into general circulation among contemporary Americans can thus be accredited with fostering both psychological and spiritual maturity among a significant sector of the general population.

Second, Esalen made this life—not the afterlife—the focus of spiritual discourse. Esalen has deemed ideas to be spiritual to the degree that they quicken life in persons and in society. While Esalen's concern with metacausation has focused a great deal of attention on higher realities, these alternate realities have never been proposed as ends in themselves.

Third, Esalen has tended to equate spirituality (coherence with metacausation) with participation in wholeness-making and world-building activities. Insofar as life can itself be defined as activity that runs counter to the second law of thermodynamics, Esalen has endeavored to show how coherence with metacauses enables persons to contribute to the cosmic process of wholeness-making and world-building. In this way, Esalen's introduction of metalanguage to psychological thinking distinguishes itself from traditional scientific (viewing the self as bound by entropy) and traditional religious (viewing the self as separated from divine causality) outlooks. Simultaneously, Esalen's culture of metalanguage has been geared to transforming persons into active agents of this wider cosmic process of wholeness-making and world-building.

Fourth, Esalen has suggested that full human maturity requires a certain openness to the metaphysical; a willingness to entertain the presence and activity of causal forces that cannot be reduced to the efficient-cause language of the natural sciences or the language of divine intervention of biblical religion. Esalen has, furthermore, championed the view that such openness to the metaphysical not only occasions qualitatively distinct kinds of joy but also promotes optimal levels of psychological health.

It has been Esalen's special role to host conversations that have sought to show how these four traits of metalanguage are simultaneously the defining traits of full psychological health and full spiritual maturity. It is unclear whether these conversations have as yet ushered in a new evolutionary era in human culture. But it is clear that they have made it possible for a significant sector of the American population to move beyond the limitations of previous cultural boundaries and forge their own original relationship to the universe.

NOTES

1. See Robert Ellwood's discussion of modernism in *The Sixties Spiritual Awakening: American Religion Moving from Modern to Postmodern* (New Brunswick, N.J.: Rutgers University Press, 1994), 10–18.

2. Some of the most helpful discussions of "causal explanation" in modern social science are found in three books by Joseph Rychlak: *A Philosophy of Science for Personality Theory* (Boston: Houghton Mifflin Company, 1968), *The Psychology of Rigorous Humanism* (New York: John Wiley & Sons, 1977), and *In Defense of Human Consciousness* (Washington, D.C.: American Psychological Association, 1997). Rychlak's

basic thesis is that although final-cause explanations are not compatible with the kinds of empirical verification typically associated with scientific inquiry, they are nonetheless compatible with certain kinds of scientific explanation with high standards of plausibility and coherence. In fact, Rychlak goes so far as to argue that "humanistic psychology is simply impossible without teleological description of human behavior" and must thus "readmit formal-and final-cause considerations as legitimate in their own right" (496).

3. William James, *The Varieties of Religious Experience* (Cambridge, Mass.: Harvard University Press, 1985), 406.

4. See Allan Hunt Badiner, "A Buddhist-Psychedelic History of Esalen Institute: An Interview with Founder Michael Murphy and President George Leonard," in Allan Hunt Badiner and Alex Grey, eds., *Zig Zag Zen* (San Francisco: Chronicle Books, 2002), 77.

5. Sri Aurobindo, cited in Sarvepali Radhakrishnan and Charles Moore, eds., *A Source Book in Indian Philosophy* (Princeton, N.J.: Princeton University Press, 1957), 581.

6. Michael Murphy, cited in Neal Vahle, "Esalen Celebrates Its Silver Anniversary," *New Realities,* September/October 1987, 31.

7. Stanislav Grof, who was in residence at Esalen for many years, recently commented that his research in the field of transpersonal psychology "is in far-reaching agreement with the image of reality found in the great spiritual and mystical traditions of the world," which he defined as "the perennial philosophy." See *The Cosmic Game* (Albany: State University of New York Press, 1998), 3.

8. The best discussion of the role of the perennial tradition in shaping the field of transpersonal psychology (closely linked with Esalen) is Jorge Ferrer's *Revisioning Transpersonal Theory* (Albany: State University of New York Press, 2002). Ferrer, who argues convincingly that "transpersonal theory was born in a perennialist world," shows just how fully perennialism has shaped transpersonal theory and may be responsible for its conceptual and practical limitations.

9. Michael Murphy, cited in Badiner, "A Buddhist-Psychedelic History of Esalen Institute," 78.

10. Jack Kornfield, "Psychedelic Experience and Spiritual Practice, A Buddhist Perspective," in Badiner and Grey, eds., *Zig Zag Zen,* 59.

11. Canadian Government's Commission of Inquiry, *The Non-Medical Use of Drugs* (New York: Penguin Books, 1971), 117.

12. William Novak, *High Culture: Marijuana in the Lives of Americans* (New York: Alfred A. Knopf, 1980), 9.

13. E-mail communication from Eugene Taylor, August 1, 2002.

14. George Leonard, cited in Badiner, "A Buddhist-Psychedelic History of Esalen Institute," 81.

15. See Alan Watts, *The Joyous Cosmology: Adventures in the Chemistry of Consciousness* (New York: Vintage Books, 1965), 40.

16. Grof, *The Cosmic Game,* 79.

17. Ibid., 268.

18. Both Mary Douglas and Mircea Eliade have observed that religious taboos often reveal fear of the unpredictability of the consequences that might result from a two-way contact with divinity. This, as I have argued in *Religion and Wine* (Knoxville:

University of Tennessee Press, 1996) and *Stairways to Heaven* (Boulder: Westview Press, 2000), helps explain part of the antipathy of established religions to mind-altering substances.

19. George Leonard, *Walking on the Edge of the World* (Boston: Houghton Mifflin Co., 1988), 248.

20. William Clebsch, *American Religious Thought* (Chicago: University of Chicago Press, 1973). In this highly regarded book, Clebsch argues that over and against the moralistic thrust of American Protestantism has been an enduring "esthetic spirituality" centered on developing "a consciousness of the beauty of living in harmony with divine things—in a word, being at home in the universe" (xvi).

21. Paul Tillich, *On the Boundary* (New York: Charles Scribner's Sons, 1966), 18.

22. See Peter Williams's helpful review essay on "Sacred Space in North America," *Journal of the American Academy of Religion* 70 (September 2002): 593–609.

23. E-mail communication from a frequent participant at Esalen programs related to the use of psychedelics.

24. Robert Wuthnow, *After Heaven: Spirituality in America Since the 1950s* (Berkeley: University of California Press, 1998), 136.

25. Meredith McGuire, "Mapping Contemporary American Spirituality: A Sociological Perspective," *Christian Spirituality Bulletin* 5 (Spring 1997): 5.

26. See my extended discussion of the religious dimension of Rogers's life and thought in "Carl Rogers, Religion, and the Role of Psychology in American Culture," *Journal of Humanistic Psychology* 22 (1982): 21–32. See also Martin Van Kalmthout, "The Religious Dimension of Rogers's Work," *Journal of Humanistic Psychology* 35 (1995): 23–38.

27. Carl Rogers, *A Way of Being* (Boston: Houghton Mifflin, 1980), 137.

28. Ibid., 228.

29. See Carl Rogers, "The Formative Tendency," *Journal of Humanistic Psychology* 18 (1978): 23–26; Rogers, "The Foundations of a Person-Centered Approach" in *A Way of Being,* 113–136; and "The Emerging Person: A New Revolution," in Richard I. Evans, *Carl Rogers: The Man and His Ideas* (New York: E. P. Dutton, 1975).

30. Rogers, "The Foundations of a Person-Centered Approach," 128.

31. Rogers, "The Emerging Person," 153.

32. Ibid.

33. Rogers, "The Formative Tendency," 25.

34. Rogers, "The Emerging Person," 153.

35. Rogers, "Foundations of a Person-Centered Approach," 122.

36. Ibid, 130.

37. Rogers, "The Emerging Person," 175.

38. James, *The Varieties of Religious Experience*, 23.

39. Timothy Leary, "Foreword" to Alan Watts's *The Joyous Cosmology*, xx.

40. Cited in Eugene Taylor's chapter "Esalen and the Counterculture Movement of the 1960s," in Taylor, *Shadow Culture: Psychology and Spirituality in America* (Washington, D. C.: Counterpoint, 1999), 236.

41. It is interesting to note that Michael Murphy speculated on the psychobiographical origins of his continuing pursuit of joy in an interview for *The New Yorker* (January 5, 1976): "My mother in particular had this gift of buoyant *joy.* . . . There

was a lot of tension in the family, too. Stormy days and sunny days, light and darkness. But through it all my parents' fidelity to each other and to us held the pain and the *joy* together and contributed, I think, to my sense of a happiness and *a meaning behind all the contrary appearances*. . . . When I was about fourteen, I began deliberately to work out a philosophy to deal with this. It became a kind of daily ritual to work at it while I walked to school—to try to come to terms with this incredible sense I had that *joy* was lurking, that there was such richness and beauty laid up at the core of life" (emphasis added; p. 32).

42. Most of the members of encounter groups operating at Esalen believed that by removing the repressive constraints imposed by culture, they were simultaneously unleashing the creativity innately present in the whole of nature. Thus, Gestalt philosophy connected with many Esalen encounter groups that were operated on the basis of a metacause ontology to the degree that it assumed that part-processes are determined by the intrinsic nature of the whole and that organisms have a natural tendency to move toward wholeness.

43. See Rychlak, *A Philosophy of Science for Personality Theory*, 74–94.

44. Jorge Ferrer, *Revisioning Transpersonal Psychology*, 82.

45. These critical observations are made clearly in Walter Anderson's *The Upstart Spring* (Reading, Mass.: Addison-Wesley, 1983), 294.

46. William James, *A Pluralistic Universe* (New York: Dutton, 1971), 270.

MICHAEL MURPHY AND THE NATURAL HISTORY OF SUPERNORMAL HUMAN ATTRIBUTES

Ann Taves

While scholars have paid some attention to the Esalen Institute at Big Sur, they have paid little or no attention to Esalen's research arm, the Esalen Center for Theory and Research (CTR). These two faces of Esalen are rather different. While the Web site for the Institute entices the browser into a site of personal transformation and growth, both literally and figuratively, the Web site for the Center invites scholars and researchers to participate in various research initiatives on topics such as the survival of life after death, integral capitalism, and evolutionary theory.[1] If the Esalen Institute at Big Sur represents the practical, experiential side of Esalen, the CTR represents its more intellectual and theoretical side. More to the point, the work of the CTR reflects in a fairly direct way the intellectual interests of Esalen cofounder Michael Murphy. This is particularly the case with the new initiative on the further evolution of human nature, which is a direct outgrowth of Murphy's most significant work, *The Future of the Body*, published in 1992. While cultural historians have paid some attention to the Esalen Institute, they have not attended to Michael Murphy as a thinker or the place of his research agenda within a larger intellectual frame of reference.

Murphy himself has articulated a clear view of where his research agenda fits into a larger frame of reference in interviews following the publication of the book and on the CTR Web site. In these contexts, he has described himself as pursuing "a natural history of supernormal human attributes" or "a natural history of extraordinary functioning."[2] In the book itself, he used the terms "extraordinary or metanormal functioning" and located his research in relation to that of Frederic Myers, William James, and Herbert Thurston, whom he described as helping "to create a new kind of natural history, as it were, showing that specimens of extraordinary functioning can be collected for comparative analysis."[3] In more recent formulations, he describes the "natural history" he is pursuing as "analogous to natural history in the life sciences in that it systematically and critically compares items of supernormal human experience (rather than plant or animal specimens) in a broadly empirical manner, collecting data from all relevant fields."[4]

On the CTR Web site, Murphy locates his research on the future evolution of human nature in relation to "groups such as the British and American Societies of Psychical Research and individuals such as William James, Frederic Myers, and Abraham Maslow."[5] In his most recent formulation, he is more expansive, including "the German and British mesmerists, such as Justinus Kerner [for more on Kerner, see Wouter Hanegraaff's chapter in this volume] and James Esdaile; Frederic Myers and other psychical researchers, pioneering psychologists such as Abraham Maslow and William James, and religious scholars who have studied the siddhis of Hindu-Buddhist lore, the charisms of Roman Catholic mystics [i.e., Herbert Thurston], and the 'adornments' of Sufi ecstatics."[6] In personal conversation, Murphy stresses that when it comes to research on the supernormal, he would put William James and Frederick Myers at the top of the list, adding, "I have to put Herbert Thurston up there, too. He had a big influence on digging this stuff up."[7]

In the book, he described the natural history of extraordinary functioning inaugurated by Myers, James, and Thurston as a "broken lineage" and tacitly positioned his own work as an effort to restore it. He now explicitly locates himself in this lineage on the CTR Web site, acknowledging as he does so that this is a lineage in the making, one which has not yet "coalesced into a universally recognized lineage of inquiry comparable to the mainstream sciences." His explicit aim at this point is to "promote such a lineage through exploratory gatherings of graduate students and experts in relevant fields, a publications series, an empirical research agenda, and internet dissemination."[8]

In this chapter, I want to explore what it means for Murphy to describe his project as a natural history of the extraordinary and to position himself in a lineage that includes Myers, James, and Thurston. Following a lead proffered by Diane Jonte-Pace in an essay on William James, I want to locate Murphy's efforts in relation to recent work on "natural history" as a modern genre and—moving between Murphy and his acknowledged precursors—explore the relationship between this genre, with its emphasis on collection, classification, and explanation, and the traditions from which his "specimens" have been extracted. I will argue that the relationship between traditional natural histories and the new kind of natural history of extraordinary functioning promoted by Murphy is largely metaphoric, both at the level of the collection (specimens) and at the level of explanation (evolution). Alternatively, the lineage in which Murphy situates himself might be understood as one that seeks to bridge the worlds of science and religion in light of two centuries of experimentation with altered states of consciousness.

"A LINEAGE OF INQUIRY"

The lineage in which Murphy locates himself is best understood as an intellectual lineage or perhaps a research tradition or, as he puts it, "a lineage of inquiry," rather than a lineage of practice, although Murphy is attempting, as we will see, to reintroduce a practice dimension.[9] When we consider Myers, James, Thurston, and Murphy as members of an lineage of inquiry, two common features stand out: their involvement with or interest in the work of the Society for Psychical Research and, following in Myers's footsteps, their interest in cataloguing the supernormal capacities of the human person.

Frederic W. H. Myers (1843–1901), the son of an Anglican clergyman, was educated in classics at Trinity College, Cambridge, during the 1860s and by the end of that decade had, through a slow and agonizing process, lost his faith.[10] In 1874, he persuaded his friend Henry Sidgwick to join him in organizing an informal organization for investigating the claims of Spiritualist mediums.[11] Myers, along with Henry Sidgwick and Edmond Gurney, was involved in the founding of the British Society for Psychical Research (SPR) in 1882. The aim of the Society was "to investigate that large body of debateable phenomena designated by such terms as mesmeric, psychical and spiritualistic."[12]

The Society's first major publication, apart from its *Proceedings*, was *Phantasms of the Living* (1886), based on some 400 accounts of "crisis apparitions" collected by Myers, Gurney, and Frank Podmore.[13] In these accounts, as Gauld explains, "a certain person, the *percipient*, sees the figure, or hears the voice, of another person (in the majority of cases well known to him), whom we will call the *agent*. It transpires that at or about the time when the percipient thought he saw the agent, or thought he heard his voice, the agent was in a totally different place, and was undergoing some singular crisis in his affairs—generally death." The thesis of the book, as articulated by Gurney and Myers in the *Proceedings* in 1884, was that "crisis apparitions are best interpreted as *hallucinations* generated in the percipient by the receipt of a *telepathic* 'message' from the dying agent." *Phantasms* can reasonably be said to mark the beginning of the lineage to which Murphy is heir. As Gauld states, with telling allusion to the tradition of natural histories, "to pass from even the ablest of previous works to *Phantasms of the Living* is like passing from a medieval bestiary or herbal to Linnaeus' *Systema Naturae*."[14] When Gurney died in 1888, possibly due to suicide, the Sidgwicks (Henry and Eleanor), Myers, and Podmore took over much of the work.

William James (1842–1910) was the most prominent member of the American Society for Psychical Research, founded in 1884. James was friends with Gurney, whom he met in 1882, and was close friends with Frederic Myers until Myers's death in 1901. Richard Hodgson, a student of Sidgwick, took over the management of the American Society in 1887. While the English researchers spent considerable time investigating mediums both before and after the founding of the SPR, William James discovered Mrs. Piper, the most notable medium investigated by either society, in 1884, following a lead from his mother-in-law. Hodgson headed up the work with Mrs. Piper after his arrival in 1887 and kept detailed records of her séances for many years beginning in the early 1890s. According to Gauld, "[N]early everyone who had extensive dealings with Mrs. Piper became convinced that she possessed supernormal powers; even Frank Podmore, the S.P.R.'s severest skeptic."[15]

In James's view, Myers's primary contribution to the SPR was theoretical rather than experimental. In a series of articles on automatic writing published in the *Proceedings* in the late 1880s, Myers brought together research the Society had done on presumptively normal subjects with that of French experimental psychologists, such as Pierre Janet, on clinical cases. Myers outlined his theory of subliminal consciousness in the *Proceedings* in 1892. His understanding of the mind as "multiplex" or "fissiparous" and, thus, capable of generating multiple centers of consciousness even in healthy individuals provided the chief alternative to the explanations of the Spiritualists (spirit communication) and the clinicians (pathological dissociation). This theory, as I have argued elsewhere, provided James with a psychological explanation for a variety of religious experiences in which persons subjectively experienced a presence that they took to be an external power.[16]

While, as Diane Jonte-Pace has argued, James's *Varieties of Religious Experience* can definitely be located in the lineage to which Murphy is heir,[17] Myers's posthumously published magnum opus *Human Personality and Its Survival of Bodily Death* (1903) is, in my view, a more direct precursor of Murphy's *Future of the Body. Human Personality,* which built upon *Phantasms of the Living,* synthesized much of the work done by the SPR between 1886 and 1900 and in many ways marked the conceptual high-water mark of the SPR's efforts. In contrast to *The Varieties,* which used psychical research to account for certain types of religious experience, *Human Personality,* like the *Future of the Body,* both catalogues and makes a case for supernormal human abilities.

Herbert Thurston (1856–1939) was a Roman Catholic historian and a member of the Society of Jesus known for much of his career for his writings on the history of liturgical and devotional practices. Starting in 1909, he also devoted attention to Christian Science, Theosophy, Spiritualism, and the physical phenomena of mysticism.[18] Thurston's contact with spiritualist phenomena went back to his childhood. In the mid-1860s, when he was eight or nine, his father, a physician on the island of Guernsey, "became interested in hypnotism, or as it was then more commonly called, mesmerism" and a friend of his father performed mesmeric experiments in the Thurstons' home.[19] While a seminarian in the late 1880s, Thurston delivered a lecture on "mesmerism, somnambulism, and thought-transference, in . . . which he took pains to deny that these were all to be explained as due to diabolical causes."[20] In 1899, his friend and fellow Jesuit George Tyrrell wrote him that he would like to join the Society for Psychical Research but would not do so unless Thurston joined with him. His biographer writes that "though Thurston did not join the Society for Psychical Research until 1919, he seems to have kept in touch with their doings through his friendship with Everard Feilding, for his first published writing on spiritualism was an account . . . of Feilding's Queen's Hall lecture on the doings of the medium Eusapia Palladino."[21]

Shortly before his death, Thurston revised his articles on the physical phenomena of mysticism for publication as a book. In the opening chapter, Thurston made it clear that he believed that the "records of Catholic mysticism" provided an important addition to the evidence so far examined by psychical researchers. He noted that

> [in] the average Saint's Life of Italian origin, even when it is based, as is often the case, upon the depositions of the witnesses in the process of Beatification, no exact references are supplied, and no indication is afforded of the value of these sources, or of the nature of the testimony, or of the circumstances under which it was given. . . . The result is certainly unfortunate, for the evidence accumulated and relatively easy [sic] of access in the processes of beatification and canonization, printed with the sanction of the Congregation of Rites, is often more remarkable, and notably better attested, than any to be found in the *Proceedings of the Society for Psychical Research*.[22]

"A NATURAL HISTORY OF THE SUPERNORMAL"

As already noted, Murphy credited "Frederic Myers, William James, Herbert Thurston and other scholars [with] . . . creat[ing] a new kind of natural history, as it were, showing that specimens of extraordinary functioning can be collected for comparative analysis. Like naturalists, who by gathering biological specimens helped reveal the fact of evolution, these researchers have prepared the way for new understandings of our human potential."[23] Just as naturalists extract living specimens from their native habitat and display the preserved specimens in a new configuration in order to make a scientific point, so too Murphy followed Myers, James, and Thurston in extracting "specimens of extraordinary functioning" from the contexts in which they were embedded, preserving them textually and arranging them in order to make a comparative point. Although there is some overlap between the "specimens" included in their various "collections," each collection is arranged differently. As is the case with natural history museums, each collection can be "read" in order to ascertain the larger point that the collection is intended to make.

Specimens of Extraordinary Functioning

Murphy's use of "specimens" is metaphoric. Where natural historians traditionally collected whole organisms, Murphy and his predecessors collected instances of unusual human functioning under various rubrics. In *Future of the Body*, Murphy used "extraordinary, or metanormal, functioning" to characterize the "specimens" that he had collected. As far as I know, the phrase "extraordinary functioning" is Murphy's. He indicates that George Leonard suggested the word "metanormal." He used the terms interchangeably in *Future of the Body* to refer to "human functioning that in some respect radically surpasses the functioning typical of most people living today."[24] In more recent formulations, perhaps out of an increased desire to locate himself in a lineage of inquiry, Murphy tends to use the term "supernormal," a term coined by Frederic Myers.[25]

Myers introduced the term "supernormal" in an essay published in the *Proceedings* in 1885. He repeated his original definition in the introductions to *Phantasms of the Living* and *Human Personality and Its Survival of Bodily Death*, where the term is also used. He coined the word, he indicated, "on the analogy of *abnormal*," to refer to "phenomena which are *beyond what usually happens—beyond*, that is, in the sense of suggesting unknown psychical laws." He went on to elaborate:

> When we speak of abnormal phenomenon we do not mean one which *contravenes* natural laws, but one which exhibits them in an unusual or inexplicable form. Similarly by a supernormal phenomenon I mean, not one which *overrides* natural laws, for I believe no such phenomenon to exist, but one which exhibits the action of laws higher, in a psychical aspect, than are

discerned in action in everyday life. By *higher* (either in a psychical or a physiological sense) I mean 'apparently belonging to a more advanced stage of evolution.' "[26]

In the late 1880s, Myers added that "[t]he word 'supernormal' is . . . meant to beg as few questions as possible; and so far as it connotes any theory as to the source or nature of apparently transcendent powers, it implies a disposition to seek the origin of those powers in some continuance of the same evolutionary process by which we explain—so far as explanation is possible—such powers as we admittedly do possess."[27] Such a formulation is in evident continuity with Murphy's "explorations of the further evolution of human nature."

The "phantasms" in the title of *Phantasms of the Living* referred to a subset of supernormal phenomena. Under this heading, the authors "propose[d] to . . . deal with all classes of cases where there is reason to suppose that the mind of one human being has affected the mind of another, without speech uttered, or word written, or sign made; has affected it, that is to say, by other means than through the recognised channels of sense." Under this heading they included instances of "telepathy"—another term coined by Myers—and "apparitions of . . . persons . . . still living . . . though they may be on the very brink and border of physical dissolution." These apparitions, Myers wrote, "are themselves extremely various in character; including not visual phenomena alone, but auditory, tactile, or even purely ideational and emotional impressions."[28] This entire range of phenomena, in other words, counted as specimens of phantasms.

When Herbert Thurston titled his collection of essays *The Physical Phenomena of Mysticism,* he borrowed a term commonly employed by psychical researchers to describe the nonmental supernormal phenomena associated with spiritualist mediums. Reported phenomena included the elongation of the body, levitation, materialization of spirits, the playing of musical instruments, the movement of objects, raps, and table-tipping.[29] The physical phenomena of mysticism discussed by Thurston included levitation, bodily elongation, stigmata, telekinesis, the odor of sanctity, and the incorruption of the body. In *Future of the Body,* Murphy includes a wide range of supernormal phenomena, both mental and physical.

The sources of the specimens collected shifts from collection to collection. *Phantasms of the Living* was based on accounts of "apparitions at or after death, and other abnormal occurrences" solicited from the general public. While Gurney, Myers, and Podmore were eager to investigate any number of phenomena—clairvoyance, haunted houses, spiritualistic phenomena, and so on—telepathy was the subject where the evidence seemed rich enough "to afford at least a solid groundwork for further inquiry."[30] Thurston, as already noted, focused on the beatification and canonization records of Roman Catholic saints, believing that the evidence of supernormal physical phenomena provided by these sources were better documented than any yet generated by the SPR. Murphy gathered evidence of supernormal phenomena from a variety of sources. He relied heavily on material collected by psychical researchers and by Thurston. To that he added more recent research drawn from medicine, anthropology, and religious studies.[31] Like his predecessors, Murphy drew much of his material from clinical, crisis, and religious contexts. Unlike his predecessors, Murphy also collected evidence from the world of sports. This is a new source of data and one that reflects Murphy's lifelong interests.[32]

Gurney, Myers, Thurston, and Murphy all evidence a high degree of concern with respect to the quality of their evidence. Gurney and Myers rejected most of the previously collected testimony of spontaneously occurring telepathy because it did not come up to their standards. According to Gurney, "The prime essentials of testimony in such matters—authorities, names, dates, corroboration, the *ipsissima verba* of the witnesses— have one or all been lacking; and there seems to have been no appreciation of the strength of the *a priori* objections which the evidence has to overmaster, nor of the possible sources of error in the evidence itself."[33] Thurston, as already noted, put forth the evidence from canonization proceedings precisely because it was so well documented. Murphy refers to three categories of evidence, ranked on the basis of reliability, and indicates that he draws only from the two more-reliable categories.[34]

A New Kind of Natural History

Murphy followed Myers, James, and Thurston in extracting "specimens of extraordinary functioning" from the contexts in which they were embedded, preserving them—so to speak—textually and rearranging them in order to make a comparative point. In so doing, Murphy consciously and the others quasi-consciously adapted the methods of natural history to a new sort of "specimen." In contrast to traditional specimens, which were, generally speaking, physical things—parts or individuals that exemplified a whole—the specimens collected by Murphy and his predecessors were phenomena—that is, occurrences in which something allegedly out of the ordinary had taken place. While I will return to this important difference later, at this point it is more crucial to observe that neither material nor metaphoric specimens exist as such independent of a research agenda or collection plan. By definition, specimens are things—literal or metaphoric—that are extracted from life by a researcher in light of the researcher's agenda. Apart from such an agenda, specimens qua specimens do not exist as such. The idea of a specimen, in other words, presupposes that things have been *extracted* from various places according to an agenda set by a researcher or collector.

Extraction

In constituting their collections, Myers, Thurston, and Murphy each made particular note of issues related to extracting "data" from religious contexts for comparative purposes. Myers noted that because of Christianity's dominance in Europe, certain questions, such as the belief in survival of life after death, had been taken as matters of faith and, as a result, experimental inquiry had been barred. "The Christian Church . . . absorbed the question into theology, and . . . treated theology as based on tradition and intuition, not on fresh experiment."[35] The increasing interest in the "comparative study of religion" was, for Myers, the chief sign of progress in this regard. For it was only with the emergence of comparative approaches that psychical researchers were able "to disengage, in a generalised form, the chief problems with which our 'psychical' science, if such could be established, would be imperatively called on to deal."[36]

Myers expected that psychical research would have a direct bearing on the underlying plausibility of revealed religions more generally, not on specific doctrines. For any revealed religion to be plausible, he said, "we have to assume, first, that human testimony to supernormal facts may be trustworthy; and secondly, that there is something in the nature of man which is capable of responding to—I may say participating in—these supernormal occurrences." Psychical research, in Myers's view, was well positioned to provide evidence that either supported or undermined these assumptions and, thus, the overall plausibility of revelation.

Thurston faced other issues. In a certain sense, his interest in the Catholic canonization proceedings made the task of extracting data easy, since the Catholic Church, perhaps more than any other tradition, had demonstrated a real interest in scrutinizing the evidence for claims of unusual physical phenomena over the centuries. As Murphy observed,

> No other tradition has collected and subjected [supernormal phenomena] to the appraisal that the Catholic Church has in its canonization proceedings. . . . Out of this has come a mass of evidence for these various holy powers or *charisms*. In terms of winnowed data, that body of evidence is unique. . . . There is probably a more complex psychology or metapsychology in Hinduism and Buddhism, but there has never been such a collection of data as the Catholic Church provides.[37]

Nonetheless, as a Jesuit historian writing in the wake of the condemnation of modernism, including the condemnation of one of his closest friends, Thurston threaded his way through this documentation with particular care. While he was open to comparing particular physical phenomena in the Catholic evidence with the evidence of physical phenomena discussed by psychical researchers, he limited his comparisons to matters that the Church deemed inessential to faith and relentlessly refused to theorize about the commonalities that he observed lest such theories have implications that might involve more sensitive topics, such as the Church's supernatural understanding of miracles. Thurston, in other words, only extracted data for comparative purposes that the Church had already been willing to concede to the comparative enterprise, and he resisted the urge to explain such phenomena insofar as explanations might pose any sort of challenge to church teaching.[38]

Murphy viewed both religious and scientific orthodoxies as potential roadblocks to new knowledge. In both cases, Murphy wrote, "[D]iscovery can be inhibited by strict adherence to particular (scientific or religious) beliefs. . . . [J]ust as potentially significant data are sometimes rejected because they cannot be explained by the conceptual system currently dominant in a particular science, extraordinary experiences that deviate from a particular religious model are sometimes neglected or suppressed."[39] In

The Future of the Body, Murphy quite consciously extracts data from the traditions in question, often noting how the phenomena were understood in their original context, and then reframes them in light of his evolutionary argument.[40]

Comparison

Researchers and collectors extracted things from their original context, thus constituting them as specimens, in order to compare them. Specimens as such have no meaning apart from the comparative agenda of the researcher or collector. Stephen Asma notes that "the odd thing about a specimen is that it's a kind of cipher when considered in isolation."

> Specimens are a lot like words: They don't mean anything unless they're in the context of a sentence or a system, and their meanings are extremely promiscuous. . . . The significance of the specimen does not inhere in the specimen itself, but is socially and theoretically constructed.[41]

As we have already seen, Murphy and his predecessors are entirely open with regard to their comparative agenda. Myers again set the agenda in this regard back in 1886 when he wrote:

> If we are to understand *supernormal* phenomena—phenomena transcending, apparently, the stage of evolution at which we have admittedly arrived,—we must first compare them, as fully as possible, both with *normal* and with *abnormal* phenomena;—meaning by abnormal phenomena those which, while diverging from the ordinary standard, fall below or, at least, do not transcend it.[42]

Organization and Display

For natural historians, comparison was a prelude to some sort of organization and display. Asma describes two stages in the development of museums, the first concerned primarily with descriptive taxonomy— the naming, describing, and classification of organisms—and the second primarily with explaining change in physiological and evolutionary terms.[43] According to Asma, "[T]he true significance of contemporary classification is that it gives us insight into the evolutionary relationships between organisms, or at least it's the starting point for asking evolutionary questions."[44] While Thurston's stated goal was simply to "state and classify facts,"[45] Gurney, Myers, and Murphy wrestled openly with theoretical explanations.

Thurston's refusal to theorize suggests something of what was at stake in moving from the collection, comparison, and evaluation of data to its organization and display. The fundamental problem for Thurston was that theories could not be strictly limited to the data at hand and thus ran the risk of suggesting explanations for phenomena that the Church had placed off limits. Because the Church recognized that the physical phenomena discussed by Thurston were "common to good and bad alike," it did not view them as miracles that could be admitted as proof of sanctity.[46] This freed Thurston to make comparisons between the physical phenomena associated with the mystics and the physical phenomena reported in the *Proceedings* and, on the basis of his comparisons, to state that he believed that both could be understood in naturalistic terms.[47] If he ventured beyond this to theorize about the underlying mechanisms that might produce such effects, he waded into more difficult waters and risked censure.

He illustrated his problem indirectly through a discussion of the theories promulgated by the Dominican Pere Mainage. Mainage was prepared not only to admit "complex telepathy" but also, according to Thurston, "a still further development which corresponds with what is called by F. W. Myers and others telekinesis."

> The eminent Dominican believes it to be conceivable that there may be an actual transference of matter from one place to another, and that this effect, though rare, may possibly not transcend man's natural powers. . . . I can only suggest that the acceptance of such a theory would seem to require a revision of the whole conception of the miraculous. Only a very slight extension of the same line of argument would be required to provide a non-supernatural interpretation of those cures of organic disorders which are allowed to rank in the Bureau des Constatations at Lourdes or are accepted as a guarantee of the divine approval in the canonization of saints.[48]

Thurston, in other words, refrained from theorizing about the causes of the phenomena he was collecting, because theories generally had implications that extended beyond the phenomena under consideration. Naturalistic explanations could not be limited to officially disputed or indifferent phenomena but threatened to account for phenomena for which the Church had offered its own definitive supernatural explanation. In contrast to Thurston, Gurney, Myers, and Murphy all went beyond collecting and comparing their data to organizing and displaying it. In doing so, they theorized, explicitly and implicitly, about the underlying causes that might account for the similarities between different "specimens" in their collections.

Reading the Collections

Although there is some overlap between the "specimens" included in the various published "collections," each is arranged differently. As is the case with natural history museums, each collection can be "read" in order to ascertain the larger point that the collection is intended to make.

Gurney's *Phantasms of the Living*

The central organizing question for *Phantasms of the Living* was whether one mind could be impressed by another independent of the "recognised channels of sense."[49] Gurney analyzed the SPR's data in relation to various categories: experimental versus spontaneous, sensory and externalized versus mental and internalized, and dreaming versus waking. When the impression is sensory and externalized, "the person seems to see, hear, or feel [something] . . . which he instinctively refers to the outer world." When the impression is mental and internalized, the person has a mental image, feels an emotion, or has "a mere blind impulse towards some sort of action." Each of these four divisions, according to Gurney, is "represented in sleeping as well as in waking life, so that *dreams* form a comprehensive class of their own," as do externalized experiences on "the borderland between "complete sleep and complete normal wakefulness."[50] Gurney laid out the evidence according to these divisions, beginning with the experimental cases, then moved through transitional cases to the spontaneous. The chapters on spontaneous telepathy began with the group that did not externalize their impressions (with chapters on "mental pictures" and "emotional and motor effects"), then transitioned through dreams and "borderland cases" to full-blown externalized impressions (or "telepathic hallucinations").

The authors advanced three main theses: (1) "Experiment proves that telepathy—the supersensory transference of thoughts and feelings from one mind to another—is a fact of Nature." (2) "Testimony proves that phantasms (impressions, voices or figures) of persons undergoing some crisis,—especially death,—are perceived by their friends and relatives with a frequency which mere chance cannot explain." (3) "These phantasms then, whatever else they may be, are instances of the supersensory action of one mind on another. The second thesis therefore confirms, and is confirmed by, the first."[51] The chapters, thus, form a sort of display in which the experimental evidence is introduced first (thesis 1) and the fully externalized spontaneous telepathic hallucinations or phantasms last (thesis 2). A series of transitional forms is presented in between in order to lead the viewer in a step-by-step fashion from one end of the display to the other. The net effect is to suggest that the cases belong on a continuum (thesis 3a) and that the evidence for spontaneous and experimental telepathy is mutually reinforcing (thesis 3b).

Myers's *Human Personality*

The central organizing question for Myers's *Human Personality and Its Survival of Bodily Death* was, as the title would suggest, the question of "whether or not [the human] personality involves any element which can survive bodily death."[52] He initially hoped to build on *Phantasms of the Living*, organizing his evidence along a continuum from "phantasms of the living to phantasms of the dead" or "from the action of embodied to the action of disembodied spirits." Over the course of his investigations, however, he concluded that the best evidence—that derived from mediums—was simply too complex to lay out on a continuum of this sort. Before the Spiritualists' claim that utterances of mediums "proceed[ed] from a disembodied source" could be evaluated, Myers decided, "there was need of a more searching review of the capacities of man's incarnate personality than psychologists unfamiliar with this new evidence had thought it worth their while to undertake."[53]

While he acknowledged that his work owed a great deal to "certain observations" made by Spiritualists, it was, he said, "in large measure a critical attack upon the main Spiritist position . . . the belief, namely, that all or almost all supernormal phenomena are due to the action of spirits of the dead. By far the larger proportion, as I hold, [of such supernormal phenomena] are due to the action of the still embodied spirit of the agent or percipient himself."[54] Myers organized his evidence with a twofold agenda in mind: first, to display the capacities of the "incarnate personality" under such headings as disintegrations of personality, genius, sleep, hypnotism, sensory automatism, phantasms of the dead, motor automatism, and trance, possession, and ecstasy; and, second, to make a scientific case for the survival of life after death.

Each chapter provides evidence of a different sort in support of Myers's understanding of the self as "multiplex"; that is, divisible into streams of consciousness (supraliminal and subliminal selves) that may operate independently and without awareness of one another.[55] He laid out his chapters along a continuum from the pathological (disintegrations of the personality) to the normal (genius, sleep, hypnotism) to the potentially supernormal (automatisms, trance possession, etc.). In the latter chapters especially, he provided evidence not only that segments of the personality may operate independently of one another but that they may also operate at times apart from the organism, thus providing evidence for the personality's survival of bodily death.[56] As was the case with *Phantasms of the Living*, *Human Personality* can be viewed as a metaphoric museum display; in this case, a series of specimens classified and displayed in order to gradually build up a case for the personality's survival of bodily death.

Murphy's *Future of the Body*

The central organizing question for Murphy's *Future of the Body* has to do with "the future evolution of human nature"; that is, with the human potential for growth and transformation. Where Myers focuses his attention on the human personality—the nature of the self—Murphy focuses on what he variously designates as human attributes, abilities, or capacities. Where Myers organizes his data to make a case for postmortem survival of the personality, Murphy organizes his data to make a case for the role of integral practices in human growth and transformation. While Murphy assumes a slightly more agnostic stance relative to postmortem survival than Myers, he indicates that we may have the opportunity to develop our metanormal capacities not only in this life but also "in worlds to come." He concludes that "no matter how life after death might proceed, there are good reasons to suppose that integral practices can facilitate our postmortem journey."[57]

Murphy organizes the data in relation to twelve attributes (perception of external events, somatic awareness and self-regulation, communication abilities, vitality, movement abilities, abilities to alter the environment directly, pain and pleasure, cognition, volition, individuation and sense of self, love, and bodily structures, states, and processes). In relation to each attribute, the data is arranged along a continuum, running from animal to normal human to extraordinary human development. This organizational framework allows for a dramatic expansion of the range of phenomena that he can display, relative to both *Phantasms* and *Human Personality*. In the *Future of the Body*, telepathy, the chief supernormal attribute discussed by both Gurney and Myers has a much more circumscribed place, appearing as one of two types of "metanormal development" under the heading of "communication abilities."

The book is divided into three parts: Part I, "the possibilities for extraordinary life," lays out various preliminary matters; Part II, "the evidence for human transformative capacity," presents the actual evidence; and Part III "transformative practices," discusses the sorts of practices most likely to promote "integral development." The evidence in Part II is not organized according to the attributes, as one might expect, but according to the disciplines or practice traditions from which the evidence has been drawn, beginning with medicine (psychosomatic changes, placebo effects, spiritual healing, capacities of disabled people), followed by alterations of consciousness (mesmerism and hypnosis, biofeedback training, psychotherapy and imagery practices), various forms of somatic training (somatic disciplines, adventure and sport, and the martial arts), and religious practices (religious adepts, saints and mystics, and scientific studies of contemplative practices). The chapters in Part II are laid out on a continuum "from disciplines that make partial claims upon their practitioners to the life-encompassing programs of certain martial arts, shamanism, yoga, and contemplative discipline." These all-encompassing programs, in his view, "promote more virtues and capacities, and embrace more human nature, than do hypnosis, biofeedback, psychotherapy, or sport."[58] They thus provide a logical bridge to a discussion of the sorts of transformative practices (Part III) that in Murphy's view are most likely to promote what he calls "integral development," or "many-sided human growth." Here, to continue with the museum metaphor, the display is configured so as to build up a case for the power of transformative practices to promote the further development of human nature.

The Limits of the Natural History Analogy

The relationship between traditional natural histories and the natural history of extraordinary functioning promoted by Murphy is, for the most part, a metaphoric one. As a metaphor, it highlights a number of intriguing similarities between the writings of Murphy, Myers, Thurston, and Gurney and the museum displays of natural historians. Granted these virtues, the metaphor should not be allowed to obscure important differences at both the level of the collection (the idea of specimens) and the level of explanation (the idea of evolution).

As noted earlier, the specimens of traditional natural historians were, generally speaking, physical things—parts or individuals that exemplified a whole, while the specimens collected by Murphy and his predecessors were phenomena—occurrences in which something allegedly out of the ordinary had taken place. While both sorts of specimens are extracted from life (i.e., from a biological ecosystem), the metaphoric specimens are extracted from a cultural ecosystem as well. All of the "specimens" collected by Myers, Gurney, Thurston, and Murphy were originally embedded in some sort of cultural ecosystem; that is, in some sort of human cultural practice. As Murphy acknowledges, his data and that of his predecessors relies "upon bodies of experience that depend upon practice."

> That was certainly true in the Myers-James era where they were surrounded by those great mediums and other activities of the Society for Psychical Research. . . . It is certainly true in the Esalen world where bodies of practice rise and then fall away and then come to be forgotten. It is kind of state dependent and the evidence doesn't rest as solidly as in physics or biology.[59]

This is a crucial point. I argued earlier that all specimens, whether material or metaphoric, are constructed by the researcher who extracts them from their original context in order to constitute them as specimens. There is a difference between extracting nonhuman organisms from a biological ecosystem and extracting state-dependent mental or physical phenomena (i.e. experiences) from a biocultural ecosystem. While it may be possible to preserve some material remains and perhaps even some biophysiological data in both cases, human experience is constituted culturally as well as biologically. Because human experience does not exist apart from cultural webs of meaning, because experience is always embedded in language and narrative, they cannot be extracted from their cultural contexts without turning them into something else.

Murphy, Myers, and Gurney all seemed conscious of this to some degree, particularly when their attempts to extract data from orthodox religious or scientific contexts met with resistance. Murphy seems particularly aware of the issue in his discussion of siddhis and charisms in the *Future of the Body*. Murphy notes that "most siddhis of Hindu-Buddhist lore, charisms of Catholic saints, and similar phenomena in other religions have been regarded in their respective traditions as inferior to enlightenment or union with God." "But," he says, "from an evolutionary perspective"—and here he consciously extracts these phenomena from their respective traditions and places them in a different (evolutionary) perspective—"they can be seen in another way—as emergent features of human development, as capacities inherent to the richer life that is available to us" (171–172). In recontextualizing the siddhis and graces as emergent features of human development, he also recognizes, at least implicitly, that he is promoting a shift in telos from a telos marked by death and suffering in traditions such as Buddhism and Christianity to a more life-affirming telos shaped by "the discoveries of modern science" (172–173). From this new vantage point, Murphy argues that "doctrines of divine mercy or grace in the Western religions, of nonattainment in Buddhism, of surrender to God's will in certain Hindu sects, and of noninterference with the Tao refer to *the same fact of human experience,* namely that unitive awareness and other extraordinary capacities often appear to be given rather than earned, spontaneously revealed rather than attained through ego-centered effort" (176, emphasis added). Murphy recognizes that some would oppose his move at this point; their argument is "that we cannot equate the Jewish, Christian, or Muslim witness to Divine mercy or grace with the arising of Buddha-nature or surrender to an impersonal Tao" (176).

My intention is not to agree or to disagree with Murphy on this point but to observe that in following out this line of thinking we have gradually moved from one discursive world into another. The question of whether siddhis and graces refer to the same fact of human experience is not a matter that is generally discussed by natural historians. It is, however, something that theologians of pluralism argue about at great length. In fact, in arguing that siddhis and graces do refer to the same fact of human experience, Murphy positions himself alongside theologians, such as John Hick and Raimon Panikkar, who discern a unity underlying all the religious traditions and in opposition to those, such as George Lindbeck or Mark Heim, who would argue that language always precedes experience and thus rules out such assertions of sameness.[60]

This brings me to the second major difference between traditional natural histories and the natural histories of the supernormal: their understanding of evolution. As Murphy, at least, is well aware, he and his predecessors are not, for the most part, referring to biological or geological evolution when they refer to evolution. He is using the term "in a very general sense, to denote different kinds of human growth." He adds: "Though the kinds of development that occur in the physical, biological, and psychosocial domains are shaped by different processes and have different patterns, they proceed in sequences that are called evolutionary" (*Future of the Body*, 24). The metaphoric extension of the concept of evolution to the human cultural domain and, specifically, to the growth and development of the individual brings an air of scientific legitimacy to a largely cultural process. Thus, when Murphy extracts graces and siddhis from their traditional contexts and views them "from an evolutionary perspective," he is not viewing them from the perspective of biological or geological evolution but from the perspective of personal or cultural evolution. This type of evolution differs in significant ways from geological or biological evolution, particularly in terms of the length of time involved in changes and the role of human agency in bringing about those changes. Conflation of these different evolutionary domains, as Murphy calls them, can obscure the role of human agency, in this case Murphy's own role, in promoting what he takes to be personal and cultural evolution and undermining what others might view as valuable forms of religious difference.

My point is simply this: in using the metaphor of natural history to illuminate what he and his predecessors are up to, Murphy frames what he is about using a scientific metaphor and obscures the extent to which his efforts and those of his predecessors might be interpreted theologically.

AN ALTERNATIVE INTERPRETATION

In thinking about the lineage in which Murphy has situated himself, two features strike me as particularly significant: 1) the centrality of psychical research and, within that tradition, the role of experimentation with altered states of consciousness (mesmerism and hypnotism) in generating new explanations of a wide range of phenomena; and 2) the persistent desire to rethink the religious life within an evolutionary paradigm.

With respect to the first issue, I am struck by the role that both Myers and Thurston thought hypnotic trance played in the rise of psychical research and the paradigm shift it effected in thinking about supernormal phenomena traditionally understood in theological terms. Thus, Thurston observed, apropos of Mollie Fancher, that

> Two centuries ago such phenomena ["those natural but unusual manifestations of man's spiritual being which science now takes account of under the name of abnormal psychology"] were summarily dismissed, by Catholics and Protestants alike, as witchcraft, sorcery, or, in brief, the work of the devil. But this was before the reality of the hypnotic trance was recognized, and before attention was thus directed to possibilities of which earlier ages had no conception.[61]

Thurston may have derived this insight from Myers, who as early as 1886 argued that "it is perhaps from the present position of *hypnotism* that the strongest argument may be drawn for the need of such researches as ours." The chief importance of "the mesmeric or hypnotic trance," he argued, was not as a therapeutic modality but as a research tool. Its value, he said, lay in its ability to allow researchers to "[shift] the threshold of consciousness" in such a way that "unnoted sensibilities, nay, perhaps even . . . new and centrally initiated powers" might emerge. Through "artificial displacements of the psycho-physical threshold," hypnotic trance freed the mind from "accustomed stimuli" so that it might "reveal those latent and delicate capacities of which [the] ordinary conscious self is unaware."[62]

As pointed out in the introduction, Murphy, in one of his more expansive versions of his lineage, begins with the German and British mesmerists, followed by Frederic Myers and other psychical researchers. This suggests that even though, in Murphy's estimation, "mesmerism and hypnosis have not produced the illumination and creativity evident, for example, in contemplative practice," he, too, acknowledges the centrality of these experimental means of inducing altered states of consciousness for the founders of his lineage as well as their role in stimulating "experiences and capacities that play an important role in transformative practice" (*Future of the Body*, 348). If we understand mesmerism and hypnosis, in Myers's words, as a means of revealing "those latent and delicate capacities of which [the] ordinary conscious self is unaware," we can see its evident continuity with what Murphy calls "transformative practices."

With respect to the second issue, I am struck by the evident desire of both Myers and Murphy to rethink the religious life within an evolutionary paradigm. Where Murphy provides us with a new vision of religious practice, Myers provides us with a new vision of the communion of the saints. The data he collected convinced Myers that "telepathic intercommunication [was a regular occurrence], not only between the minds of men still on earth, but between minds or spirits still on earth and spirits departed." While he rejected much of traditional Christian teaching, the evidence of telepathy between spirits living and dead revitalized Myers's understanding of the communion of the saints. On the basis of "observation without the veil, and by utterance from within," that is, utterances from departed spirits, Myers felt he had evidence to believe that life after death was a "state . . . of endless evolution in wisdom and in love." "[T]he Communion of Saints," he wrote, "not only adorns but constitutes the Life Everlasting. Nay, from the law of telepathy it follows that that communion is valid for us here and now."[63] Waxing poetic, he linked this intercourse between the living and the dead with the evolutionary process in which "science and religion" ultimately "fuse in one."

> We hope that the intercourse, now at last consciously begun . . . between discarnate and incarnate souls, may through long effort clarify into a directer communion, so that they shall teach us all they will. . . . Evolution will no longer appear as a truncated process, an ever-arrested movement upon an unknown goal. Rather we may gain a glimpse of an ultimate incandescence where science and religion fuse in one; a cosmic evolution of Energy into Life, and of Life into Love, which is Joy.[64]

The evidence that Murphy collected convinced him that transformative practice can play a crucial role in the emergence of our full human potential. A developing awareness with an evident debt to Eastern meditation lies at the heart of Murphy's understanding of transformative practice.

> Such awareness [he writes] can disidentify itself from all images, thoughts, impulses, feelings, and sensations by noninterfering self-observation. It comes into its own, so to speak, through a choiceless awareness in action or repose that relinquishes attachment to particular events, either psychic or physical. It provides a growing freedom from mental, emotional, and physical habits, as well as brief moments of joy and recognition of deeper freedom still. With cultivation, it opens onto larger vistas and becomes a boundless subjectivity that realizes unity everywhere. (*Future of the Body*, 585–586)

Both Myers and Murphy stress the importance of looking forward, not back. "We should look, not backward to fading tradition," Myers admonished, "but onward to dawning experience."[65] In a similar vein, Murphy reminds us that "we need not be limited by the achievements of the past."

> Indeed, most traditional spiritual programs don't translate well when imported uncritically into our modern culture. In this age of great religious reinvention, we need discrimination and wisdom to synthesize the best of the old and the new to forge modern yogas. We need to leave the certainty of the old ways, at times, for adventurous journeying into the further reaches of our human nature.[66]

While the idea of natural history does illuminate significant continuities between Murphy's research and earlier figures such as Gurney, Myers, and Thurston, the use of a scientific metaphor to describe those continuities obscures the extent to which their work wrestled with theological issues as well. Based on these two features just highlighted, the lineage in which Murphy situates himself can also be interpreted as one that seeks to bridge the worlds of science and religion in light of two centuries of experimentation with altered states of consciousness.

Notes

1. See Esalen's Web site at www.esalen.org and the Esalen Center's Web site at www.esalenctr.org.
2. Joan Smith, "Making the Next Evolutionary Leap," *San Francisco Examiner*,

Sunday, July 26, 1992, D:1; "The Esalen Institute Study of Human Nature's Further Evolution," available online at http://www.esalenctr.org/display/research1.cfm; Michael Murphy, "Toward a Natural History of Supernormal Attributes," 2002, available online at http://www.esalenctr.org/display/paper.cfm?ID 8.

3. Michael Murphy, *The Future of the Body* (New York: Tarcher, 1992), 9.

4. "The Esalen Institute Study of Human Nature's Further Evolution."

5. Ibid.

6. Murphy, "Toward a Natural History of Supernormal Attributes."

7. Michael Murphy, telephone conversation with author, January 18, 2003.

8. "The Esalen Institute Study of Human Nature's Further Evolution."

9. Where the latter transmits spiritual authority as in the case of mind-to-mind transmission from master to student in Zen Buddhist lineages or apostolic succession from apostles to bishops in Christianity, the former transmits ideas and, in some cases, methods of investigation.

10. Alan Gauld, *The Founders of Psychical Research* (New York: Schocken Books, 1968), 37–44, 64, 89–99, 137–138.

11. Ibid., 103–106.

12. Ibid., 137–138, 46–47, 53–54, quote on 38.

13. Edward Gurney, Frederic W. H. Myers, and Frank Podmore, *Phantasms of the Living*, 2 vols. (London: SPR, 1886).

14. Gauld, *The Founders of Psychical Research*, 160, 162, 164.

15. Ibid., 252–258, 261.

16. Ann Taves, "Religious Experience and the Divisible Self: William James (and Frederic Myers) as Theorist(s) of Religion," *Journal of the American Academy of Religion* 71, no. 2 (2003): 318–319; see also Adam Crabtree, "Models of the Mind," 2001, available online at http://www.esalenctr.org/display/papers.cfm.

17. Diane Jonte-Pace compares James's *Varieties* to a "cabinet of curiosities," an early genre in the tradition of natural histories; see Diane Jonte-Pace, "Amnesias and Ideologies in the Psychology of Religion," paper presented at the annual meeting of the American Academy of Religion, Toronto, Canada, 2002.

18. For a complete listing, see Joseph Crehan, S.J., *Father Thurston: A Memoir with a Bibliography of His Writings* (London and New York: Sheed and Ward, 1952), 185–222.

19. Ibid., 134–135; Herbert Thurston, S.J., *The Church and Spiritualism*, ed. Joseph Husslein, S.J., Science and Culture Series (Milwaukee: Bruce Publishing Company, 1933), xi–xii; on Spiritualism in England in the 1860s, see Gauld, *The Founders of Psychical Research*, 70–77.

20. Crehan, *Father Thurston*, 32.

21. Ibid., 136–138; on Feilding, see also Gauld, *The Founders of Psychical Research*, 243–245.

22. Herbert Thurston, S.J., *The Physical Phenomena of Mysticism*, ed. J. H. Crehan, S.J. (London: Burnes Oates, 1952), 2, see also 141, 233.

23. Murphy, *The Future of the Body*, 9.

24. Ibid., 587.

25. Murphy, "Toward a Natural History of Supernormal Attributes"; Murphy, "The Esalen Institute Study of Human Nature's Further Evolution." When Bill Parsons referred to the "paranormal" in our conversation with Murphy, Murphy re-

sponded, "I'd rather use the word supernormal." He indicated that the meaning of "paranormal" is limited to "telepathy, clairvoyance, [and] precognition." He prefers "supernormal or extraordinary" because they are more inclusive. Conversation with Michael Murphy, William Parsons, Diane Jonte-Pace, and Ann Taves, Sausalito, Calif., July 25, 2002.

26. Frederic W. Myers, "Automatic Writing—II," *Proceedings of the Society for Psychical Research* 3 (1885): 30. See also Myers's introduction to Gurney, *Phantasms of the Living*, xvii, note 2; and Frederic W. Myers, *Human Personality and Its Survival of Bodily Death*, vol. 1 (1903; reprint, New York: Longmans, Green and Co., 1954), xxii.

27. Frederic W. Myers, "Automatic Writing—IV—the Daemon of Socrates," *Proceedings of the Society for Psychical Research* 5 (1888–89): 525.

28. Myers introduction to Gurney, *Phantasms of the Living*, ix. Myers introduced the term "telepathy" in 1882, see Myers, *Human Personality*, 1: xxii.

29. Gauld, *Founders.*

30. Myers's introduction to Gurney, *Phantasms of the Living*, xxviii–xxix.

31. Murphy, *The Future of the Body*, 14–15, 23.

32. Michael Murphy and J. Brodie, "I Experience a Kind of Clarity," *Intellectual Digest* 3, no. 5 (1973); Michael Murphy, *Jacob Atabet* (New York: Tarcher, 1977); Michael Murphy and R. White, *The Psychic Side of Sports* (Reading, Mass.: Addison-Wesley, 1978).

33. Gurney, *Phantasms of the Living*, 6.

34. Murphy, *The Future of the Body*, 9.

35. Myers, *Human Personality*, 1: xxiv.

36. Myers, introduction to Gurney, *Phantasms of the Living*, xvii–xviii.

37. John Maniatis and Sw. Virato, "The Future of the Body: An Interview with Michael Murphy," *New Frontier*, May/June 1992, 13.

38. Thurston, *The Physical Phenomena of Mysticism*, 141, 233.

39. Murphy, *The Future of the Body*, 12.

40. See ibid., 171–179.

41. Stephen T. Asma, *Stuffed Animals and Pickled Heads: The Culture and Evolution of Natural History Museums* (New York: Oxford University Press, 2001), xiii.

42. Frederic W. Myers, "Automatic Writing—III," *Proceedings of the Society for Psychical Research* 4 (1886): 213.

43. Asma, *Stuffed Animals and Pickled Heads*, 128–129.

44. Ibid., 19.

45. Thurston, *The Physical Phenomena of Mysticism*, 233.

46. Ibid., 141, 233.

47. Ibid., 128, 92.

48. Ibid., 14–15.

49. Gurney, *Phantasms of the Living*, 5.

50. Ibid., 6–7, 131–132.

51. Ibid., xxxii.

52. Myers, *Human Personality*, 1: 1.

53. Ibid., 1: 8–9.

54. Ibid., 1: 6.

55. Ibid., 1: 14–17; Taves, "Religious Experience."

56. Myers, *Human Personality,* 1: 14–15, 249–51, 2: 74–75.

57. Murphy, *The Future of the Body,* 230.

58. Ibid., 546.

59. Telephone conversation with Michael Murphy, January 28, 2003.

60. Paul F. Knitter, *Introducing Theologies of Religions* (Maryknoll, N.Y.: Orbis, 2002), 109–149, 173–215.

61. Thurston, *The Physical Phenomena of Mysticism,* 294.

62. Myers, introduction to Gurney, *Phantasms,* xiv–xv. Mollie Fancher was a celebrated invalid with alleged clairvoyant faculties. See Judge Abraham H. Dailey, *Mollie Fancher, the Brooklyn Enigma* (Brooklyn, 1894).

63. Myers, *Human Personality,* 2: 287.

64. Ibid., 290.

65. Ibid.

66. Ronald S. Miller, "The Future of the Body: A Conversation with Michael Murphy," *Noetic Sciences Review* (Summer 1992): 12.

FROM SARX TO SOMA: ESALEN'S ROLE IN RECOVERING THE BODY FOR SPIRITUAL DEVELOPMENT

Don Hanlon Johnson

At the time of Esalen's founding in the early 1960s, discourse about the experienced body was hard to come by. On the intellectual front, there were a few phenomenologists lurking quietly among the linguistic analysts and logicians so as to avoid notice and keep their jobs. In the realm of praxis, a few teachers, many of them refugees from World War II Europe, were working with small groups in private studios in New York, Boston, and San Francisco. Since that time there has been a proliferation of serious intellectual studies of the experienced body.[1] Alongside that more well-known development has been the rapid growth of a new field of practical experiential studies of the human body that includes tens of thousands of practitioners scattered throughout the world, a growing body of literature, yearly international conferences, a professional journal, and a handful of graduate academic degree programs. Esalen has played a major role in the shaping of this field and its growing impact on the consciousness of the role of bodily experience in the life of the intellect and the life of the spirit.

THE RECOVERY OF A BODY-BASED INTELLIGENCE

The experienced body has not fared well in modern culture—the body that has lived successfully through challenges of physical difficulty and disease, the body of sensual delights, the body of physical achievement, the body of bright inquiry. Like the voices of women and marginalized cultures, the voice of the experienced body has been severely muted against the backdrop of the louder and generously funded voices of object-bodies—the genomic body, the electronically imaged body, the matrix body of artificial intelligence, even the more sophisticated body of behavioral and complementary medicine. Needless to say, there is ample room in the culture for good sex, fine eating, massage, and physical fitness. But these bodily activities seem to have nothing to do with the development of our communal store of intelligence and the evolution of science.

And yet our most primal sources of intelligence lie within bodily experience. Eugene Gendlin, one of the most prolific writers about the role of experience in the development of intelligence, puts it this way:

> Our bodies sense themselves in living in our situations. Our bodies do our living. Our bodies are interaction in the environment. . . . The body is an interaction in that it breathes, not only in that it senses the cold of the air. It feeds; it does not only see and smell food. It grows and sweats. It walks; it does not only perceive the hard resistance of the ground. And it walks not just as a displacement between two points in empty space, rather to go somewhere. The body senses the whole situation, and it urges, it implicitly shapes our next action. It senses itself living in its whole context—the situation.[2]

The ancient and wise knowing of the situation that is carried by the body cannot be revealed by objective analysis alone. Deliberate skillful cultivation is necessary to dredge it up. The widespread intellectual assaults on Platonic, Christian, and Cartesian dualisms require practical methodologies if they are to be any more than flights of academic fancy. It is in this arena of practical knowing that Esalen's unique role comes to light.

Growing quietly alongside the bewildering effervescence of sciences of the object-body has been a shadow movement that has developed the knowledge inherent in bodily experience. From the mid-1800s until the beginnings of World War II, there was a widespread and vibrant counterculture of the experiential body throughout Europe and the United States. It was set in motion by a number of teachers who traveled back and forth between northern Europe and the eastern seaboard of the United States during the mid- and late nineteenth century: François Delsarte, Genevieve Stebbins, Bess Mensendieck, Leo Kofler, and Emile Jacques-Dalcroze, to name a few.[3] These people shared a new vision of embodiment that was at odds with the dominant models found in classical ballet, physical education, religion, and biomedicine. Instead of training dancers and athletes to shape their bodies to fit a classical form that was considered normative for all, they encouraged individual expressiveness and a return to a more "natural" body. Rejecting biomedicine and religion's separation of the human spirit from a mechanistically conceived body, they envisioned an intimate unity among movement, body structure, health, and spiritual consciousness under the rubric of "gymnastic." At a time when medical doctors were still engaged in the most crude uses of surgery and medication, the practitioners of various branches of gymnastic were already doing sophisticated healing work using expressive movement, sensory awareness, sound, music, and touch.

An early pioneer of the gymnastic movement was François Delsarte, born in 1811, a Parisian actor and director of a school of drama. In the course of his job of teaching actors, he became fascinated with how certain movements could be expressive and others unexpressive. He gradually developed a method that emphasized the relationship between movement and breathing. He was such a failure in Paris that he decided to emigrate to New York around 1860, where he rapidly gained a number of devoted students, including Steele McKay and Genevieve Stebbins. In the last years of his life, Delsarte returned to Paris, where he died in 1871, forgotten and alone.[4] At the same time, Stebbins had managed to gain such wide acceptance for the work that two German women, Hede Kallmeyer and Bess Mensendieck, came to New York to study with her. They took the work back to Germany, where they developed their own systems. Mensendieck's work once again crossed the Atlantic and eventually became the basis for the widely influential posture-training method used in East Coast prep schools and private universities. For some three decades, before-and-after photos of incoming students in the buff were taken and subjected to analysis by William Sheldon for his visual studies of the human form. They were also widely traded among men and women of the Ivy League schools until the salacious underground activity reached the news media and was stopped.

Another pioneer in the gymnastic movement was the Swiss Leo Kofler. He emigrated to Kansas, where he contracted tuberculosis of the larynx. When he gained a position as organist and choirmaster at St. Paul's Chapel, Trinity Parish, in New York in 1877, he consulted a throat specialist, who inspired him to immerse himself in studies of the anatomy and physiology of the larynx, the voice, and respiration. Out of those studies he healed himself and developed a system for exploring the relationships between what he identified as "natural" breathing and voice. He described this system in his *The Art of Breathing,* translated into German in 1897 by Clara Schlaffhorst and Hedwig Andersen, who used it as the inspiration for their Rotenburger School.[5] This same translation has persisted through thirty-six editions, and the School still flourishes in Germany. Significant for what it indicates about the lack of American intellectual interest in this kind of serious bodily exploration is the fact that the book rapidly passed out of print in English.

A third major innovator in gymnastic was Émile Jacques-Dalcroze, a musician who lived in Geneva and developed a method of education based on combining rhythmic movements with music. In his Hellerau School, he counted among his students Rudolf von Laban and Mary Wigman, who were among the principal creators of modern dance and dance therapy.[6]

The world wars loom large in the shaping of this movement. The first war divided the international and interdisciplinary community of dancers, physical therapists, craftspeople, artists, and scientists, leaving the schools of body-teaching more isolated but still intact. Before and between the two wars, western Europe had witnessed the beginnings of a widespread practical and theoretical critique of the entrenchment of body-mind dualism in medicine, education, philosophy, and the bodily practices of dance, exercise, and sports. The rise of Hitler and Stalin, who put in place severely puritanical measures against the sensuality of artistic expression of any kind, had a devastating impact on this movement. Many of the innovators had to flee from their homelands, dispersing throughout the Americas and Australia, where they set aside the more visionary aspects of their work to eke out a living by practicing what looked like physical rehabilitation or psychotherapy. Refugees such as Charlotte Selver, Carola Speads, Wilhelm Reich, Fritz Perls, and Marion Rosen went from being active participants in a vital cultural movement to practicing their work in isolation with handfuls of students while trying to gain a financial foothold in their new and unfamiliar homes.

It is difficult to understand the decline in the value placed on first-person experiential knowledge of the body without noticing another significant result of the wars. The enormous stores of money and intellectual talent brought to bear on the creation of weaponry and detection devices had the unforeseen results of electronic technologies that would revolutionize biomedical research. New possibilities of exploring the submicroscopic interstices of the living body by advances in imaging devices—Computeried Axial Tomography scans, and a host of other electronic innovations—enabled researchers to produce a practical science of the object-body to an extent unimaginable at the beginning of the twentieth century. While the increase in knowledge of the object-body, supported by rapidly growing funding and institutional culture, provided one of the most dramatic stories of the postwar era, practices for furthering the experienced body remained on the sidelines.[7] There was indeed a vital subculture of dance, massage, and exercise, but it had little effect on the intellectual climate.[8]

One aspect of Esalen Institute's historical role can be understood in this recovery of a momentum for exploring direct experience. In the 1960s, the hospitality of Esalen and a counterculture that was exploring different states of consciousness provided the opportunity to regather strands of the widely shared vision that had been lost. A new cooperative venture began to form. Some of the old pioneers, such as Charlotte Selver,[9] Alexander Lowen,[10] Moshe Feldenkrais, and Ida Rolf,[11] traveled westward from the East Coast and Europe, gathered large numbers of students, returned to their homes, established new schools, and often eventually brought their work back to its sources in Europe, where it had been forgotten.

Because my professional life was formed within the atmosphere of the early years of Esalen, I took for granted much of what we were learning there and developing. It was only in later years that I gained some perspective on its significance. For example, in November 1988, I was invited to give the keynote address for the first annual conference of the European Association of Somatic Therapy in Paris. There were some 500 people at the conference, mostly scholars and university students. There were also a small group of the prewar pioneers who developed training institutes whose graduates have long been well established within postwar European culture. In addition, there were many of the first-generation students of Moshe Feldenkrais, Wilhelm Reich, Elsa Gindler, Mary Wigman, and Rudolf von Laban.

The organizer, a Lacanian psychoanalyst, had written an introduction to the conference program which attempted to situate this new movement in human transformation within a historical context. I was somewhat startled when I read his summary, where he argued that there are three sources for the field: Wilhelm Reich, American Indians, and Esalen.

Easy enough to understand the first. There is a dramatic contrast between the image of Wilhelm Reich in Europe and the United States. Here he is either regarded as an eccentric quack who advocated unbridled sexual activity as the key to social and personal problems or as the founder of an approach to individual psychotherapy developed under the name of bioenergetics.[12] In Europe, by contrast, his work inspired widespread movements based on his vision that Freud's psychoanalytic theory had to be combined with a reform of social structures if there was to be any genuine change in the psychological health of large populations, not just among a few bourgeois individuals. He argued that the healthy adult sexuality which Freud outlined was impossible without improvements in economic conditions, education, and perinatal care. To this day, one finds throughout Europe birth control clinics, preschools, birthing centers, and grade schools inspired by his ideas as well as political movements oriented toward changing laws surrounding birth control, abortion, divorce, and sexual behavior. There has been an easy relationship between Reichian theory and the many methods of working with the body-personality using breath, sensory awareness, manipulative strategies, movement practices, and visualization.

With not too great a mental stretch, I was able to make sense of the American Indian factor. There is a perception that the Native Americans have maintained a sense of connection with the body and the earth that was lost by the Christianized and scientized Western Europeans and the early colonists. The sweats and fasts, journeys alone in the wilds, and emphasis on the presence of the divine in direct perception of nature create a very different context for understanding the transcendent significance of bodily reality.

BUT WHAT ABOUT ESALEN?

In puzzling over this question, I came to realize that Esalen was in some ways like a Wild West version of the 1920s German Bauhaus, which was a haven for a remarkable number of creative thinkers and artists who would eventually, as refugees, leave their marks on contemporary architecture, music, dance, and philosophy. Although the United States was politically a safe refuge for many such innovators, it did not offer a supportive environment for the work of these scattered teachers. Between the two world wars, the institutionalized approach to the human body had been medicalized according to the European model. In the early 1920s, John D. Rockefeller and Andrew Carnegie had commissioned Frederick Gates and Abraham Flexner to purify the protean medical practices, which were then characteristic of the New World's democratic ideals, and establish the hegemony of European academic medicine rooted in the Cartesian division between the mechanistic body and the mind. Flexner and Gates went about state-by-state lobbying for the passing of laws outlawing those practices that were judged to be at odds with this imported biomedicine. Like midwives and indigenous healers, the many teachers of body practices were confined to quiet teaching and work in anonymous offices far from the public dialogue, often living for years within blocks of one another without any contact. In this environment, somewhat like an alchemical alembic, the various works did indeed simmer quietly, with skills being honed and goals purified. But they had little, if any, effect on the larger culture.

In December 1963, in the second year of Esalen's formal programs, Michael Murphy set in motion a regathering of the fragments dispersed by the war by inviting Charlotte Selver, a refugee from Nazi Germany, to offer workshops. Charlotte, who died at 102 years in 2003, is the clearest embodiment of this rich movement. She had been an active par-

ticipant in the summer rallies of the *Wandervögel,* where she encountered
the sensory awareness work of Elsa Gindler, who soon became her teacher.
Selver taught at the Bauhaus during the fertile Weimar period and finally
left Germany for New York in 1938 when her own University of Hei-
delberg required her to wear the Jewish star. Supporting herself by cleaning apartments, she slowly worked her way into the intellectual community of New York and began teaching her work more publicly, attracting
the support of better-known refugees such as Erich Fromm. Alan Watts,
then living on a houseboat in Sausalito, heard of her work and invited
her to California, where she met Michael Murphy.

Charlotte was the first in a long series of teachers of body practices
who would visit Esalen regularly: Moshe Feldenkrais, Ida Rolf, Alexander
Lowen, Anna Halprin, Gabrielle Roth, Ilana Rubenfeld, Judith Aston,
Bonnie Bainbridge Cohen, Emilie Conrad, and Fritz Smith, to name a
few.

At that time, the scars resulting from the postwar fragmentation of
these various schools brought about a cultish attitude which was redolent
of the theological disputes of the late Middle Ages, almost surreal in
specificity about body parts. Ida Rolf dismissed F. Matthias Alexander as
having the third lumbar and third cervical vertebrae move back too far
from an imaginary vertical plumb line through the body; Moshe Feldenkrais argued that there was no point working on body structure, which
could only be changed through changing function, and made fun of Rolfers and Aston Patterners as people who were devoid of imagination about
all the possible ways one might move. Rolf and Aston countered that
functional changes were trivial and evanescent. Stanley Keleman argued
that Rolfers and Alexander teachers were like crazed arborists crashing
into forests to straighten out the redwood trees. Charlotte Selver disdained
them all as vulgar and insensitive louts. Most of them argued that their
practices made psychotherapy and spiritual teaching irrelevant, since all
emotional health and enlightenment could now be attained by improving
the flow of cerebrospinous fluid, aligning the body with gravity, or introducing more flexibility into the joints. Ida Rolf summed up their attitude
in her oft-repeated phrase, "There ain't no psychology, just biology." The
claims of each bordered on the megalomania bred of isolation. Not only
did they reject the methods of their peers, they also disdained older cul-

tural practices such as hatha yoga and tai chi chuan, which they considered anachronistic. It was a collection of body churches, each arguing dogmatic superiority.

What happened in the late 1960s and throughout the 1970s at Esalen was something akin to the parallel ecumenical movement in religion. This strange collection of weird inventors suddenly found themselves in the same dining room, sometimes crowded into seats next to undesirables of a competing school. When they relaxed from their teaching roles as they ate and drank, they found that other very creative and courageous people had ideas about the body that were not all that different from their own and that they too had something important to offer a damaged world. Even when they did not directly interact, they could not avoid thinking about each other because their students were always interacting and posing questions that arose from the different teachings. Which was primary— structure or function? Was catharsis necessary or not? Does direct work with the body displace the need for depth psychoanalysis? Is touch inherently intrusive? And like embattled Christians, they began to realize that their differences were trivial compared to the radical gap between their shared vision of the human body and the dominant paradigm.

At this stage, which lasted throughout the 1970s, there was only an inchoate community organized around these practices, formed by students who were cross-training and raising questions about apparent theoretical and practical conflicts among the methods they were studying. But there was little conceptual work moving toward an understanding of what the various works shared. Esalen entered here to play a crucial role in bringing together senior teachers and practitioners of the various schools for study seminars that were dialogues among humanistic scholars, biomedical researchers, and social scientists.

The late Thomas Hanna made his first visit to Esalen in 1972, a short time after he had published his groundbreaking *Bodies in Revolt*[13] while he was chair of the philosophy department at the University of Florida. This book was a reflection on the common ground among a series of thinkers, from Charles Darwin to Maurice Merleau-Ponty, who represented an organized resistance to the mind-body dualism infecting Western thought. He argued that these figures set the stage for a radical revolution in the way our culture thinks about bodily existence and shapes institutions rooted in that thinking.

Like many of us at the time who went to Esalen as professional philosophers, Hanna was surprised to find nonacademic artisans in the massage rooms actually doing existentialism and phenomenology in the flesh without knowing much about the larger philosophical, historical, and cultural significance of their skillful work. Partly inspired by what he saw there and by the opportunities Esalen gave him to gather outstanding teachers, he went on to create the journal *Somatics* in 1976, the first public forum in which practitioners of individual schools could engage in dialogue. He wrote a seminal series of essays on the unity of the field, using the neologism "Somatics" in contrast to the more common "somatic" (an adjective synonymous with "physical" or, more technically, "the musculoskeletal frame of the body") to define the field as the study of first-person bodily experience, in distinction to biomedical sciences of third-person object-bodies. The term was inspired by the Greek *soma*, which was used throughout the classical era to signify the whole person. As the Christian era began, Paul argued that the essence of Christianity lay in the transformation of a raw secular body, *sarx*, into the immortal body, *soma*, of the Christian community. Hanna's term was also inspired by Edmund Husserl's earlier vision of a "somatology," a science that would unite knowledge from both the object-body and the subject-body.[14] With Thomas Hanna's journal, his philosophical essays, and my own,[15] in addition to the ongoing proliferation of skill development in different methods of body practice, the conditions were set for the marriage of the two prongs of this movement, practice and theory, that resulted in a new field of inquiry with Esalen as its first home.

In 1983, I founded the first graduate studies program in the field, which is now located at the California Institute of Integral Studies, a fully accredited graduate school in San Francisco. At the same time, I was invited by State Assemblyman John Vasconcellos, a longtime Esalen visitor, to be a member of a three-person task force of the California state legislature charged with revising the laws governing the practice of counseling. That appointment enabled me to make the legal space to incorporate body practices within the scope of practice of counseling psychology. In 1987, at Michael Murphy's invitation, I organized at Esalen the first of many ecumenical seminars in the field, inviting scholars and scientists in many fields to interact with the creators of the major schools of Somatics. These seminars resulted in the publishing of historical and theoretical essays that defined the field.[16]

Hanna's journal, the graduate program at CIIS, the ongoing Esalen seminars, the Somatics book series, and Michael Murphy's publication of *The Future of the Body* have resulted in a dramatic change in the way these schools viewed their interrelationships. It is now commonplace for teachers and practitioners both to consider themselves as specialists in a more generalized field and to engage in collaborative activities involving shared needs for education and research. There are now a number of graduate programs in the field, yearly national and international congresses, and a growing body of books and articles.[17]

THE PRACTICAL GAP BETWEEN BODY AND INTELLIGENCE

It cannot be denied that Esalen's role in this history is due in part to its extraordinary natural beauty. While it is very difficult to gather in urban academic settings outstanding scholars, scientists, and educators who are typically busy and charge high fees, the unique beauty of Big Sur and Esalen's salutary hot springs entice such people to donate their time to meetings there. This obvious factor makes it easy to miss a more profound epistemological role Esalen has played in bridging the enormous gap between practical and intellectual knowledge; in this case, between body workers who are typically unskilled in language and its nuances and academically trained scholars and scientists who are awash in concepts that are untethered from their experiential sources. Thus, the development of the field of Somatics is not understood properly if it is seen only as one of many alternative kinds of therapy that evolved during the past century. Nor is Esalen's unique role in the gradual shift of an intellectual and spiritual climate intelligible in that context. The nurturing of a sophisticated field of body practices formed the necessary correlate to the explosion of academic interest in the body among social thinkers that occurred during this same period.

When I first went to Esalen in 1967 and encountered these practices, I was a Jesuit seminarian in my final stages of preparation for ordination to the priesthood, already indoctrinated for some twelve years in a body-oriented spirituality. This spiritual tradition took literally the Pauline claim that the resurrection of Christ's body is the promise of our immortal existence in the flesh. In light of that fundamental notion, we believed that taking the Eucharist was actually eating Christ's body to transform our own bodies into the immortal body of Christ. Our spiritual teachers put great emphasis on the belief that meditation and the sacraments were effecting this transformation. We were enticed to cultivate a life of extreme asceticism with promises of the kinds of bodily transformation that occur in the documentation of the lives of the saints: teleportation, elongation, levitation, sweet-smelling body odor, and ultimately an immortal body of blissful pleasure (or excruciating pain!). In this vein, we learned meditation practices grounded in sensory awareness and we practiced deliberate postures in meditation associated with desired states of consciousness. Because of the central importance of our bodies in the spiritual journey, emphasis was also given to diet, relaxation methods, visualization, hypnosis, and exercise as useful adjuncts to the great transformative process.

But there was a profound contradiction between being taught to cultivate our bodies and the institutional context, which enshrined radical dualisms between body and soul, between a time-bound earth and the eternal realms of heaven and hell. The practices designed for embodiment were paradoxically disembodied, existing in an ethereal closet, neither densely physical nor spaciously spiritual. Although we were taught the importance of standing, kneeling, prostrating, and giving attention to breathing and the cadences of silent walking, we lacked a practical education in how to draw our chronically dissociated mental attention into those realms. As a result, I performed those supposedly bodily activities as if I were sleepwalking. Even after my mystical training was supplemented by philosophical studies of Husserl, Heidegger, Merleau-Ponty, and Sartre, where I learned to think even more intellectually about the centrality of the human body in the life-world, my own flesh and blood still felt like a distant planet.

But as soon as I encountered various teachers of body practices and learned how to saturate these seemingly banal activities with consciousness, my fourteen years of spiritual teaching began literally to make sense. Deliberately attending to a certain posture, a quiet movement, or the rhythms of my breathing evoked, at long last, the experiential states with which spiritual teachings associated them: peacefulness, spaciousness, no-mindedness, bare presence.

It was hard for me to articulate this strange phenomenon until I came across a small community of sociologists, anthropologists, and philosophers who had begun to take seriously the inherent intellectual meaning of practices—Marcel Mauss, Mary Douglas, Maurice Merleau-Ponty, Michel Foucault, Susan Bordo, and Pierre Bourdieu.[18] In the dominant mode of thinking, practices are always being interpreted in light of pre-existing theory as instances or concretizations of intellectually articulated structures without any intrinsic intelligibility apart from theory. Marcel Mauss initiated a study of the intricacies of specific practices as matrices of new understandings, arguing that typical practices contained within themselves notions not fully articulated in theory unless the practices are investigated in their own right. For example, he examined patterns of diving, wielding shovels, and walking as emblematic of differences between British and French cultures and education.

Yasuo Yuasa, a scholar of Asian bodily practices, argues that the most profound difference between Asian and European intellectual traditions lies in the priority given to practice in the process of developing theory.[19] In Asian theory and practice, flesh, blood, genitals, and lungs are the raw materials to be cultivated by meditation, the martial arts, ethical behavior, and the other aesthetic practices to bring about a flowering of pleasure, intelligence, and (it is to be hoped) wisdom.[20] The break between theory and practice in Western thought, he argues, reflects the Cartesian gap between mind and body, where theory is the principle of rational order, while practice is merely the shaping of so-called chaotic experience by the mind. In that view, experiential practices have no intrinsic intelligibility apart from the theories that shape them; they illustrate theory rather than generate it. Asian practices, by contrast, are thought to be the seedbed for intellectual and spiritual development. If you examine any of the Asian practices—tea ceremony, calligraphy, poetry writing, martial arts, meditation, healing practices—you find a seamless continuum from what

Westerners would call the "physical" through the "intellectual" to the "spiritual." There is, for example, a highly refined emphasis on bodily posture, diet, and tonicity that is reflected in the minute attention to aesthetic detail. At the same time, a practitioner is required to deal with mental and emotional barriers to ethical behavior. Ultimately, any of these practices contain within the practice itself a cosmic dimension, a sense of harmony with reality and all that entails. There is no division of worlds in which some activities are thought to be purely physical, others emotional, others mental, others spiritual. These are all aspects of a sustained practice of cultivation.

Yuasa's analysis illuminates the peculiar nature of Somatics, which is more accurately understood by comparison with body practices in Asia than with so-called healing practices alternative to biomedicine or with Western physical therapy. From the perspective that views practices as naturally prompting the evolution of new theory, it becomes clearer how the seemingly chaotic mix of charismatic teachers and their newly trained practitioners mixing together on the Esalen grounds led to the creation of a new academic discipline with advanced university degree programs, publicly sanctioned forms of therapy, and scientific inquiry. The progress over a 35-year period at Esalen of a two-pronged movement—the one reflective, theoretical, and scientific; the other, a progressive refinement of practical skills—represents a characteristically American approach to theory construction, the robust intellectual pragmatist tradition articulated by William James, C. S. Peirce, and John Dewey. Knowledge in this tradition gets its validation in experiential action, which, upon reflection, reshapes preexisting words and theories.[21]

BODY SPIRITUALITY

What is little known to the public is that each of the various founders and pioneers of the Somatics methods considered that their works implied a transgressive spiritual vision that remained undeveloped and problematic within established institutions. One of the most profoundly unifying notions of the field is the idea that experiential and methodical journeys into breathing, sensing, moving, touching, cellular pulsation, and countless other interstices of bodily experience reveal not just emotional stories and releases from traumatic scars but also the depths of what people in various traditions have called the corridors of spirit: spaciousness, cosmic connection, compassion, and the acceptance of what is. Those of us who were attracted to these teachers in the 1960s were refugees from one or another formal religion, unable to find a fitting home in a foreign-grown tradition such as Vedanta or Buddhism. We were more drawn by those visions of a new kind of grounded spirituality, longing as we were for something to fill the emptiness we felt after leaving behind the religions of our forefathers, than we were by any therapeutic claims.

But because the languages of these various works are in the vocabularies of the body—names of muscles, bones, senses, anatomical parts, cells, organs—those who stand outside these works easily pigeonhole them into the old mailboxes of "body," "mind," and "spirit." For example, the experiential methods developed by Bonnie Bainbridge Cohen are as specifically anatomical as one can get, focused in minute detail on body parts, processes, and regions; at the same time, they are as spiritual in content as any classical meditation practice. Here is how she puts it in a typical passage:

> Working with the glands, there was a body that I began to experience in myself and to see in others, that lay between the pituitary and the pineal on a diagonal line going up through the nose and through the back of the head. As we got in touch with that body, we found that the present, past and future all began to merge. Now, always and never.[22]

Scholars trying to conceptualize the significance of the vast number of body-oriented practices crafted in the West during the past 100 years (but who have not experienced these worlds) can be trapped within either the classic Platonic animalistic framework or the more modern Cartesian mechanistic grid. In the Platonic view of the perennialists and Christian monasticism, these body practices—movement, sensory awareness, breathing, touch—are seen as new forms of Athenian gymnastics where oiled naked men wrestled with each other, preparing their bodies for the musical, mathematical, and mystical arts of the spirit. The body is thought of as a wild and vital animal with juices that needed to be kept from spilling over into mind and spirit. The mind needs quiet and discipline if it is to learn anything complicated, and spirit requires a purging of gross stuff. To the more modern thinker under the sway of Descartes and Galileo, the body has been purged of animal mythology and remains a stark machine—pumps, pulleys, chips, electronic signals. Like computers and automobiles, our bodies must indeed be kept in good shape so that we can engage in the truly human level of reading, writing, and thinking. Without health and vitality, those important activities cannot take place.

And yet, to those of us on the inside, something else more profound is afoot that is hard to express in old phrases. Perhaps it would be easiest to approach such realms by imitating the older Martin Heidegger, who waited silently in the Black Forest for those poets who would extricate new phrases from the soil. Best perhaps to adopt a linguistic ascetic where "body," "spirit," "mind," and "soul" are eschewed through a refusal to indulge in such easy phrases as "integrating body, mind, and spirit." Instead we might pay attention to the face, seeing there the bony prominences covered with a textured derma revealing its neuromuscular maps in its nuanced movements; its smiles and expressions of grief; its rapturous expression of orgastic release; its radiance of longing and hope. Where in that terrain does one point at "body," "mind," or "spirit"? As some of us have forced ourselves to find other phrases to describe what is going on here, we have begun to articulate the richness of the knowledge that has grown in this unique and beautiful place on the edge of the Western world that is closer to Kyoto than to Athens. The late Charlotte Selver put it this way:

> What people call "mystic"—the experiences one has, for instance in breathing, in balance, or whatever it is, on contact with another person— this can be very clearly experienced and yet experienced as a wonder, too. In other words, I feel it would be marvelous if one could work to pinpoint certain very clear revelations, which come out of experience and which in themselves are astonishing. The revelations can come from the very smallest experience. For instance, eating.[23]

Notes

1. Among the seminal works in this vital intellectual revolution are Maurice Merleau-Ponty, *Phenomenology of Perception,* trans. Colin Smith (London: Routledge and Kegan Paul, 1962); Eugene Gendlin, *Experiencing and the Creation of Meaning: A Philosophical and Psychological Approach to the Subjective* (New York: Glencoe Press, 1962); Michel Foucault, *The History of Sexuality,* vol. 1, *An Introduction,* trans. Robert

Hurley (New York: Random House, 1978); David Michael Levin, *The Body's Recollection of Being: Phenomenological Psychology and the Deconstruction of Nihilism* (London: Routledge and Kegan Paul, 1985); Michel Feher, Ramona Naddaff, and Nadia Tazi, eds., *Fragments for a History of the Human Body*, 3 vols. (New York: Zone Press, 1989); Jonathan Crary and Sanford Kwinter, eds., *Incorporations* (New York: Zone Press, 1992).

2. Eugene T. Gendlin, "The Primacy of the Body, Not the Primacy of Perception: How the Body Knows the Situation and Philosophy," *Man and World* 25, nos. 3–4 (1992): 341–353.

3. For fragments of this forgotten lineage, I am indebted to two lovely books written by its direct heirs: Carola H. Speads, *Ways to Better Breathing* (Great Neck, N.Y.: Felix Morrow, 1986), xxi ff.; and Dr. Lilly Ehrenfried, *De l'éducation du corps à l'équilibre de l'esprit* (Paris: Editions Montaigne, 1956), 133–139. The task of uncovering the history of Somatics depends on oral history, fragments mentioned by the way in exercise books or in histories of dance, a teacher mentioned in passing.

4. The development of the Delsarte System is described in Ted Shawn's *Every Little Movement* (New York: M. Wittmark, 1954), which also has a bibliography of the work.

5. Leo Kofler, *The Art of Breathing* (New York: Edgar S. Werner, 1889). The German edition was published in Kassel, Germany, by Baerenreiter Verlag, 23rd ed., 1966.

6. An extremely valuable book for a study of this period is Karl Toepfer's *The Empire of Ecstasy: Nudity and Movement in German Body Culture, 1910–1935* (Berkeley: University of California Press, 1997).

7. An insightful book for gaining a view of the burst of creative technical invention during and after the war and its effects on research in physics, is Peter Galison's *Image and Logic: A Material Culture of Microphysics* (Chicago: University of Chicago Press, 1997).

8. Hillel Schwartz describes the robust body culture present in modern dance, the martial arts, and individual sports in "Torque: The New Kinaesthetic of the Twentieth Century," in Jonathan Crary and Sanford Kwinter, eds. *Incorporations* (New York: Urzone, 1992), 70–126.

9. Charlotte Selver brought to the United States the radical bodily practices of sensory awareness, which was developed by the Berliner Elsa Gindler. See Charles V. W. Brooks, *Sensory Awareness: The Rediscovery of Experiencing through the Workshops of Charlotte Selver* (Great Neck, N.Y.: Felix Morrow, 1986).

10. Alexander Lowen studied with Wilhelm Reich and developed a secularized, less mystical version of Reich's bioenergetic approach to psychoanalysis. He has written extensively on his synthesis. See *The Language of the Body* (New York: Collier Books, 1958).

11. Ida Rolf, *Rolfing: The Integration of Human Structures* (New York: Harper & Row, 1979).

12. His book *Character Analysis,* trans. Vincent Carfagno (New York: Simon and Schuster, 1972), is an account of his evolution from psychoanalysis to bioenergetics.

13. Thomas Hanna, *Bodies in Revolt: A Primer in Somatic Thinking* (San Francisco: Holt, Rinehart, and Winston, 1970).

14. Thomas Hanna, "What Is Somatics?" *Somatics* (Spring/Summer 1986): 4–8;

Edmund Husserl, *Ideas Pertaining to a Pure Phenomenology and to Phenomenology and to a Phenomenological Philosophy: Third Book. Phenomenology and the Foundations of the Sciences*, trans. Ted E. Klein and William E. Pohl (The Hague: Martinus Nijhoff, 1980), paras. 2, 3. Cited by Elizabeth Behnke, "On the Intertwining of Phenomenology and Somatics," *The Newsletter of the Study Project in Phenomenology of the Body* 6, no. 1 (Spring 1993): 11. For an analysis of the Greek tradition, see the references in Dale B. Martin, *The Corinthian Body* (New Haven: Yale, 1995), 271n9.

15. *The Protean Body* (New York: Harper and Row, 1978); *Body: Recovering Our Sensual Wisdom* (Boston: Beacon Press, 1983; Berkeley, Calif.: North Atlantic Books, 1992, paperback); "Principles and Techniques: Towards the Unity of the Somatics Field," *Somatics* 6, no. 1 (1987): 4–8.

16. David Michael Levin and George Solomon, "The Discursive Formation of the Body in the History of Medicine," *The Journal of Medicine and Philosophy* 15 (1990): 515–537. To date, these have been co-published by North Atlantic Books and CIIS, edited by Don Hanlon Johnson: *Bone, Breath, and Gesture: Practices of Embodiment* (1995); *Groundworks: Narratives of Embodiment* (1997); *The Body in Psychotherapy: Inquiries in Somatic Psychology*, ed. with Ian J. Grand (1998).

17. For example, as this book goes to press, a major collection of articles by some seventy Somatics theorists and practitioners is being published in Germany: Gustl Marlock and Halko Weiss, ed., *The Handbook of Body Psychotherapy* (Berlin: Hogrefe Verlag, forthcoming).

18. Marcel Mauss, "The Techniques of the Body," trans. B. Brewer, *Economy and Society* 2 (1973): 70–88. See also the subsequent work of Mary Douglas, *Natural Symbols: Explorations in Cosmology* (London: Barrie and Rockliff, 1970); and Pierre Bourdieu, *Distinction: A Social Critique of the Judgement of Taste*, trans. Richard Nice (Cambridge, Mass.: Harvard University Press, 1984); and *Outline of a Theory of Practice*, trans. Richard Nice (Cambridge, Mass.: Harvard University Press, 1972).

19. Yasuo Yuasa, *The Body: Toward an Eastern Mind-Body Theory*, trans. Nagatomo Shigenori and T. P. Kasulis (New York: State University of New York Press, 1987), 25. See also his *The Body, Self-Cultivation, and Ki-Energy*, trans. Nagatomo Shigenori and Monte Hull (New York: State University of New York Press, 1993).

20. For example, see Shigehisa Kuriyama, *The Expressiveness of the Body and the Divergence of Greek and Chinese Medicine* (New York: Zone Books, 1999).

21. A book that gives a picture of the relationships between American philosophy and Somatics is Bruce W. Wilshire's *The Primal Roots of American Philosophy: Pragmatism, Phenomenology, and Native American Thought* (Harrisburg: University of Pennsylvania Press, 2000).

22. Bonnie Bainbridge Cohen and Nancy Stark Smith, "Interview with Bonnie Bainbridge Cohen," *Contact Quarterly*, no. 1 (1981): 7.

23. Charlotte Selver, "Interview with Ilana Rubenfeld," in Johnson, ed., *Bone, Breath, and Gesture*, 17.

SATAN'S HOT SPRINGS: ESALEN IN THE POPULAR EVANGELICAL IMAGINATION

Glenn W. Shuck

The bathhouse, extensively remodeled, with redwood, new tiled floors, and some new tubs, was originally a humble concrete-block structure built by a group of Christian fundamentalists in Fresno. They would have thrown down their trowels in disgust if they had known that they were erecting what would one day become America's best-known center of public and coeducational nudity.

—Walter Truett Anderson,
The Upstart Spring[1]

Educators, statesmen, jurists, entertainers, corporate moguls, and financiers were gathering just a mile up the valley from Summit at the Summit Institute for Humanistic Studies. Their semiannual conference was just getting underway, and as these global planners gathered, demon lords and warriors of the most conniving sort gathered with them, filling the valley with a swirling, sooty, steadily thickening cloud of spirits.

—Frank Peretti, *Piercing the Darkness*[2]

As I prepared a topic for this volume, I remembered a novel I had read when beginning my dissertation research on evangelical prophecy fiction. Written by Oregon pastor-turned-novelist Frank Peretti, *Piercing the Darkness* condemns much of modernity; it was difficult at the time for me to isolate one conspiracy theory from the other. But as I looked back I remembered that Peretti described a place very much like Esalen, only from a quite different perspective. Thus, when Jeffrey Kripal asked me to contribute a chapter to the present volume, it seemed reasonable enough to explore how writers from a major subsection of American popular religion view Esalen.[3] Here, then, I track the attitudes of popular evangelical writers toward Esalen, ultimately asking why they see something so menacing when they consider Esalen and its offshoots in the American religious landscape.

PERETTI AND EVANGELICAL RESPONSES TO ESALEN

Evangelical novelist Frank Peretti surprised many cultural observers during the 1980s when he rose from obscurity to achieve bestseller status—a rarity at that time among evangelical novelists. His two groundbreaking novels, *This Present Darkness* and *Piercing the Darkness,* feature small towns shrouded in demonic shadows, hostages to forces well beyond their control or understanding.[4] Besides the abundant conspiracy theories and general cultural pessimism, Peretti's novels are also unique because of the cosmology he envisions. Accidents do not just happen. Demons and angels, unseen to the human eye, fight over people and institutions, bringing about subtle and occasionally profound changes to the human world. At times their warfare seems downright trivial. In *Piercing the Darkness,* angels and demons struggle over the status of a traffic signal, for example, with the angels ultimately prevailing, giving a believer a green light.[5] Despite the deterministic implications of hordes of powerful demons and angels, we learn that humans either empower or disempower them through their prayers and allegiances. Of greater interest, however, is the fact that Peretti attributes demons to people and institutions that are not faithful to conservative evangelical belief.

In *Piercing the Darkness,* demons infiltrate the quiet town of Bacon's Corner, wreaking havoc in the community, the nondenominational Bible church, and the Christian school. They occupy the post office, the police headquarters, and, especially, the public school. At issue is a seemingly harmless curriculum developed by one Sally Beth Roe entitled "Finding the Real Me."[6] Apparently the curriculum encourages students, especially little Amber Brandon, to channel spirit guides, who invariably turn out to be demons. Amber channels Amethyst, a demon who presents itself as a harmless pony accented by rainbows and sunshine but who turns out to be a menacing little imp. After her mother, the local postmaster, recognizes something askew in Amber, she takes her to the local Christian academy. There, headmaster Tom Harris recognizes her demonic state and attempts an exorcism, which sets off a mighty chain of events that starts with abuse charges against Harris and eventually leads to nefarious conspiracies at the highest levels of power.[7]

In Peretti's imagination, the chain of demonic power leading out of Bacon's Corner is quite extensive. Peretti uses the figure of Sally Beth Roe, who becomes an aimless drifter, to illuminate the journey through the hierarchy of darkness. Essentially, Roe traces out her old stomping grounds and patterns, this time leading not to demonic possession but rather to Christian deliverance. First she returns to her alma mater, Bentmore University—a paradigmatic secular university devoted to preparing leaders for their role in building the New Age. Next, Roe's journey takes her to the Omega Center, an East Coast New Age–oriented educational facility and think tank. It was there that she developed the "Finding the Real Me" curriculum. Digging ever deeper into the conspiracy, she finds herself drawn to Chicago and the legal headquarters of the American Citizens' Freedom Association, or ACFA. Finally, Sally's demonic pursuers catch up to her and take her to their headquarters: the Summit Institute for Humanistic Studies. The greatest demon of them all, "Strongman," aka Ba'al, also makes Summit his base of operations.

Summit hosts a series of conferences for academics and those of similar nefarious influence. At the same time, it features workshops that include famous celebrities, as Peretti describes in the following passage:

> A group of about thirty conferees gathered in the crisp, scented air for a workshop led by a well-known recording artist. The young, blond-haired man had his guitar along, and some songs were planned before his talk on "Ecology: The Merging of Earth and Spirit."

There was a certain giddiness in the group. The people had never been this close to such a famous person before, and he was not the only famous person sitting there amid the rosemary, thyme, and lamb's ears. Two news-making clergymen of global stature were also in attendance, as well as a director of mystical science-fiction films whose name was a household word and whose film characters were now plastic toys in every kid's room in this country and abroad.

The blond singer strummed his guitar, and they all began to sing one of his well-known ballads. The moment was magical.

The demons among them were enjoying it as well. Such worship and attention as they were now receiving was like getting a good back rub, and they even twitched and squirmed with delight at every bar of the song's carefully shaded double meanings.[8]

When Peretti tells us that "Krystalsong," a well-known witch and scholar, is also in attendance, the temptation to translate Peretti's thinly veiled references becomes unbearable. Peretti obviously has the late John Denver in mind as his ballad singer, while the film director sounds a lot like the genius behind the *Star Wars* phenomenon, George Lucas. The "newsmaking clergymen" could include a number of figures associated with the Esalen Institute, especially the late Anglican bishop James Pike, but possibly also well-known theologians Harvey Cox and the late Paul Tillich. Krystalsong is less obvious but might point to the famous Wiccan priestess and scholar Starhawk (Miriam Simos). Finally, in case his descriptions are not obvious enough, Peretti suggests that the de-mons at this well-known retreat center for humanistic psychology also enjoy a good back rub—likely a devilish reference to Esalen's pioneering work in massage therapy and many different forms of bodywork, or So-matics, that Don Hanlon Johnson explores in his contribution to this volume.

While the fictive nature of Peretti's work makes a foolproof correla-tion with Esalen impossible, it is very evident that Peretti has a distaste for everything associated with a place remarkably similar to Esalen.[9] The combination of the importance of Peretti's fictional Summit Institute to the human potential movement along with its gardenlike resort atmo-sphere, academic conferences and workshops, emphasis on Asian religions and mystical traditions, celebrity sightings, "back rubs," and mountains, among other similarities, all tend to indicate the centrality of Esalen to Peretti's demonic landscape.[10]

Peretti is certainly not the only evangelical writer to target Esalen. Writer, talk-show host, Christian motivational speaker, and purported exorcist Bob Larson has also included Esalen in his "anti-cult" encyclopedia, *Larson's New Book of Cults*.[11] As with many such accounts, Larson gets the surface facts right but misses badly on their interpretations. He writes, for example, that "the hot baths, which initiated members may attend in the nude, are considered a rite of passage into a new life (These are not so popular now, in the age of AIDS)."[12] Actually, the hot baths remain extremely popular and have been recently remodeled. As for the rest of the quote, Larson twists the meaning and purpose of the baths, confining his summation to a few stereotypes that he apparently believes will resonate with his readers. The rest of Larson's entry on Esalen attempts to shock the reader with a lurid account of Esalen's emphasis on bodywork (a practice involving potentially unclad practitioners and clients), and he also makes generic mention of Esalen's importance to the human potential movement.

Prolific evangelical writer Dave Hunt also notes Esalen's centrality to the human potential movement, calling it "The Mecca of Human Potential."[13] Hunt, though, after briefly mentioning Esalen's origins and a few of the celebrities known to stop by, focuses on spirit channeling. He writes that "Esalen was into 'channeling' spirit entities long before it became popular."[14] Drawing data from older Esalen catalogs and Walter Truett Anderson's book about Esalen's early years, *The Upstart Spring*, Hunt discusses in particular a group of "spirit entities" called "The Nine." Hunt continues:

> Esalen had its own resident "channeler," a young English woman named Jenny O'Connor. By means of automatic writing, a group of nonhuman entities calling themselves "The Nine" (and allegedly based on the star Sirius), delivered regular messages through Jenny and were at times quite remarkable for their uncanny precognitive accuracy.[15]

Hunt goes on to write that The Nine (via Jenny O'Connor) played a significant role in Esalen's course offerings before influencing a leadership shakeup.[16] Hunt also links the power of The Nine with the late *Star Trek* developer Gene Roddenberry. Finally, Hunt closes his discussion of Esalen by associating the group with demonic entities discussed in Ephesians

6:12—the (in)famous powers and principalities of darkness dwelling in high places. Hunt's concerns do not differ substantially from those of Peretti or Larson; all worry that Esalen continues to channel, succor, and distribute powerful demonic forces.[17]

Douglas R. Groothuis, author of *Unmasking the New Age*, offers a more nuanced and restrained account of Esalen, although his ultimate analysis does not differ appreciably from the previously noted writers.[18] Groothuis briefly describes Esalen's centrality to the human potential movement:

> The Esalen Institute in Big Sur, California has been a potential "hothouse" for over three decades. Prominent at Esalen have been Michael Murphy and George Leonard, both pioneers of the New Age movement in America. Esalen has also sponsored Swami Muktananda and other assorted holy men, swamis, yogis and gurus.[19]

Groothuis also reinforces a basic evangelical suspicion of humanistic psychology, noting that "[a] recent Esalen catalog of events promises an experience where 'your discoveries are your truth without outside validation.' "[20] This is anathema for an evangelical such as Groothuis, for whom truth always requires "outside validation."

More significant, Groothuis moves from a criticism of Esalen itself to criticism of its cofounder, Michael Murphy. In analyzing the writings of Murphy, Groothuis finds that the human potential movement has crept into one of the most sacred chambers of American cultural life: sports. Murphy, as Groothuis points out, suggests that sports "can induce a mystical state of consciousness much like that spoken of in Eastern religions."[21] Groothuis further comments on Murphy's implicit goal of merging aspects of Eastern and Western religion through an emphasis on the wondrous capacities of the human body. Groothuis is also bothered by the intensity of Murphy's admiration of sports, declaring that "Murphy is almost messianic about the potential that sports unleashes."

One may not find in Groothuis's description the sort of alarm one finds in Peretti, Larson, and Hunt, but one nevertheless sees a profound suspicion of the human potential movement, a movement which takes the form of a gradual "change in consciousness."[22] Leaders in the human potential movement, Groothuis suggests, especially those at Esalen, seek to bring forth a powerful change in human consciousness in what could be described as an evolutionary process. Groothuis thus ties the human potential movement to another of popular evangelicalism's most potent enemies: evolutionary theory. He writes that "whether Darwin realized it or not, the mystical goal of the theory of evolution he championed has always been to become 'God.' "[23] Here we have an unmistakable statement of what bothers Groothuis that conspicuously omits any overt discussion of demons and spirits. The previous writers, however, beneath such mythological trappings, share Groothuis's suspicions. To further illuminate their concerns, I now turn to the more general attitudes of popular evangelical writers to the closely related "evils" of the New Age, humanism, and human potential.

HUMANISM AND THE HUMAN POTENTIAL MOVEMENT

My goal here is not to provide an analysis of what scholars of North American religion consider the human potential movement. Certainly the description which follows will not resemble what Esalen cofounders Michael Murphy and Richard Price had in mind when they took Aldous Huxley's notion of "human potentiality" and attempted to transform and apply it, with the help of George Leonard, into "the human potential."[24] Rather, I seek to relate an account of how popular evangelical writers articulate the "evils" of the New Age movement, humanism, and human potential. It is not so important here, for that matter, to understand how leaders of the human potential movement have perceived themselves (several of the contributions to this volume already cover this ground); it is much more important—at least for the purposes of this chapter—to understand how popular evangelical writers view the New Age, humanism, and, especially, the human potential movements and their potential consequences. Only through such an analysis can we gather a clearer sense of why evangelical writers are so bothered by places like Esalen and the cultural and spiritual attitudes they allegedly foster.

Perhaps the first thing one notices when evaluating the attitudes of popular evangelical writers vis-à-vis questions of humanism and human potential is that it becomes difficult to differentiate the expository accounts of many writers from Peretti's ostensibly fictive content. That is, fictional narratives read a lot like expository accounts, and expository accounts, in turn, increasingly present readers with mythological trappings that fit nicely with the mythological worldviews of many readers. Expository accounts often begin with a somewhat analytical tone, explaining what the future holds for their readers in a rather matter-of-fact style, and end up with a message and style quite a bit like Peretti's, albeit lacking his more colorful narrative.

The next trait one will likely notice is that the literature often either fails to account for the diversity of belief and practice among those associated with the "New Age" or blatantly overlooks it. Texe Marrs, a popular and prolific evangelical writer, conflates the enemies of Christianity under one rubric: the New Age movement. He writes:

> The New Age is a universal, open-arms religion that excludes from its ranks only those who believe in Jesus Christ and a personal God. Buddhists, Shintoists, Satanists, Secular Humanists, witches, witch doctors, and shamans— all who reject Christianity are invited to become trusted members of the New Age family. Worshippers of separate faiths and denominations are to be unified in a common purpose: the glorification of man.[25]

Elsewhere, Marrs seems to recognize the inherent unwieldiness of such a combination, admitting that diversity exists within the New Age and writing that "there is no one organizational hierarchy or any document or statement of belief that unites all such groups."[26] Yet Marrs goes on to make the conflation, claiming that "most of the groups alleged to be autonomous are, in fact, integral components of the apparatus opposed to biblical Christianity."[27] Marrs thus lumps together divergent groups out of the conviction that they engage in, as he phrases it, the anti-Christian "glorification of man."[28]

Discussing actress Shirley MacLaine and her well-known New Age affinities, evangelical writers John Ankerberg and John Weldon go "out on a limb" to make Marrs's point even more explicitly, conveying "human potential" as a powerful subset of the New Age, one that necessarily grows out of any involvement with New Age ideas. They write that "mystical experiences have led New Agers to believe that they truly are one with the universe and are part of God. It has also led them to believe that they have uncovered 'human potential,' an alleged divine power within themselves that, they think, exists in all men."[29] The present section—at least for the purpose of description—takes such writers at their word, no matter how questionable their observations may appear.

The negative response of popular evangelical writers to the human potential movement is more deep-seated than spontaneous. This is to say, even if they lacked the New Age or human potential as all-encompassing organizational categories, popular evangelical writers would still require such an oppositional force to help them express their reservations about modernity. Notions of human potential challenge the Calvinist heritage of many conservative evangelicals, confronting their deeply rooted belief that humans, although they are made "in the image of God," ultimately occupy an ontological sphere wholly other from that of God that prevents them from building the Tower of Babel and reaching up to Godhood. The human potential movement, in contrast, seeks to blur such hard ontological boundaries. Put simply—although more will be said about this shortly—evangelicals are much more concerned with describing the nature of God and what they associate with God's own "potential" than "human potential" in and of itself. The New Age movement, humanism, and the human potential movement are all just different names for a continuum of hostile cultural forces that promote a worldview quite opposed to that of popular evangelicalism, or so at least many of their writers insist.

The allegedly vile agenda of such an axis of evil is certainly under-scored by one of popular evangelicalism's most prominent figures, Tim LaHaye. LaHaye, who is best known for his megaselling *Left Behind* series of novels, which was co-written with Jerry Jenkins, was a cultural and political activist many years before he became a novelist. Indeed, historian Larry Eskridge has called LaHaye "the most influential American evangelical of the last twenty-five years."[30] LaHaye's nonfiction titles, beginning especially with *The Battle for the Mind*, published in 1980, lay out his considerable agenda.[31] Although LaHaye impugns a number of cultural forces he views as antagonistic to the values of evangelicalism, he focuses on a particularly insidious and vile threat he calls "secular humanism." Secular humanism subsumes for LaHaye a number of other problematic areas. He offers a concise definition:

> Secular humanism is the philosophic base of liberalism and is easily defined. I call it a Godless, man-centered philosophy of life that rejects moral ab-

solutes and traditional values. It makes man the measure of all things rather than God. It is usually hostile toward religion in general, with a particular hatred toward Christianity. I consider this worldview to be the most harmful, anti-American, anti-Christian philosophy in our country today. Most of society's current evils can be traced to secular humanist thinkers or liberals whose theories originated in that philosophy.[32]

LaHaye's objections to modernity in *Battle for the Mind,* although extensive, can be summed up by his objection to the sentiments expressed by the ancient Greek philosopher Protagoras that "man is the measure of all things."[33] The steady insidious slide of the nation into the pit of humanism, LaHaye believes, threatens to turn Americans away from God as the measure of all things and toward nothing other than themselves.

LaHaye provides his readers with a historical background of humanism. He claims that the apostle Paul, who opposed "the wisdom of man," and the vigor of the early Church helped to minimize the harmful effects of humanism—at least until Thomas Aquinas came on the scene in the thirteenth century.[34] LaHaye writes that "Aquinas opened the door for free-thinking educators to gradually implant more of the wisdom of man, as they discarded the wisdom of God. Eventually, man's wisdom became truth to secular man."[35] LaHaye moves quickly from Aquinas on to the Renaissance before attacking the humanistic contributions of nineteenth-century German philosophers Georg Friedrich Hegel, Ludwig Feuerbach, and Friedrich Nietzsche.[36] Finally, LaHaye condemns the educational philosophy of John Dewey before tying contemporary intellectuals and educators to the ancient and self-perpetuating heresy of humanism.

Humanism as a category is incredibly vast, which gives LaHaye the opportunity to take his critique in any number of directions. It is no surprise that his concerns settle on the religious and cultural realms. He cites humanism as a new religion, one that will ultimately rally the world around the banner of humanity and its inherent goodness and potential before paving the way for the ascent of the antichrist. LaHaye quotes part of Oliver Reiser's *Humanist Manifesto,* a collection LaHaye views as the bible of humanism:

> While this age does owe a vast debt to traditional religions, it is none the less [*sic*] obvious that any religion that can hope to be a synthesizing and dynamic force for today must be shaped for the needs of this age. To establish such a religion is a major necessity of the present.[37]

LaHaye's suggestion is quite clear: humanism is a powerful, dangerous, and deceptive religious movement. But what kind of religion is it, besides one that promotes the interests of autonomous humanity vis-à-vis notions of a God-centered cosmos? LaHaye makes a case for humanism as a religion in itself, which is fair enough, but, like Marrs, he also considers humanism a form of paganism and associates it with religions such as "Babylonian mysticism"—a catch-all term for religions that present options to the Judeo-Christian worldview and which also auger the arrival of the End Times.[38] For example, LaHaye's critique—more fully developed in the *Left Behind* series and its accompanying expository volumes— extends to the religions associated with the New Age movement.[39] Yet their notion of humanism is quite different and not readily compatible with what LaHaye associates with the *Humanist Manifesto*. Both may share a long trajectory anchored by Protagoras's proclamation of man as the measure of all things, but there are important differences. For example, Prometheus Books, a publishing house associated with skeptics and "debunkers" who tend to sneer at New Age claims of human potential, publishes the *Humanist Manifesto*. This incongruity obviously does not faze LaHaye, who sees a much stronger thread of Satanic conspiracy undergirding all of it. It is a truism that friends seem to possess great internal diversity while enemies often appear monolithic. Humanism, for LaHaye, is the deadly worship of humanity and its alleged ability to dispense with God—whatever the particular nuances.

This brings me, finally, to a brief description of how popular evangelical writers view the human potential movement. Much of this has already been covered and may appear obvious, given the content of the last several pages. Nevertheless, there are a few angles yet to explore. We have seen that Tim LaHaye uses the *Humanist Manifesto* to condemn the New Age and humanism and, tangentially, notions of human potential. Bob Larson makes the connection even more obvious, however. For Larson, the human potential movement is an outgrowth of the *Humanist Manifestoes I* and *II*, published in 1933 and 1973, respectively. The movement began in earnest with mid-century developments in humanistic psychology before intensifying and assuming greater definition along the idyllic shores of Big Sur at the Esalen Institute during the 1960s.[40] Never mind that placing representatives from Esalen together in a small room alongside researchers associated with Prometheus Press would likely bring forth bloodshed, intellectual or otherwise. Larson, like his fellows in popular evangelical literature, tends to overlook the differences of their enemies, who favor a global conspiracy aimed against evangelicals and their notion of God. Larson writes that "[t]he error of Eden was the serpent's lie that man's understanding would allow him to be a god. Human Potential Movement courses resurrect this falsehood with supposedly pure motives of enhancing self-esteem and improving business environments."[41] But the result, Larson implies, is just another demonically inspired heresy of human perfectionism.

Douglas Groothuis again provides a cogent summary of evangelical views on human potential, writing an account that uncannily parallels the descriptions and beliefs of those associated with Esalen and the broader human potential movement.[42] In a section he titles "The Politics of Transformation," Groothuis impugns the notion of evolution. While this is nothing new for an evangelical writer, Groothuis appears most concerned with a subtler form of evolution than the much more popularized biological version. He worries, in other words, about the gradual yet profound transformation of consciousness sought by leaders of the human potential movement. Starting with a critique of such seemingly benign methods as changing human consciousness, Groothuis makes the connection between the pursuit of deeply personal transformations and the transformation of culture on a large scale. Indeed, Groothuis appears to place more faith in the ultimate political efficacy of the human potential movement than many of its critics on the left who suspect that such introspective methods of fomenting change amount to little more than political quietism.[43] Groothuis obviously believes differently. Although he writes that this new consciousness will help bring forth such traditional evangelical bugaboos as "a new economic order, a stronger United Nations and a centralized government,"[44] it might be best to leave aside the specifics and focus on the simple fact that he believes—and worries—that something important may indeed be happening because of the human potential movement. Thus Groothuis on a more sophisticated level shares the suspicions of his fellow evangelical writers when he takes Esalen and the human potential movement at their respective words. Whatever else popular evangelical writers think of Esalen, they believe that it is having a major personal, cultural, and political impact in the contemporary world.

The previous section noted most of the reasons why popular evangelical writers have responded so critically to Esalen and the workings of the human potential movements. These writers tie Esalen into a much larger conspiracy that threatens basic evangelical beliefs and values. Besides the trepidations of modernity—its global plots, secret organizations, and the consolidation of power into the hands of the few—one also finds a stronger condemnation of a basic move toward the autonomy of humans at the expense of beliefs in an all-powerful yet still personal God. Whatever else the global conspirators may be up to, in other words, their chief aim is to delude humanity into believing that it is capable of great things, discarding God in the process. Popular evangelical writers, obviously, are vehemently opposed to such trends.

Another factor may be at work, however. I have written elsewhere that popular evangelical identity is a fragile construct that requires a clear articulation of "the enemy" in order to define what it means to be an evangelical in good standing.[45] Writers such as Frank Peretti and Bob Larson, for example, go to great lengths to demonize their enemies, articulating in the process what is unacceptable belief or behavior for the true followers of God. It is a convenient strategy, but one that presents great risks to those who take it too seriously. After all, believers may come to rely too much on external forces for self-definition, getting caught up with and evolving alongside their cultural foes.[46] A simpler explanation involves the fear of evangelical writers that New Age practices may creep into the churches, corrupting true belief with, as one writer puts it, "ancient evil."[47] Either way, the growth of the New Age and its human potential wing threaten the integrity of popular evangelicalism—according to the latter's most ardent defenders.

There is yet another related reason that plays a role in the opposition of popular evangelical writers to Esalen. Esalen and the human potential movement, to put it succinctly, represent competent adversaries in the quest for spiritual seekers. The late evangelical writer Randall Baer, an expert on crystals and other aspects of the New Age movement before his conversion to conservative Protestantism, explicitly denied this. He wrote that it was quite rare for a former New Ager such as himself to make the journey into conservative Protestantism.[48] Yet Baer's case demonstrates that evangelicals recognize the potential for significant movement between the New Age and evangelical worlds. For example, Sally Beth Roe, makes the (literal) journey from the New Age into the waiting arms of Bible-believing evangelicalism. Such spiritual fluidity is not lost on evangelical literati, who worry that their literary sheep might find different flocks. Bob Larson warns his readers against a wide variety of "cults," while Dave Hunt and Douglas Groothuis point out the insidious and seductive nature of New Age beliefs. Clearly evangelical writers believe that rank-and-file believers are not immune to the temptations (or competition) peddled by the purveyors of New Age ideas, to say nothing of spiritual seekers who have yet to make a commitment one way or the other.

Sociologist Wade Clark Roof notes the seeker orientation of many Baby Boomer evangelicals, who could easily slip between either worldview. He points out that various evangelical megachurches and nondenominational "seeker churches" appeal to those looking for self-transformation and profound spiritual connections, often without either high pressure or traditional "churchy" elements.[49] The human potential movement offers seekers many of the same things, albeit with certain variations that popular evangelical writers are all too eager to point out. Competition in the spiritual marketplace may in the final analysis provide just as significant an explanation for the evangelical antipathy toward Esalen as any of their own justifications.

In sum, we must take both explanations seriously because they are two sides of the same coin. Popular evangelical writers worry that Esalen and its relatives within the human potential movement pose a dire threaten to their core values, especially if left unchecked. But they also worry that potential believers—perhaps even those already in the fold—may choose other shepherds unless they are sufficiently deterred. Thus, Esalen, that legendary bohemian experiment of human consciousness situated precariously between the cold vast expanse of the Pacific Ocean and the rapidly rising Santa Lucia Range, provides an ideal adversary for those unable or unwilling to answer the challenges posed to their own world-views by the relentlessly encroaching forces of modernity.

NOTES

1. Walter Truett Anderson, *The Upstart Spring: Esalen and the American Awakening* (Reading, Mass.: Addison Wesley, 1983).

2. Frank E. Peretti, *Piercing the Darkness* (Westchester, Ill.: Crossway Books, 1989), 363.

3. I define "popular evangelicals" as those who hold several, if not most, of the following traits: 1) they take the Bible as a guiding, and perhaps inerrant, authority; 2) they believe that one must be saved and have a second birth in Christ—that is, have a "born again" experience; 3) they feel the need to "witness," or offer their faith to others; 4) they believe that each individual must freely choose for or against Christ; 5) and they believe that Christ will return soon to reclaim his earthly kingdom. Since I am writing here about a form of *popular* religion, the precise beliefs of any one believer may deviate somewhat from this formula but still fall under the evangelical label. Moreover, I am not attempting an all-purpose definition of *evangelicalism proper* (it excludes certain Christian Reformed groups, for example, although these groups share many of the concerns raised in this chapter by their more popularized cousins). Rather, again, I am trying to describe for readers the outlines of a popular religious movement; really, a "folk religion" as historian George Marsden has described it, not simply a denomination or continuum of denominations. Moreover, much symbolic blood has been spilled on this issue; thus I want to make my "popular" usage as clear as possible. See George Marsden, ed., *Evangelicalism and Modern America* (Grand Rapids, Mich.: Eerdman's, 1984), x. Finally, in terms of numbers, estimates place the total number of American popular evangelicals at between 60 million to 80 million, depending largely upon the methods and categories one uses. For more on the definitions and the demographics of American evangelicals, see James Davison Hunter, *Evangelicalism: The Coming Generation* (New York: Oxford University Press, 1987); and Christian Smith, *Christian America? What Evangelicals Really Want* (Berkeley: University of California Press, 2000), 16.

4. Frank E. Peretti, *This Present Darkness* (Westchester, Ill.: Crossway Books, 1986). Peretti's first bestseller originated the formula found in *Piercing the Darkness,* that of small towns embattled by demons and conspiratorial forces outside the understanding of common folk. Notably, *This Present Darkness* received a major boost when Christian pop star Amy Grant began promoting the novel at her concerts.

5. Peretti, *Piercing the Darkness,* 383.

6. The name Sally Beth Roe is evocative of Jane Roe, the pseudonym used by Norma McCorvey in the landmark 1973 Supreme Court decision expanding the scope of pro-choice rights. Peretti creates a character whose struggles also bear remarkable resemblance to those of McCorvey. Peretti's Roe has an abortion before regretting that decision and, like McCorvey, struggles with an extended crisis of values. More-

over, Peretti's fictional character, using the language McCorvey's Web site deploys to describe her crisis of values, is "a helpless pawn in a powerful game." Finally, like the fictional Roe, McCorvey has done an about-face, becoming an outspoken pro-life activist. See McCorvey's Web site at http://www.roenomore.org (accessed March 2, 2004).

7. What Peretti describes in his paranoid though remarkably gripping prose is not unlike what happened with the infamous Salem witch trials of 1692. For an especially solid historical and psychosociological account of the Salem witch trials, see Paul S. Boyer and Stephen Nissenbaum, *Salem Possessed: The Social Origins of Witchcraft* (Cambridge, Mass.: Harvard University Press, 1974).

8. Peretti, *Piercing the Darkness,* 378.

9. While Peretti's attention to Esalen is obvious, his Summit Institute may incorporate the activities of any number of other centers of the human potential movement, including especially the Omega Institute for Holistic Studies in Rhinebeck, New York, and Naropa University in Boulder, Colorado. I should also mention the Summit Lighthouse of Mark (d. 1973) and Elizabeth Clare Prophet headquartered in Gardiner, Montana. Summit has run afoul of popular evangelical writers for promoting theosophical ideas, including alleged contact with ascended spiritual masters. Evangelical writers, of course, view such masters as demons. Summit's description of Mark Prophet is especially suggestive of a relational pattern between New Age leaders and evangelical Protestantism, a theme I take up later in the chapter: "Mark L. Prophet (1918–1973) was a mystic, a Messenger for the ascended masters and the late husband of Elizabeth Clare Prophet. When Mark was about 17, he was contacted by the ascended Master El Morya. *Because of his fundamentalist Christian upbringing* [emphasis added], Mark sent the master away. Years later, Mark decided to pursue El Morya and the master resumed his contact with him." See the Web site of the Summit Lighthouse at http://www.tsl.org/messengers/mlp.asp (accessed February 25, 2004).

10. For the sake of those interested in the plotlines of *Piercing the Darkness,* Sally is taken to the Summit Institute, where she is tortured in a cottage while the conference goes on outside. The angels quickly achieve dominance, however, and swoop down upon all of the institutions in Peretti's hierarchy, finally attacking Summit, where they allow Sally to escape through the gates and into the nearby forest. Sally symbolically escapes the clutches of the New Age and enters the waiting arms of evangelical Protestantism.

11. Bob Larson, *Larson's New Book of Cults* (Wheaton, Ill.: Tyndale House, 1982), 212–213. See also Bob Larson, *Abaddon* (Nashville, Tenn.: Thomas Nelson, 1983). Larson, like Peretti, has tried has hand with evangelical fiction, focusing on problems of demonic possession allegedly induced by childhood abuse and death metal music. Larson's exorcism operations have thrived; Larson now operates a training program for hopeful exorcists called Do What Jesus Did. See also Bob Larson's Web site, http://www.boblarson.org (accessed February 25, 2004).

12. Larson, *Larson's New Book of Cults,* 212.

13. Dave Hunt, *Occult Invasion* (Eugene, Ore.: Harvest House, 1998), 444–445.

14. Ibid, 445.

15. Ibid. See also Anderson, *The Upstart Spring,* 305. According to Anderson (whom Hunt cites) Jenny's remarkable prediction involved the Washington Redskins defeating the Miami Dolphins 27–21, a score that while closer than the actual final

score, was still closer than the outcome predicted by veteran football analysts and professional gamblers. In this case, Jenny merely beat the spread. Her prediction might have been genuinely otherworldly had she successfully picked the American Football Conference champions, the Dolphins.

16. Hunt, *Occult Invasion*, 445. See also Anderson, *The Upstart Spring*, 304–305. Hunt uses Anderson as his source for the leadership shake-up and the prominent role played by Jenny O'Connor and "The Nine."

17. It is also interesting that while Hunt admits that the late Esalen cofounder Richard Price may have thought of The Nine as "unconscious projections," Hunt gives credulity to a supernatural explanation. I find this point interesting because evangelical writers such as Hunt do not consider demons to be mythological forces that symbolize psychological or cultural anxieties. Their writings make it evident that they believe in *real* personified demons.

18. Douglas R. Groothuis, *Unmasking the New Age* (Downer's Grove, Ill.: InterVarsity Press, 1986), 22–23, 79.

19. Ibid, 79.

20. Ibid.

21. Ibid, 23.

22. Ibid.

23. Ibid, 20.

24. Anderson, *The Upstart Spring*, 10–11, 64–65, 121. Also, although Murphy and Leonard understood their work as dealing with *the* human potential—maintaining the definite article, in other words—evangelical writers invariably drop the article in their own descriptions. Thus to maintain consistency with my sources, I, too, drop the article out of *the* human potential, at least when describing it from an evangelical perspective.

25. Texe Marrs, *Dark Secrets of the New Age: Satan's Plan for a One World Religion* (Westchester, Ill.: Crossway, 1987), 13.

26. Texe Marrs, *Mega Forces: Signs and Wonders of the Coming Chaos* (Austin, Tex.: Living Truth, 1987), 245.

27. Ibid, 246.

28. Marrs, *Dark Secrets of the New Age*, 13.

29. John Ankerberg and John Weldon, *The Facts on the New Age Movement* (Eugene, Ore.: Harvest House, 1988), 7.

30. Larry Eskridge quoted in *Rolling Stone*, "Reverend Doomsday: According to Tim LaHaye, the Apocalypse Is Now," January 28, 2004. Available online at http:www.rollingstone.com (accessed March 3, 2004).

31. Tim LaHaye, *You Are Engaged in the Battle for the Mind: A Subtle Warfare* (Old Tappan, N.J.: Revell, 1980).

32. Tim LaHaye, *The Race for the 21st Century* (Nashville, Tenn.: Thomas Nelson, 1986), 139–140.

33. LaHaye, *The Battle for the Mind*, 28. See also Wouter J. Hanegraaff's contribution to this volume, "Human Potential Before Esalen: An Experiment in Anachronism," for historical background on the roots of the human potential movement.

34. LaHaye, *The Battle for the Mind*, 27–46, 57–83.

35. Ibid, 29.

36. Ibid, 59. It is interesting, especially in the case of Nietzsche, that LaHaye refers to them as "German *rationalists* [emphasis added]."

37. Ibid, 94.

38. Ibid, 133.

39. For more on LaHaye and his critique of New Age religion, see Glenn W. Shuck, *Marks of the Beast: Left Behind and the Struggle for Evangelical Identity* (New York: New York University Press, 2004). Chapter 4 is especially relevant.

40. Larson, *Larson's New Book of Cults*, 251–253.

41. Ibid, 253.

42. Groothuis, *Unmasking the New Age*, 118–119.

43. Anderson, *The Upstart Spring*, 281–283, 304.

44. Groothuis, *Unmasking the New Age*, 119.

45. Shuck, *Marks of the Beast*. See especially Chapters 5 and 6.

46. This reminds me of a car-bumper decoration that has grown more popular in recent years. Especially in the Bible Belt of the southern United States, many evangelicals have placed fish symbols on their cars for years to identify themselves as Christians. Recently, a variation has appeared featuring a bigger fish with legs with its body marked "Darwin" eating the smaller fish. Some evangelicals, not to be out-done, have added a still larger fish marked "Truth" eating the evolved "Darwin" fish. Believers may not be aware, however, that they have been drawn ironically into the very sort of evolutionary process they would so fervently oppose. Such is a danger of incautious opposition.

47. Joseph Carr, *The Lucifer Connection* (Lafayette, La.: Huntington House, 1987), 97–101. Carr is especially concerned about the practice of "visualization," which he claims is rampant in many churches. My personal experience with an evangelical secondary school attests to this, as one coach encouraged students to visualize them-selves becoming better basketball players. In any event, it was woefully unsuccessful in my case.

48. Randall Baer, *Inside the New Age Nightmare* (Lafayette, La.: Huntington House, 1989), 73. Baer writes that "in the New Age context, converts to Christianity are rare; and former leaders converting to the Christian faith are unheard-of. To totally cut all ties with the subculture seemed a radically backward spiritual move to make." Yet Baer's obsession with the possibility of such movement appears to provide the impetus for his ministry. See also Hal Lindsey with C. C. Carlson, *Satan Is Alive and Well on Planet Earth* (Grand Rapids, Mich.: Zondervan, 1972), 15–17. To cite a contrary anecdote, Hal Lindsey, writing on the New Age movement, describes a woman who renounced satanically derived psychic powers once she discovered the truth from Lindsey. Lindsey fills his book, in fact, with accounts of those who have "overcome" New Age beliefs. His strategy in using the anecdotes is no doubt evan-gelical in purpose. Still, he deploys it for a reason: there are believers to be won among adherents of the New Age. He must also account for current believers who require stern reinforcement against New Age temptations.

49. Wade Clark Roof, *Spiritual Marketplace: Baby Boomers and the Remaking of American Religion* (Princeton, N.J.: Princeton University Press, 1999), 94–96.

ESALEN INSTITUTE, ESSENCE FAITHS, AND THE RELIGIOUS MARKETPLACE

Marion S. Goldman

Esalen brings together essence faiths from both eastern and western spiritual traditions. These religions do not have deities who reveal ultimate truths, nor do they provide for personal relationships with deities. Instead, essence religions posit ephemeral, omnipresent supernatural essences within individuals and, in some traditions, corresponding divine essences in the natural world.[1] Sociologists define essence religious traditions as spiritual practices that involve impersonal forces which rule or order all life on earth. These forces are remote, intangible divine elements which human beings can feel and experience but which elude possibilities for explicit social interaction.

Most theory and research about successful religious groups looks at western monotheistic faiths that grow and prosper over many generations to become widely accepted religions. Contemporary sociologists often discount the impact of both western and eastern essence religions in the United States, noting their small membership and limited influence.[2] However, these religious traditions have continued over generations, shaping a variety of new religious movements, revitalizing liberal mainstream religions, and influencing the dominant culture.

The category of essence faith includes a range of spiritual traditions, many of which differ with one another in significant matters of doctrine. Some, such as Gnosticism, which Wouter Hanegraaff discusses in this volume, were all but invisible in the United States. But a vast number of faiths from Unitarianism to Americanized Zen to the philosophies of Bhagwan Shree Rajneesh/Osho to Scientology fall into the broad category of essence religions. Some essence groups focus on a small number of elect with divine possibilities, but most American essence traditions democratically affirm potential for growth and godliness in everyone.

American essence traditions are in medium to high tension with conservative Christian doctrine, which affirms one *true* God and offers strict guidelines for steps to salvation.[3] Usually, in both East and West, essence faiths are elite faiths; most of their founders and core members are educated members of the upper and upper-middle classes. Central members of Esalen's founding generation were drawn from liberal Protestant and Jewish denominations and ultraliberal post–Vatican II Roman Catholics. During the 1960s, these groups or parts of them substituted moral principles for experience of the supernatural. By exposing individuals to a vast range of supernatural and transpersonal experiences drawn from emerging essence traditions, Esalen revitalized the spiritual lives of disaffected members of liberal denominations and brought members to novel faiths which emerged during the 1960s and 1970s.

I will consider Esalen as a spiritual retreat, think tank, and pilgrimage center and as an example of the relatively recent phenomenon of personal growth centers which revitalize parts of established liberal denominations and support and create networks among influential members of established essence faiths. This chapter examines Esalen as an example that enables us to consider ties between liberal philosophies and denominations and the numerous novel essence faiths which have spread throughout the United States since the 1960s.

Esalen is an appropriate case because it is the longest established and most influential North American personal growth center and retreat center with an explicit spiritual agenda. Over four decades, two major North American growth centers and two major alternative educational institutions drew from both Esalen's model and its constituencies. Informal exchanges and cross-membership in leadership roles link Esalen with Hollyhock Institute, Omega Institute, the California Institute of Integral Studies, and Naropa University.

The Institute is a crucible for contemporary essence religion and quest culture. I will describe Esalen, its role in the cultural history of American religion, and its underlying belief system. I posit that Esalen and a handful of other spiritual growth centers and alternative institutions bring together, revitalize, and increase the cultural influence of established and innovative essence faiths.

RESEARCH

In the 1970s and early 1980s, Esalen provided a gateway to a number of novel spiritual groups, introducing seekers to new religious experiences and emergent gurus in scheduled workshops and lectures. The movements nurtured at Esalen included Erhard training seminars, psychosynthesis, Arica, Fritz Perls's Gestalt approach and the Rajneesh movement. My interest in Esalen developed in response to the Institute's pivotal role in the spiritual marketplace as a fertile birthplace of or bridge to emerging new religious movements.[4] I shifted to closer examination of Esalen as an example of institutions that sustain markets for elite essence religions and spiritual services.

I locate Esalen at the center of a web of related institutions. This partially visible network includes alternative colleges and graduate schools, foundations that fund spiritual research and practice, and recognized professional organizations that bring unconventional physical and health practices into the mainstream. Sometimes intersecting with the edges of this network, liberal denominations and religious organizations, such as the National Council of Churches (NCC), have drawn from and contributed to Esalen.[5]

Data for this chapter came from Esalen catalogues from 1964 through 2002, with particular emphasis on the 1970s, when Esalen had its greatest international visibility. I examined those materials in terms of workshops offered, board members, and central themes. I also interviewed a number of individuals, including Walter Truett Anderson and Michael Murphy. Over the past two and a half years, I participated and observed at Esalen and at related alternative spiritual establishments ranging from bookstores to psychodrama workshops to yoga classes.

ELITE TRADITIONS

Essence faiths have been active throughout the world for centuries.[6] A number of sociologists[7] assert that essence traditions appeal to only limited numbers of intellectuals while mass faiths with many committed members thrive because they have one or more deities who embody rewards on earth and in the afterlife. Stark charts the rise of popular Buddhism in India and China,[8] illustrating how it developed into a mass faith only after a pantheon of gods and goddesses superseded some amorphous divine essence. A number of small contemporary novel religions based on divine essence eventually created a single powerful deity.[9] According to this theoretical tradition, the most culturally influential and personally meaningful faiths involve a unique deity who provides rigorous moral rules and requires singular belief and personal action grounded in spiritual conviction.[10]

The idea of "one and only one true God," however, may have little appeal to wide segments of the American population, particularly those reared in liberal or eclectic religious traditions. These individuals are usually educated and relatively affluent.[11] Beginning in the early nineteenth century, urban intellectuals in large American cities generated and spread essence traditions, encouraging similar seekers toward spiritual exploration and theoretical speculation.

The first major group to develop unique American essence traditions emerged around Boston, where varied American transcendentalisms appeared in the early nineteenth century.[12] Both the Transcendentalists and those who founded Esalen more than a century later shared much in common with Max Weber's nineteenth-century South Asian elites, whose religious virtuosity rested on their belief in divine essence. Describing their symbolic system, Weber noted, "It unites a virtuoso-like self-redemption by man's own effort with universal accessibility of salvation."[13] He also described the importance of contemplation and inner-worldly vocational ethics for religious virtuosi who gave up possibilities of worldly success in order to pursue spiritual goals.

Contemporary essence religions attract and hold financially, intellectually, and culturally empowered seekers, whose religious quests usually eclipse their material ambitions. The Institute attracts talented seekers, and its workshops and conferences create professional pathways for the most-dedicated virtuosi, whose economic and social lives revolve around spiritual pursuits. Esalen's recent catalogues (2002–2003) reveal complicated sets of workshops, conferences, publications, and spiritual services that serve both full-time virtuosi and part-time seekers. The Institute functions like a bazaar, offering dozens of different spiritual traditions, all of which involve belief in divinity within individuals and often in the natural world as well.

As other authors in this volume note, Esalen emerged in the 1960s along with other political and cultural social movements. From its beginnings in the early 1960s, the Institute provided a space for pursuit of shared personal visions and ideas of collective good. The affluent individuals who made up Esalen's founding generation defined spirituality in ways that resonated with them and made sense of their personal experiences.[14] Their characterizations and implementation of spirituality inevitably reflected their own social and spiritual experiences.[15] Founding members symbolically separated themselves from the crass materialism of the late 1950s, although not necessarily from material comforts or pursuit of socially responsible, esthetically satisfying rewards.[16]

The rise and fall of different groups, ranging from the Rajneeshees to Christian Science to the Mormons, has often been described in terms of shifts in the religious marketplace.[17] Both national and local religious marketplaces involve a range of spiritual organizations that seek to attract or hold religious adherents and the unchurched believers seeking affiliations with one group over another. Like mid-nineteenth-century Boston, the mid-twentieth-century San Francisco Bay area was a vital marketplace for religious ideas and spiritual practices because of its rapid population growth and its major universities with surrounding campus communities. The University of California to the east and Stanford to the south contributed members and ideas to emerging movements that helped generate Esalen and which were in turn energized by the Institute. Bay Area intelligentsia were far more geographically and intellectually diverse than those of the Back Bay of a century before. And the Bay Area's geographic and intellectual dispersion generated demand for a pilgrimage center which could draw together established and emerging essence spiritualities.

Cultivating that essential spark of divinity remains central to Esalen's foundational doctrine, although Michael Murphy, Esalen's cofounder, emphasized the idea of an evolutionary leap forward that might be hastened if human abilities could reach their optimal levels.[18] Esalen began as an intellectual seminar center at Big Sur Hot Springs in 1962, and it was formally incorporated and renamed Esalen Institute by 1964 as programs expanded to include experience-based workshops that encouraged personal growth and collective discoveries of eternal spiritual truths.[19] As the flagship of the human potential movement, Esalen significantly influenced contemporary American spirituality, personal growth psychologies, and bodywork.[20] The multifaceted approach involves emotion, body, and intellect integrated around a spiritual core. One early Esalen catalogue (Fall 1964–Winter 1965), offered a "promise of a new sanctity and the good life."

Throughout its first decade, Esalen had a number of explicit ties to liberal essence traditions. The Institute received grants from the National Council of Churches in 1969, which also sent representatives to Esalen from its Department of Educational Development.[21] Liberal essence-oriented Protestant and Roman Catholic clergy came to Esalen, attempting to deepen their spiritual practice and explore and apply techniques from encounter groups. Several novel spiritual groups emerged directly from Esalen, notably Arica.[22]

ESALEN'S NICHE

Situated on a breathtaking stretch of the Pacific Coast less than three hours south of San Francisco, Esalen has been a magnet for four decades, attracting a wide range of teachers, artists, philosophers, and writers to lead workshops and lecture to participants ranging from seasoned practitioners to novice seekers. Green hills and pine, cypress, and eucalyptus trees surround rocky cliffs and create an enchanted landscape. The crucial markers of that landscape are natural hot springs, which are channeled into tubs overlooking the sea. Fragrances from the trees mingle with salt spray, sulfurous fumes from the springs, and smoke from woodstoves and other sources, creating a place where all senses can be revived and cultivated.

Landscape is Esalen's keystone; the spectacular setting dramatically adds to the Institute's allure and mythology. According to legend, the long-vanished Esselen Indians valued the extraordinary stretch of coastline along the fifty-three miles of Big Sur as a sacred space which was special, different, and invested with meaning.[23] Jack London, Lillian Ross, and Robinson Jeffers wrote about Big Sur's magic in the early twentieth century, and the region gained literary notoriety in the late 1940s when bohemian writers, musicians, and poets such as Henry Miller and Anaïs Nin settled along the fifty miles of Big Sur coastline.[24] Coastal cottages and motels attracted Hollywood celebrities such as Rita Hayworth and Orson Welles and, later in the 1960s, Richard Burton and Elizabeth Taylor.[25] Most of the area, however, was populated by woodsmen, farmers, and small businesspeople who gathered at the local Grange and usually distanced themselves from the bohemian culture. Today, Esalen's interdependent internal cultures are as numerous as those in the Big Sur area, although less than seventy staff members or work-study interns live on site or in nearby communities at any given time.[26]

This chapter considers only the segment of Esalen which is directed toward educated seekers. The focus, therefore, is on general religious foundations rather than on specific spiritual practices, although the two are almost inevitably intermeshed at Esalen. I also focus on public presentations rather than personal engagement, although I recognize that public, political, and personal cannot be separated fully.

Cofounder Michael Murphy's original vision was of a seminar center that dealt with spiritual growth and human possibilities. Soon after Esalen started, however, his cofounder, Richard Price, began to emphasize the experiential aspects of personal growth, particularly as they were framed through encounter groups and early versions of Gestalt therapy.[27] These dramatic experiential approaches shaped Esalen's public image, although essence spirituality was implicitly part of them. A third significant part of Esalen since shortly after its founding involves body work, particularly Esalen massage, which developed from a number of resources, especially Charlotte Selver's sensory work and Ida Rolf's deep-tissue approaches.[28] While Esalen massage is internationally known and branded, the Esalen bodyworkers are relatively tangential to Murphy's vision and to the Institute's current governing board.[29]

The fourth overlapping group that is part of Esalen's core includes its long-term community, who live in the Big Sur area or at Esalen itself. They deal with Esalen's operations—its gardens, buildings, hot springs, kitchens, guest relations, and myriad other parts of the spiritual retreat—supporting the infrastructure of the idyllic countercultural haven. A number of bodyworkers also live in the Big Sur area, as do some workshop leaders and board members.

Those who live and work at Esalen share visions of diffuse spirituality involving sparks of divinity within each human and correspondence with divinity in the natural environment. All of the three dozen people living at or near Esalen whom I interviewed formally or informally engage in daily spiritual practice, ranging from dancing to meditation to performing jazz. Sam Keen, a longtime presence at Esalen noted, "Everything is a manifestation of a single divine substance."

Throughout his youth, Murphy regularly visited his grandparents' country retreat at Big Sur Hot Springs, long before his first sustained exposure to eastern spirituality.[30] His return to California corresponded with the intellectual and spiritual ferment in San Francisco and its environs. Big Sur Hot Springs and early Esalen attracted lecturers and participants from intersecting groups of academics, religious leaders, and mental health professionals affiliated with Bay Area organizations, ranging from San Francisco's elite Grace Cathedral to the Beat generation's landmark City Lights Bookstore.[31] The intersection of formal and informal institutions, recognized networks, and talented outsiders created a supply of wide-ranging spiritual resources.

Most of the early seekers in the 1960s came to Big Sur from the San Francisco vicinity's intellectual/spiritual/political scene, although some journeyed from southern California, influenced by philosophers Aldous Huxley and Gerald Heard. Widespread public attention in the mid-1960s expanded national and international interest in Esalen. Increased prominence followed George Leonard's *Look Magazine* articles in 1966[32] and Leo Litwak's 1967 *New York Times* article, "Joy Is the Prize."[33] Hollywood generated more exposure because longtime seeker Jennifer Jones, an Oscar-winning actress and major mogul's widow, introduced movie stars and screenwriters to Esalen and they in turn publicized the Institute.[34] Whether from Hollywood, San Francisco, New York City, or beyond, the vast majority of Esalen's leaders, residents, and visitors in its first two decades were drawn from America's floundering mainstream religious faiths.[35] Other articles and observations suggest that this continues to be the pattern.

ESALEN AND THE PROTESTANT MAINLINE

Esalen developed during a period of religious reconfiguration that began during the 1960s as mainline Protestant denominations lost members and evangelical faiths grew dramatically.[36] Many members of the Protestant mainline switched to stricter, but also more rewarding, evangelical and fundamentalist religious groups, which called for greater commitment and offered community and potential salvation in return for a high level of commitment. Others remained believers, and not belongers, cobbling together personal spiritual practices from a variety of resources and sometimes rejoining the liberal denominations they had dropped earlier. This was the broad group that was especially attracted to Esalen.

Esalen's cofounders were reared in Methodist/Jewish and Episcopal liberal religious traditions. As Barclay James Erickson explores in greater detail in his chapter in this volume, Richard Price came from a family that was nominally Protestant, although his father was an assimilated Jewish immigrant. Growing up in a Chicago suburb which informally barred Jews and African Americans, Price turned toward philosophy and psychology for answers about life's meanings and value. After dropping out of Harvard graduate school, he moved to San Francisco and drifted into the Beat scene and its ancillary Zen community, where he connected with Michael Murphy.[37] A series of psychotic episodes drove Price back to the Midwest, where his family annulled his brief marriage and coerced him into a series of cruel insulin shock treatments at a residential clinic. About three years after his discharge from the clinic, Price quit his job in Chicago and returned to San Francisco, where he and Michael Murphy laid the groundwork for Esalen.

Price sought alternatives to coercive psychiatry through the creation of a new kind of community where emotional and spiritual growth were intertwined. During a 1985 interview with Wade Hudson, a patients' rights writer/activist, Price described how gestalt practice at Esalen also had a spiritual dimension:

> So it's a paradox, so it's almost like Akido, there's a certain kind of Taoism that by allowing change, [change] happens. With allowing and with contact rather than forcing[,] change happens.[38]

More-explicit spirituality, the potential for connection with psychic phenomena, and evolution toward extraordinary human functioning defined Michael Murphy's search. Murphy articulated a lifelong spiritually grounded vision:

> I had this feeling that we all had access to, the ground of being, or God, or light. Our job in life was to get in touch with it and to bring it into the world—through meditation, friendship, prayer, music, even sports.[39]

Both Price and Murphy dedicated Esalen as a retreat where theorists, practitioners, and short- and long-term participants could cultivate the empathy, selflessness, and self-transcendence implicitly grounded in basic spiritual foundations.[40] Luminaries from psychology, bodywork, experiential education, creativity, and psychedelic experimentation all contributed to Esalen's rapid visibility and shaped the Institute's residential community and external networks.

During its formative decade, however, Protestant theologians and clergy were essential to Esalen's ethos and growing fame, sending word of new kinds of spiritual practice to their congregations and the media. They brought Esalen religiously informed concerns about life's meanings, and they took away innovative approaches that integrated bodywork and psychologies of personal growth with their theological approaches. The Protestant mainline helped shape Esalen, and Esalen in turn briefly renewed segments of the Protestant mainline and offered possibilities to individuals disillusioned with established liberal faiths.

Episcopal Bishop James Pike and former Episcopal priest and Zen popularizer Alan Watts were among the first and most famous of these clergy. Both engaged in theological reforms and social outreach designed to restore attendance and commitment to West Coast liberal religious traditions. Alan Watts was unaffiliated with any church when he became one of Esalen's godfathers, participating in the first set of 1962 seminars. Many San Franciscans knew of Watts as a notorious libertine, but he was also widely recognized as a Zen sage whose popular Sunday-morning radio series *Way beyond the West* and widely read books and pamphlets on Zen Buddhism established his reputation and influence on liberal Christianity and innovative novel religions in the late 1950s and early 1960s.[41] An ordained priest, Watts served as Northwestern University's Episcopal chaplain for five years before resigning the priesthood. He continued to identify himself as a theologian who sought higher consciousness and connection to supernatural powers by every means possible, including meditation, sex, and psychedelics.[42] Watts died in 1973, but he sustained a continuing reputation through publication and audio recordings, adding to Esalen's visibility.

In the early 1960s, James Pike was by far the most famous liberal clergyman associated with Esalen, although Watts's published legacy and influence became much greater over time. Despite opposition from theological conservatives, Pike was selected as Bishop Coadjutor and subsequently Bishop of California in 1958. His increasingly critical stance toward Episcopal doctrine shook the denomination. As Bishop of California, Pike appeared on the cover of *Time* magazine during the period when the Episcopal House of Bishops moved toward censuring him for critiquing central doctrines such as original sin, the trinity, and the virgin birth. His call for greater spiritual dedication and doctrinal pluralism fueled the spiritual "revolution" within the Bay Area.[43] He died in 1967, a year after resigning as Bishop of California.

Pike offered Esalen explicit institutional links to the Episcopal Church. He participated at the Institute in Big Sur, offering workshops and seminars about spirituality and heterodoxy as early as 1964.[44] Pike also spread the word about Esalen from his pulpit in Grace Cathedral, at the epicenter of San Francisco's elite Protestant congregations. Late in 1966, he volunteered to provide seminar rooms and headquarters for Esalen's short-lived San Francisco branch (1967–1977). Pike's offer was rescinded by members of Grace's board, who tendered meeting rooms for Esalen's programs but insisted that the Institute's San Francisco headquarters be located elsewhere.[45]

During his association with Esalen, Bishop Pike attracted other Protestant theologians to Big Sur. Another renegade bishop, England's James Robinson, led seminars, as did Harvey Cox, the Harvard Divinity School professor who described the challenges of inevitable secularization in *The Secular City*. The spirituality of experience and personal essence these individuals advocated was nothing new to American Protestantism, but it took on extraordinary importance in the 1960s and 1970s as the declining membership in liberal congregations forced reexamination of established religious forms.

While Esalen's spiritual grounding may not have been apparent to casual visitors or the general public, visiting religious seekers were keenly attuned to the Institute's spiritual foundations. In 1966, shortly after Esalen began, Allen Ginsberg, renowned American poet and Zen ambassador, participated in an Esalen panel about religion with poet Gary Snyder, Bishop Pike, and Harvey Cox. During that visit to Esalen, Ginsberg joined a group of visiting Episcopal ministers and their wives for a soak in the hot springs. Asked to identify his religion while steeping in the springs, Ginsberg said he was probably a Buddhist Jew with attachments to Krishna, Shiva, Allah, Coyote, and the Sacred Heart. Then he added that he was on a pilgrimage. In a minute he corrected himself again, saying that he really thought all the gods were "groovy" and so he was more of a Buddhist Jewish pantheist. Ginsberg asserted, "I figure one sacrament's as good as the next one if it works."[46] In that single offhand statement, Ginsberg captured the consistent pulse of established and new essence religions beneath Esalen's seemingly haphazard history. Like the hot springs, essence religion is indispensable to Esalen's identity.

RECENT RELIGIOUS TRENDS

Since 1998, close to 90 percent of Esalen's clients live in the United States, with the vast majority residing on the West Coast.[47] They are believers, not belongers, hoping to revitalize their own spiritual lives and possibly the religious institutions with which they identify. As a center for personal and spiritual exploration, Esalen both sustains and generates cultural innovation in liberal American religions at the present time, when renewal is critical.

Between 1965 and 2000, vast numbers of Americans moved away

from established liberal faiths in Protestant, Roman Catholic, and Jewish traditions. Many sought religious experience, intensity, and community.[48] A small portion reaffiliated with more-conservative denominations, sparking growth in Orthodox Judaism, strict Protestant denominations, and Roman Catholic sects. However, most disillusioned religious liberals either minimized their affiliation to nominal membership with declining participation or dropped out entirely. Liberal clergy and their dissatisfied congregants came to Esalen seeking spiritual revival. Recent patterns of disaffiliation suggest that Esalen and similar centers may experience a surge in demand from disillusioned and unaffiliated liberals.

Between 1991 and 1998, the number of American adults with no religious preference doubled from seven to fourteen percent.[49] During the same decade, a quest culture grew dramatically, allowing individuals to explore various essence religions through centers such as Esalen, the Internet, specialty magazines such as *Yoga Journal,* or traveling workshops and speakers.[50] So long as Esalen remains the "Harvard of the human potential movement,"[51] it is likely to fulfill important functions for these unaffiliated individuals. Unaffiliated Americans are by no means disbelievers, and only five percent of them fail to have faith in a higher power.[52] Moreover, 40 percent of those with no religious preference explicitly define themselves as spiritual, albeit not religious. Esalen may attract a new generation, drawing together unaffiliated seekers from the mainstream and desperate clergy striving to rejuvenate their denominations.

FOUNDATIONAL DOCTRINE

In the late 1960s, Charles Glock and Robert Bellah forecasted the growth of a vital new religious consciousness throughout America.[53] This prediction did not come to pass, but their volume serves as documentation of the era when Esalen emerged at the forefront of the human potential movement. Mid-twentieth-century human potential movements restated the basic assumptions underlying American essence religions:

> Many participants in transpersonal religions say the word God is not meaningful to them. Those who do relate to the term rarely have an anthropomorphic image in mind. Rather than Father, Lord, or Friend, the image is more likely to be "my ground of being, my true nature, the ultimate energy."[54]

This doctrinal foundation shaped Esalen's history, framed its definition of success, and continues to sustain its influence on American spirituality and culture. Esalen resonates with refugees from the religious mainstream because it rests on a doctrine of human and natural divinity that is similar to their earlier religious socialization. They may retain their cultural capital and sustain their social networks[55] while revitalizing their faith with spiritual experience and physical and emotional engagement. Essence doctrine, in other words, forms a robust framework for Esalen's changing interpretations and practices.

Five central beliefs ground Esalen's myriad approaches to spirituality and personal transformation. Sometimes those beliefs are clearly articulated, while at other times an emphasis on well-known workshop leaders or on techniques such as Gestalt psychology masks them. Nevertheless, they are a constant at the ostensibly ever-changing Institute and help account for Esalen's decades of cultural influence. They are:

1. There is essential divinity within every person.

2. There is fundamental unity and interdependence of mind, body, spirit, and psyche.

3. Hard work and sustained practice provide means through which individuals may reach the full potential of their divine essence.

4. Extraordinary functioning and mystical communion with divine essence are direct and experiential rather than cognitive realizations.

5. When humans cultivate their extraordinary abilities, the collective may evolve to higher levels of functioning. Thus, personal transformations will generate social evolution.

The *a priori* assumption of divinity within the individual is the absolute postulate grounding all other elements of Esalen's core doctrine. A spark of divinity resides within each person. As a pilgrimage center, Esalen facilitates connection and cultivation of that very personal essence. Esalen's cofounders provided their own unique spiritual spin on divine human essence by locating inner godliness beyond the domain of spirit alone and specifying the interdependence of spirit that centers mind, body, and psyche to form the whole self. Each of these seats of human divinity can be recognized and cultivated separately. Ultimately, however, each would influence the others, and all four must receive the individual's attention, particularly the spirit and the spiritual dimensions of the other three. The unity of spirit and body receives particular emphasis both in terms of sport[56] and in relation to somatic practices such as sensory awareness, body/mind realignment, and meditative massage.[57] Workshops supply varied means for seekers to explore unseen mystical powers within themselves and others, providing a rich soil for cultivating one's own abilities and intuitions while observing similar extraordinary possibilities in others.

Within a decade of its founding and the demise of a problematic residential program, Esalen became a combination resort, spiritual spa, research center, and think tank rather than a closed institution in the traditions of Roman Catholic monasteries or isolated mystery schools such as Gerald Heard's short-lived Trabuco College discussed by Timothy Miller in this volume. Visitors and residents alike were encouraged to move on with their new insights and experience, becoming "missionaries" for Esalen's doctrines of essence spirituality.[58]

Over the past forty years, the vast majority of individuals who visited Esalen or contributed to its varied programs have journeyed far from Big Sur and made their homes elsewhere. Some central participants who live away from Esalen, such as Murphy, consider the Institute as a headquarters and the seat of a far-reaching spiritual movement. Other devout adherents regard Esalen and its Center for Theory and Research (CTR) as a place to develop and share themselves and their own distinctive practice without calling it home.

Most Esalen visitors, even committed ones, are not spiritual virtuosi embedded in a religious existence. However, many leaders and pilgrims who return again and again conduct their lives in terms of Esalen's core essence doctrine, which is articulated at a distance from Esalen in their own spiritual affiliations, which range from the Episcopal Church to Sivananda Yoga. They may embark on the householders' paths found in both Buddhist and Hindu essence traditions.[59] While involved with other work and obligations, they take on some spiritual practice(s) as fundamental to their lives, informing all other activities.

The Esalen Institute represents the hub of a wide-ranging spiritual movement that is recasting contemporary essence religiosity. James Beckford examined this broad postmodern spirituality and defined it as "parallel religion."[60] This recent religious approach, according to Beckford, emphasizes the interconnectedness of the physical, spiritual, and intellectual. Parallel religions encourage every participant to meld diverse spiritual practices into personalized paths. Because Esalen's spiritual approach is inclusive, allowing practitioners to affiliate with more than one group at a time, it is at the forefront of the trend toward parallel religion. Esalen's foundational doctrine emphasizes complementarities of different approaches and interconnections among varied groups and individuals.

It is rare for a spiritual approach that demands neither militant monotheism nor allegiance to a single leader to exert such profound influence on a large religious subculture. Esalen's pivotal historic and geographical location and resources play some part in the development and spread of holistic approaches to American spirituality. Essence doctrine resonates with millions of Americans, allowing them to interpret their lives and reach beyond themselves. William Sims Bainbridge documents the wide appeal of contemporary essence doctrines and speculates on their importance to religious innovation in the spiritual marketplace.[61] Esalen's emphasis on mysticism and experience adds weight and personal meaning to established essence traditions. The doctrine of body, mind, and psyche around a core of personal and natural divinity adds immeasurably to Esalen's historic and contemporary appeal to Americans searching for something to enrich their spiritual experience.

NOTES

1. Rodney Stark, *One True God: Historical Consequences of Monotheism* (Princeton, N.J.: Princeton University Press, 2001), 9–18.

2. Ibid.

3. Bryan R. Wilson, *The Sociology of Religion* (Oxford: Oxford University Press, 1985).

4. Marion S. Goldman, *Passionate Journeys: Why Successful Women Joined a Cult* (Ann Arbor: University of Michigan Press, 1999).

5. Richard John Carter, "Re-Invention and Paradox: The Esalen Institute in the 1990s" (Master of Business thesis, Swinburne University of Technology, Australia, 1997).

6. Ninian Smart, *The Religious Experience of Mankind,* 3rd ed. (New York: Charles Scribner's Sons, 1984); Paul Tillich, *The Courage to Be* (New Haven, Conn.: Yale University Press, 1966).

7. Rodney Stark and Roger Finke, *Acts of Faith: Explaining the Human Side of Religion* (Berkeley: University of California Press, 2000); Stark, *One True God.*

8. Stark, *One True God,* 9–29.

9. William Sims Bainbridge, *Satan's Power: Ethnography of a Deviant Psychotherapy Cult* (Berkeley: University of California Press, 1978).

10. Stark and Finke, *Acts of Faith.*

11. Goldman, *Passionate Journeys;* Stark, *One True God,* 9–29.

12. Louis Menand, *The Metaphysical Club: A Story of Ideas in America* (New York: Farrar, Straus, and Giroux, 2001); Catherine L. Albanese, *Corresponding Motion: Transcendental Religion and the New America* (Philadelphia: Temple University Press, 1977).

13. Max Weber, *Economy and Society: An Outline of Interpretive Sociology,* vol. 3 (New York: Bedminster Press, 1968), 359.

14. Clifford Geertz, *The Interpretation of Cultures: Selected Essays* (New York: Basic Books, 1973); Walter Truett Anderson, *The Upstart Spring: Esalen and the American Awakening* (Reading, Mass: Addison Wesley, 1983).

15. Ken Wilber, *One Taste: The Journals of Ken Wilber* (Boston: Shambhala, 1999), 7–37.

16. Anderson, *The Upstart Spring;* David Brooks, *Bobos in Paradise: The New Upper Class and How They Got There* (New York: Simon and Schuster, 2000).

17. Stark and Finke, *Acts of Faith.*

18. Calvin Tompkins, "Profiles: New Paradigms; Michael Murphy," *New Yorker Magazine,* January 5, 1976, 30–45.

19. George Leonard, *Walking on the Edge of the World: A Memoir of the Sixties and Beyond* (Boston: Houghton Mifflin, 1988), 197–217.

20. Anderson, *The Upstart Spring;* Harvey Gallagher Cox, *The Way East: The Promise and Peril of the New Orientalism* (New York: Simon and Schuster, 1977); Jacob Needleman and Dennis Lewis, *Sacred Tradition and Present Need* (New York: Viking, 1975).

21. National Council of Churches Archives 1960–1970, Philadelphia, Pennsylvania.

22. Anderson, *The Upstart Spring,* 220–222, 223–229.

23. Ibid, 18–19.

24. Stories of celebrity visits to the area are chronicled on the Web site of Nepenthe Restaurant, at http://www.nepenthebigsur.com.

25. Henry Miller, *Big Sur and the Oranges of Hieronymus Bosch* (New York: New Directions, 1957), 3–4.

26. Carter, "Re-Invention and Paradox."

27. Anderson, *The Upstart Spring.*

28. Don Hanlon Johnson, *Body, Spirit and Democracy* (Berkeley: North Atlantic Books Somatic Resources, 1994).

29. Carter, "Re-Invention and Paradox."

30. Anderson, *The Upstart Spring,* 15–42.

31. Ibid., 15–43.

32. Leonard, *Walking on the Edge of the World*, 234–248.

33. Leo Litwak, "The Esalen Foundation: 'Joy Is the Prize,' " in Dennis Hale and Jonathan Eisen, eds., *The California Dream* (New York: Collier Books, 1968), 308–318.

34. Anderson, *The Upstart Spring*, 137–140.

35. Ibid.

36. Finke and Stark, *The Churching of America 1776–1990* (New Brunswick, N.J.: Rutgers University Press, 1992), 247–249.

37. Anderson, *The Upstart Spring*, 34–36; Michael Downing, *Shoes Outside the Door* (San Francisco: Counterpoint, 2001).

38. Wade Hudson, interview with Richard Price, April 1985, cassette tape, transcript available through Esalen, Big Sur, California.

39. Michael Murphy quoted in Michael Schwartz, *What Really Matters: Searching for Wisdom in America* (New York: Bantam Books, 1996), 78.

40. Schwartz, *What Really Matters*, 92.

41. Alan Watts, *The Culture of the Counter-Culture* (Boston: Charles Tuttle, 1999), vii–ix.

42. Anderson, *The Upstart Spring*, 55–58.

43. David M. Robertson, *A Passionate Pilgrim: A Biography of James A. Pike* (New York: Alfred Knopf, 2004).

44. Anderson, *The Upstart Spring*, 103, 211.

45. Ibid, 148–149.

46. Allen Ginsberg quoted in Jane Kramer, *Allen Ginsberg in America* (New York: From International Publishing, 1969), 22–23.

47. Taped interviews with two Esalen staff members by Marion S. Goldman, February 24, 2000, at Esalen, Big Sur. Transcript kept to protect anonymity of interviewees.

48. Goldman, *Passionate Journeys*, 16–18; Finke and Stark, *The Churching of America 1776–1990*, 246–249.

49. Michael Hout and Claude Fischer, "Why More Americans Have No Religious Preference: Politics and Generations," *American Sociological Review* 67 (April 2002): 165.

50. Wade Clark Roof, *Spiritual Marketplace: Baby Boomers and the Remaking of American Religion* (Princeton, N.J.: Princeton University Press, 1999).

51. Anderson, *The Upstart Spring*, 276.

52. Hout and Fischer, "Why More Americans Have No Religious Preference," 173–174.

53. Charles Y. Glock and Robert Bellah, eds., *The New Religious Consciousness* (Berkeley: University of California Press, 1976), ix–xvii.

54. Donald Stone "The Human Potential Movement," in *The New Religious Consciousness*, ed. Charles Glock and Robert N. Bellah (Berkeley: University of California Press, 1976), 93–115.

55. Pierre Bourdieu, *Distinction: A Social Critique of the Judgment of Taste* (Cambridge, Mass.: Harvard University Press, 1984).

56. Michael Murphy and Rhea A. White, *The Psychic Side of Sports* (New York: Addison Wesley Publishing Company, 1978).

57. Johnson, *Body, Spirit and Democracy*.

58. Carter, "Re-Invention and Paradox," 68.

59. George Leonard and Michael Murphy, *The Life We Are Given* (New York: G. P. Putnam's Sons, 1995), 19.

60. James Beckford, *Religion in Advanced Industrial Society* (London: Unwin Hyman, 1989).

61. William Sims Bainbridge, "After the New Age," *Journal for the Scientific Study of Religion* 43 (Summer 2004): 381–394.

Michael Murphy

By the time the media discovered it in 1968, Esalen had inspired the formation of more than fifty centers for personal growth, received foundation grants to pursue research in education and alternative medicine, and attracted eminent program leaders from many parts of the world. But these facts were not widely featured in the first wave of articles about the institute. Newspaper and magazine coverage of Esalen until the late 1970s ranged from balanced, insightful pieces such as Leo Litvak's *New York Times Magazine* essay "Surprised by Joy" and Calvin Tomkins's *New Yorker* profile "New Paradigms" to sensational accounts of Esalen's uninhibited encounter groups, body therapies, and nude bathing. Attitudes in these articles ran the gamut from celebration to disgust. An approving story in the *New York Times,* for example, called an early Esalen conference on sport the athletic equivalent of "the Bastille's fall," whereas a banner headline in the *Miami Herald* proclaimed that the institute was "A Dark and Dirty Place" and *The Village Voice* welcomed our demise in a piece titled "Esalen: A Slow Death." Eventually, a few memoirs by people close to Esalen as well as three book-length journalistic accounts provided more-thorough accounts of our activities (most notably George Leonard's eloquent *Walking on the Edge of the World* and Walt Anderson's *The Upstart Spring*), but until now the institute has received little philosophic or scholarly appraisal.

This book, as well as Jeff Kripal's forthcoming *The Enlightenment of the Body,* begins to make up for the deficit. As you might imagine, they are greatly welcomed by those of us associated with Esalen. It is good to be less voyeuristically viewed and (if we are honest with ourselves) to be brought to some degree in from outlaw country. The essays collected here begin to examine historic currents which some of us have long thought were part of our story. They sometimes provide new insights about what we've done. And they come at a fortunate moment, as the institute undergoes the most thorough reorganization since its founding. During the past two years, we have rewritten our bylaws, strengthened our board, restructured our staff, created long-term master plans for our programs and facilities, and thought long and hard about our past and future. These essays reinforce our attempts to see Esalen with fresh eyes. Thoughtful appraisals such as these contribute to our renewal.

But this book only marks a beginning. Various explorations of the human potential that we've worked to promote are not widely understood as yet by mainstream social scientists. The larger cultural changes in which we're involved have not been adequately described by sociologists or historians. This collection, for example, insightful and welcome as it is, does not include reviews of our work in Soviet-American relations, education, ecology, and alternative medicine, nor does it examine in depth the many lessons we've learned about the strengths and weaknesses of transformative practices and the role of individual differences in programs for personal growth. I hope that these essays and Kripal's forthcoming book will stimulate research and commentary that make up for this lack. A broader conversation about the cultural movements in which Esalen is involved will serve more than academic interests. It could have significant practical consequences.

The world today cries out for ways to join often-clashing peoples, religious views, and cultures through visions that embrace both our capacities for greater life and our glorious complexities. Esalen, and many groups with which it is affiliated, have worked to embody such visions and in so doing find ways past the differences between East and West, honored traditions and modernity, science and religion. In this effort, by trial and error, and with plenty of failures as well as success, we have found ways to address the great divides that now exist between cultures and different ways of knowing. Essays such as those in this book help illuminate these efforts.

Like a gradually emerging digital photograph, the picture of Esalen's work held by those of us close to the institute has grown richer through the years, remaining constant in its fundamental contours while, pixel by pixel, it grows in texture and depth. Though we began, for example, with the belief that human nature harbors more capacities for growth than is generally appreciated, we found that such potentials are more complex and varied than we'd thought. And we have learned much about the limitations and shadow sides of programs for personal growth so that our picture is more sharply defined.

These essays contribute to this developing view of the institute's activities in two ways I want to emphasize here, first by illuminating certain patterns in the institute's activities that most people don't recognize, and second by highlighting Esalen's relation to larger historic and cultural developments. The first kind of insight is developed by Robert Fuller in his chapter on "metalanguage" and by Gordon Wheeler in his examination of Gestalt therapy, the second by Catherine Albanese's description of Esalen's role in the American acceptance of physical yogas, by Marion Goldman's characterization of American "essence religions," by Jeff Kripal's appraisal of Esalen in relation to the incarnational mysticism of Indian Tantra, and by Wouter Hannegraaf's breathtaking proposal that our work is related to a Gnostic turn from world-negation to world-embrace that has been developing in the West since ancient times.

Fuller's chapter held a surprise for me, namely, that Carl Rogers in his last years embraced transpersonal, even mystical, aspects of human nature which he had once rejected. Fuller describes this shift in Rogers's thinking to highlight a feature of Esalen activities that no one else, I think, has described so clearly. This aspect of our work involves what he calls a "metalanguage" that facilitates dialogue and cooperative work among widely disparate people, among them atheists, agnostics, and mystics, who have held in their various ways that humankind is informed by a telos, a "metacausality," or Aristotelian final cause, as well as by the strictly material, or efficient, causes recognized by mainstream science. Fuller sheds new light on this, helping me better understand the often-intuitive criteria we used in shaping our program.

For example, during Esalen's first decade, though I chose and invited most of our program leaders and wrote most of their course descriptions,

I did not apply a litmus test to their beliefs about God or humankind. Aldous Huxley, Gerald Heard, Frederic Spiegelberg, Alan Watts, Paul Tillich, and Arnold Toynbee each in their own way believed in a Transcendent order; whereas Fritz Perls, Abraham Maslow, and Rogers, among others, declared themselves to be either atheists or agnostics and some, such as Gregory Bateson and Buckminster Fuller, were either undecided or unwilling to speak clearly about such matters. Nevertheless, all of them shared a basic, if sometimes unspoken, assumption that human nature is essentially oriented toward further development and harbors an essential impulse to greater life that can be enlisted through somatic, psychological, cognitive, and spiritual practices.

This was the case even among leaders central to Esalen who dismissed overtly spiritual practice and evolutionary worldviews such as Sri Aurobindo's. Fritz Perls, for example, halted a Gestalt awareness session with me because, as he told Dick Price later, he had experienced an overwhelming "satori." Hearing this, I felt confirmed in my belief, which was shared by many others, that Fritz was a cryptomystic. Though he regularly claimed that meditation was "neither shitting nor getting off the pot" and tried to persuade us that there should be fewer "mystics and occultists" among our program leaders, he at times enjoyed moments of extraordinary illumination, either during working sessions where his mood was obvious to all or in private with psychedelics. And Abe Maslow too came out of the mystical closet, increasingly so as he developed his ideas about "peak experience" and self-transcendence. Near the end of his life he told me that it was time to go beyond both the humanistic and transpersonal psychologies he had helped to initiate toward a "fifth force" in psychology that would explore the connections between individual self-actualization, cultural development, and cosmic evolution. Though he died before he developed this proposal and as far as I know had not discussed it with many people, he had, like Carl Rogers, it seems, begun to embrace a worldview that saw personal growth aligned with some sort of universal telos.

In organizing our first programs, Dick Price and I operated intuitively, without a blueprint. We had sworn to prevent a "capture the flag" mentality. And we celebrated intellectual diversity. But we believed with nearly every one of our program leaders, whatever their scientific or religious faith, that humankind has a drive or attraction toward further development. Fuller is right about that. We wanted to do more than "illuminate facts already given," to quote William James. Most Esalen leaders and seminar participants wanted to postulate new facts and new horizons. In this we were, as Fuller puts it, committed to an integral, deeply optimistic vision of personal and social transformation, believing that body, mind, emotions, and spirit are inextricably entwined in human nature.

These founding views and intentions have remained constant for Esalen since its programs began. (Our early holism, for example, is reflected in the confluent education for affective and cognitive learning created by George Brown at Esalen and the University of California, Santa Barbara; in the psychosynthesis of Robert Assagioli; by the integral transformative practice that George Leonard and I are developing; and in other projects Esalen has promoted). However, it is also the case that our programs have evolved in response to the interests and needs of our program participants. In describing the relationship between Gestalt therapy and Esalen (see Chapter 6), Gordon Wheeler highlights the interplay between what is constant and changing in our work, showing among other things that Gestalt training has gradually shifted its emphasis from the "me" to the "we." In the 1960s, we responded to the widespread call among our seminarians for liberation from the deadening inhibitions of American life that had prevailed for them in the 1950s. Interest in new vistas of personal growth, altered states of consciousness, and liberating self-awareness was more evident in our early brochures than our programs for social action. Nevertheless, beginning in 1963, we sponsored both public and invitational programs to promote ecology, Chinese-American relations, racial understanding in the United States, and other social causes; and by the 1970s we had initiated programs with the Ford Foundation, the National Institute of Mental Health, the National Council of Churches, and other institutions to broaden elementary and secondary school curricula, foster what is now called alternative medicine, develop better approaches to the cure of mental illness, broaden theological dialogue in mainstream churches, improve Soviet-American relations, and promote pioneer citizen, or "track-two," diplomacy. Gestalt therapists and other psychologists have through the years shifted their emphasis at Esalen from self-expression to relationship-building, but the institute has from its start fostered programs for social betterment.

In 1962, as Esalen's programs began, most of our leaders entertained bold hopes and visions of the future, many of which have been fulfilled. In numerous essays, for example, Aldous Huxley had envisioned a pioneering education in the "non-verbal humanities" that would cultivate capacities Western culture tended to neglect, and his call has been fulfilled to a large degree by the development of alternative medicine, the appearance of Somatics as a recognized field, and the proliferation of meditation practices and other ways of growth. Arnold Toynbee predicted correctly that the coming of Buddhism (and by implication other Eastern philosophies) to the West might turn out to be a transformative event of the twentieth century, opening new vistas of spiritual vision and practice. During his seminar at Esalen (and in conversations afterward), Paul Tillich proposed that the merging of Eastern contemplative philosophies with Western notions of the world's advance (or, as he put it, the joining of "circular" and "linear" images of history) would broaden philosophic and theological dialogue and deepen our sense of human possibility. And Abraham Maslow, with Tony Sutich, Carl Rogers, Rollo May, and others, had initiated a new field in psychology that would eventually help to broaden and enliven personality theory and therapeutic practice. Implicit in these ideas, hopes, and initiatives was the sense that we were part of something that eluded the categories of most journalists, social scientists, and historians. The reflections in this book by Jeff Kripal and Wouter Hanegraaff have a similar boldness and sweep. They resonate strongly with Esalen's vision.

Kripal, for example, in aligning our work with the Indian Tantric embrace of the divine immanence and its summoning of new life from our secret depths, illuminates more of our intentions and activities than any psychologist or sociologist I can think of. He reveals, to use Gregory Bateson's phrase, a pattern that connects Esalen practices as seemingly disparate as zen Buddhist meditation, sensory-awareness exercises, strenuously cathartic Reichian therapies, and sport psychology. Whatever their temperament and philosophy, nearly every Esalen leader has believed, like

Tantric philosophers, that something greater is pressing for birth in us, new solidarities with our fellows, a deeper joy, more life. Kripal contextualizes this fact in relation to one of humankind's greatest spiritual traditions. The "Bengali connection" we share adds to my enjoyment of these insights. That we come to our work via Sri Ramakrishna and Sri Aurobindo, two giants from Calcutta with Tantric roots (with Voltaire, Foucault, and William James added) makes our collaboration in these reflections a happy enterprise for me.

Which leads me to Hanegraaff's chapter, in which he proposes that Esalen's work is related to Gnosticism's progressive world engagement. Few people have recognized this turn by Gnostics in the West from world negation toward what might be called a Tantric embrace of the divine immanence, and Hanegraaff's proposal is bound to be questioned. But I want him to be right. My reasons for starting Esalen were rooted in the evolutionary world-engaging vision of Sri Aurobindo, who saw the development of Indian spirituality in much the same way as Hanegraaff views the development of Gnosticism, namely as a "descent" of spiritual illumination and practice into the world at large. (More specifically, Aurobindo proposed that Indian spirituality deepened its embrace of human nature in the course of time in a "downward" movement into the intuitive mind via the Upanishads, the reasoning intellect with the Vedantic systematic philosophies, then into the emotions through Sri Chaitanya and other devotional geniuses of the Indian Middle Age, and finally into the body and its powerful energies by way of the Tantras.) Though few religious and cultural historians have viewed the history of Gnostic vision as have Aurobindo and Hanegraaff, it is not implausible that mystic sensibilities East and West have more and more embraced the world as a field of spiritual embodiment.

As life expectancy, wealth generation, and material conditions in general improved in Europe and other parts of the world, Gnostics such as those Hanegraaff names as well as philosophers such as Hegel, Schelling, Bergson, Teilhard, and Aurobindo came to view the world as a progressive manifestation of its latent divinity. In spite of the horrors and difficulties humankind faces, certain discoveries of recent decades continue to invite visions of this kind. Never before has there been so much publicly accessible knowledge about our capacities for extraordinary life, from the study of exceptional human functioning in many fields, from comparative analyses of Eastern and Western contemplative lore, from burgeoning experimental research with meditation and other transformative disciplines, and from our dawning recognition that each social group nurtures only some of our potentials for growth while neglecting or suppressing others. Though dreams of further human development can seem far-fetched, many conditions exist to support them. My colleagues at Esalen and I have always believed that.

Catherine L. Albanese is professor of Religious Studies at the University of California, Santa Barbara. Her many publications include *Nature Religion in America: From the Algonquin Indians to the New Age*. Professor Albanese is a past president of the American Academy of Religion.

Barclay James Erickson holds a doctorate in Clinical Psychology from The Fielding Institute in Santa Barbara, California. He began his involvement with Esalen in 1976 when he took a month-long workshop in which Dick Price led gestalt sessions. Eric has continued his involvement at Esalen and is currently on the staff there, leading groups and teaching workshops.

Robert Fuller is Caterpillar Professor of Religious Studies at Bradley University. His recent books include *Naming the Antichrist: The History of an American Obsession* and *Spiritual, But Not Religious: Understanding Unchurched America*.

Marion S. Goldman is professor of Sociology and Religious Studies at the University of Oregon. Her research involves gender, spirituality, and the American cultural context. She is author of *Gold Diggers & Silver Miners*, co-winner of the Hamilton Prize, and *Passionate Journeys: Why Successful Women Joined a Cult*.

Wouter J. Hanegraaff is professor at the University of Amsterdam in the Faculty of Humanities. Trained as a historian of religions, Hanegraaff's area of specialization is the history of Western esoteric currents from the early Renaissance to the present. Among other works, he is author of *New Age Religion and Western Culture: Esotericism in the Mirror of Secular Thought.*

Don Hanlon Johnson is professor of Somatics at the California Institute of Integral Studies. He founded the first graduate degree program in the field of Somatics, which was housed at Antioch University before it moved to CIIS. He is the author of three books and several journal articles on the central role of bodily experience in providing a unique understanding of critical social, spiritual, and psychological issues.

Jeffrey J. Kripal is J. Newton Rayzor Professor of Religious Studies and Chair of the Department of Religious Studies at Rice University. He is author of *Roads of Excess, Palaces of Wisdom: Eroticism and Reflexivity in the Study of Mysticism* and *Kali's Child: The Mystical and the Erotic in the Life and Teachings of Ramakrishna,* and the coeditor of three collections of essays on the ethical status of mysticism, the psychology of religion, and the Hindu Goddess Kali.

Timothy Miller is professor of Religious Studies at the University of Kansas. His recent publications include: *The Hippies and American Values, The Quest for Utopia in Twentieth-Century America,* and *The 60s Communes: Hippies and Beyond.*

Michael Murphy is the cofounder and chairman of Esalen Institute. In the 1980s, he helped organize Esalen's pioneering Soviet-American Exchange Program, which became a premiere vehicle for citizen-to-citizen relations between Russians and Americans. Murphy's publications include *The Future of the Body* and four novels, including *Golf in the Kingdom* and *An End to Ordinary History.*

Glenn W. Shuck is assistant professor of religion at Williams College. In addition to a number of published essays, he is author of *Marks of the Beast: The Left Behind Novels and the Struggle for Evangelical Identity.*

Ann Taves is Professor of the History of Christianity and American Religion at Claremont School of Theology and Claremont Graduate University. Her books include *Fits, Trances and Visions: Experiencing Religion and Explaining Experience from Wesley to James,* which won the Association of American Publishers Award for Best Professional/Scholarly Book in Philosophy and Religion in 2000.

Gordon Wheeler teaches and trains widely around the world, drawing on Gestalt, constructivist, and intersubjective traditions to present a new development model of relational psychology. He is author or editor of over a dozen books in the field, including recently *Beyond Individualism* and *The Heart of Development,* as well as several works of translation and fiction.

Index

Numbers in italics refer to illustrations.